Marie Kasibvy

# COLLINS GUIDE
## TO BULBS

# COLLINS GUIDE TO

# BULBS

*By*

## PATRICK M. SYNGE

—

WITH 330 BULBS ILLUSTRATED
IN COLOUR

27 IN BLACK AND WHITE

—

COLLINS
ST JAMES'S PLACE, LONDON
1961

# Acknowledgments

THE author wishes to acknowledge with warmest thanks the aid of many friends who have helped him over this book in various ways ; in particular Mr. E. B. Anderson who has read and commented on the larger part of the manuscript and whose knowledge of bulbous plants is unrivalled in this country, Mr. T. T. Barnard for help and advice on *Gladiolus* species, *Moraea* and *Watsonia*, the late Miss C. Beck and Rear-Admiral P. Furse on *Fritillaria*, Mr. John Gilmour, V.M.H., on *Tulipa*, Mr. Eliot Hodgkin who has read and commented on some sections, the Hon. Lewis Palmer, V.M.H., for help and advice on *Cyclamen*, Sir Frederick Stern, V.M.H., on *Iris* and *Lilium*, Mr. C. F. Coleman on *Narcissus* and Mr. T. Hoog of Messrs. Van Tubergen who gave up a day to showing us the plants in his famous nursery. He would also like to acknowledge the trouble and care that the artists have taken over the plates, especially Paul Furse who has drawn on his immense series of drawings of many rare and unusual plants made over the years and has so enabled us to illustrate many plants which are not so often seen as well as those which are shown freely each year.

He also acknowledges with thanks the permission of Sir Frederick Stern to use two photographs taken at Highdown, Mr. Oliver Wyatt for one taken at Maidwell Hall and the work of Mr. J. E. Downward, F.R.P.S., who has been responsible for the majority of the black and white plates and also several of the colour ones.

He would also like to acknowledge with thanks the permission of the Council of The Royal Horticultural Society for him to undertake this book.

# CONTENTS

## INTRODUCTION

## ALPHABETICAL LIST OF BULBS

# Contents

# LIST OF COLOUR PLATES

# Colour Plates

Plates 1, 3, 4, 6, 7, 8, 9, 11, 13, 14, 17, 24, 29 and 32 are from paintings by Rear-Admiral J. P. W. Furse ; plates 5, 12, 16, 19, 20, 21, 25, 30 and 31 are from paintings by Paul Jones ; plates 26 and 27 from paintings by Pamela Freeman ; plates 2 and 28 from paintings by Margaret Stones

Plates 10*a*, 15, 18*a* and *b*, 22 and 23 are from colour photographs taken by Mr. J. E. Downward ; plate 10*b* is from a colour photograph by the author

The line drawings on pages 37, 38 and 40 are by Pamela Freeman

# LIST OF BLACK AND WHITE PLATES

11

# Black and White Plates

All the photographs were taken by Mr. J. E. Downward except for Plate IX, which is from the R.H.S. collections, Plate XXI, which is by Mr. R. A. Adam and Plate XXIV, which is by Mr. T. C. Clare

# PREFACE

BULBOUS FLOWERS are undoubtedly among the most rewarding kinds of plants that we can grow in our gardens and no gardener would wish to be without them. They present such great variation, ranging from the smallest crocus species, under an inch in height, to the largest lily, maybe eight feet in height. The great majority also are easy to grow and there are bulbs for every month of the year, from the crocuses and snowdrops of January to the cyclamen and freesias and forced hyacinths of December. Some find their greatest delight in the smooth and regular form and clear colour of the exhibition daffodil, or even the frilled extravagance of the show begonia; others prefer the graceful icy perfection of the snowdrop or the delicate feathered markings of the crocus species. Again others are delighted most by a meadow full of naturalised daffodils, all tossing and waving in the breeze. The Victorian gardener found satisfaction and beauty in a formal bedding scheme of regimented hyacinths or tulips, each exactly in its position and each exactly the same height. Such a scheme still has its place in some gardens as well as in many parks and it requires skill and care to carry it out to perfection. I myself find my greatest gardening pleasure in a naturalised woodland scheme, a glorified piece of nature where the art and the craft of gardening is so masked that everything appears as if it might be growing wild, a scene where bulbs of many sorts are mingled in loose drifts as an underplanting and as a complement to flowering trees and shrubs and backed by the deep rich green of conifers and evergreens. There is infinite scope in such an arrangement and once established, apart from an annual mulching and perhaps an annual weeding, it will come nearer to looking after itself than any other form of gardening. It is the nearest approach to the labour-saving garden that the economic situations of this epoch permit for the majority of those of us who wish to garden on anything more than a very restricted scale.

For the purposes of this book the term bulbous plant will be interpreted liberally and not in the strict botanical sense. As well as the true bulbous plants we will include those other subjects which have corms or even tubers or rhizomes, but which require the same kind of treatment and which are generally offered by nurserymen in the same catalogue with bulbs. It is purely an arbitrary distinction, and certain large groups of tuberous plants such as the bearded irises and the dahlias are not included since they can usually be discussed more conveniently with the group of herbaceous plants and there has to be a limit to the length of any one book.

# *Preface*

Again, a complete treatment showing all the bulbous and allied plants of the world already described and of which specimens are available in herbaria would fill many volumes the size of this one and be a lifetime's task. The intention of this book is more modest, namely to describe for the gardener in Great Britain and North America a selected list of bulbous plants which are suitable for growing in his garden or greenhouse. It is hoped that all the genera and species of bulbs which the average gardener is likely to meet have been included, but the specialist in a particular genus will of course find others outside our range. Again the numbers of horticultural varieties, or cultivars as they should now be described to distinguish them from botanical varieties, which have been raised in such genera as *Narcissus* and *Tulipa* runs into many thousands. Classified lists have been published of these names and no good purpose would be served by recapitulating even a large proportion of these names. So a selection has been made of these which the author considers the best available at the time of publication. Many cultivars are introduced each year and many varying names will be found in the catalogues. The purpose of this book is to deal rather with those of proven merit than to chase after the very latest and most expensive. More reliance has been placed on the results of the R.H.S. trials at Wisley in recent years and the plants seen there than on the awards given to flowers shown for exhibition. A few of the newer and more costly daffodils and tulips have, however, been included in the hope that these may become the flowers for every man in another decade. In less than one generation we have seen the spread of such a bulb as *Narcissus* 'Fortune' from a single bulb, through a small stock, at a price not less than £50 a bulb, to one of the most widely grown of all bulbs and priced at less than one shilling a bulb.

The nomenclature of the species and botanical varieties is based for the most part on that adopted in The Royal Horticultural Society's Dictionary of Gardening and its Supplement, and only departs from it where the author has good personal reason to do so or where other more recently published work makes it seem to him desirable to do so. He cannot claim to have made the critical herbarium and library study of each genus that would be required for a monographic work of one genus, however much such works may be needed. The bibliography has intentionally been made of some length so that he who is keen for more information on any particular group or genus may as far as possible be guided where to look for it if it exists. In many cases it just does not. There are some who will consider that a challenge and find these the more interesting genera and they are much to be encouraged. The wonderful collection of coloured plates and accurate descriptions contained in The Botanical Magazine has been a great help in the case of many rarer species where living material was not available. These plates have all been drawn from living material.

Again the emphasis of the book is rather on the hardy or nearly hardy than on the tender bulb and only a few are included that need to be grown

# Preface

in warm greenhouses or stove houses. These few are of such outstanding interest or merit that their inclusion seems necessary.

The majority of bulbous plants are easy to grow in gardens situated in a very wide range of positions and certainly from no other group of plants can one obtain a quicker return, since the embryo flower is already present in the bulb when we buy it. Colchicums probably win this race, often flowering within a few days of planting or sometimes even producing flowers when dry on the counter of the bulb store. From bulbs the impatient gardener, and we all come into that category at times, can obtain a quick effect and if he wishes it brilliant colour in a new garden. The larger effects of naturalised bulbs spread into a carpet require of course much more patience but still each year the reward should be greater, increasing by compound interest and multiplying fast as the seedlings from the flowers of earlier years begin to flower themselves.

The use of abbreviations and technical terms has been kept down as far as possible but some technical terms are necessary for clarity and some abbreviations for saving of space and also to avoid wearisome repetition. The system of spelling all specific epithets with a small letter has been adopted since this is now the practice of the main botanical institutions of the world and is now followed by The Royal Horticultural Society as well as being a recommendation of the International Code of Botanical Nomenclature. It comes as a shock to many of the older gardeners to see such epithets as *smithii* spelt with a small letter but still that is now the established custom and it serves no useful purpose to rail against it as uncouth or to continue to ignore it, even though I myself, in company with that grand old gardener, the late Mr. E. A. Bowles, would have preferred that the older system had remained the general custom and counted it worth the slight extra trouble.

# INTRODUCTION

## (1) BEDDING

IN OUR parks and public gardens and to a lesser extent in many private gardens we still see a wide use of bulbs for spring bedding and there is no other class of plant which can quite take their place and give the same brilliant show in April and May. Elaborate schemes of bedding with thousands of hyacinths in serried rows are now largely only a memory but small beds with tulips coming up through foamy blue clouds of forget-me-not are still worth their space in nearly every garden that has some small area around the house devoted to more formal gardening. Even with the present devotion to wild and woodland gardens the transition from the formality of the house to the wild garden generally seems to me to require a small intervening part that is treated semi-formally, maybe with paving stones and small beds and even backed by low yew hedges. It is in this part that the place still remains in small and medium-sized English gardens for the use of bulbs in a bedding scheme. It is not necessary to have large blocks of any one colour, "cheque book" gardening as some call it, and a judicious use of planning can insure a display of varied and harmonious colour for two months at least.

Tulips and hyacinths are the two classes of bulbs most used for bedding schemes, but there is a place also for smaller groups of anemones, crocuses, daffodils, grape hyacinths and even tigridias, lilies or galtonias in the summer in more informal arrangements.

### Preparation of beds

This should be thorough and they should be dug through and allowed to settle for at least a week before planting. Large quantities of very fresh manure are not desirable, but the digging in of some *well-rotted* manure or compost will benefit most beds, especially if a crop of summer bedding plants has just been lifted. An application of bone meal in autumn or dried blood in early spring can also not fail to benefit the bulbs. If the bulbs are to be mixed with such plants as forget-me-nots, these are best planted before the bulbs. Tulips combine well with these and almost the classic combination is the pink Darwin tulip 'Clara Butt' and a blue forget-me-not. Dwarf wallflowers will also provide a suitable underplanting for the tulips, especially the very pale yellow 'Primrose

Monarch'; but the giant wallflowers are rather too tall and compete too much with the tulips unless these are widely spaced. Double white arabis also provides a good foil for tulips of nearly all colours.

Hyacinths are often used as an underplanting in rose beds and lifted soon after flowering. When it was the habit to cut nearly all roses practically down to the ground in spring pruning, they certainly made more beautiful and interesting a very dull area. With the present practice of less severe pruning of roses there is perhaps not so much room for them and with present costs bedded hyacinths are now largely a memory of my childhood, except for displays in the parks and public gardens. However, a few in small beds around the house can still be very beautiful in combination with other flowers and will scent the area around. It is not necessary for this to buy the very largest bulbs or to produce the massive exhibition spikes of the florist.

The use of other spring bulbs such as crocuses, daffodils and even muscari (grape hyacinths) will be discussed more under the section dealing with naturalisation. But the lovely carpet of colour that can be given by masses of golden *Crocus aureus* mixed with mauve *Crocus tomasinianus*, dramatically opening as the sun comes out, from a slender suede-grey bud to a wide mauve flower in February or early March, or with the deep rich colour of the dark purple 'Nigger Boy' or 'Purpureus grandiflorus,' or the pale dove-blue-grey 'Vanguard' which flowers as early as the Dutch yellow crocuses, will make a sight of interest much earlier in the year than the other bedding plants which can follow later. By the end of May the foliage will almost have died down sufficiently to enable the corms to be lifted without damage. Daffodils or anemones could be grown to follow on, but like all flowers which look only one way when in flower, they are better placed in beds against a wall or with other background than in beds which are seen from all sides. The same applies to gladioli.

The use of bulbs for summer bedding is not practised as widely as I feel it deserves. A bed of exotic tigridias seeming to hover like great tropical butterflies over an underplanting of blue lobelia would give us an effect like a Persian carpet and would flower over quite a long season. Lilies can very successfully be planted out from pots in the spring and such species as *L. regale* can easily and cheaply be raised from seed in three years in sufficient numbers to make a fine show. They are probably, however, better mixed with other plants than planted on their own. How lovely they would be with salpiglossis and underplanted with dark heliotrope. A bed of Tiger lilies can present a very exotic sight and I have always remembered several such beds at Government House, Ottawa, which I saw when a boy.

The creamy-white galtonias flower in August and September and give a certain statuesque quality to any bedding scheme. They are well worth

considering for this purpose, rising above some dwarf plants such as mauve petunias or crimson *Phlox drummondii* or merely growing up through silver foliage in an all-white garden.

Tuberous begonias are also widely used for bedding and can present a very lovely effect, like a coat of many colours. For outside planting generally the single or semi-double ones stand up to the weather better than the very large full doubles. A hot summer suits them as long as they can be given plenty of water. They can be raised from seed sown in February in a heated propagating frame and will flower the same year, but of course, an earlier effect will be obtained by starting the tubers into growth in a box of sand and peat during March or April and then planting them out at the end of May or early June, about nine inches apart.

### (2) BULBS IN THE BORDER

Many of the same principles apply to the use of bulbs in the border as to their use for bedding, and their treatment will be very similar, although a wider variety of choice can be made and more informality used in the planting. The background which can be provided by shrubs in a mixed shrub, bulb and herbaceous plant border can be very pleasing and many prefer this method to the more formal bedding schemes. Groups of tulips either of one colour or even mixed can look very effective along the front of a border and will provide colour before the herbaceous plants. After flowering they can be lifted and plunged in a reserve patch or annuals can be planted out and allowed to grow over the bulbs. Probably, however, it is better to lift them in most cases. The effect of an old cottage garden bright in colour for many months, lavishly filled and varied with all manner of plants is one with which it is not easy to succeed, but bulbs can contribute largely to it.

Later-flowering groups of gladioli, lilies, galtonias and even tigridias will look well and add an extra interest and distinction to the border. These can all be planted in the spring, or the lilies may be planted in the autumn. Clumps of crown imperials (*Fritillaria imperialis*) in both the lemon-yellow and the orange-red forms look very well in the border but care must be taken not to fork into their large bulbs. A most evil foxy smell will quickly warn any offender.

A narrow border under a wall or in front of a greenhouse will provide an excellent site for those bulbs which benefit from a little extra warmth, tulip species and the many very lovely hybrids of *T. kaufmanniana*, *T. fosteriana* and *T. greigii* which are now available, later crinums, *Amaryllis belladonna* and nerines.

The crinums especially do well planted right up against the wall. In the front of such a border try groups of small bulbs and corms such as crocuses, snowdrops (and there are many good kinds of these beyond the ordinary *G. nivalis*) and anemones. Even some dwarf narcissi will look well and can be left in place to increase from year to year, perhaps coming up through a carpet of dwarf thymes or pinks. An early spring border of this kind can be of interest from February till May and again in the late summer. The invasive grape hyacinths and garlics should be left out of such a border if the choicer bulbs are wanted, but for spreading widely and providing a mass of colour they are unexcelled.

## (3) BULBS NATURALISED IN GRASS

Here daffodils and crocuses are pre-eminent, and the effects of wide spreading drifts of golden daffodils following yellow or mauve crocuses coming through short green grass is one that is difficult to surpass in any other form of gardening. It is an effect that is predominantly seen in English gardens and especially the gardens and parks of the great English country houses or colleges, but there is no reason why this need be. It is, however, an effect for which time is essential, but provided a good start can be made it is surprising how much effect can be obtained in a space as short as five years, especially if, after the third or fourth year, some of the clumps be lifted and divided.

The one essential requirement for the continuance of naturalised bulbs is that the grass be not cut until the leaves of the bulbs have died down and, in the case of daffodils, this usually means the end of June or even later; in the case of crocuses the end of May. It will not then be possible in the rest of the summer to obtain that short velvety effect attained by old lawns which are consistently mowed and rolled throughout the year. In these days, however, of the necessity of labour-saving this is probably no great disadvantage and it is surprising how quickly the brown effects of cutting long grass passes off. In the case of damp meadows it is also sometimes possible to carry on the interest a month after the daffodils by simulating some of the effect of an alpine meadow with trollius, astrantia and blue geraniums. This is unlikely, however, to be successful in dry sites.

The grouping of daffodils will always remain a matter of taste, but most gardeners prefer to group together the yellow varieties apart from the white ones, while it is generally better not to group them in regular or solid masses, but in a more informal way. The classical and most often repeated advice is to throw the bulbs in loose drifts on the ground and plant them as they fall, but I suspect that few actually follow this advice and it would be difficult to avoid leaving some bulbs unplanted if the throwing ranged widely. It is important not to plant too thickly at the beginning. Leave room for the natural increase.

## Bulbs Naturalised in Grass

The earliest flowering species of narcissus suitable for naturalisation is the *N. bulbocodium*, which exists in an infinite variety of forms and colours from palest cream to a deep citron-yellow. One of the most beautiful sights at Wisley during the whole year is the bulbocodium meadow, but it is a very damp meadow with water constantly draining down the slope through the upper layers and this is undoubtedly one of the secrets of its success (Pl. **18***a*). It is unlikely that such a planting would be successful on a dry slope.

The bulbocodiums will be quickly followed by the dwarf wild daffodil *N. pseudo-narcissus* and by *N. lobularis*. These delightful little Lent lilies are some of the most beautiful of all daffodils for naturalising, flowering at least a fortnight before the bigger kinds and standing up to all kinds of rough weather. The trumpets are golden-yellow and the perianths a paler cream.

For naturalisation in grass one does not want the exhibition daffodil with its perfect orb of smooth petals and corona and long stem. Its perfections would be lost in the mass. Rather should one choose some of the older kinds with shorter stems and perhaps tougher constitutions. There are few better for this purpose than the golden double trumpet 'Van Sion' and it makes a wonderful mass of yellow, nor should the old 'Sir Watkin' or 'Golden Spur' or 'Empress' be left out. Among the newer varieties 'Carlton' is a very strong grower and with a short stem should be good for this purpose. A planting of the short cupped white forms and even some of the Poeticus can also be very lovely, giving the Wordsworthian effect of dancing in the breeze in a way which the great new exhibition trumpets can never do. In my opinion the very brilliant yellows with flaming red cups should be avoided also for this purpose.

For crocuses the large-flowered hybrids are the best and it is preferable to keep the Dutch yellow away from the purples and the whites. They will also flower earlier by ten days or so, except for that unusual pale mauve form of *C. vernus* called 'Vanguard' which flowers very early and is very reliable. The purples and mauves and whites can be mingled together but to be effective both they and the yellows need to be planted in a good mass. The species crocus are mostly more suited to the rock garden or to open parts of a woodland garden, but *C. tomasinianus* can, in favourable situations, be established so that it will grow through short grass.

Sometimes bluebells, scillas, anemones, chionodoxa and cyclamen can be established in grass but their place is better in the woodland or rock garden and under that section they will be considered. The dwarf blue wild scilla is often seen to most excellent effect in short grass by the sea.

All bulbs will need to be planted carefully either with a trowel or a bulb planter that will remove a small nest of turf and then replace it. A top dressing of the grass in early spring with a good fertiliser will also

21

greatly help the bulbs. Daffodils should be planted with the nose of the bulb about three inches deep while crocuses need not be planted more than an inch to an inch and a half below the surface. It is wonderful, however, how bulbs will adjust themselves in successive years to their most suitable depths.

### (4) BULBS IN THE WOODLAND GARDEN

Many bulbs such as lilies, daffodils and trilliums seem to be a natural complement of a woodland garden and form a most satisfying part of it. Few will grow in deep shade but in semi-shade or in an open glade the number that will thrive is very great. In some cases the sharper competition for moisture, particularly in the summer, and so the increased drainage that the roots of the trees or shrubs provide, is a benefit to the bulbs.

Under the branches or close to the roots of an old beech-tree there is only one plant that I know which is likely to grow and spread satisfactorily and that is *Cyclamen neapolitanum* whose leaves are active during the winter and early spring months, but there are few flowers more lovely when they have spread widely. Winter aconites will sometimes also flourish and spread in quite heavy shade, even that of horse-chestnuts, and here few are likely to disturb their seedlings by weeding since few weeds will grow.

For woodland planting, however, it is desirable as in border planting to break up the ground first and perhaps dig in some extra peat or leaf-mould and in the case of rather heavy clay or in places where the drainage is bad one can either plant in a small mound or surround the bulb, particularly the lily bulb, with sharp sand.

Throughout the year it is possible to have almost a continuous succession of flowers in an open woodland that is not too dry. The best trees are the oaks which are deep rooting and come into leaf late, but pines, provided that they are not thick, also give a leaf-mould which is acceptable to many plants. Beeches give too deep a shade for the majority of bulbs but are the perfect background. Birches tend to be surface rooting and often the ground under them is dry. Sorbus and wild cherries are usually a good complement and do not usually grow too big.

The essence of successful woodland planting is informality. The regularly-spaced group either in a circle or a rectangle should be avoided. Rather should one try to plant irregular groups often with an outlier or two a little way off from the main group.

In the first months of the year snowdrops, aconites, then crocuses will form the main show. Snowdrops rarely increase widely in very dry or overshaded positions, but in richer positions they generally grow well and do as well on lime as off it. All snowdrops are best divided and planted when they are going out of flower rather than as dry bulbs in the autumn. A succession over several months can be obtained by planting the different species and varieties. The late autumn-flowering snowdrops from Greece are not suitable for woodland conditions but by January the delicate *Galanthus rhizehensis* and the stouter *G. byzantinus* will usually be coming into flower. In February and early March comes the great profusion of snowdrops. Usually the forms of *G. plicatus* are the latest to flower.

Of the early crocuses a mixture of *C. tomasinianus*, the delightful little mauve "tommies" that spread so fast and the real golden *C. aureus* is excellent but it must have at least some sun overhead. They will both grow in grass. The daffodils are woodland plants especially but again they need some sun, although not necessarily sun all the day.

It is probably better to keep the dwarf species and their little hybrids away from the larger hybrids. *N. cyclamineus* with its very bright, almost acid, yellow flowers is always one of the first and it flourishes best in a damp peaty position, as does also the hoop petticoat, *N. bulbocodium* with its many forms. The naturalised masses of these in the old woodland garden at the bottom of the rock garden at Wisley give me as much pleasure during the year as any other plantings I know. Of the larger daffodils for woodland planting it is not necessary to buy the latest, largest or newest varieties. In fact it is probably wiser not to do so. These grow better in specially prepared beds. Even the old double 'Van Sion' is excellent as a woodland plant and seems to have great persistence and vigour. Of some of the others I have found 'Polindra' with its white perianth and lemon cup a good plant which does nobly each year and always fits in well.

Of the fritillaries probably our native *F. meleagris* is the most suitable, the majority of the others preferring more sun but *F. pyrenaica* is also well worth trying to establish.

Bluebells and anemones will look after themselves if it is a suitable area for them ; if not there is probably little to be done about it as even though one may plant them, like primroses, they will not often spread freely away from their own formations. Luckily, however, their areas are very widespread. Really it is only the very hot and dry which need to be avoided.

Lilies are, of course, the most superb of all woodland plants and nowhere do they look better or more at home, but they must have some sun, careful placing and some preparation of the soil, while their roots must be kept clear of grasses and other competition. It is not by any means so with lilies in the wild but in gardens it seems to be desirable, except in the case of a few very strong growing ones such as the martagons. After these *L. pardalinum* and the Bellingham hybrids will be the most likely to spread freely and increase and they are very spectacular in a mass. *L. superbum* and *L. canadense* are also both woodland plants and have more perfection and grace and poise of flower but do not usually spread so widely; nevertheless they should be planted for their beauty, as should also the little pink trumpet *L. rubellum.* It is a real triumph if one can get a clump of this to persist over the years but it sometimes happens. The great white trumpets of *Cardiocrinum giganteum*, followed by their statuesque candelabra seed heads, find their perfect background in the trunk of an old oak but they need a good rich and rather moist position and some feeding with well-rotted manure to attain their greatest size. Then one may expect spikes of 6 or 7 ft. or even more. The tallest have usually been grown from seed.

In the autumn the colchicums look well at the edges of a woodland or in an open glade but they must definitely have some sun. And so the season comes round again to the snowdrops.

## (5) BULBS IN THE ROCK GARDEN

The large rock garden is an excellent place for the dwarfer bulbs and they will provide colour there both early in the year and late in the autumn when there are few other rock plants in flower. In the small rock garden bulbs are best kept either to a narrow border along the top or bottom or to groups between the rock plants. The common idea that most bulbs will thrive and flower each year through a thick carpet of dwarf perennials or shrubs such as pinks, thymes or helianthemums unfortunately only applies to a very few of the most vigorous. Probably grape hyacinths will survive such treatment and a very few crocus such as *C. tomasinianus* and *C. aureus* and a few dwarf narcissi, but the majority will not obtain the summer ripening that they need. The choicer kinds all need to be grown where the ground above them is open after their flowering and where they can mature their foliage and bulbs without too much interference from other plants. This particularly applies to the majority of bulbs from the Mediterranean regions which need a hot summer ripening. Often, though, to plant a slightly tender tuber or bulb such as *Cyclamen graecum* just underneath a rock will ensure its survival and success-ful flowering outside in areas where otherwise a greenhouse would be needed.

A raised bed or mound will often assist greatly in maturing the bulb, particularly in the damper areas of the West. In the drier parts such as East Anglia this is probably not needed. The majority of sun-loving bulbous plants do not need, in fact definitely should not have, the summer watering that many choice alpine plants will require in a dry season. They are labour-saving in this respect and some bare patches in summer will be more than compensated for by the extra interest and colour they provide in winter, early spring or even autumn. Here the genus crocus is invaluable; one should plant in a sunny place *C. laevigatus* and *C. imperati* for literal winter flowering with the snowdrops, then *C. aureus,* forms of *C. chrysanthus* and the deeper forms of *C. tomasinianus* for late winter and early spring together with the hybrid winter aconite *Eranthis tubergenii.* The dwarf cyclamen are also excellent and long-lived. Grow *C. orbiculatum* in its various forms for late winter and early spring flowering, while for late summer and autumn *C. europaeum, C. neapolitanum* and *C. cilicium* usually flower well in that order and are quite hardy. *Crocus asturicus* and *C. salzmannii* are rarely seen but are very reliable for autumn flowering in most gardens. Bulbs and tubers that seed and spread very freely, like the grape hyacinth 'Heavenly Blue,' 'Star of Bethlehem' (the white ornithogalum), some of the alliums and *Anemone nemorosa,* are probably best avoided for the rock garden of choicer plants. But species such as *Muscari tubergenianum* and *M. botryoides* will spread rather less freely and be worth their space. If a collection of choice crocuses is to be grown it is also better to avoid planting *C. tomasinianus* or *C. speciosus* as well since, lovely as they are, they will quickly swamp the others. Colchicums should also be treated with care owing to their large summer foliage which may smother other small plants as it dies off. There are no real rock garden lilies either, although the scarlet *L. pomponium* may sometimes be used. Bone meal will form an excellent top dressing for all of these.

(6) BULBS IN PANS IN THE ALPINE HOUSE

An alpine house with pans of bulbs in flower can be a great delight during the late winter and early spring months from January to mid-April and again in the autumn. No heat is generally given but the protection from storms and wind and some degree of frost freedom will be a great help and enable the flowers to be seen at their best and raised up to waist level. In the alpine house plants will also flower rather earlier than in the open garden.

The essential points about alpine house culture are plenty of ventilation, good drainage in the pans and careful watering. The ventilators should be opened in all mild spells and may then also be left open at night. Some alpine houses even have permanently open ventilators under the benches but this is not necessary for the majority of the bulbs we might be likely to want to grow. It is important not to include tender bulbs which need a little heat to mature their flowers satisfactorily such as freesias and some of the gladiolus species. The majority of bulbs will grow quite successfully in the John Innes Potting Mixture but it is important to give them good drainage at the base in the form of both crocks and sharp grit or crushed brick. It is generally better also to use pots or pans rather on the small side for the particular bulbs than to over-pot them. A sour compost will cause trouble immediately and probably the leaves will die off and the bulb be weakened for the next season. Watering also needs to be carefully controlled and it is often better, particularly in cold weather, to keep the pans on the dry side rather than the opposite. Some of the choicer cyclamen such as *C. libanoticum* and *C. persicum* resent very much having water sloshed over the leaves and corms and should only be watered from below by standing the pan in a tray or bath of water or very carefully round the edge, so that the top of the corm is not wetted. A few of the earlier flowering tulips and the more dwarf narcissi should be treated in the same way, although in both genera the larger members will require larger amounts of water and do not need nearly such careful treatment. It is a considerable advantage to plunge the bases of the pans in shingle which can be kept damp or even to dig them in up to the brim in sand. If the sand be watered from time to time the pan will not require nearly so much. One must ensure, however, good support for the benches since the weight will be quite considerable.

Many growers prefer to use the alpine house primarily as a place for displaying plants in flower or coming into flower rather than as a place to grow them throughout the year and undoubtedly this method is the most satisfactory. It also means that quite a small alpine house supported by several frames will suffice. Resting bulbs are better plunged in a frame rather than left in the house and may often be grown on there till they are coming into flower. Often ten months can be spent in the frame and two months in the alpine house. After flowering it is important to keep the bulbs growing until the foliage dies down naturally. They should on no account be placed under the bench and forgotten as soon as the flowers are over or one's hobby will become a very expensive one, since fresh bulbs will need to be purchased each year. The resting period of all bulbs is very important. Some will require as much heat as possible, such as an upper shelf in a greenhouse, others a much more gentle drying such as being placed under the bench with the pans on their sides or plunged in a frame in semi-shade but shielded from the rain. This is the kind of characteristic one gets to know with experience and some indications for particular bulbs are given later in this book. In general, however, the pans are best outside a small alpine house during this period.

The choice of bulbs for the alpine house is very large. It is possible to start the display in January with pans of the Palestine *Iris vartani* and its lovely white form and also the variable *Crocus laevigatus* from Greece. Often this will start flowering before the old year is out. Some of the earliest snowdrops such as *Galanthus rhizehensis, G. corcyrensis* and the stouter *G. byzantinus* and the early flowering forms of *G. caucasicus* follow very soon. A few dwarf conifers in pans will often help the display of the house at this season. In February there comes great abundance, crocuses such as the manifold forms of *C. chrysanthus*, the deeper mauve and purple forms of *C. tomasinianus*, the true *C. aureus* are all most rewarding. Later will come some of the more delicate and rarer species such as *C. minimus* and *C. corsicus*. On the whole though crocuses are not very permanent when grown in pans. They are excellent the first year provided there is no attempt to force them on with heat, but in subsequent years tend to dwindle. However, some are so cheap that it is no great hardship to replace them annually and then plant them out after flowering into the garden. The choicer and more expensive crocuses will generally last longer planted in a bulb frame. Iris and cyclamen are two other most rewarding genera for the alpine house. In the house at Wisley the large pans of *Cyclamen libanoticum* each year seem to increase in beauty. An excellent effect can be obtained by spacing several corms out, around a large pan. It need not be very deep. *Iris histrioides* will probably be the first to flower in February, if not in January and will be quickly followed by *Iris reticulata* and *Iris danfordiae*. The hybrids such as ' Joyce,' ' Harmony ' and ' Wentworth ' are particularly fine in pans and there is perhaps little to choose between them. The recently introduced forms of *Cyclamen pseudibericum* make their buds in the autumn and keep them lying flat all the winter. Then in February and March they turn upwards to flower magnificently, a deep and rich magenta-purple on a stout four- or even six-inch stem.

The dwarf narcissi should not be omitted, starting with the early white hoop petticoats such as *N. cantabricus monophyllus* and the creamy-yellow *romieuxii* in December or January. Then come the smallest trumpet, *N. asturiensis*, a true golden little frilled beauty, closely followed by *N. cyclamineus* which requires a good deal of moisture when growing, and its numerous hybrids, all of which seem worth growing. Minicycla is particularly attractive though rather variable in size. The Angel's Tears *N. triandrus albus* come nearer the end of the dwarf daffodil season but are very rewarding in pans and also lovely to bring into the house. In the alpine house at Wisley large pans of *Anemone blanda* are like patches of bright sky when they open in the sun and always spectacular in late March. In March and April some of the dwarfer tulips such as the forms of *T. pulchella* and *T. humilis* will make a strong splash of magenta-purple and yellow while in April the excessively brilliant scarlet *T. linifolia* and the creamy-yellow *T. batalinii* give bright splashes of colour.

Some of the fritillaries also show off well their more sombre charms in March and April.

During the summer the interest will largely shift to the open garden, but in the autumn there will be flowers again, the choicer forms of *Crocus speciosus* possibly and later in October the Spanish beauties *C. nudiflorus* with its deepest mauve-purple flowers bare of leaves and *C. salzmannii*. Then later the snowy white *C. niveus* from Greece is very beautiful, and so we get round to the late winter and spring flowers again.

The pans should be repotted every second or third year and when not repotted the top soil should be shaken off and replaced with fresh, in which some bone meal has been mixed. A little dressing of sulphate of potash when the pans are in flower will also help them to build up the bulbs for the next year. The narcissi should be the first pans to be repotted since they start to make new roots in August or September. The compost should be only slightly moist and further water need not be given until rooting has become well established. Some recommend giving no water until top growth shows above the ground but sometimes this may be unduly weakening to the bulb and probably a little moisture earlier will be a help. The experienced grower will soon become able to judge this for himself.

### (7) BULBS IN THE GREENHOUSE

*The cool greenhouse*

Under this category I include all houses in which there is a little heat, probably sufficient to keep out the frost and to maintain a minimum temperature of not less than 40°F. This small amount of heat will make a great difference to the bulbs which can be grown. Freesias and other South African bulbs should do well although if freesia flower is wanted very early in the year more heat will be required, but not too much must be given in the earlier stages of growth. Some of the choicer daffodils are very rewarding when grown in pots in a cool greenhouse and one can obtain flowers in the best possible state. The dwarf bulbs have mostly been dealt with under the alpine house but some of the cyclamen such as *C. persicum, C. libanoticum* and the autumn *C. rohlfsianum* will not be averse to the extra heat of the greenhouse as long as they are given plenty of ventilation. In general bulbs in pots will require more ventilation than will many other greenhouse plants such as primulas or cinerarias. Drainage is also important. In general the John Innes Potting Compost will suit most bulbs and once potbound they can be given extra feeding with liquid manures, bone meal, dried blood, etc.

In the autumn the hybrid nerines will make a magnificent show with their glistening petals provided careful attention has been given to their resting period during the summer. This resting period is really the main key to the successful growth of bulbs in the greenhouse and each species is peculiar to its requirements. It is important, however, to keep them watered and growing after flowering until the leaves die down naturally. If space is available the bigeneric hybrid *Crinodonna corsii* is also an excellent plant for autumn flowering in the greenhouse but it is a big grower.

In the summer some lilies in pots will decorate such a house but they must be given some shading and plenty of ventilation in the summer. Also it is important to spray constantly to keep down the aphids which so quickly spread virus disease among lilies. The white *L. longiflorum* and *L. formosanum* should do well in such conditions and so will *L. auratum* and *L. speciosum* and also such choice beauties as the Golden Clarion strains or *L. brownii*, the white waxy trumpet with the deep maroon outside.

In general a large number of choice bulbs can be grown in such a house with certainly no more difficulty than would be occasioned by a house of other plants — probably rather less.

A most interesting cool house could also be obtained from a selection of the early spring flowering South African gladiolus and moraea species and hybrids, but it requires special attention and in general these plants do not mix well with other bulbs. Another group of plants which would repay collecting in a cool greenhouse are the South American amaryllids such as *Habranthus*, *Phaedranassa* and *Zephyranthes*.

## The warm greenhouse and the stove house

Here one can grow such exotic plants as the gloriosas, although these can be moved into the cool greenhouse when in flower; *Eucharis amazonica* the white Easter lily; in a really warm or stove house *Pamianthe peruviana*; and some of the tropical African crinums with their massive bulbs and foliage. During the growing season they will benefit from a high humidity and plenty of moisture. Probably they never require to be dried off completely but the water can be diminished during their resting period. In such a house also the vast hybrid hippeastrums will do best although they can be grown in a cool greenhouse.

## (8) BULBS IN BOWLS

The cultivation of bulbs in ornamental bowls of fibre for flowering in the house during the winter is a popular practice and presents no great difficulties in the case of hyacinths, daffodils and a number of other bulbs. It is particularly suitable for those who live in towns or have no greenhouse in which to bring on the bulbs. Since there is no drainage hole at the bottom of the bowl there is no mess from water running through.

The fibre generally contains a small amount of charcoal and shell which helps to keep it sweet. It is made from peat moss and bought dry. If it appears rather coarse it can easily be broken up. The fibre should then be damped thoroughly and mixed until it is wet all through. It should be wet enough to stick together in lumps but not so wet that water comes out when squeezed. Any surplus water can, however, be squeezed out before it is put in the bowl. No chemicals need to be added. The fibre should be pressed down firmly and the bulbs planted so that the upper half of hyacinths and the nose of daffodil bulbs are above the surface of the fibre. Fibre must be pressed into the spaces around the bottom of the bulbs and it is important not to leave any airholes below the bulbs. It is only worth planting good sound bulbs which are quite hard and firm and of flowering size. A small bulb will not build up to a big one in a bowl of fibre.

After planting they must be placed in a cool and dark place in order that a good rooting system may be formed. During this time the fibre must not be allowed to dry out. They may be placed in the garden and covered with ashes or peat moss, in a box on a verandah covered with the same or in a cool shed. A hot dry cupboard is not a suitable place for them since this will encourage top growth before good roots are formed. They must be protected from mice and rats. The former seem particularly to like crocus corms. This rooting will take two months at least and the bowls should be brought into the light when an inch or so of top growth is showing. By this time the bowl should be full of white roots and these can in most cases easily be examined by turning the bowl out. The bulbs should come to no harm if it is done carefully. If the roots are brown and not white it generally indicates that they have rotted in a sour fibre and have been over-watered. They should not be placed in a high temperature and for the next two weeks 40°F. by night and 50°F. by day is quite sufficient. This can be raised later if the bulbs are wanted to flower early in the year. If they are given too high a temperature too early the flowers may fail to develop and they will come " blind." For Christmas and early January flowering the bulbs need to be planted at the end of August or early in September and only a few kinds are suitable.

Among narcissi the bunch flowered tazettas such as ' Scilly Isles White,' ' Paper White ' and ' Soleil d'Or ' are the earliest. Among hyacinths the small flowered Roman kinds or specially prepared bulbs should be bought. The white variety ' L'Innocence ' is generally one of the earliest. The earliest tulips to flower are the single early flowering such as ' Brilliant Star,' ' Prince of Austria ' and ' General de Wet ' but the amateur does not often get them to flower as early as Christmas. For later flowering in the second half of January and February all the hyacinths should be successful, the deep blue ' Ostara ' being particularly good. Among the narcissi there is an ample choice. It is not worth buying expensive novelties for growing in bowls since afterwards the bulbs will take at least a year in the garden to recover and build up again. Such varieties as ' Carlton,' ' Rustom Pasha,' ' Fermoy ' and the large jonquil ' Trevithian ' will usually make excellent bowls for the house several weeks before they would flower outside.

Crocuses are nice in bowls too, but one must be careful not to grow them too hot or without plenty of ventilation or they will be likely to be blind. They may even be left plunged outside until the buds are showing. Also they tend to attract aphids in large quantities if grown in a warm house. *Fritillaria meleagris* are lovely in a bowl and for them the fibre can be kept rather damper than with other bulbs. The Spanish bluebells also do well in bowls but should be grown rather cool until the flower buds are showing.

### (9) THE BULB FRAME

A number of bulbs such as species of crocuses, irises and tulips seem to be more permanent and to grow and flower better from year to year when planted out into a frame rather than grown in pots and pans. They are also very much less trouble to look after and if arranged carefully their resting periods can be easily controlled by keeping the lights on. It is a more natural way of growing them. The kind of frame I would advocate is one raised so that the flowers are at waist level. In fact in this way it can be planted and viewed like a bulb bed in an alpine house and with a few small rocks made into a miniature garden. It is not the intention of such a frame to provide any great heat protection in winter and so it need not be air tight. In fact it is better if it is well ventilated. For ease of maintenance of the bed the kind of frame I would advocate is a metal one on small wheels which run along a metal bar on the top of the supporting wall. If this is built of breeze blocks it is quite adequate and quicker than building with bricks. Such a frame can be bought in sections and a new section added as the collection increases. It will, however, always be necessary to build the side wall one section at least longer than the frame so as to allow space for one section of glass to run along for opening. Such frames can generally be opened at the ends also by taking off the end glass and this is necessary as well when the bulbs inside have grown tall in order to avoid damage when running the frame along its rail.

In such a frame drainage is very important and this will of course be improved by raising the surface of the soil above ground level, but even so six inches of broken brick, stones and such material at the bottom is by no means too much. On top of this I would place a layer of rough compost from the compost heap or even old turves if available. The main bulk of the frame can then be filled with a mixture mainly composed of good loam but with some peat and coarse sand as well. For the majority of bulbs it is probably not too much to incorporate a good layer of old mushroom compost or really well broken down old manure among the soil a few inches below the depth at which the bulbs will be planted.

But it must be kept definitely below their planting depth or they may rot, and fresh manure must on no account be used. A top dressing of light shingle or granite or limestone chips after planting will also help to keep bulbs from rotting around the collar.

Such a frame should grow well all the small bulbs mentioned in the previous section as well as such difficult but beautiful irises as the Onco-cyclus group. It is important, however, to keep together all plants requiring similar resting periods; in general such plants as irises of the reticulata group, early crocus species and *chrysanthus* hybrids and some of the dwarf early daffodils will mix successfully together and will benefit from the protection of the frame. Early in June at the latest the lights should be run back over them and left in position till September to ensure a good ripening period. A thorough damping will be required then to start the bulbs off again into growth and at intervals through the winter and spring the lights may be run along in mild spells to allow the rain to water the frame for one. As long as the drainage is good it is unlikely to become too wet, and such bulbs require plenty of moisture when growing. During late March, April or May if the weather is good the lights can be left off entirely or, if there is not space to run them along, the top glass can be taken out.

Tulips, Juno irises and fritillaries which flower a little later will not require to start their ripening period till later, probably mid-June and so are best kept together. The earliest tulips such as the *violacea* forms of *T. pulchella* and *T. humilis* should, however, be grown with the first section. Cyclamen such as *C. pseudibericum* will also do well there but real spreaders such as some of the ornithogalum and muscari should be avoided. In such a frame one will probably obtain a good harvest also of seedlings as well as young bulbs arising from division. These can generally be left to grow on but every third or fourth year some groups may become so thick as to need lifting and dividing: then the surplus can be tried in the open garden without fears of losing one's entire stock. Such a frame is probably best suited to the winter and early spring flowers which require summer resting, but one section may be devoted also to late summer flowering plants such as zephyranthes and nerines which grow during the early part of the summer and can be kept dry during the winter. The hybrid *Amaryllis belladonna* forms are also excellent but make rather rank and extensive foliage in the summer and so should be kept separate from more delicate bulbs. Such a frame can house a large collection of rare and choice bulbs in quite a small space and can be maintained with a minimum of trouble.

(10) PROPAGATION OF BULBS

The main methods of propagation are by division and seed.

*Division*

This is undoubtedly the commonest and the easiest method, but it is sometimes slow to build up a stock of a choice bulb in this way. Bulbs vary considerably in the speed at which they divide and produce offsets. Some like muscari proliferate with bulblets like the frog spawning. Others like some of the choicer lilies will come up with single stems from year to year.

The majority of bulbs will, however, increase by division sufficiently rapidly for the clump to need lifting and dividing every third or fourth year and it is desirable to know when to do this for bulbs vary. Snowdrops are best lifted and divided when the flowers begin to fade and will then take little or no check. Narcissi are best lifted and divided in July and replanted in late August or early September. Lilies are best divided and replanted when growth begins to die down in September or early October or in spring when the young shoots appear. It should not be done during the winter months. Lilies can of course be propagated also from scales and this method is described under the genus. Stem bulblets also suffice in some species. Tulips should be lifted after they die down in June and need not be replanted till mid-October.

There is also a method of cutting up bulbs and inducing the section to produce bulblets and this is used by nurserymen for hyacinths but can be extended to other bulbs. A good description of it will be found in Mr. E. B. Anderson's excellent book *Dwarf Bulbs for the Rock Garden* and there is little point in my repeating his directions here since I have not had any personal experience of this method which is not much used by amateurs.

*Seed*

This is a most important method of increase and I would like to encourage more gardeners to undertake the growing of the rarer bulbs from seed. Only in this way can a large stock be built up and also interesting variations in colour, size, form and even hardiness and vigour may be obtained. Admittedly it is a slow process, three to five years to flowering size in most cases, in a few even more. The majority of seeds of bulbs are best sown as soon as they are ripe and in the case of hardy bulbs the pans can be plunged outside in a cold frame. If there is snow during the winter the frames can be opened and the snow will do no harm. In fact it may help to hasten germination when the spring comes. Many growers do not even use a glass but just protect the pans from leaves and mice by a fine meshed wire netting letting all the rain and weather fall on the pans. Although the seeds may have been sown in the summer there will probably be little germination till the following spring and some may even take two or three seasons. It is generally worth keeping such pans for three seasons before turning them out.

Slugs are the biggest enemy of young bulb seedlings and it is important to guard against these with slug bait or by watering with a slug repellent and killer. A covering on the pots of sharp coarse sand will also help in this connection and in keeping the pots clear of moss.

If it is desired to accelerate growth as much as possible the pans may be brought into a cool greenhouse when germination is seen but they will probably come to no harm if left outside in their frame or plunge bed. It is not generally desirable to prick them out the first year after germination but to wait another year until a small bulb has been formed when they can be turned out, sorted carefully and planted out in the autumn either into further pans or into the garden. One tends to lose them, however, if they are planted out in the open too young before a small bulb or corm has been made. If the pots are small they can be fed slightly with bone meal during growth. It follows from this that it is desirable to sow the seeds as thinly as possible. Tender bulbs will of course require greenhouse treatment in their seedling stages. In Anderson's *Dwarf Bulbs for the Rock Garden* will be found a useful table of the approximate times in years that various genera will take to reach flowering size. Such a table can, however, only be very approximate. It is a pity that *Tulipa* is one of the slowest genera.

## (11) ON COLLECTING BULBS

The natural habitats of bulbs throughout the world are very widespread and equally varied. In central and southern Europe and Asia Minor, where the majority of British gardeners may be tempted to collect, the bulbs will mostly be found in the mountain meadows often damp with running water in the early spring, at the edge of sub-alpine woodlands, on strong rocky slopes, particularly in Iran and parts of Turkey, but even in this case the melting snow will provide ample moisture though later the sun will bake the ground almost rock hard. More often the bulbs will be found on a slope where the drainage is good than on flat ground. Generally the bulbs will be much deeper than it is the custom to plant them in gardens. Often tulips will be found eight inches or even a foot down and crocuses and cyclamen nearly as deep. If the bulbs are collected when in flower or green leaf it is desirable not to break the stalk, but if one does do so then it is still worth while digging down carefully until one can find the base of it and so the bulb.

A narrow, long trowel like a fern trowel is generally the most useful implement and it is best to dig all round so that the bulb comes up with its basal plate and roots intact. A bulb from which the basal plate has been detached will nearly always fail to grow again.

Of course the best time to collect a bulb is after it has begun to die down and has become ripened and at this stage the flower for the next season will have already begun to form. After a little practice one becomes quite adept at recognising slightly withered leaves of crocus, tulip, colchicum and a number of others. The crocus leaf is distinguished from a grass leaf by the middle band of silvery green along the centre. The tulip leaf is nearly always glaucous and in many species often has a conspicuous undulating edge.

Bulbs in this condition can be cut directly off from their stem, cleared of their old outer covers, but not stripped quite bare, and placed in paper or other bags and left dry. It is not important to plant these again quickly; in fact they may often be left out of the ground in their bags until autumn. In the case of such bulbs as the Juno irises which have fleshy roots below the bulb it is important to keep as many of these intact as possible. They can be planted direct in the autumn into their final positions in the rock garden or bulb frame. With such bulbs it is often impossible to recognise the species from the withered leaf and there is no information about the colour of the flower, so it will be an added excitement the next spring to see what one has got when they flower.

The ideal method, of course, is to visit the collecting area in the spring and to mark the areas of desirable bulbs when they are in flower and then to return two or three months later to collect the bulbs when they are mature. However, the majority of collectors, especially amateurs—and very many species, and especially selected fine forms of species, have been brought into cultivation by amateurs—will only pass that way once and will need to collect their bulbs when they see them, perhaps in flower or even in bud. This will mean, particularly in the case of crocuses, reticulate irises and spring flowering colchicums, that only a little corm, bulb or tuber has already been built up for the following year. After digging the flower or seed head should be cut off since it is very unlikely to ripen its seed and would weaken the young bulb in so doing. The bulbs with leaves and stem should be placed in a polythene bag, preferably large enough to contain it all. A piece of newspaper may be wrapped round the bulb and base of the stem and secured with an elastic band. The top of the bag should be closed with another elastic band but it is generally well worth while to examine such bags each evening and if they are showing signs of becoming very damp and sweating so that there are drops of water inside the bag it should be left open overnight. Trouble arises in such bags far more often through the contents becoming too damp and beginning to rot rather than through their being too dry. It is important to allow plenty of air round the bag. If one merely throws all the bags one collects in a tight mass, one on top of the other, into a box or into the boot of a car, and then forgets them for a week or so, the chances are that all the leaves will have become a rotten mass and much will need to be thrown out. Such bulbs on one's return will need careful attention and are not ready to be planted direct into the open garden. It is best to plant them in a box of soil which is kept rather on the dry side and is made up with a high proportion of sand and drainage material. If the foliage is already beginning to brown and die down, then no further water should be given until the autumn or until they show signs of beginning to grow again. Such boxes should be placed in the shade and not baked in full sun and the rain must be kept off them in the summer. If the leaves, however, are still green and fresh the bulbs may well be given some water and grown on until the leaves begin to turn brown. In the case of bulbs collected in flower it is often an advantage to keep them in these boxes for a full season and let them flower there the next year if they will. In the late autumn when the bulbs are beginning to grow again a sprinkling of some fertiliser such as bone meal will help them. If, however, a flowering size bulb has been built up it can either be potted up or planted out into the open garden. It will do no harm to shake out the boxes of dry soil in the autumn and sort the bulbs out according to their size. It is most important though to keep the bulbs firm; a flabby bulb seldom grows successfully.

## (12) STRUCTURE AND ANATOMY

In this book are included plants which have bulbs, corms and a few with tubers or rhizomes.

A *bulb* is defined as a modified shoot with a disc-like basal plate and above it a number of fleshy scales which take the place of leaves and contain foods such as starch and sugar and some proteins. Each year from near the centre a new stem with or without flower bud arises, remains dormant or grows slightly through the winter and then grows away in the spring. Thus the rudimentary flower for the next season is developed at the end of the previous season and depends on the good cultivation and feeding of the bulb during the previous season rather than on the current season. The main examples given in this book are daffodils, tulips, scillas, hyacinths, irises, lilies and fritillaries. In the former the outside scale leaves of the bulb have become dry and membranous and provide an outer tunic but this is absent in lilies and fritillaries. Lilies have a large number of scales but in fritillaries the bulb is made up of

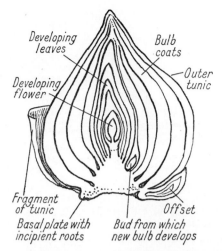

Fig. 1. A tulip bulb cut across to show the developing bud and the offset from which the bulb of the succeeding year will grow. The old tulip bulb dies after flowering and a new bulb is developed each year.

Developing leaves
Bulb coats
Developing flower
Outer tunic
Fragment of tunic
Offset
Basal plate with incipient roots
Bud from which new bulb develops

only two or three or in some of a number of rice grain bulblets around a small central bulb. A new bulb is formed from a lateral bud arising on the basal plate. In the case of a tulip the old bulb dies after flowering, leaving one or more newly formed bulbs in the tunic. A daffodil bulb, however, remains for several seasons, the young bulbs growing and developing by its side and eventually forming a clump if not divided.

A *corm* consists of the swollen base of a stem in which reserve food materials are stored. It is generally rounded or flattened at the top and surrounded by a membranous tunic. A new corm is formed each year on top of or beside the old one, which withers away though sometimes taking more than one year to fade away completely. The main examples in the book are crocus, gladiolus, watsonia and also colchicum which has a corm shaped irregularly like a tuber, one side of which projects downwards to form a foot-like part.

A *tuber* or rhizome is not the base of a stem but a swollen part of an underground stem. A tuber is usually roundish and often knobby as in

Fig. 2. A gladiolus corm cut across to show the young bud from which the flower spike will grow. A new corm is developed each year on top of the old corm which gradually withers away.

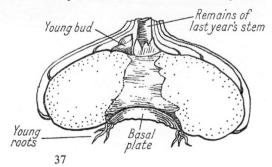

Young bud
Remains of last year's stem
Young roots
Basal plate

37

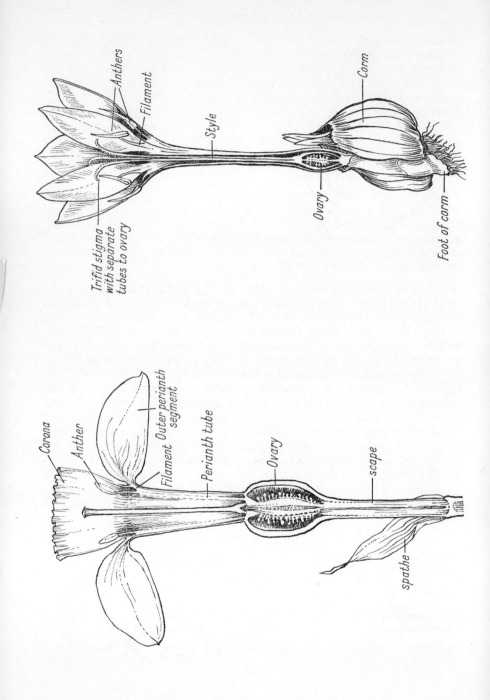

*Anemone coronaria* or an Arum lily, or trillium or a cyclamen and buds off other tubers in the three former examples form knobby eyes or buds. Cyclamen can only be propagated from seed or from cutting up the tuber, sometimes rather a risky operation. A *rhizome* is narrower and elongated and spreads widely underground sending up at intervals flowering stems or leafy stems and then spreading further underground beyond them. *Anemone nemorosa,* our common wild anemone is a good example of this.

### *Flower structure*

The three main families represented in this book are monocotyledons, that is, their seedlings come up with one initial seed leaf only. They are:

*Amaryllidaceae,* a very large family with about 75 genera in which the ovary is generally inferior, that is, the other floral parts are inserted above it. The flowers are either in an umbel or single as in many narcissi, while the stamens are usually six. In 1934 in his important work on the *Families of Flowering Plants,* J. Hutchinson redefined the older definition of the *Amaryllidaceae* laying more stress on the form of the inflorescence to include some genera in which the ovary is superior and then included in it *Allium, Brodiaea, Ipheion* and several other genera more usually included in *Liliaceae.*

*Liliaceae* is an even larger family with about 200 genera. The perianth segments are generally six arranged in two series, the stamens six and the carpel three and the ovary superior. The family includes such important bulbs as hyacinths, lilies, colchicums, fritillaries and tulips.

*Iridaceae* is a smaller family with between 50 and 60 genera. The perianth has six segments united below into a tube which may be long or short. There are *only three* stamens thus distinguishing it from the *Liliaceae* and the ovary is inferior. It includes such important genera as crocus, freesia, gladiolus and iris.

*Cyclamen* is quite outside these families and belongs to the *Primulaceae* as does the primrose.

### (13) PESTS AND DISEASES

Bulbs are fortunately subject to fewer troubles of this nature than the majority of plants. As long as they are purchased from a reliable source

Fig. 3 (*Left*) Diagrammatic section of flower of a narcissus to show arrangement of parts in the *Amaryllidaceae.*

Fig. 4 (*Right*) Diagrammatic section of flower of a Colchicum to show arrangement of parts in the *Liliaceae* and differences from the crocus flower of the *Iridaceae.*

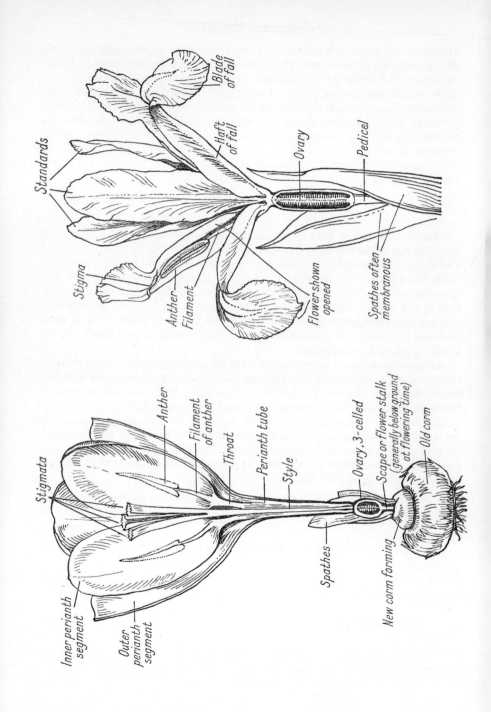

in nearly all cases the buyer can safely rely on the dry bulbs or corms being free of disease, the only exception being unfortunately the lily bulbs in which some stocks still have much virus infection. However, even in that case, suppliers are mostly now alive to the danger and rogue out any infected plants as soon as they detect them. Probably the worst enemies are slugs and aphids and in these cases bulbs are no exception to the majority of other plants. Mice and occasionally squirrels also may burrow down and eat the bulb and many of the disappearances which otherwise appear mysterious may be caused by them. For further information on pests the late Mr. Fox Wilson's excellent book *Horticultural Pests: detection and control* should be consulted. It has recently been revised and brought up-to-date by Dr. P. Becker. For disease there is a useful bulletin from the Ministry of Agriculture entitled " Diseases of Bulbs " by Mr. W. C. Moore. It is Bulletin No. 117. Information will also be found in the R.H.S. Dictionary of Gardening under each genus. So we will only deal here with the main sources of trouble. Pests are usually regarded as including all insect and animal predators while diseases cover fungus, bacterial and virus troubles. The number of proprietary insecticides and fungicides is now very vast and the field changes from year to year. The Ministry of Agriculture runs an approval scheme for tested chemicals and those with the approved mark, a prominent diamond-shaped label with a crown in the centre, can be relied upon. Here only a small number can be mentioned and recommended which are known to be effective and there are probably many more which would serve as well.

Prevention, however, rather than cure is still the aim to be achieved and for this a high standard of garden and particularly greenhouse and frame cleanliness is very important. All rotten or diseased material or dead or diseased plants should be cleared away as soon as they are observed and burnt before they spread infection. Regular use of Meta bait against slugs and snails and spraying against aphids is also well worth while in the greenhouse and frame and in some cases in the rock garden as well.

Damage from one cause, particularly a boring or sucking insect, may well lay open the path by which other organisms or parasites enter the tissues of the plant and cause much worse damage than the initial. Any bulbs that are soft after storage or on lifting should be examined carefully and nearly always rejected.

In cases of doubt competent and practised advice is generally readily available to Fellows of The Royal Horticultural Society from their

---

Fig. 5 (*Left*) Diagrammatic section of flower of a crocus to show arrangement of parts in the *Iridaceae*.

Fig. 6 (*Right*) Diagrammatic section of flower of a bulbous iris to show arrangements of parts.

# Pests and Diseases

technical advisory officers at Wisley who are specialists in the field of ornamental plant troubles, and anybody can consult the Ministry of Agriculture advisory pest control and other officers. Several large firms of insecticide makers also give such advisory service. The pests are dealt with here in order of size rather than of importance.

## Pests

*Squirrels, rabbits* and *hares.* Sometimes they will dig up a bulb in soft soil, particularly a lily bulb, or they may eat the young shoots. Rabbits especially seem to be partial to young lily shoots. Squirrels, however, do far more damage to young trees and shrubs than to bulbs. The only cure is trapping or shooting but if one is lucky enough to live in a part of the country where the red squirrel still survives, one must simply put up with the bulb damage in order to preserve this delightful little animal which is now unfortunately so rare in this country. Very choice bulbs can be surrounded with wire netting dug into the soil and turned over at the top.

*Mice.* These are probably more destructive than most gardeners realise. Bulbs in store are particularly tempting to them. Traps can be set or poisoned baits containing a substance called " Warfarin " can be used, preferably placed in an old drain pipe or under a jar or tin lying on its side to protect it from the rain. It is claimed that small doses do not harm dogs, cats or birds. Such baits should be protected from the rain.

*Slugs and snails.* These cause perhaps the greatest damage of all pests by eating the young shoots of bulbs and particularly the first leaves of seedlings soon after they have emerged from the ground. Collapse of a stem may also be due to slug damage, one side of the stem having been eaten away. Generally their presence can be detected by a trail of slime in the morning. In a greenhouse small numbers can often be picked up and squashed after dark with the aid of a torch but continuous prevention with baits is much better and a number of effective ones are available containing Meta. Although there are several species both of slugs and of snails which cause damage the result and the treatment are much the same.

*Aphids.* There are many different species and races of aphids, but their differentiation is not usually important to the gardener since all are deleterious and should be destroyed where seen. They multiply with incredible rapidity and through their sucking out of the cell sap cause malformation, twisting of leaves, yellowing and premature wilting and leaf fall, greatly reducing the vigour of growth. Both the aphids and the symptoms are generally easily seen by the naked eye. Virus diseases are spread by aphids and this forms a second very strong reason for keeping

42

one's plants clean from them, particularly in the case of lilies which are very susceptible. The honeydew secreted by the aphids also encourages the growth of sooty moulds as well as the presence of ants. Fortunately there are now many chemical sprays which destroy aphids very effectively and prevent colonies being built up. In summer, however, a fortnightly precautionary spray is not too frequent. Lindane which contains Gamma BHC, Sybol and Malathion which contains a more potent organophosphorus poison are the substances most used by amateurs. Nicotine used to be the main insecticide of this type but has now largely been superseded. The newer systemic insecticides which are taken up into the cell sap of the plant are also most effective, often keeping a plant clean for a month or longer but must be used with care strictly according to the makers' instructions.

*Root aphids.* These are generally detected by wilting and loss of vigour of the plant. When it is lifted for examination the roots may be covered with grey aphids. Really badly infested plants should be destroyed but a reasonable control of less infected plants can be obtained by spraying the roots with Malathion and then washing them clean before replanting in fresh uninfected soil. It is advisable to control ants in neighbouring colonies since these may be closely associated with the aphids.

There are, of course, many other causes for wilting which is the result of insufficient root absorbtion ranging from lack of water, to root damage, from damage by wireworms, cockchafer grubs etc., to rotting of roots caused by lack of aeration in sour soil.

*Mites.* Bulb mites are small yellowish-white, rounded arachnids. They are not true insects but belong to the same order as the spiders. The bulb mites are just visible to the naked eye and attack bulbs especially in winter and where there has been some previous injury. Badly infested bulbs should be destroyed. Bulb scale mites are smaller and their effect shows as yellowish-brown streaks or flecks on the scales and in the neck of the bulb. The markings are often red in amaryllids. The hot water treatment as recommended for narcissus flies will also be effective for control of such mites.

*White grubs and leatherjackets.* These are respectively the larvae of Cockchafers and Crane Flies or Daddy Long Legs. The former are large, very fat, white soft grubs, the latter greyish and with a tough skin. The white grubs live in the soil for several years and are particularly prevalent in old grassland and also close to large hedges. Both feed on roots of grasses, bulbs and other plants and will bore into the bulb as well. When one sees a plant wilting unexpectedly they are often the cause. No really satisfactory remedy has been yet found for them but probably the best is to turn up the soil, squash such grubs as one sees and leave the birds to get some more. Some measure of control can also be obtained by working DDT or Aldrin in dust form into the upper layers of the soil but it is expensive over any large area. This should be done either in autumn or spring when they are nearest to the surface.

*Narcissus flies.* There are three of these, a large and two small. The large is placed in the genus *Merodon*, but the small have now been transferred to *Eumerus*. The large narcissus fly has a fat, grub-like whitish larva which burrows into bulbs which become soft and spongy and decay from the basal place. The leaves if any, are weak and may also be twisted. Any such bulbs found should be burnt. The adults lay the eggs between late April and the end of June and in this time it is worth dusting rows of narcissi with Lindane around the tops of the bulbs. Professional, and some of the larger amateur, growers also lift their bulbs every third or fourth year and then immerse them for an hour in hot water. The recommended temperature is now 110°F. and this kills all grubs without harming the bulbs too much. They are seldom, however, quite so good in the succeeding year. These flies also attack hyacinths, scillas and occasionally lilies.

The grub of the smaller narcissus fly is rather like a much smaller version of the large one but several may occupy one bulb so the result is the same. The treatment is also the same. They attack hyacinths as well.

*Stem and bulb eelworm.* These are minute nematode worms, usually only visible under a microscope but multiplying very fast and capable of doing much damage. This is usually first noticed in the leaves which become twisted and malformed and sometimes streaked. The bulb when dug up will show brown patches or rings in the scales and in the case of tulips this flower may also be distorted. The forms of eelworms are numerous and several appear to be specific only to one plant. Tulips, irises, hyacinths, narcissi and snowdrops are the main bulbs attacked. At present there is no easy chemical cure, although the hot water treatment of narcissus bulbs has diminished the infection very much in most professional growers' stocks. It is possible that treatment along the same lines may in the future be recommended for tulips also. Otherwise infected bulbs should be burnt and if possible the ground used for something different for the next few years.

*Thrips.* These are very small flies which produce a white mottling or streaking on the leaves. The flowers can also be attacked with the same result. Gladioli are the most frequent hosts among the range of plants dealt with here but hippeastrum and cyclamen may also be attacked. The flies also hibernate on the dried corms of the gladioli during the winter and cause dark rough patches where the corm becomes hard and dead. Spraying the foliage with Lindane or Malathion at rather frequent intervals will keep the pests under control and the corms can be dusted with DDT.

# Pests and Diseases

## Diseases

These are not so numerous as the pests but nevertheless there are a few fungus diseases which are worth attention, while virus diseases are becoming very serious in many genera.

*Botrytis.* This is probably the most serious of the fungus diseases, particularly on bulbs such as lilies, snowdrops and tulips. In each case a different species is involved, but the symptoms always involve brown spotted or mottled areas on the leaves and stems. The disease can usually be checked by spraying with a copper spray such as Bordeaux Mixture and in the case of lilies preventive spraying throughout the season is worth while. The disease is usually more prevalent in a damp season and tends to spread very fast once established.

*Lilies.* The fungus is *Botrytis elliptica* and the disease first shows as circular pale brown areas which later turn grey as the spores develop until finally the whole leaf turns brown and droops and may even fall off or the stem may collapse prematurely. This considerably weakens the bulb for next year. It particularly attacks Madonna lily *L. candidum* and precautions against this must start with spraying of the overwintering green basal rosettes of leaves. It is important to burn all dead leaves and stems rather than leave them on the ground for the spores to collect.

*Tulips.* The disease called " Fire " in tulips is caused by *Botrytis tulipae.* It is also sometimes known as " Tulip Mould " and shows first on stunted plants which become withered and show greyish diseased areas. This can spread very quickly especially in boxes of tulips used for forcing and in damp weather. The disease can also attack both the flowers and the bulbs and can be seen as brownish round lesions below the tunic, which may spread to infect the whole of the fleshy part of the bulb. Such bulbs should be burnt and infected plants rogued out and burnt as soon as they are noticed. Once the disease has become epidemic no spraying is likely to cure it but if there are only spasmodic diseased plants it is worth spraying the others with Tulisan after the malformed ones have been rogued out.

*Other bulbs.* " Fire " disease also occurs in hyacinths and in narcissi where it is called " Smoulder " but in this country it is not so serious as on lilies and tulips. As above any malformed plants should be rogued out and burnt, especially if the leaves are yellow and wilted. In snowdrops " Grey Mould " is caused by *Botrytis galanthina* and can be a killer, the leaves, and then the whole bulb, rotting away.

*Basal rots.* This is a fairly wide term used for a number of fungus diseases affecting the basal plate of bulbs. In narcissus it is caused by *Fusarium bulbigenum*, which appears first usually in bulbs in storage and then spreads upwards throughout the bulb causing a brown decay of the

45

tissues. Such bulbs will be soft at planting time and should be discarded as even a slightly attacked bulb will be unlikely to recover completely or produce sound foliage or flower. There is no known cure at present.

In lilies the basal plate may be attacked by a *Fusarium* fungus causing the scales of the bulb to fall apart after the base has disintegrated. This is fatal and unfortunately the resting spores of the disease can remain in the soil for several years so new lilies should be planted in a different place. Lilies seem to be particularly susceptible in their younger stages and after moving.

*Ink disease.* This is confined to the reticulate bulbous section of iris and is caused by a species of *Mystrosporium*. It appears as dark black patches over the outer tunic of the bulb and then spreads inwards causing the bulb to rot. It is particularly prevalent on *Iris reticulata*. No satisfactory control is known and diseased bulbs should be discarded.

*Plant viruses.* These present some of the most serious problems to the gardener of all diseases. There are numerous strains of virus which can infect the cells of plants. Some are specific only to one type of plant while others such as the tomato mosaic virus can infect a number of plants. Under an electronic microscope, which has very high power, some viruses can be seen as crystalline bodies in the cell nucleus or plasma, but their exact structure is barely known although very considerable advances have been made on this side in recent years.

The symptoms usually associated with virus diseases are distortion and twisting of the stem, leaves or flowers, flecking and streaking of the flowers such as in " broken " tulips and yellow mottling and streaking or ringed spots on the leaves generally coupled with the death and rotting of the cells in the mottled patches. These often spread along the veins. The symptoms seem to vary also with conditions of light and heat and in some cases may be partially suppressed by a very low or very high temperature. In this perhaps lies our best hopes of a cure in the future. General loss of vigour results in very varying degrees. A virus disease is the cause of broken colour in tulips and such bulbs seem able to continue although with decreased vigour for many years. Again lilies are very subject to virus diseases of several strains. With one of them the lily seems able to live without too much damage but when a separate strain infects it as well the collapse becomes rapid. Curiously, however, the masked virus can be transmitted and show symptoms in other plants. More discussion of lily viruses will be found in the lily section.

Viruses are transmitted chiefly by insect carriers and these are mainly aphids, hence the importance of spraying constantly against these pests. Viruses can also be spread by mechanical means such as a knife blade which has been used to cut an infected plant. They are perpetuated by vegetative propagation as well as by cuttings and grafting and so it is important to weed out and burn all infected plants. A very few viruses have been found to be spread through seeds or transmitted through the soil but so far this means has not applied to any of those now known to infect bulbs.

It is often difficult for the gardener to identify with certainty a virus infection in the early stages. Some of the symptoms could be caused either by a simple aphid attack or even by unsatisfactory weather or nutritional troubles. In a valuable stock of bulbs it is better, however, to lift and isolate any suspected plants and above all to try and keep down all agents of infection such as aphids. In the case of a more common bulb it is better to destroy it on the first suspicion of the disease. This applies particularly to narcissi infected with stripe disease in which the leaves come up distorted and with longitudinal pale, or even bright, yellow stripes and raised ridges on the surface. At present there is no known cure for virus infected plants that can be carried out by the average gardener at home.

# *Alphabetical List of Bulbs*

# ABBREVIATIONS

\* Species and varieties especially recommended

† Species and varieties which need some protection in colder areas and are more suitable for specially protected and warm gardens when grown outside

*fl.* flower or flowers

*l.* leaf or leaves

sp. species

Syn. Synonym, another name given to the same plant, but now discarded for one of several reasons.

# NAMES OF PLANTS

Generic and specific names and those of botanical varieties are given in bold type where described, elsewhere in italics. Names of horticultural varieties which are thought to be clones, and which will therefore not be expected to vary, are printed in small capitals in single quotation marks. Names of Group Hybrids or Grexes, as they are often called, are in small caps but without quotation marks. They may be expected to show variation.

*Throughout this book plate numbers in arabic figures refer to colour plates, while roman numerals are used for black and white plates*

# ACHIMENES *Gesneriaceae*

GREENHOUSE tuberous perennials requiring a temperature of 60 to 65°F. while they are making their growth. They provide useful colour in the greenhouse in summer and when in flower may be transferred to a cooler house. Flower funnel-shaped or tubular with prominent corolla lobes, mauve, blue, pink, red or white. Most of those now grown are nurserymen's hybrids but *A. longiflora* with large solitary violet-blue flowers is also worth growing and is probably the best species. There are also white, pink and red forms of it. Most of the species are native to Central and S. America. *A. tubiflora* has 2 ft. spikes of large waxy-white flowers with a fine scent. Syn. *Gloxinia tubiflora, Dolichoderia tubiflora.*

Achimenes should be dried off and allowed to rest in the winter and started into growth in the spring, planting the tubers 1 to 1½ in. deep. They should be grown in a generous potting compost and assisted with some extra feeding when in full growth and not allowed to become dry. Several small tubers may be set together in a pot or basket. They are less common now than formerly owing to the expense of retaining heated houses. The tips of the first young shoots should be pinched out so as to induce a bushy growth.

Achimenes are usually grown from tubers but may also be grown from seed. The tubers or rhizomes can also be cut up and divided like a potato in the spring or they can be grown from leaf cuttings like a saint-paulia, or ordinary cuttings taken during the summer. Seeds will only germinate in a high temperature and the plants should bloom in the second year.

# ACIDANTHERA *Iridaceae*

THESE are closely related to *Gladiolus* and the corms require similar treatment except that they are not so hardy and flower later in the summer. Only one species *A. bicolor* from Abyssinia is generally grown and a larger and more vigorous variety *\*murielae* has almost superseded the type (Pl. 5, 1). This has large white, slightly drooping flowers about 2 in. across with a large perianth tube; each petal has a large dark purple blotch at its base. Fragrant. Stem 2½ to 3½ ft. and six or more flowers to a stem. Leaves narrow, like those of a gladiolus. *A. bicolor* is hardy

51

in the warmer parts of this country and in the West of N. America, but in colder areas the corms should be lifted annually and planted in spring about the end of April or early May. They are slow developers and often do not flower before the end of September or early October, so it is sometimes advisable to start them in pots in a greenhouse. They are also suitable for a cool greenhouse or can be grown in a frame.

# ALBUCA *Liliaceae*

COOL greenhouse bulbous plants with white, greenish-white or yellowish flowers in loose racemes from South and Tropical Africa; somewhat resembling galtonias, to which they are nearly related. In very mild areas or in California and the West of U.S.A. they may be grown out-doors provided they are given some winter protection. Bulbs should be potted in early autumn in a good compost and watered and fertilised during the growing period. Resting period is in late summer when no water is required.

A. **nelsonii** is the commonest sp.; *fl.* white with a brick-red stripe down outside of each segment, fragrant. Flowering scapes and racemes up to 5 ft. in height May-June; *l.* long, narrow. Natal. Other species occasionally found are:

A. **altissima**. White with green back to petals; 1½ to 2 ft.

A. **aurea**. Pale yellow with greenish ray on outside of each petal; 12 in.

A. **major**. Greenish-yellow with green stripe on outside.

A. **minor**. Similar to *A. major*, but smaller in both *l.* and *fl.* 12 in., drooping. May. Known in S. Africa as " soldiers in the box."

# ALLIUM *Liliaceae*

A VERY LARGE genus of bulbous plants mostly hardy, ranging over Europe, N. Africa, Asia and N. America to Mexico. The onion, leek, garlic, chive and shallot all belong to this genus but are considered to fall out-side the scope of this book. Although no species are very conspicuous a number are well worth growing for their soft colourings, while the bold globular heads of the ordinary onion are not in any way a mean decora-tion when in flower. They mostly grow well in a well-drained position, the Asiatic species being rather less vigorous than the European and including several most graceful little species with linear leaves like tufts of fine grass and best suited for the rock garden. For the most part the

*Plate* 1: ALLIUM. 1, *A. pulchellum*. 2, *A. siculum*. 3, *A. ostrowskyanum*. 4, *A. beesianum*. 5, *A. moly*. 6, *A. murrayanum*. 7, *A. caeruleum*. 8, *A. triquetrum*. 9, *A. cyaneum*. 10, *A. neapolitanum*. 11, *A. narcissiflorum*. 12, *A. cyaphorum*. var. *farreri*. 13, *A. falcifolium*

*Plate* 2: 1, *Amaryllis belladonna*, typical form. 2, *A. belladonna* ‘ Parkeri ’. 3, *Crinodonna corsii*

# *Allium*

onion scent is only noticeable when the leaves are bruised or the bulbs lifted. Only a small selection of the species which could be obtained by anyone concentrating on the genus can be included here. Propagation is by offsets from the bulb or by seeds sown in spring or late summer. The commonest species is the yellow *A. moly* and this spreads very freely and is suitable for naturalising in meadows or open woodlands.

**A. acuminatum.** Light to deep lilac, sometimes pink or deep rose-purple in flattish heads 1–2 in. across, 6–12 in. *L*. linear. July-August. Western N. America. This sp. is distinguished by the three outer segments being recurved and large while the inner are acuminate, hence the name, and stand erect over the gynoecium. It was discovered by Archibald Menzies during Dr. Vancouver's famous voyage of discovery. A pleasant though not very spectacular plant for the large rock garden.

\* **A. albopilosum.** Violet-blue and with a metallic sheen, tepals narrow, pointed, in very large globose heads up to 8 in. across and with up to 80 *fl*. in one head. Stem 1–2 ft. *L*. strap-shaped, slightly glaucous and hairy below. A peculiar plant of very considerable distinction, the flower heads looking like glossy violet footballs, always noticed in the garden. Not as vigorous a grower or spreader as some species but well worth a place in a sunny border. Turkestan.

**A. amabile.** Deep rose to magneta-red, spotted on inside, petals recurved near tips when *fl*. fully open, pendulous, bell-shaped in umbels of 2–5 *fl*.; 4–8 in. *L*. linear; stem slender. Late summer. China, N.W. Yunnan. Found by G. Forrest. A plant for a well-drained place on the rock garden and a true alpine. *A. mairei* is very similar and is sometimes regarded as being synonymous, the *fl*. being lighter in colour, white to pale rose, and the *l*. stiffer and broader. Syn. *A. yunnanense*.

**A. azureum.** Syn. of *A. caeruleum*.

**A. beesianum.** A graceful sp. from Yunnan and W. China. *Fl*. bright blue, sometimes purplish-blue, pendulous in small umbels on 9–12 in. stems. *L*. linear and growing in tufts. A delightful and rather unusual late summer flowering plant, suitable for a warm place on the rock garden. Collected by G. Forrest who also collected a white form but unfortunately this is not known in cultivation. (Pl. **1**, 4)

**A. caeruleum.** Deep sky-blue, *fl*. star-like in small but dense umbels. 1–2 ft. *L*. linear. June-July. Turkestan. A plant for the large rock garden or sunny border. Syn. *A. azureum*. (Pl. **1**, 7)

**A. cernuum.** A very variable and widespread N. American sp. *Fl*. rose, whitish with rose-pink base to tepals or purple, in pendulous umbels, rather loose, of 30–40 *fl*. Scape 1–1½ ft. June-July. Scent of plant strong. *L*. linear. A beautiful and easily cultivated plant.

**A. cyaneum.** Brilliant turquoise-blue, probably the strongest in colour of the genus. Flower-heads small, stem 9–12 in. Suitable for the rock garden and one of the most attractive, if not most spectacular sp. Introduced first by Farrer from Kansu who described the *fl.* as " very beautiful with its heads of rich bluebell blue in August." *L.* linear. Well illustrated in Col. Grey's *Hardy Bulbs.* (Pl. **1**, 9)

**A. cyathophorum** var. **farreri.** A slightly larger plant with reddish-purple bell-shaped *fl.* in umbels of up to 30 to a head. 12–15 in. Also collected by Farrer in Kansu. Early summer. *L.* linear. (Pl. **1**, 12) Syn. *A. farreri.*

**A. falcifolium.** A dwarf sp. from Western N. America. Stem up to 3 in. with a small umbel of star-like pinkish-purple *fl.* with yellow pollen. *L.* broadly linear. Suitable for the rock garden or alpine house, rare in cultivation. (Pl. **1**, 13)

**A. flavum.** A small yellow-flowered sp. from S. Europe. 12–15 in. *Fl.* small, bell-shaped; up to 30 in an umbel. *L.* linear.

**A. giganteum.** One of the larger onions, as its name implies. Stem up to 4 ft. with large, globose heads up to 4 in. in diameter of closely packed little lilac-coloured *fl.* An effective plant for sunny places in the wild garden or border. June.

**A. kansuense.** Another delicate blue-flowered sp. for the rock garden or alpine house, introduced by Farrer from high altitudes and screes in Kansu. *Fl.* pale blue, drooping in a many-flowered umbel. Late summer. 4–12 in. *L.* linear. There is also a violet-blue form.

\* **A. karataviense.** A very fine sp. with decorative, very broad, glaucous, sometimes variegated, leaves lying flat usually in pairs. *Fl.* white, sometimes pink, in a large dense umbel like a big ball up to 1 ft. in circumference, on stout stems 6–8 in. *L.* broad, glaucous, slightly mottled. May-June. Suitable for the front of a sunny border or a large rock garden. (Pl. I)

**A. macranthum.** An unusual sp. in that its root is fleshy and almost rhizomatous. A tall plant up to 3 ft. with a large head of bell-shaped pendulous *fl.* up to 50 in a head and each ½ in. long, mauve-purple. Sikkim. June-July.

**A. moly.** Probably the best known of the wild garlics. Golden-yellow, star-like, in many-flowered umbels on 6–12 in. stems. Increasing very rapidly and suitable for naturalising in open sunny places or in light woodland. June-July. *L.* lanceolate, deep green. South and South-West Europe. (Pl. **1**, 5)

**A. murrayanum.** Closely allied to the better known *A. acuminatum* and like it a good garden plant for the front of the sunny border or large rock garden. Stem 1 ft. with an umbel of many pale pink or purplish-pink *fl.* May-June. North America. (Pl. **1**, 6)

**A. narcissiflorum.** A common plant of the North Italian Alps with bright pinkish-purple, bell-shaped, somewhat pendulous *fl.*, 8–12 in. Described, perhaps not unjustly, by Farrer as "the glory of its race." A plant from the stony screes but nevertheless suitable to a sheltered warm place in the rock garden or a pan in the alpine house. *L.* strap-shaped. June-July. Syn. *A. pedemontanum.* (Pl. **1**, 11)

**A. neapolitanum.** One of the most early-flowering of the genus, common in

Southern Europe, especially in moist places. *Fl.* white, about ½–¾ in. in diameter, in loose umbels on 8–12 in. stems. *L.* linear or strap-shaped. March-May. Tender except in sheltered situations but good as a pot plant in the cool greenhouse, and almost without the characteristic onion scent. In fact it is sold as a cut flower in Southern Europe. (Pl. **1**, 10)

**A. oreophilum** var. **ostrowskianum.** A beautiful plant with large round umbels of many pink or purple *fl.* each rather larger than is usual in the genus. 8–12 in. June-July. Suitable for the large rock garden or front of the border. Turkestan. (Pl. **1**, 3). Syn. *A. ostrowskianum.*

**A. pulchellum.** *Fl.* small, reddish-violet, with stamens projecting as far again as the segments of the perianth; *fl.* in a loose umbel with pedicels of uneven length. 1–2 ft. May-June. Eastern Mediterranean regions. (Pl. **1**, 1)

**A. rosenbachianum.** One of the stout large-flowered onions from Central Asia and the regions of Bokhara. *Fl.* purplish-violet or rose-purple in round heads. 2–2½ ft. June-July. A decorative plant for the border and one of the most handsome members of the genus.

**A. roseum.** Star-like, bright pink *fl.* up to 20 in loose umbels. 8–12 in. S. Europe and N. Africa. A good sp. for a warm position in the large rock garden, spreading freely.

* **A. siculum.** A tall sp. up to 3 ft. with large blue-green, broad bell-shaped, almost squarish *fl.* broadly striped with dark red on the outside, borne on long curving pedicels in large loose umbels of up to 30 flowers. May-June. A striking and graceful plant for the border, practically scentless in the flowers, though not in the stem and leaves if bruised. Sicily and S. France. (Pl. **1**, 2)

**A. sphaerocephalum.** *Fl.* dark purple, bell-shaped in dense umbels on stems 1–2 ft. July-August. Widely distributed in Europe and Asia Minor and a rare native in Britain.

**A. tibeticum.** A beautiful sp. with deep blue or purple *fl.* suitable for the rock garden or even large scree. 6 in. *Fl.* bell-shaped, large for an *Allium*, but only a few to the umbel. *L.* linear. Summer. Tibet.

**A. triquetrum.** A white-flowered sp. with a strong scent, distinguished by its three-angled stems, common in S. Europe and generally spreading freely when admitted to the garden, so better suited for naturalising in the wild garden. Regarded by many gardeners as a menace. Umbel with 6–10 large bell-shaped *fl.* on 1 ft. stems. May-June. (Pl. **1**, 8)

**A. victorialis.** *Fl.* yellowish, sometimes white, small but numerous in large umbels, 1–2 ft. Mediterranean. May. *L.* oblong-lanceolate, wider than in most sp.

**A. zebdanense.** This white flowered sp. derives its name from Zebdan a place in the Lebanon, the *fl.* being large and bell-shaped. 1–2 ft. May-June. Requires a very warm and sheltered position.

**Amarcrinum howardii.** See under *Crinodonna.*

# AMARYLLIS *Amaryllidaceae*

A MONOTYPIC genus as now generally understood and containing that very fine bulbous plant from S. Africa, *A. belladonna*. Flower pale pink with a slight mauvish tinge, 2–2½ ft., September-October, flowering before the leaves appear. Each flower trumpet-shaped, paler at the throat; 2–4 flowers to a stem; leaf strap-shaped appearing in winter and early spring. Bulbs very large. (Pl. **2**, 1)

A. belladonna should be planted in as warm a border as possible, that outside the wall of a heated greenhouse being particularly suitable. Once planted the bulbs should be left alone for many years. They are unlikely to flower the first season after planting. Good drainage is required and also a good measure of feeding with bone meal, dried blood and even some well-rotted stable manure once the bulbs are established. They flower best after a really hot summer and for the same reason seem to grow even better in California, Australia and New Zealand and S. France than they do in this country. It is sometimes suggested that if there is no heavy rain they should be flooded about mid-August so as to start the flower spikes into growth and provided they have been well baked during the summer I think that this is a good practice. In cold areas some protection for the young foliage from the frost should be given with dry bracken, straw or cloches. Propagation is chiefly by division of the bulbs but they can be raised from seed ; this is very slow indeed in this country, the young bulbs not flowering for seven years generally and often taking longer.

Several selected forms have been named and these are definitely finer than the type. They are however still uncommon plants for the most part, but are well worth making an effort to obtain.

elata. A tall form up to 3 ft., flowering earlier than the type and slightly paler in colour but with a pronounced central streak of darker colour down the centre of each tepal. Stems brownish-maroon.

* ' HATHOR ' A very fine pure white form with a yellow throat and large heads of *fl.*

kewensis. A very late flowering dark pink form with yellow at the throat.

* multiflora. A fine strain of varying shades and with large *fl.* head, raised in Australia and probably originally of the same parentage as Parkeri, recently much developed in California where great globular heads of *fl.* of better colour than the sp. have been produced and appear to be a considerable improvement on the type.

* ' PARKERI' A vigorous plant with large flower-heads of a deep pink with yellow at the throat, up to 12 *fl.* to a stem. This is generally considered to have been raised in Sydney, Australia, from a cross between *A. belladonna* and *Brunsvigia josephinae*. It however resembles the *Amaryllis*, and it may possibly have been produced parthenogenetically. (Pl. **2**, 2)

**rubra.** Flowering later than the type; *fl.* deep vivid pink, white at the throat. A fine tall-growing form, sometimes up to 3 ft. Flower-stalk reddish.

# ANEMONE  *Ranunculaceae*

WINDFLOWERS. Daisy-like flowers with broad or narrow petaloid sepals taking the place of the petals and often yellow or white centres.

The tuberous and rhizomatous rooted anemones give us some of the most delightful of all spring flowers and are suited for a wide variety of situations. One species, *A. nemorosa*, is the common wild anemone of our woodlands, but for gardens there are several selected forms of it which are even more beautiful than the wild species. The other species which we grow are for the most part natives of the Mediterranean countries, S. France, Italy and especially Greece, and are therefore best planted in open situations where the soil is well drained and the tubers may be well ripened in the summer. Anemones are especially plants to be grown in large masses and a small colony, if left undisturbed, will often spread to carpet with colour a large area. One of the finest flower spectacles that I know is in a Sussex garden near the coast where a few corms of the dark blue form of *A. blanda* have spread to form a solid mass of blue in a wide border. They now cover many square yards and even tend to spread out into the neighbouring grass walks. On a sunny day in March, flowering generally at the same time as a nearby pink almond, they are a wonderful sight and it is a planting which never fails, provides flower for three weeks to a month and requires the minimum of upkeep.

Another good combination is the planting of anemones under old fruit trees where the soil needs little disturbance and where they will flower before the trees open their leaves. They combine well in rock gardens with many dwarf bulbs such as the species of *Narcissus* and the early tulips.

The Poppy anemones, hybrids and strains developed from *A. coronaria*, *A. hortensis*, *A. pavonina* and *A. fulgens*, are very widely grown for the flower market especially in Cornwall and the Scilly Isles, where they flower from October till April depending on the month in which the tubers are planted. Many commercial growers, however, find it most satisfactory to plant fresh tubers each year from stocks developed on the rich soils of the bulb areas of East Anglia or Holland.

Although authorities differ on the origin of the name, anemones are popularly and most appropriately regarded as the Windflowers, being derived from *anemos*, the Greek word for wind. Another derivation, and probably the prior and correct one, is from the Syrian word " Na-ma'an," the annual cry of lament for the dead Adonis whose blood is described by legend as flaming yearly back to life in the flowers of the scarlet anemones.

The hepaticas are regarded as a separate genus but are fibrous rather than tuberous rooted while the Pulsatilla group (also now treated by most botanists under a separate genus *Pulsatilla*) are regarded as being more herbaceous perennials than tuberous plants and so both fall outside the scope of this book.

Most anemones are easily grown from seed, which in the species considered here, is contained in small achenes and should be sown as fresh as possible. The seedlings do not transplant easily when small and it is probably better to leave the box or pan until the green leaves have died down and then shake out the little tubers for replanting.

The flowers of all the tuberous anemones only open in the sun. The leaves are finely divided and provide a pleasant complement to the flowers.

\* **A. appenina.** The bright sky-blue anemone of open woodland of S. Europe, often found naturalised in English woods. *Fl.* blue, single, but white, pink and double forms are also known: 6 in. March-April. Slightly taller than *A. blanda* but with *fl.* a little smaller, up to 1½ in. across, and tepals 10–18 and narrower. Flowering later. Rhizome is thick, almost black and cylindrical and more like a tuber than in *A. nemorosa* and has finger-like projections easily broken off to form new plants, but it is less like a tuber than in *A. blanda* or *A. coronaria*. A lovely *fl.*, spreading widely either in half shade or sun, best moved soon after flowering and rhizomes should not be allowed to dry out. Once planted they should be left undisturbed and may be naturalised in rough grass. (Pl. 3, 6a–b)

\* **A. blanda.** The mountain anemone of Greece. March-April. *Fl.* deep blue, pale blue, mauve, pink or white, 1½–2 in. across. (Pl. 3, 9a-d) Up to 6 in. *L.* finely divided into 3 leaflets. February-April. One of the finest sp., growing and spreading particularly well on the warm chalk soils near the south coast. Tuber almost globose but somewhat flattened above and below. Should be planted in full sun; in Greece, however, it grows most frequently in semi-shade or even full shade among bushes or in coniferous woodland on the mountains.

　\* Var. **atrocoerulea** (syn. *ingramii*). The deepest blue form. (Pl. 3, 9a)
　　Var. **scythinica.** Paler sapphire-blue on outside and generally flowering later, inner side of tepals white. A delightful variety but rather less vigorous than var. *atrocoerulea*. N. Kurdistan. (Pl. 3, 9d)
　' White Beauty ' *Fl.* very large, nearly twice the size of the normal form. A very promising new variety.

\* **A. coronaria.** The Poppy anemones of gardens, which have been developed from the wild and nearly equally fine forms of this species from S. France and Italy and from hybrids, many occurring naturally, between it and *A.*

# Anemone

*pavonina, A. hortensis* and *A. fulgens. Fl.* up to 3 in. across with 6 or more wide tepals, stems 6–18 in. in height, scarlet, crimson, blue, mauve or white, single, semi-double or double. (Pl. 3, 2*a-e*). Specially good strains are St. Brigid, mostly semi-double, and Creagh Castle and De Caen or Giant French, single, while named single varieties include ' His Excellency ' (Syn. ' Hollandia '), scarlet with white centre, ' Mr. Fokker,' blue, ' Sylphide,' violet, and ' The Bride,' white, while good semi-double St. Brigid anemones are ' The Admiral,' violet-mauve, ' The Governor,' scarlet, and ' Lord Lieutenant,' blue. These anemones form knobbly tubers which can be dried and planted in April for flowering in June-July, in June for September-flowering and in September-October for late winter and spring flowering. They thrive best in rich vegetable-garden soil, not too dry. In light sandy soils an addition of peat and loam helps them, also bone meal and dried blood. Protection with cloches is also a help to those planted for winter flowering. Undoubtedly they grow and flower best in gardens in the South and West of the country and in Holland and in very cold gardens they are hardly worth growing unless they can be given cloche protection. They are easily grown from seed, flowering after 18 months, and many growers prefer this method. Others lift and dry off the tubers each year while many commercial growers find it most economical to buy in fresh tubers for forcing each year.

**A. fulgens.** Probably a naturally occurring hybrid between *A. pavonina* and *A. hortensis.* S. France. A very lovely *fl.* with tepals a little narrower than those of *A. coronaria*, brilliant scarlet, up to 2 in. across, 9–15 in. in height. Tuberous and requiring same conditions as *A. pavonina. L.* often appearing in the autumn. (Pl. 3, 5*a*)
> Var. **annulata grandiflora.** Scarlet with a yellow centre and slightly larger *fl.* Var. *multipetala*, semi-double (Pl. 3, 5*b*). Probably the same as *A. pavonina* var. *pavonina* (see p. 60).

**A. hortensis.** In spite of its name a wild anemone from the Mediterranean coast, extending from the South of France to Albania. Tepals narrow and *fl.* without a pale centre. Stem 12–15 in. *Fl.* pink, lilac or mauve, like a more starry and less robust *A. pavonina.* (Pl. 3, 3*a-c*). Syn. *A. stellata.*

**A. nemorosa.** Our wild anemone and one of the most graceful and lovely of all wild *fl.* (Pl. 3, 4*a-d*). *Fl.* white, often flushed with mauve or pink on the outside, about 1 in. across; tepals 6 or more. 6–8 in. March-April. Stem slender so that the flowers appear to dance in the breeze. A woodland plant, naturalising and spreading freely once it is happy, but generally not thriving in very dry situations. Rhizome horizontal, cylindrical and rather slender. Therefore it should not be allowed to dry out on moving and clumps are best transplanted soon after flowering before the foliage has completely died down. The seed should be sown when still green. A number of specially fine forms have been selected, of which perhaps the finest is *' Allenii ' after the late Mr. Allen of Shepton Mallet, who raised and selected many good forms of bulbous plants, especially Snowdrops. *Fl.* pale rosy-lilac outside and soft lavender-blue inside and larger than the type; *flore-pleno* a fine form with double white *fl.* slightly smaller than the single (Pl. 3, 4*b*); ' Blue Bonnet,' good pale lavender-blue flushed with crimson outside; ' Leeds Variety,' described as the best of the white forms, with broad overlapping tepals but

59

unfortunately not now easily available though it may still exist in some older gardens; *'Robinsoniana,' large flower, pale lavender-blue (Pl. **3**, 4*a*). 'Royal Blue,' the deepest blue; 'Vestal,' pure white without coloured flush on outside.

**A. pavoniana.** A Spanish sp. with white *fl.* and quite distinct from the succeeding. Named after the Spanish botanist Pavon. Rarely found in gardens.

* **A. pavonina.** The anemone of the Great Peacock (*Pavo major*) or with the peacock eye. Widespread in Greece and Macedonia and Western Asia Minor where it flowers very early in the spring. *Fl.* with 7–12 rather broad tepals, 6–15 in., scarlet, pink, mauve or purple. February-April. Var. *ocellata* with golden eye in centre, sometimes described as a yellow claw at the base of the tepal. (Pl. **3**, 1). Var. *purpureo-violacea*, violet or rosy-violet with a white centre.

Many double forms have also been raised and are portrayed particularly in old herbals and Dutch flower paintings. St. Bravo strain raised by Messrs. van Tubergen has been specially selected and tends to have longer stems and slightly larger *fl.* than the type. They include all the colours of the type and the actual botanical type figured first in Clusius' great herbal is a full double with 20 or more tepals and distinguished as *A. pavonina* var. *pavonina* and probably the same as *A. fulgens* var. *multipetala* Needs to be treated generously as *A. coronaria* and in a sunny open position.

**A. quinquefolia.** The American wood anemone, but with *fl.* and growth smaller and more slender than in *A. nemorosa*. *Fl.* white. Not so vigorous in England as *A. nemorosa*.

**A. ranunculoides.** The Buttercup anemone. Yellow, with 5–6 tepals, up to 8 in. high. March-April. Rhizome slender, growing horizontally. S. Europe. Var. *superba*; *fl.* deeper yellow, larger, and leaf with a bronzy tinge. Should be grown in an open sunny position. Hybrids between this and *A. nemorosa* are called *A. lipsiensis* and the best form has sulphur-yellow *fl.* slightly larger than those of *A. ranunculoides*. Syn. *A. ranunculoides pallida*. (Pl. **3**, 8)

**A. trifolia.** Close to *A. nemorosa*, but with slightly larger pure white *fl.* with white anthers and three undivided leaflets. S.E. Europe, Dolomites, where it replaces *A. nemorosa*. It requires similar conditions. Very pale blue forms have also been found in the Dolomites, notably in the woods above Misurina (near Cortina). (Pl. **3**, 7)

# ANTHERICUM *Liliaceae*

A LARGE genus found in S. Africa, Mexico and Europe, but only one species *A. liliago*, St. Bernard's lily, is generally grown in English gardens. It is a common plant in alpine meadows and bears in June or early July a raceme of white lily-like flowers of considerable grace and charm. Height up to 2 ft.; flower up to 1½ in. diam., open trumpet-shaped,

*Plate* 3: ANEMONES. 1*a-d*, *A. pavonina*, blue, pink, scarlet and magenta forms. 2*a-e*, *A. coronaria*, scarlet, flame, pale yellow, blue and white forms. 3*a-c*, *A. hortensis*, lilac, magenta and pink forms. 4*a*, *A. nemorosa* 'Robinsoniana'. 4*b*, *A. nemorosa*, double form. 4*c-d*, *A. nemorosa*. 5*a*, *A. fulgens*. 5*b*, *A. fulgens* var. *multipetala*. 6*a*, *A. appenina* var. *alba*. 6*b*, *A. appenina*. 7, *A. trifolia*. 8, *A. ranunculoides*. 9*a*, *A. blanda* var. *ingramii*. 9*b*, *A. blanda* var. *rosea*. 9*c*, *A. blanda* var. *alba*. 9*d*, *A. blanda* var. *scythinica*

*Plate* 4: Colchicum. 1, *C. cilicium* (usually this species does not show so much chequering). 2, *C. autumnale fl. pleno*. 3, *C. cilicium purpureum*. 4, *C. autumnale fl. pleno album*. 5, *C. autumnale*. 6, *C. speciosum* 'Disraeli'. 7, *C. speciosum album*. 8, *C. byzantinum*. 9, *C. speciosum bornmulleri*. 10, *C. speciosum*. 11, *C. agrippinum*. 12, *C. variegatum*

anthers golden, leaves narrow, rush-like. Root a cluster of fleshy tubers, plant 3–6 in. deep. It is best grown either on the rock garden or near the front of the border and appreciates plenty of feeding and moisture during the growing season. This is a really choice plant which is not seen in English gardens nearly as much as its beauty would justify. Propagate by seed or by division, but it generally needs a year to settle down again before flowering.

**A. liliastrum.** St. Bruno's lily. See under *Paradisea.*

**A. ramosum.** An alpine plant with smaller, more starlike white *fl.* than St. Bernard's lily and branched stems. An interesting but not very conspicuous plant, suitable for the wild garden, but very rarely seen.

# ANTHOLYZA *Iridaceae*

A GENUS now reduced to a single species, *A. ringens*, owing to the transfer to other genera of species formerly included in it. The name is given from the supposed resemblance of the flower to the open mouth of an enraged beast.

**A. ringens.** Known rather unkindly as Rat's-tail in S. Africa, has a head of curious bright red and greenish-yellow *fl.* of an asymmetric shape which may appeal to some people. It is described as one of the most spectacular of the early spring *fl.* of the Cape, but is now very seldom seen in this country where it is doubtfully hardy except in very warm situations in full sunshine. It can, however, be grown in a cool greenhouse or grown outside and lifted for the winter like a gladiolus. One segment of the *fl.* is much enlarged and elongated beyond all the others, a brilliant scarlet in colour, while the stamens project even further. The tube of the *fl.* is a light yellowish-green and up to 8 *fl.* are borne together tightly packed on an 18 in. stem. Beyond the spike projects a barren flower-spike which, it has been suggested, is adapted as a bird-perch for the honey-birds or sun-birds which fertilise it. Flowers in early summer. Corm large globose and should be planted about 6 in. deep if planted outside. *L.* linear, ribbed up to 1 ft. long growing from the base. Syn. *Babiana ringens.* Can be propagated from seed.

**A. aethiopica, A. bicolor, A. caffra, A. floribunda.** See under *Chasmanthe.*

**A. paniculata.** See under *Curtonus.*

# ARISAEMA *Araceae*

A FASCINATING and large genus, especially for those who have a partiality for green and dull purple flowers of bizarre shape and fine foliage. They are distinguished from *Arum* by the usually monoecious character of the flowers, i.e. on the spadix they have either male or female flowers but not both and also by their leaves being divided into several lobes. The hardy and nearly hardy species are treated first, then a few of the greenhouse and stove house species from Malaya and India. The flowers are usually hooded and the hood often curls over and ends in a long tail.

## (*a*) Hardy and nearly hardy species

These are primarily plants for the dampish woodland and look best in the company of small ferns and other plants with ornamental foliage such as Hostas. The root is tuberous, generally rounded and they should be planted several inches deep and given plenty of leaf-mould or peat.

**A. candidissimum.** One of the most decorative of the sp. with a spathe white, or in one form veined with pink and green, up to 3 in. long including tube, spadix pale greenish-yellow, slightly scented. June. *L.* three lobed and large. Tuber globose. Quite hardy and suitable for bog or dampish positions. W. China. (Pl. II)

† **A. concinnum.** An exception in the genus in that it has dioecious *fl.* Spathe greenish-yellow and white in the female *fl.*, bluish-purple and striped white in the male *fl.* and twined into a long tail in both. *L.* solitary, much divided, large, up to 2 ft. long with stalk and brown or purple spotted. Himalaya and E. Asia. Likely to be rather tender except in very sheltered gardens and rarely seen. Tuber globose.

† **A. consanguineum.** A large sp. with leaf stalk up to 3 ft. long and mottled with dark pink and brown and much divided leaves. Spathe up to 7 in. long, green, striped with deep purple and white on the inside. E. Asia, Yunnan. Reported to have been hardy at Glasnevin Botanic Garden, near Dublin, but rarely seen. Early summer. Tuber flattish, up to 4 in. across.

**A. dracontium.** North American Dragon Root. Leaf-stalk up to 1 ft., mottled; *l.* much divided. Spathe and spadix both green and borne below the height of the leaves. Hardy. Tuber oblong.

**A. griffithii.** One of the most decorative sp., which has been compared to a giant hooded cobra. Leaf-stalk up to 2 ft.; *l.* divided into three ovate leaflets margined with red. Spathe up to 6 in. long with a tube of 3 in. and up to 5 in. across, lined and spotted with violet. Spring flowering. Himalayas, Sikkim. Hardy.

**A. hookeri.** Allied to *A. griffithii* but from higher Himalayan regions.

**A. japonicum.** Another dioecious sp. *L.* divided into five or more leaflets. 2–3 ft. in height. Spathe green with white veins and stripes, about 4 in. long and with a long tube. Height 9 in.–1 ft. Flowering early spring, March–April. Japan. Tuber globose.

**A. sikokianum.** A striking sp. from Japan with spathe and tube dark brownish-purple outside, striped white and brown inside, blade of spathe undulating, spadix white. Hardy. Syn. *A. sazensoo.*

† **A. speciosum.** *L.* solitary with stalk up to 2 ft. and spotted with deep purple. Spathe hooded, greenish-purple outside and deep violet within; tube green, striped with white or pale purple; spadix deep glossy purple, prolonged, with a long point, tall and narrow, tail up to 20 in. long. March–April. Himalayas. Tender, but suitable for a cool greenhouse. In warmer areas worth trying outside in a damp place. Tuber elongated, rhizome-like.

**A. triphyllum.** The American ' Jack in the Pulpit.' *L.* divided into three leaflets. Spathe green; striped purple on inside, up to 6 in. long, spadix spotted brown about 3 in. long. Hood bright green outside, purplish-brown below forming the " sounding board " of this realistic pulpit. Height 1 ft. Flowering June-July. Eastern N. America. Hardy. Sometimes produces scarlet berries in autumn. Starts into growth late, sometimes not till May. Tuber roundish, flat, turnip-like. Syn. *A. atrorubens.*

## (*b*) Species for warm greenhouse or stovehouse

Some of these plants have large pitchers, striped purple and green and decorative foliage, but they tend to grow large and are only suitable for planting out in a large tropical house. They require a minimum winter temperature of 50° F. and should be planted in a mixture of loam well enriched with leaf-mould and old manure. They can also be grown in large pots in which case repotting is best done in spring when the fresh growth is just starting. They require plenty of water in the summer, but may be left nearly dry in winter when the growth has died down.

† **A. anomalum.** Malaya. 1 ft. Spathe dark brownish- or greenish-purple, striped white. Flowers with the leaves. Rootstock tuberous and elongated.

† **A. fimbriatum.** Malaya. 1–2 ft. Spathe brownish-purple with white stripes, spadix slender and near top end covered with slender purplish threads. A rare but distinctive plant.

† **A. tortuosum.** India. Height up to 2 ft. Spathe green, rounded, purplish inside, deeper purple in var. *helleborifolium* which also has smaller leaflets and used to be grown under the name *A. curvatum.* Tuber up to 4 in. across, flat, round.

# ARUM  *Araceae*

THE AROIDS are a peculiar family, having in the genera dealt with here and in most other cases also no normal flowers with sepals and petals. Instead, they have separate male and female flowers, without the usual petals or sepals, and set on a round, club-shaped central organ, called a spadix. This is mainly covered and shielded by a large curved sheath called a spathe. The male flowers are always the uppermost below a sterile tip, then there is a zone of neutral and sterile flowers and below that the female ones. The seeds are borne in fleshy berries, often scarlet. The root is a tuber or rhizome and the leaves are generally easily recognised, being hastate and often mottled in the genera dealt with here—*Arum, Dracunculus, Sauromatum* and *Zantedeschia*, all of which have been in the past included in *Arum* and are still popularly described as Arum lilies. One of our best-known wild flowers is the Cuckoo Pint or Lords-and-ladies, *A. maculatum*, and the arrangement of its spathe and flowers is typical of that in the other members of the genus. All are primarily plants of the hedgerow and semi-shade but in the case of the Mediterranean species they do better in more open sunny places in our gardens. The Lords-and-ladies are only suitable for the wild garden. They can easily be increased by detaching parts of the tubers. *Arum* is distinguished from *Arisaema* by the leaves which are divided into three or more sections in the latter and by the flowers which in *Arisaema* have the sexes on different plants.

**A. aethiopicum.**  See under *Zantedeschia aethiopica*.

**A. cornutum.**  See under *Sauromatum guttatum*.

**A. creticum.**  Spathe pale lemon-yellow or creamy-white, perhaps the best colour in the genus but variable in its depth; spadix slightly deeper golden-yellow; up to 1 ft. with spathe 4 in. across. Tuber roundish; *l.* hastate with base cordate and widely diverging lobes, unmottled. March-April. Crete in the mountains and also recorded from Samos and a few other Greek islands. Hardy but unsuitable for very cold situations, probably best grown in full sun in a border under a wall. The higher altitude form has whitish spathes and a purple spadix.

**A. dioscoridis.**  A very variable plant from the E. Mediterranean regions. Spathe large, appearing before the *l.*, green, mottled with purple or darkish-purple, paler inside. Tuber flattened on top; *l.* large, hastate, stem 8 in. to 1 ft. Not a very distinctive or distinguished plant for the garden and rarely seen in cultivation.

**A. dracunculus.**  See under *Dracunculus vulgaris*.

**A. elliottianum.**  See under *Zantedeschia elliottiana*.

*Plate* 5: CRINUM AND ACIDANTHERA. 1, *A. bicolor murielae.* 2, *C. powellii album.* 3, *C. powellii*
'Harlemense'. 4, *C. powellii roseum*

*Plate* 6: CROCUS, AUTUMN-FLOWERING. 1, *C. cancellatus.* 2, *C. kotschyanus.* 3, *C. speciosus*, 3 forms ; the deep blue in centre is 'Oxonian'. 4, *C. pulchellus.* 5, *C. cancellatus* var. *cilicicus.* 6, *C. salzmanii.* 7, *C. byzantinus.* 8a, *C. longiflorus.* 8b, *C. longiflorus* var. *melitensis.* 9, *C. medius.* 10, *C. nudiflorus.* 11, *C. asturicus*, 3 forms. 12, *C. hadriaticus.* 13, *C. kotschyanus* var. *leucopharynx.* 14, *C. sativus* 2 forms. 15, *C. tournfortii.* 16, *C. niveus.* 17, *C. laevigatus* var. *fontenayi.* 18, *C. ochroleucus*

## Babiana

**A. italicum.** The Italian Arum. Resembling our native Lords-and-ladies but much larger. Spathe large, 7 in. long and 4 in. across, pale yellowish-green, first erect, then later rolled back at the tip. Upper part of spadix club-shaped, pale yellow, but deeper in colour than the spathe; *l.* large, hastate, veined with white, autumnal and in a warm place lasting throughout the winter and so more decorative than our native sp. both in leaf and fruit. Southern Europe from Spain to Caucasus, Morocco and parts of Asia Minor.
\* Var. **marmoratum.** *L.* marbled and distinctly veined with white. Useful for flower arrangements. Syn. var. *pictum.*

**A. maculatum.** Our native Lords-and-ladies. Decorative but often spreading freely and best kept to the wild garden or enjoyed in the hedgerows.

**A. melanoleucum.** See under *Zantedeschia melanoleuca.*

**A. nigrum.** This is not really the maroon-black arum, which is *A. pictum.* Stem up to 8 in. with spathe green in lower part and purplish in upper part, *l.* hastate, largely unmottled. S. Europe. Not a very striking sp. for the garden.

**A. palaestinum.** The Jerusalem Arum, native of Palestine. A striking plant with spathe 6 in. long by 3 in. broad, purplish-green outside but inside a deep purplish-black, unspotted, with spadix long but still shorter than spathe, appearing bluish-black in colour. *L.* bright green, slightly fleshy. Spring. Rather tender except in very warm situations, probably best suited to a cool greenhouse. Syn. *A. sanctum.*

**A. pentlandii.** See under *Zantedeschia angustiloba.*

**A. pictum.** Differing from other sp. in its autumnal flowering. Spathe produced before *l.*; green and white at base and outside, purple inside. Stem up to 10 in.; *l.* large, cordate at base. Hardy. Spain and Corsica.

**A. rehmannii.** See under *Zantedeschia rehmannii.*

# † BABIANA *Iridaceae*

I⊤ IS claimed that this beautiful genus of S. African corms is so named because they are readily eaten by baboons, the Afrikaans for baboon being " babianer." It is curious that there is one outlying species in the Island of Socotra but this has very small flowers and is likely to be of little horticultural value. The flowers are funnel-shaped and generally irregular in their perianth segments, often brightly coloured and somewhat resembling ixias, although their stems are usually much shorter and stouter. The leaves are plaited like those of a gladiolus, generally ciliate and the corms small and reticulate. In this country they are usually grown in the cool greenhouse, being planted in pots in the autumn for flowering in late spring or early summer. In the warmer parts of the country and in the Scilly Isles the forms of *B. stricta* may be grown outdoors in a sunny border under a wall, planted deeply, about 6 in., but will generally need some winter protection of ashes or bracken or cloche. When grown in pots they should be watered very sparingly until they begin to grow actively, but then they should not be allowed to become dry again until they begin to die down after flowering, when they should be given a complete rest. There are about 30 species but those available in this country are for the most part forms or varieties of *B. stricta*, some of which are very brilliant in colour. Many of these were formerly given separate specific rank.

**B. disticha.** The Hyacinth-scented Babiana. Stem up to 1 ft.; *fl.* regular with segments strap-shaped and partly recurved and long tube 1½–2 in. across when open, pale blue with pale yellow throat; *l.* broad, plaited, ciliate. Close to *B. plicata* of which it is sometimes considered as a variety. June. Cape Province where it flowers in August, early spring there.

**B. gawleri.** Dwarf. *Fl.* lilac-mauve, the segments having dark purple and white markings at base, the short spikes emerging from large spathes. *L.* narrow, villose. Cape Province.

**B. hypogaea.** Dwarf with upward-facing *fl.* rich bluish-mauve with white markings in clusters at base of *l.*; tube long and *fl.* like a small gladiolus. Flowers in autumn in S. Africa but probably not now in cultivation in this country. Syn. *B. bainesii.* Corms sub-globose, usually deeply buried and not readily transplanted in flower, widely spreading in S. Africa.

**B. plicata.** Dwarf, generally not over 6 in. *Fl.* 2 in. across, pale lilac-mauve with dark markings at base of three lower segments which have also a narrow median yellow stripe. Sweet-scented. May-June. Cape Province where it flowers in August.

**B. sambucina,** the Elder-scented Babiana. Dwarf. *Fl.* deep mauvish-purple, large and handsome, up to 2½ in. across. Stem 6 in. with several *fl.* Spathe large.

**B. socotrana.** Dwarf with solitary small lilac *fl.*, ½ to ¾ in. across on very short stem and almost hidden by *l.* which are broad and plicate. Sept. Isle of Socotra. Probably requiring intermediate greenhouse and it is doubtful whether this is now in cultivation. Not a very striking plant.

**B. stricta.** Probably the finest sp. but very variable in colour. Stem up to 12 in. with 4 or 5 cup-shaped *fl.* about 1½ in. across, bright blue, pale lilac, crimson or creamy-yellow. A number of these variants have been separated as distinct sp. in the past and were so featured in the Botanical Magazine towards the end of the eighteenth century when plants from the Cape were very popular for English greenhouses but are here treated as varieties as in most modern works. Spathe and *l.* ciliate. Var. *angustifolia*, *fl.* bright caerulean-blue with black markings on 3 petals. *L.* narrow.

    Var. **rubro-cyanea.** One of the most brilliant. *Fl.* deep caerulean-blue or ultramarine with bright crimson centre on short stems. Dwarf.

    Var. **sulphurea.** Cream with turquoise-blue markings at base on tube and deep mauve stigmas.

Var. **villosa.** Deep crimson with deep violet-blue anthers. Taller than var. *rubro-cyanea.*

**B. tubata.** Long-tubed Babiana. Tube up to 2½ in., narrow, pale purple, upper part of perianth segments pale creamy-yellow with red markings on base of three lower segments, stained red or lilac-red outside. *Fl.* 5-7 on a short stem. *L.* broad, plicate, ciliate.

**B. tubiflora.** Close to preceeding sp. Tube very long but *fl.* smaller, creamy-white with red markings from inside and outside.

# BRODIAEA *Liliaceae*

A LARGE genus of Western N. American plants growing from corms, mostly hardy in this country but apart from a few species not very showy and flowering in mid-summer from late May till the end of July. Consequently they have never become as popular in English gardens as their descriptions in Californian books would suggest they merit. In the wooded slopes and meadows of California and Oregon they appear to play the part of the English bluebell, being known by such names as Fool's Onion and Nigger's Toes. In England they are usually seen at their best in gardens in the warmer parts of the country where they increase by offsets and can form large clumps. The flowers are borne in umbels as in *Allium* on stems 1 to 3 ft. high and are mostly in shades of blue, purple and mauve, with the exception of one species, the Californian firecracker, which has bright crimson flowers. The leaves are linear, rather grass-like and die away before the flowers open, thus leaving a slightly naked appearance to the stems. Thus they are best planted in groups rather than singly. The corms are rounded and slightly gladiolus like. Brodiaeas should be planted in full sun either in the herbaceous border where their space can be covered after they have finished flowering or in patches towards the front of shrubs. They need dividing after three or four years but otherwise should be left undisturbed. They do better after a good summer's ripening as in their native habitat. In very cold areas some of the species should have the protection of a heap of ashes or covering of bracken in winter. Lester Rowntree in her book *Hardy Californians* particularly recommends them for gardens with heavy soils.

*Brodiaea* is not a very homogeneous genus and some American botanists have split off from *Brodiaea* into separate genera a number of the species depending on the number of fertile anthers, those with three fertile stamens with anthers fixed at the base and dark brown corm being retained in *Brodiaea* but those with six fertile stamens being referred to *Triteleia*. Other species including those with long tubular flowers have

67

# Brodiaea

been placed in *Dichelostemma*. There seems, however, little agreement between authorities and in this book I have retained them all under *Brodiaea* following J. G. Baker's plan since the revised classification has not yet been generally accepted in horticultural literature or books of reference and there still seems considerable differences, as will be seen from the range of synonyms quoted. One species, formerly known as *B. uniflora* is, however, very distinct, having single trumpet-shaped flowers on 8 in. stems, bulbous rootstocks and a S. American distribution. It is a delightful little garden plant and will now be found in the monotypic genus *Ipheion*, having been treated variously as *Brodiaea*, *Triteleia* and *Milla*.

**B. bridgesii.** One of the more commonly grown sp. *Fl.* lilac-mauve, blue or reddish-lilac, star-like when open, in small umbels on stems 8–12 in. California and Oregon. Like a smaller *B. laxa.* June. Syn. *Triteleia bridgesii.*

**B. californica.** Usually blue-purple but a pink form has been recorded; tubular funnel-shaped *fl.* with perianth segments about three times as long as tube, in small umbels of up to 12, on stems up to 1½ ft. June. California. An attractive sp. like a small and more delicate *Agapanthus*, but probably only suitable for gardens in the warmer parts of the country and rarely seen. Syn. *Hookera californica.*

**B. capitata.** See under *B. pulchella.*

**B. coccinea.** A syn. of *B. ida-maia.*

**B. coronaria.** *Fl.* bluish-purple with a whitish throat; long tubes, perianth segments rather narrow, opening at the end into a star-like flower, borne on long pedicels in a few-flowered, loose umbel on slightly succulent stems up to 1 ft. *L.* very narrow. June-July. Western N. America from British Columbia to California, where it grows in hayfields and is known as the Harvest Brodiaea. Syns. *B. grandiflora* Smith non Lindley, *Hookera coronaria.*

Var. **rosea.** Pale lavender to pinkish-lavender, becoming pinker on drying.

**B. crocea.** Known in its native country as " Old Maids." *Fl.* yellow in a small loose umbel on stem up to 1 ft. high. California. May-June. Syn. *Triteleia crocea.*

**B. grandiflora** Smith non Lindley. A syn. of *B. coronaria.*

† **B. ida-maia.** Californian or Floral Firecracker. A well-named plant, the drooping *fl.* of which are long tubed up to 1½ in., bright crimson-red topped with bright yellow and yellow-green, the ends of the perianth segments opening to show a star of yellowish-green and a white throat. Umbels rather tight with up to 15 *fl.* on stem up to 3 ft. but generally less. California. June. Syn. *Brodiaea coccinea, Brevoortia ida-maia, Dichelostemma ida-maia.* Unfortunately this spectacular sp. is only hardy in the milder parts of the country and even there appears to be very shy flowering. In its native areas it is said to grow in heavy soil.

## Brunsvigia

**B. ixioides.** Known in its native country as " Pretty Face." *Fl.* yellow or pinkish-yellow with heavy purplish-brown stripes outside, stem up to 18 in. Variable. Tender since it is a coastal sp. Close to *B. crocea* in appearance. July. Oregon. California. Syns. *B. lutea, Calliprora ixioides.*

* **B. laxa.** Probably the finest of all the sp., like a small early flowering *Agapanthus*, although a variable plant both in colour and size of umbel. In the best forms *fl.* deep violet-blue or white, tubular, funnel-shaped up to 1½ in. long, on long pedicels and in large umbels up to 1 ft. across. Stems up to 3 ft. but generally less. June-July. Hardy. California. Syn. *Triteleia laxa,* A lighter blue hybrid *B.* × *tubergenii* has been raised between this and *B. peduncularis,* a sp. with rosy-white *fl.* in large umbels.

**B. multiflora.** *Fl.* lavender to deep purple in quite large umbels and on long stems up to 3 ft. Syn. *Dichelostemma multiflorum.*

**B. pulchella.** Blue Dicks or Wild Hyacinth in its native country. *Fl.* bright violet-blue, rather papery and with deep violet spathes in small tight umbels about 1½ in. across on stem 1–2 ft. May-June. California, where it is abundant. One corm will throw several stems. Var. *alba,* white. Sometimes grown as *B. capitata.* Syns. *Dichelostemma pulchellum, Hookera pulchella.*

**B. uniflora.** See under *Ipheion uniflorum.*

**B. volubilis.** A very distinct sp. sometimes placed in a separate genus of its own. Stem weak and partly twining around neighbouring plants, often the stouter *B. laxa,* up to several ft. in length. *Fl.* pale pinkish-mauve in dense umbels up to 3 in. across but not usually a very strong colour. Corm large, said to reach the size of a walnut. Rather tender and probably the least useful of those mentioned. July. California. Syn. *Stropholirion californicum, Dichelostemma volubile.*

# †BRUNSVIGIA *Amaryllidaceae*

A GENUS of S. African bulbous plants with enormous bulbs sometimes 1 ft. in length and 6 in. in diameter, closely related to *Amaryllis* and *Crinum* but differing in having irregularly shaped flowers. These are borne in a large round umbel on long pedicels, though individually they are not so large or conspicuous as those of *Crinum* and appear before the leaves. They are mostly pink or purplish-red and are irregular in length and width with a long tube. The bulbs are more tender than those of *Crinum powellii* or *Amaryllis belladonna* and are seldom seen in this country since they need to be grown in a warm frame or a cool greenhouse which gets plenty of sun. They need a complete resting dry period after the leaves have died down. Plenty of water, however, is required during their growing period and they are said to do best in a mixture of sand

and peat. They usually take a long time to settle down again after moving and flower sparsely in this country.

**B. gigantea.** A syn. of *B. orientalis*.

**B. josephinae.** Stems up to 2½ ft. with a large umbel of scarlet or purplish-red *fl.* with some white streaks towards the base, 2–3 in. long, ends of segments reflexed, pedicels very long, up to 8 in. but varying in length. Late summer. Bulb very large; *l.* strap-shaped, 2–3 ft. long. Seeds fleshy. Cape Province, Natal where it flowers in March. Probably the finest horticultural sp. and considered by some to have been one of the parents of the possibly hybrid *Amaryllis* forms with yellow throats such as *A. parkeri* and the *multiflora* strain, but there is no certain evidence of this and it seems to me unlikely. *Brunsdonna tubergenii*, however, is definitely a hybrid of this cross and has violet-pink *fl.* in large heads.

**B. orientalis.** " The Candelabra or Chandelier Flower." *Fl.* red but flushed yellowish-green towards base, 2½ in. long, up to 2 in. across on long pedicels of varying length in a loose umbel up to 2 ft. across which later becomes detached and carried by the wind across the veldt. Stem 1 ft. Sept. Bulb very large; *l.* spreading on ground, broad, tongue-shaped. Grows on fixed sand dunes in Cape Districts, flowering there in February-March. Syns. *B. gigantea, B. multiflora*.

# BULBOCODIUM *Liliaceae*

A SMALL monotypic genus related closely to *Colchicum* and *Merendera*, distinguished from *Crocus* by the six stamens and superior ovary and from *Merendera* and *Colchicum* by the styles which are joined together instead of free and from *Colchicum* by the segments of the flower being divided right down to the base.

**B. vernum.** *Fl.* of rather reddish-violet-purple with a white base but variable in colour, almost sessile on the ground and funnel-shaped, up to 4 in. high, crocus-like when first opening. Petals rather narrow and strap-shaped, recurving when fully open and falling apart rather untidily. March-April. Tuber ovoid, dark brown or blackish. *Fl.* rises from base of tuber on flatter side as in *Colchicum*. *L.* broadly strap-shaped, produced generally after *fl.* Spain, Alps and mountains of Europe eastwards to Russia. Quite hardy but not very conspicuous nor very often seen as a garden plant. Generally not a very vigorous grower in gardens and said to require frequent lifting and replanting. Described by Parkinson as " Meadowe Saffron of the spring."

# CALOCHORTUS *Liliaceae*

THIS GENUS stretches from British Columbia along the Pacific coast of N. America right down to Mexico and Guatemala and includes some of the most beautiful and also conspicuous of the American bulbous plants, rivalled only by the lilies and erythroniums. Unfortunately, however, they are not nearly so amenable to cultivation away from their own environment, either in this country or in the eastern part of N. America. Records of their continued and successful cultivation are rare. In their home they are mostly found in dry places. Some of the species appear to be slightly tender and all require a warm position and very quick drainage with adequate moisture in the growing season. Afterwards they must be dry. The Mexican species are probably best treated like tigridias and lifted in November for replanting in the spring while for the others some growers have recommended lifting for a period after they have died down, drying off well and then replanting in the late autumn. They may also be grown in pans in the cool greenhouse. The latest revision gives 57 species in the genus but in view of their rarity and difficulty it is only proposed to describe a few here. Further information will readily be found in Lester Rowntree's *Hardy Californians*, in articles by Carl Purdy, who collected a number and especially in a recent very thorough monographic treatment by Marion Ownbey in the *Annals of the Missouri Botanical Garden*, Vol. 27, pp. 371–560. He divides the genus, which is a very variable one, into three quite well-defined sections, *Mariposa*, *Eucalochortus* and *Cyclobothra*. It is in the first section of the Mariposa lilies or Mariposa tulips that we chiefly find the most outstanding horticultural plants. In this section the flowers are mostly upright, several to a stem, and passing through a wide range of colours, with prominent blotches. Some of the species are reported from the wild as variable in colour depending on the reaction and type of soil. In shape they are narrowly or broadly campanulate and the perianth segments are divided into quite well-defined sepals and petals. At the base of each petal is generally a conspicuous structure usually called a gland. The leaves are narrow and linear and the bulbs tunicated and for the most part not very large. Seeds are often rather slow to germinate but probably this is the best way of building up a stock and some may bloom in the fourth year. Col. Grey in his *Hardy Bulbs* reported that he was able to grow twenty species in Kent and that they seeded themselves. They can also be increased from the offsets, while some species bear aerial bulblets in the axils of the leaves.

## (*a*) Mariposa

Distinguished by the membranaceous bulb coats, the upright conspicuous flowers and the oblong-linear fruits, usually three-angled. The most widespread section, ranging from Canada to Mexico and east to the Dakotas.

**C. clavatus.** The largest sp. in the genus. *Fl.* large, cup-shaped, yellow with club-shaped hairs at the base and reddish-brown veins. Stem up to 3 ft. with up to 6 *fl.* California.

**C. concolor.** A slender sp. with up to 4 *fl.* to a stem; lemon-yellow, usually marked with a dark red blotch near the base of each sepal, petals bearded above the gland.

**C. kennedyi.** Dazzling vermilion-scarlet in colour, a plant of the dry desert slopes, but perhaps the most striking member of the genus and worth considerable care. Very variable in height from being almost sessile on the ground up to 2 ft. Sepals striped grey and white, petals orange-scarlet with a dark purple blotch at the base of each.

**C. leichtlinii.** One of the commoner sp. in California, but growing on the higher mountain slopes and so one of the hardiest. Stem 2 in. to 2 ft. depending on the altitude and conditions, *fl.* up to 2½ in. across, creamy-yellow or white with brighter yellow hairs covering the base of the petals inside and a deep reddish-purple blotch above which is a fringe of darker markings. A graceful and handsome plant first introduced by Douglas and allied to *C. venustus*, but rather smaller.

**C. luteus.** A handsome sp. with large deep yellow *fl.* up to 4 in. in diam. when fully open; 1–4 to a stem, which sometimes needs support. They are variable in size and markings but towards the base they are hairy and also lined with brownish-purple markings. June-July. California.

**C. macrocarpus.** *Fl.* 1–3 to a stem, purple, large, saucer-like when open, each petal with a green stripe along the centre and sometimes also with a darker purple band above the gland at the base; the sepals are unusually narrow for the genus. British Columbia to California. Said to like a dry sandy soil. June-July.

**C. nuttallii.** White, tinged and often veined with lilac, yellow at base and marked with a reddish-brown or purple band above the gland; 1–4 to a stem. Widely distributed in dry places from N. Dakota to New Mexico, mostly on high mountains slopes. June-July. Known locally as the " Sego Lily." A pink form has also been recorded.

**C. oculatus.** A syn. of *C. vestae*.

**C. splendens.** Large, pale lavender or pinkish-lilac *fl.*, usually with a purple spot above the gland on the petals and also on the sepals. California. May-June.

## Calochortus

**C. venustus.** One of the largest and best-known members of the genus. Very variable. Stem up to 2 ft. *Fl.* white, but sometimes yellow, purple or even dark red, each petal having a prominent dark red blotch and sometimes a second paler blotch above, hairy. California, usually in a light sandy soil. Colour variations may possibly be due to soil conditions. One of the more amenable to cultivation but should always be kept dry in winter. June-July.

**C. vestae.** *Fl.* large, white or pale purplish, petals pencilled with red or purple and with a conspicuous reddish-brown blotch; 1–3 to a stem. Stem strongly bulbiferous. California. A tetraploid sometimes confused both with *C. luteus* and *C. venustus*. Syn. *C. oculatus*.

## (b) Eucalochortus

The Fairy lanterns differ from the Mariposa tulips in that the flowers are usually nodding or pendulous rather than erect, rather globose and generally not so large or conspicuous. However they have a delicate charm of their own. Probably also they are slightly easier of cultivation in most cases since they come from more lightly wooded or scrub areas of hillside. Consequently they do better with some leaf-mould in their compost, although still requiring very good drainage. The majority are furry inside the flowers and therefore have also earned the name of Cats' Ears. The leaves of this section are mostly shining green, wider and more conspicuous than those of the Mariposas. They come from the northern part of the *Calochortus* regions.

**C. albus.** Pearly-white, the petals fringed with white hairs and almost translucent, yellow or pink or purple at base, nodding and with up to 25 *fl.* to a stem. Variable. This is reputed to be one of the most reliable sp. to grow in an open border. California. May-June.

**C. caeruleus.** *Fl.* small and delicate, petals conspicuously fringed, pale blue or lilac, with darker purple hairs and large purple blotch at base, 1–5 to a stem, generally rather dwarf, not over 6 in. Plants described under the name *mauweanus* are either this sp. or *C. tolmiei*, a closely related sp. with whiter or creamy *fl.* tinged with purple or rose and less prominent fringing to the petals. California from higher slopes.

**C. elegans.** Closely related to previous sp. but less conspicuously fringed petals. *Fl.* white or greenish-white with a purple base. June. California. Dwarf, 4–8 in. high, sometimes only 1 in. in higher regions by the snow.

**C. lilacinus.** A syn. of *C. uniflorus*.

**C. pulchellus.** Golden Lantern. Golden-yellow with a delicate frill of hairs on the edges of the petals. Up to 1 ft. with a much branched stem, each branch ending in a small umbel of 2–4 pendulous and fragrant *fl.* May-June. California. Reputed to be one of the most reliable for cultivation in the open ground.

**C. uniflorus.** Lilac or pale pink, outside veined with pale crimson, inside

73

hairy towards base and with a purple spot above gland at base of each petal. Stem normally unbranched, often very short. 1–2 *fl.* on long pedicels, often erect rather than nodding. It usually bears more than one. One of the easier sp. to grow.

## (*c*) Cyclobothra

This is the most southern section of the genus and so its members cannot be considered hardy in English gardens and are even more rarely seen than the members of the two other sections. The flowers of this section are not very uniform, those of the subsection *Weediani* having erect flowers not unlike the Mariposa tulips while those of the subsection *Barbatus* and *Purpureus* have nodding or pendulous flowers and have sometimes been confused with fritillaries. Probably they are all best treated like Oncocyclus irises and either lifted or dried off well after flowering. It has been recommended that they should be planted in May and lifted in November for the winter.

† **C. barbatus.** *Fl.* campanulate, nodding, yellow often with purplish markings, 1–2 *fl.* to a stem, petals densely bearded, broad. Mexico. Tender. Syns. *Fritillaria barbata, Calochortus flavus.*

† **C. purpureus.** *Fl.* campanulate, nodding, purplish-brown, 1–2 to a stem, bulbiferous. Mexico. Tender. Syns. *Fritillaria purpurea, Calochortus grandiflorus.* Closely related in the same section are the more tender †*C. cernuus*, also with smaller purplish *fl.*, and †*C. hartwegii* with slightly larger purplish-brown *fl.* Late flowering. July–September.

† **C. weedii.** Probably the best sp. in this section. *Fl.* erect, large, lemon-yellow or orange, up to 3½ in. across and covered inside with large bristly purple hairs; petals usually fimbriate, broad, with conspicuous claw at base and deep yellow blotch with purple border. Stems up to 18 in. high, branching low, with 3–4 *fl.* on each. Probably best grown in a cool greenhouse. S. California on dry rocky hills.

# CAMASSIA *Liliaceae*

DISTINGUISHED by the N. American Indian name of Quamash or Camass this is a small genus allied to *Scilla*, of about five species only, confined except for one species to Central and Western N. America. The bulbs are mostly large and edible and the flowers star-like in varying shades of white, cream and blue-mauve, borne in straight spikes up to 2 or occasionally 3 ft. They are not very showy and flowering in June or early July when there are so many more striking flowers they have never become very popular in English gardens. In their wild habitats, where they are said to cover whole meadows, they must be very beautiful. They are easy of cultivation and quite hardy, but do best in a rather moist border of good or heavy loam or with some clay and will tolerate winter wet. They do not attain their full size on hot or dry sandy soils. The bulbs do not increase much by division but they can easily be grown from seed which is freely produced and will flower in 3–4 years. They should be left undisturbed if possible and grown in full or at least half sun, the bulbs being planted in autumn about 4 in. deep. The leaves are all radical and narrowly linear or strap-shaped, the flower spikes usually rising well above them.

**C. cusickii.** Bulb very large, even up to half a pound. Stem up to 3 ft. with numerous star-like *fl.*, pale blue, about 1½ in. across. *L.* somewhat glaucous.

**C. esculenta.** Probably the best-known name in the genus but owing to early confusion *C. esculenta* Lindley is now regarded as a syn. of the variable *C. quamash*, while *C. esculenta* (Ker-Gawl) Colville is a syn. of *C. scillioides.*

**C. fraseri.** Also a syn. of *C. scillioides.*

**C. howellii.** Bulb rather small, stem up to 2 ft. but generally less with pale purple, regular, star-like *fl.* about 1 in. across on long pedicels, generally not opening till the afternoon. S. Oregon.

\* **C. leichtlinii.** Bulb large with stout stem up to 3 ft. Very variable in colour. *Fl.* regular and white, cream, blue or purple, the segments broad and twisting together as they wither, a diagnostic character.

> Var. **atroviolacea.** Deep purple. California to British Columbia. Carl Purdy, who knew these plants well in their native habitat, regarded this as the finest of all camassias and compared it to a small eremurus.

**C. quamash.** Common Camass. Bulb large. Stem 2–3 ft. Variable in colour from white to ultramarine-blue, perianth irregular, all *fl.* opening at the same time. Eight subspecies have been differentiated by American botanists. Western N. America from California and Utah to British Columbia.

**C. scillioides.** A smaller sp. with narrow *l.* and rather slender stem, up to 18 in. *fl.* star-like, pale blue, smaller than those of *C. quamash.* Eastern N. America. Better known under its syn. *C. fraseri.*

# CARDIOCRINUM *Liliaceae*

THIS GENUS has long been included in *Lilium*, to which it is obviously very closely related, and the majority of gardeners talk of *Lilium giganteum*, rather than *Cardiocrinum giganteum*. However, in the majority of recent botanical and serious horticultural literature it is treated as a separate genus and so it seems to be best to follow this arrangement here. There is little doubt that if it had never been included in *Lilium* there would likely be little argument over its status as a separate genus and even 100 years ago John Lindley so regarded it. It contains three species of which only one, *C. giganteum*, is widely grown in gardens, but it is one of the finest and noblest of the plants which most of us call "lilies" and well worth the generous cultivation which it requires. The other two species are neither nearly so fine nor such good garden plants.

The main differences between *Cardiocrinum* and *Lilium* lie in the following points:

|  | *Cardiocrinum* | *Lilium* |
|---|---|---|
| BULBS | Contain only a few scales which are formed from the base of leaves of previous years | Generally with numerous scales at base of stem axis |
| LEAVES | Basal leaves broad and cordate. The only type of leaves developed for several years till flowering size is reached. Stem leaves similar | Basal leaves not really distinct from stem leaves and usually not present in mature bulbs |
| SEED CAPSULES | Prominently toothed | Not toothed |

The flowers in *Lilium* are so varied that it would not be possible to separate *Cardiocrinum* off on this character. The flowers in the latter are trumpet-shaped, very large and opening wide with segments slightly reflexed at tips.

All the species are woodland plants and are best so planted and generally do better without lime in the soil. The bulbs should be planted shallowly and are gross feeders and will do well in heavily manured ground which would probably kill out most lilies very rapidly. They are not suitable plants for hot dry positions or for very sandy soils.

**C. cathayanum.** The Chinese sp. of this genus and probably the least fine of the three. Stem up to 4 ft. with up to 5 funnel-shaped trumpets, creamy-white inside and white outside with a greenish flush towards the base, about $4\frac{1}{2}$ in. long and clustered together at top of stem. Like the succeeding sp. but unlike *C. giganteum* in the arrangement of its main stem leaves which are carried in a loose whorl about half way up, large, broadly oblong and pointed. A rare plant in cultivation.

**C. cordatum.** The Japanese counterpart of the preceding. Stem up to 6ft. with up to 10 creamy-white trumpets up to 6 in. long but lacking the fine symmetry of the flower of *C. giganteum*. Bulb whitish, of medium size and *l.* broad and heart-shaped at base, arranged in a whorl half way up the stem. Basal *l.* rather tender and appearing early in the year which tends to make it an unsatisfactory garden plant.

**\* C. giganteum.** The finest sp. of the genus and found all along the Himalayan range from Nepal to N.E. Burma and S.E. Tibet. The stately spike in a good specimen will often reach 10 ft., with up to 20 *fl.* of regular trumpet shape, horizontal or slightly pendulous and each 6 in. in length, glistening pure white outside, white inside with some red markings towards the base. Stem stout and usually standing erect without any staking. *L.* large, cordate at base and arranged irregularly up the stem, bright green, shining; basal *l.* larger, up to 1 ft. in length and nearly as broad, on long petioles. Bulb large, dark green. The mature bulbs are not generally transplanted but smaller ones obtained from offsets or seeds are usually grown in their flowering, positions. Those from seed take seven or even more years before flowering those from offsets about four years, but the ones from seed give the biggest spikes. After flowering the main bulb dies but leaves behind several offsets which should be divided up and replanted. This lily associates very well with rhododendrons and meconopsis and looks its best in dells in the wood-land garden where the *fl.* can be seen against dark foliage or against a tree trunk. After flowering the seed capsules which are carried upright on the spike have a considerable dignity which prolongs the decorative effect. July. (Pl. III)

 Var. **yunnanense.** A variety from W. China and N.W. Burma, generally rather smaller in growth and with flowers without any red markings on the inside. Rare in cultivation and not such a good garden plant as the type.

# CHASMANTHE *Iridaceae*

A SMALL genus of S. African plants with flattened corms closely allied to *Antholyza*, in which genus the majority of its members were formerly placed. The stem ends in a spike or a panicle but without the curious zigzag spacing of *Antholyza ringens.* The flowers are mostly reddish-orange and have a long tube opening out with spreading lobes at the end. None of the species are reliably hardy in this country but may be grown successfully in a cold frame or outside and lifted in the winter, the corms being then planted in a frame or in a box of light soil or sand and kept rather dry.

**C. aethiopica.** Stem up to 4 ft. with a one-sided spike of reddish-orange *fl.* tubular and curved over in outer part, 1½ in. long, top petal much prolonged beyond rest and shielding the long style and stamens. July-August. Corm large, globose; *l.* linear but not plicate, arranged in a fan. S.W. Cape Districts.

**C. bicolor.** Much smaller than above, but otherwise rather similar. *Fl.* deep scarlet, narrow, tubular, with lower segments greenish-purple, toothed and much shorter. May-June. Stem up to 2 ft.

**C. caffra.** Stem up to 1½ ft. with bright red tubular *fl.*, about 2 in. long, arranged in two ranks on the spike, the upper petal being prolonged and curved. June. Cape Province, Natal.

**C. floribunda.** Probably the best sp. Flower-spike larger than in *C. aethiopica* and with more *fl.* open together. Orange, though a yellow form is also recorded. *L.* broader up to 2 in. across. May-June. Cape Province.


# CHIONODOXA *Liliaceae*

A SMALL and very homogeneous genus of eight species, well named ' Glory of the Snow' from their native habitat in Crete and the mountains of W. Turkey where they flower as the snow melts like the soldanellas and crocuses in the Alps. They are among our best early flowering bulbs. All are quite hardy and easily grown, preferably in full sun in a well-drained position, where they spread freely and their brilliant blue almost rivals a patch of *Gentiana verna* or a summer sky. They also make good plants for a pan in the alpine house but such protection is not necessary. *Chionodoxa* is closely related to *Scilla* but is distinguished by the perianth segments being joined at the base instead of being separate and by the broader filaments of the anthers. The flowers are borne in a loose raceme on stems 4–10 in. high and from a small campanulate base open into a flat star of varying shades of blue. The leaves are strap-shaped and deep green, the bulbs globular and fleshy. A large bulb will usually produce several flower-stems. They should be planted in early autumn not more than 3 in. deep. They are excellent for the rock garden or for naturalising in more open places in the wild garden and can be left for a number of years undisturbed. They will even grow in grass but do not there attain their full size. Those from Crete, *C. cretica* and *C. nana,* are less conspicuous than the species from Turkey. It is unfortunate that *C. luciliae* is the only one usually offered in most bulb catalogues since the others are equally fine. There is a group of hybrids between *Chionodoxa* and *Scilla* which will be found under *Chionoscilla.*

C. cretica. A slender sp. with stems up to 8 in. but generally less bearing 1 or 2 *fl.*, occasionally more, pale blue or white flushed with blue or mauve and with a white centre and about ½ in. across. Not a very robust plant and not nearly such a good garden plant as *C. luciliae.* Crete; mountain slopes.

C. gigantea. A larger plant than *C. luciliae* to which it is closely related, but not generally quite such a brilliant colour, *fl.* pale purple-blue with only a very small white eye. Late March-early April. Turkey: Anatolian Mountains. Unfortunately rare in cultivation. Var. *grandiflora* has broader petals and is described as brighter and richer in colour. There is also a good white form. (Pl. **24,** 8)

# Chionodoxa

**C. lochiae.** A recently discovered sp. from the pine forests of the Troödos mountains of Cyprus. Distinguished by its uniformly bright blue *fl.* without white centre and with blue anthers and narrow filaments. Stem up to 6 in. with up to five *fl.*, usually fewer, rather loosely disposed, similar in size and form to those of *C. luciliae*; *l.* linear, usually erect. Still a very rare and reputedly difficult plant in cultivation. The only sp. to be found on igneous rather than calcareous rocks.

\* **C. luciliae,** the only sp. commonly grown and described by the late Henry Elwes, no inconsiderable authority, as " one of the best, if not the best of all its class, far surpassing any of the squills and apparently as hardy and as easy to increase as *Scilla sibirica*," while George Maw, that great authority on Crocus who saw it flowering high up at 7,000 ft. on a Turkish mountain, described it as " one of the most sumptuous displays of floral beauty I ever beheld, a mass of blue and white resembling *Nemophila insignis* in colour, but more intense and brilliant." Stem up to 6 in. with up to 10 *fl.*, star-like, bright blue or mauvish-blue with white centre, ¾ in. across. *L.* strap-shaped, bright green, bulb fleshy, globose. Late March-early April. Turkey, mountains of Anatolia, from 3,000–7,000 ft. There are also pink and white forms and one ' Pink Giant ' has been named and is usually taller than the type. (Pl. **24**, 6)

**C. nana.** The smallest sp. and resembling *C. cretica* but even smaller in all its parts. Stem rarely exceeding 4 in., *fl.* white, pale blue or pale lilac. Cretan Mountains. (Pl. **24**, 21)

\* **C. sardensis.** Distinguished from *C. luciliae* by its deeper coloured and almost entirely porcelain-blue petals and very small white eye—a deeper and more intense blue. Stem purplish-brown, up to 8 in. but usually less, with a loose raceme of 6 or more *fl.*, star-like when open, ¾ in. across, late March-early May. Turkey: Anatolian mountains. Pink and white forms also exist. Unfortunately rare in cultivation. (Pl. **24**, 18)

\* **C. siehei.** Probably the largest and most conspicuous member of the genus. Stem to 8 or 10 in. with up to 15 *fl.*, but generally fewer. *Fl.* 1¼ in. across with oblong segments, violet-blue or deep, almost prussian blue with conspicuous white centre. *L.* long, linear, tapering at end; bulb large, fleshy. Unfortunately, this fine plant is rarely seen in English gardens and further stock would be well worth collecting. Turkey: E. Anatolian Mountains, 7,000–8,000 ft. Late March-April. Possibly the fine variety \*' Naburn Blue ' with deep sky blue *fl.* and white centres belongs to this sp.

**C. tmoli.** A dwarfer plant than *C. luciliae*, which it otherwise much resembles but even more brilliant vivid blue in colouring, centre white. Bulb small. Unfortunately very rare in cultivation. Turkey, mountains of Anatolia where it is said to grow in deep gorges. In cultivation it is reputed to need a damper position than the other sp. (Pl. **24**, 16)

## × CHIONOSCILLA *Liliaceae*

A SMALL group of bigeneric hybrids of which so far only one has been described, × *C. allenii*.

× **C. allenii,** a hybrid group between *Chionodoxa luciliae* and *Scilla bifolia,* the cross having arisen several times and possibly also in the wild. Closely resembling *Chionodoxa luciliae,* but with perianth segments joined at the base up to 1·5 mm. generally darker blue, becoming violet-blue as they age and with no white at base. Stem up to 8 in., quite stout and with up to 7 *fl.,* each 1 in. across. Leaves narrowly strap-shaped but still rather broader than in its parents. March. A very handsome plant but rare in cultivation, which should be the same as for *Chionodoxa.*

## CHLIDANTHUS *Amaryllidaceae*

A SMALL genus of bulbous plants from the Andes and mountains of S. America and Mexico. Only one species, *C. fragrans,* is in cultivation and even it is rarely seen. It is slightly tender and usually given the protection of a frame or cool greenhouse or lifted in winter but it has been reported as growing successfully outside in a very warm border against a greenhouse wall.

† **C. fragrans.** Stem 6–12 in. with a small loose umbel of erect or slightly drooping *fl.* of medium or pale yellow, each with a long perianth tube up to 3 in. and 6 small lobes, star-shaped at the mouth. Fragrant. Peduncle short. Bulb tunicated, ovoid. *L.* linear, appearing after *fl.,* slightly glaucous. June-July. Andes of Peru and Chile. Bulbs should be kept dry and rested in winter after *l.* have died down. They increase freely by division. Not very free-flowering. Var. *ehrenbergii* from Mexico is very similar, but is sometimes described as a separate sp. *Fl.* slightly more erect.

---

*Plate* 7 (*Opposite*) : CROCUS, WINTER AND EARLY SPRING FLOWERING. 1, *C. tomasinianus* ' Taplow Ruby'. 2, *C. korolkowii.* 3, *C. imperati.* 4, *C. imperati* form without feathering. 5, *C. stellaris.* 6, *C. etruscus.* 7, *C. tomasinianus.* 8, *C. versicolor.* 9, *C. dalmaticus.* 10, *C. fleischeri.* 11, *C. balansae.* 12, *C. aureus.* 13, *C. danfordiae.* 14, *C. chrysanthus* seedling. 15, *C. corsicus.* 16, *C. chrysanthus* ' Sultan.' 17, Anther of above. 18, *C. chrysanthus* ' E. A. Bowles.' 19, *C. chrysanthus* ' Warley White.' 20, *C. chrysanthus* ' Snow Bunting.' 21, *C. biflorus* var. *weldenii albus.* 22, *C. sieberi* var. *versicolor.* 23, *C. minimus.* 24, *C. sieberi* ' Hubert Edelsten.' 25, *C. olivieri.* 26, *C. susianus.* 27, *C. sieberi* ' Violet Queen.' 28, *C. biflorus* var. *weldenii.* 29, *C. chrysanthus* ' Blue Butterfly.' 30, *C. biflorus* var. *argenteus* 31, *C. suterianus* ' Golden Bunch.' 32, *C. suterianus* ' Jamie.' 33, *C. aerius* ' Celeste.' 34, *C. cambessedesii.*

*Plate* 7: Crocus, Winter and Early Spring-Flowering

*Plate* 8: CYCLAMEN, WINTER AND SPRING-FLOWERING. 1, *C. repandum.* 2, *C. persicum.* 3, *C. persicum*, broad-leaved form from Cyprus. 4, *C. creticum.* 5, *C. balearicum.* 6, *C. orbiculatum* var. *hiemale.* 7, *C. pseudibericum.* 8, *C. orbiculatum.* 9, *C. orbiculatum* var. *coum.* 10, *C. libanoticum*

*Plate* 9: CYCLAMEN, AUTUMN-FLOWERING. 1, *C. cilicium*. 2, *C. graecum*. 3, *C. africanum*. 4, *C. neapolitanum*. 5, *C. rohlfsianum*. 6, *C. graecum*, form from Crete, sometimes know as *C. pseudo-graecum*. 7, *C. europaeum*. 8, *C. cyprium*

*Plate 10:* Above, *Crocus speciosus* at Myddelton House in September. Left, *Crocus tomasinianus* and *Crocus aureus* in mid-February at Highdown, Goring-by-Sea

# COLCHICUM *Liliaceae*

ALTHOUGH generally known in gardens as autumn crocuses, the species of this genus are really very distinct from the crocus both in the tuber, flower and leaves. It also has winter and spring flowering species, less spectacular than the autumnal ones, but still attractive little plants and too rarely seen in alpine houses or gardens.

The botanical differences of the flower between the two genera are easily shown: in brief, like the lilies, a colchicum flower has six stamens arranged in two ranks while a crocus has only three like an iris; in the colchicum the ovary or seed capsule is described botanically as superior, that is. it is inside the perianth tube, while in crocus it is inferior or below the perianth tube. In practice in both genera the seed capsules are often found right down at ground level. The large and unsymmetrically shaped tuber of colchicum is very distinct from the neat corm of crocus, while many may have wished that the large spring leaves of colchicum could be replaced by the fine grass-like leaves of crocus.

Nevertheless colchicums are most valuable autumn-flowering plants, not planted nearly as widely as their merits would indicate, very tolerant of a wide range of conditions, in most cases increasing rapidly and flowering very freely.

Their big leaves do, however, to a large extent govern the places in the garden where they should be planted. They always look well along the edge of a shrubbery and they do not require full sun. They will grow satisfactorily among grass round a tree trunk as long as the grass is not cut before the leaves have not only died down but also shrivelled, i.e. at the beginning of July. It is most important not to cut their leaves off when they are green.

Again they look well as an edging to parts of the kitchen garden or even a mixed shrub and herbaceous plant border. At Wisley they are grown very well near the edges of the beds in the old Azalea garden and this part of the garden is well worth a visit for their sake during September. The species of *C. autumnale* and *C. speciosum* and their varieties are those most commonly grown and they are splendid plants for many forms of gardening other than the purely formal. Nor are they suitable for the rock garden where their large leaves will fall over and may smother many other choice and more delicate treasures.

There are very few finer white flowers in the whole garden than those of *C. speciosum album*, tulip-shaped like a beautiful goblet and as large as a good tulip flower, though without its long stem, an unusually pure

C.G.B.                                    81                                    F white in colour with just a faint tinge of pale green in the perianth tube and at the base of the flower.

For purposes of description it seems better to divide the colchicums into three groups:

(*a*) The large autumn flowering species, varieties and hybrids centring round *C. autumnale* and *C. speciosum* and chiefly without distinct tessellation and flowering without leaves.

(*b*) The late autumn and winter flowering species with large tessellated flowers, a very beautiful group but of not nearly such easy cultivation as the first group, also flowering without leaves.

(*c*) The smaller spring flowering species. These are hardly known in gardens but contain some attractive and quite hardy plants as well as several treasures for the alpine house. They mostly flower with the young leaves. In cultivation, however, they do not have the vigour of the first group.

The genus is well covered in the second edition of E. A. Bowles' *Handbook of Crocus and Colchicum*, and all gardeners who are interested in the less common species of these two genera will find in it the best account available and one based on an experience which no one else is likely to acquire in this generation.

Colchicums can be propagated from seed but are rather slower than crocus seedlings, generally taking five years to flower.

## (*a*) Autumn flowering species

The tubers of this group are mostly large and should be planted at least 3–5 in. deep.

**C. alpinum.** An abundant plant in the alpine and sub-alpine pastures, flowering freely in August and September, sometimes even in July. *Fl.* small-medium in size, generally rosy-purple in colour. Unfortunately, although often collected, this attractive and delicate sp. does not seem to make a good garden plant in England and does not display either the vigour with which it grows in the alps or that of most of the other sp. of this group. Two, occasionally three *l.* to a tuber, long but narrow, appearing after *fl.*

**C. autumnale.** A sp. native to Gt. Britain as well as to much of Europe; sometimes known as "Naked Boys" from the rather naked pale pinkish appearance of the buds and *fl.* without any *l.* They have also been called "the son before the father" perhaps from the illusion that the seed heads were produced before the *fl. Fl.* about 2 in. long with rather narrow, starry segments, soft rosy-lilac in colour, growing in clusters from a single tuber and tending to fall over after they have matured. (Pl. **4**, **5**). This is generally the earliest garden sp. to appear as soon as the first rains of late summer penetrate the soil. Like those of *C. speciosum* the tubers will often sprout and even flower on a dry shelf of a shop and if bought and planted in early September they will come into flower very quickly often within a few days.

There are very fine doubles, both purple and white, which are well worth growing (Pl. **4**, 2, 4). The single white variety is generally rather small in flower and not of a very clean white. This sp. is easily grown and suited to a wide variety of places in the garden or at the edge of open woodland glades, where it will never look out of place. It flowers most freely, however, in full or almost full sun.

**C. atropurpureum.** Rather similar to the preceding sp. of which it has sometimes been regarded as a variety, but perianth tube shorter and segments deeper in colour, reddish-magenta, pale in bud. Origin unknown. A rare plant.

**C. bornmuelleri.** See under *C. speciosum*.

\* **C. byzantinum.** Allied to *C. autumnale* and one of the largest and most free flowering of all this group, producing up to 20 *fl.* in a spathe, pale rosy-lilac, stigmas curved at end and tipped with crimson. September. *L.* very large, broad and pleated like a *Veratrum* leaf, but not appearing before early spring. This sp. does not appear to set seed and Mr. Bowles suggested that the garden stock may even have been all descended as a clone from a tuber sent to Clusius from near Constantinople, as it increases so freely by division. (Pl. **4**, 8)

\* **C. cilicium.** Rather similar to preceding sp. but flowering slightly later and with darker pinkish-purple or more rosy *fl.*, stigmas not crooked and with dull purple tips. *L.* large and generally produced in autumn soon after flowering. A very free flowering and desirable sp. from Turkey which is not grown nor offered nearly so widely as its merits deserve. (Pl. **4**, 1)

Var. **purpureum,** deep reddish-purple, one of the finest of all colchicums. Tuber large, ovoid. (Pl. **4**, 3)

**C. giganteum.** Very closely allied to *C. speciosum* but flowering later. *Fl.* large, soft rosy-purple with petals opening out more widely. A strong free-flowering plant, sometimes offered under the name *C. illyricum superbum*. Throat white, distinct in the wide, almost horizontal opening of the petals.

**C. lingulatum.** *Fl.* smaller than in *C. autumnale*, petals narrow, strap-shaped, rosy-lilac, or faintly tessellated. Sept.-Oct. Greece. A rarely seen sp.

**C. lusitanum.** *Fl.* medium-large, deep purplish-pink with slight tessellation, of the same group as *C. autumnale* but with larger *fl.* appearing later. Oct.-Nov. S. Spain, Portugal and possibly North Africa. *L.* appearing also in winter, linear-lanceolate.

**C. speciosum.** As a garden plant this is probably the finest of the genus. *Fl.* large, globose, tulip-like, up to 1 ft. in height on long stout perianth tubes, variable in colour from pale rosy-lilac with a pale or white throat to deep reddish-purple (Pl. **4**, 10) or, in var. \**album*, white. (Pl. **4**, 7) Sept.-Oct., following *C. autumnale* in flower. Asia Minor, Caucasus. *L.* large but not appearing till spring. Tuber large.

# Colchicum

A number of hybrids and garden forms have been raised from crosses made between this sp., *C. giganteum* and the large flowered tessellated sp. from Greece *C. sibthorpii* and *C. bowlesianum.* They have, however, inherited the good garden constitution of *C. speciosum* and have rather varying, although rarely very conspicuous tessellated petals. It is these forms which are most commonly found in gardens. Several of them, however, are so close to each other in colour, season of flowering and habit that it is hardly possible to tell them apart, far less to describe on paper the differences. The following, however, are all worth growing.

* ' ATRORUBENS ' Rich purplish-crimson without tessellation, a very fine variety of the sp., *rubrum* is very close to this but according to Mr. Bowles very slightly paler.

' AUTUMN QUEEN ' Rosy-violet with white throat and some tessellation. Early flowering: end of August to September.

Var. **bornmuelleri.** An early flowering variety of *C. speciosum*, distinguished by its pale, almost white buds and greenish, not purple perianth tube; *fl.* large, pale rosy-lilac with conspicuous white throat. Turkey. (Pl. **4**, 9)

' CONQUEST ' Late flowering, deep violet-mauve, tessellated.

* ' DISRAELI ' Large *fl.*, segments slightly waved at the edges, deep violet-mauve and prominently tessellated. A very fine variety. Mid-September. (Pl. **4**, 6)

* ' HUXLEY ' One of the largest in *fl.*, globular, deep rosy-lilac, only slightly tessellated; rarely offered but one of the finest.

' LILAC WONDER ' Very free flowering, less globular and with pointed petals, rosy-violet, perianth tube rather slender so that the *fl.* are not so long lasting; tessellation very light.

' PREMIER ' Large-flowered, pale rosy-lilac with white throat, strong perianth tube; only very slight tessellation.

' PRINCESS ASTRID ' Light rosy-violet, closely resembling ' Autumn Queen.' Early flowering.

* ' THE GIANT ' *Fl.* large on stout perianth tube, warm rosy-lilac with prominent white throat and only very faint tessellation on the inside of the *fl.* A strong grower, excellent for naturalising in grass.

' VIOLET QUEEN ' Deep purplish-violet with pointed petals and conspicuous white throat, moderately tessellated. Mid-September.

' WATER LILY ' Large, double, with up to 20 warm rosy-lilac petals and so quite distinct from all the other varieties described. From their weight the *fl.* tend to fall over soon after opening although the perianth tubes are stout; said to have been derived from a cross between *C. speciosum album* and the white form of *C. autumnale flore-pleno.* The comparison with a small water lily is not inapt.

## (b) Tessellated species

These are undoubtedly the glories of the genus, having large flowers, the petals of which are covered with a chequer-board tessellated pattern in dark and light rosy-mauve. Unfortunately they are not nearly so hardy as the species of the previous group and also flower rather later, often into November and December. In consequence they are more suited to culture in the frame or alpine house than in the open ground. They are also more sensitive over drainage and considerably less vigorous than the preceding species. Perhaps this gives an extra spice to their cultivation if one can get hold of them, for they are mostly rare even in their native habitats of Greece and Crete. In the past they have been much confused in nomenclature but this has been satisfactorily dealt with in Mr. Bowles' handbook and I propose to follow him in this respect as in so many others.

C. agrippinum. This is the sp. often offered and figured under the name *variegatum* which rightly belongs to another plant described later. *Fl.* medium in size with petals rather narrow and pointed, pale rosy-lilac heavily chequered with deeper lilac-purple, perianth tube whitish, rather weak, so that the *fl.* is often seen after it has fallen over, in which state unfortunately it seems to be a favourite for slugs. Hardy. Autumnal: Sept.-Oct. Native habitat not known. Possibly a hybrid between *C. autumnale* and *C. variegatum.* (Pl. 4, 11)

\* C. bowlesianum. Very large, egg-shaped, petals 2 in. in length, broad but pointed at apex, rosy-lilac unevenly chequered with darker purplish-violet markings, November. *L.* numerous, nearly erect, rich green, 1 in. wide and up to 10 in. long, margins not waved. N. Greece around Salonika. A very fine plant but rarely seen in cultivation.

\* C. macrophyllum. *Fl.* very large, funnel-shaped, pale lilac, more faintly tessellated than the preceding sp. Nov.-Dec. *L.* large, up to 2 ft. in height, pleated as in a *Veratrum.* Crete, Rhodes. Probably tender.

\* C. sibthorpii. *Fl.* large, rosy-lilac, rather lightly tessellated, not so deep in colour nor quite so large as the two preceding sp. but still one of the finest and also less rare and probably easier to grow than these as it flowers earlier. October. *L.* bluish-green, wavy on the margins and spreading horizontally when fully grown, each leaf up to 1 in. wide and 6 in. in length. Greece, Mt. Parnes. This sp. has also been known and figured as *C. latifolium*, unfortunately an invalid name.

C. variegatum. This has been much confused with *C. agrippinum*, but is much later flowering, generally not till December, and can also be distinguished by the more distinct pattern and darkness of the chequering and by the wider outer petals, especially near their base; perianth tube short. *L.* fewer than in *C. agrippinum*, spreading on the ground and with waved edges. A plant for the alpine house rather than the open rock garden. Greece, Greek islands. (Pl. 4, 12)

## (c) Winter and spring flowering species

These carry on the season after the great tessellated winter flowering species and several of them are rather charming and beautiful little species with flowers considerably smaller than those previously described. For this reason and also because of their early flowering they are best suited to the alpine house. They are for the most part mountain plants in their own habitats often to be found flowering at the edge of melting patches of snow like a *Soldanella* and so obviously requiring much moisture when in growth. This section also contains the only yellow-flowering species, but it is more curious than beautiful. Good drainage is essential for all these plants which seem to lack in cultivation the vigour of the autumnal flowering ones.

**C. catacuzenium.** Pale rosy-lilac, globular, petals about 1 in. in length and ½ in. in width; *fl.* borne generally in a large cluster practically on the ground and with *l.* just appearing. *L.* three to a tuber, narrow, linear. March-April. Mountains of Greece.

I found this plant flowering freely towards the end of April high up on Mt. Chelmos in the Northern Peloponnese of Greece. The snow had only just melted from this area about 7,000 ft. and it was growing in very damp shale, almost scree—the kind of position in which one might find *Androsace alpina* and this may be a clue to its requirements in cultivation. Tuber small and shoot emerging from side of it. Specimens of this sp. have been confused both with *C. bulbocodioides* and " *C. montanum.*"

**C. decaisnei.** *Fl.* medium in size, star-like, petals rather narrow, pale pink or white, dwarf, 1 to 3 in. only. Nov.-Dec. Lebanon.

**C. fasciculare** var. **brachyphyllum.** *Fl.* white, globular, 3 in. high and 1 in. across. November-January. Lebanon. Alpine house. A beautiful plant.

**C. hungaricum.** This is the correct name for the sp. often described as *C. montanum*, a name whose use is so confused that it has now been abandoned. *Fl.* small, very pale lilac or whitish with conspicuous dark anthers. Two *fl.*, occasionally three, narrow, almost linear.

**C. luteum.** *Fl.* medium in size, but petals narrow, strap-shaped up to 1 in. long, bright yellow, 2 to 3 *fl.* to a spathe. February. Kashmir. A sp. best suited to the alpine house and more curious than beautiful. The plate in the Botanical Magazine flatters it over much or else we have lost this fine form. Syn: *Synsiphon luteum.*

" **C. montanum.**" A confused name, now best disregarded or treated as a synonym of *Merendera montana.*

There are a number of other sp. in this group but since these are very rarely indeed to be seen in gardens or obtained and are for the most part described both in Mr. Bowles' Handbook and in the Botanical Magazine I have not described them here for the added reason that in most cases I have not seen living material. These include *C. ancyrense* from Asia Minor sometimes described as *C. biebersteinii* or *C. bulbocodioides*, *C. cupani* from Greece, *C. doerfleri* from Bulgaria, Sicily, S. France and N. Africa, *C. kesselringii* from Russian Turkestan (also described as *C. regelii*), *C. hydrophilum* from Asia Minor, *C. libanoticum* from the Mountains of Lebanon, *C. pusillum* from Crete, *C. steveni* from Syria and Lebanon and *C. troodi* from Cyprus.

# × CRINODONNA *Amaryllidaceae*

A BIGENERIC hybrid group raised between *Amaryllis belladonna* as the female parent and *Crinum moorei* as the male. It was raised twice about the same time, probably first near Florence in Italy where it was called *C. corsii* and described in 1921 and then in California by a Mr. F. Howard whose plants were known as *Amarcrinum howardii*. However, it is a very uniform group and the Italian name has preference by date of first publication. They are very handsome autumn flowering plants intermediate between the two parents, having the persistent long green leaves of a *Crinum* and the large heads of flowers combined with the pink funnel-shaped flowers of *Amaryllis belladonna* although the sometimes rather harsh colour of the latter has been modified into a softer pink. There are records of *Crinodonna* surviving out of doors for several winters in a warm sheltered situation and flowering satisfactorily and it is worth trying in a warm place such as one would give to *Amaryllis belladonna*. Generally, however, they are grown in beds or tubs in a cool greenhouse or in a frame. They are too large for most pots. Some summer ripening seems to be required but perhaps not so much as for the *Amaryllis*. Very fine specimens with shell-pink flowers can be seen each autumn in the first greenhouse at Wisley flowering freely for quite a long period.

×**C. corsii.** Stem up to 2½ ft. with a large umbel rather closely packed with large funnel-shaped pink *fl.* about 4 in. across, tube short. A number of *fl.* open together. Sept.-Oct. Bulb large, ovoid; *l.* strap-shaped, long, persistent, distichous. (Pl. **2, 3**). Syn. × *Amarcrinum howardii*.

# CRINUM *Amaryllidaceae*

A LARGE genus of S. African, Central African and Asiatic bulbs with large umbels of lily-like pink or white flowers. Unfortunately only a very few of these are hardy or nearly hardy. One, a hybrid, *C. powellii*, is among the very best of our late summer bulbous plants and rivals even many of the lilies in beauty.

All the species have very large bulbs, rounded at the base like footballs and little smaller, but at the upper ends prolonged into long necks often up to a foot in length. From this emerges a number of long strap-shaped, bright shining green leaves and among these the flowers are borne on stout stems, an umbel at the end emerging from a large scaly spathe or

87

spathes. The hardy species are best placed in a warm sunny position, preferably at the foot of a south wall and the bulbs should be planted deeply enough for the majority of the neck to be in the ground. Then they are best left undisturbed for many years, so it is desirable to enrich the ground well before planting. In cold areas a covering of bracken in winter will help but this is not necessary in the South of England or in the Home Counties around London in the case of *C. powellii* or its parents *C. bulbispermum* and *C. moorei*. These latter, however, are rarely seen now in cultivation so popular has the hybrid become. The bulbs increase rapidly by offsets but flower all the better for being crowded. The pink form of *C. powellii* makes a lovely picture behind blue agapanthus seen against a grey stone wall or even a white one, and the two will usually flower together. There are many flowers in an umbel of the crinum and they open in succession so the flowering season is a long one. Since the more tropical species require either very large tubs or to be planted out in a warm greenhouse or a stove house and then will each require at least a square yard, a space which few can afford to-day, they are not dealt with here and only the hardy or nearly hardy species are included.

† **C. asiaticum.** Described in an early issue of the Botanical Magazine as "The Largest Crinum." This may not be literally true but the size is certainly quite massive. It is also known as the " Asiatic Poison Bulb." Up to 50 *fl.* in a large umbel on a stout stem 3–4 ft. tall with a 3 in. pedicel, petals narrow and strap-shaped, 3–4 in. long by ¼–½ in. wide, strongly recurved and divided to the base, white, flushed pink outside near tips, showing the prominent pink filaments of the stamens, sweetly scented. Summer flowering. Very variable and extending over a large range from the Himalayas to the East Indies and China. Cool or intermediate greenhouse but there are records of its having been grown outside in very mild areas of England. Several varieties have been given separate names.

    Var. **anomalum.** *Fl.* similar to above but *l.* with a most curious broad striated or plaited and variegated wing along each margin.

    Var. **procerum.** Very large, with pedicels of 5 in., petals very strongly recurved and more heavily striped with pink on outside. Burma.

**C. bulbispermum.** This is the sp. more frequently known as *C. capense* or *C. longifolium*. *Fl.* shell-pink, veined with deeper pink, petals 3 in. long. Up to 20 *fl.* in an umbel, on long pedicels of 3 in.; stem 2–3 ft. well above *l.* Fragrant. Early to mid-summer. Bulb ovoid, 3–4 in. in diam. *L.* lorate, 2–3 ft. long with wavy edge. Hardy. S. Africa, S. Transvaal, Natal, Basutoland, often growing on river banks and there flowering in their spring, i.e. Sept.-Oct.

**C. capense.** A syn. of *C. bulbispermum*.

**C. longifolium.** A syn. of *C. bulbispermum*.

† **C. macowanii.** Distinguished by its black anthers. *Fl.* pale mauvish-pink or pale pink or white with red stripes outside, on long pedicels up to 4 in.

# Crocosmia

Stem 2–4 ft. with an umbel up to 15 *fl.* Bulb very large with diameter up to 10 in. and a long neck. *L.* lorate, bright green, 3–4 in. wide. S.W. Natal. Generally regarded as a cool greenhouse plant but nearly hardy and worth trying in a warm position under a wall.

**C. moorei.** Large, generally a good rosy-pink or white with pink flush and slightly larger than those of *C. bulbispermum.* Six to eight *fl.* in a head with only short pedicels. Perianth tube 3 in. long and upper part of segments 4 in. very broadly campanulate, spreading wide as *fl.* open. Bulb very large, ovoid, 6 in. across. *L.* 2–3 ft. long, strap-shaped. Summer but there are also records of its flowering in spring. Generally treated as a cool greenhouse plant but there are records of its flowering satisfactorily outside. In general it has now been superseded in gardens by the forms of its hybrid *C. powellii* which are hardier and more free flowering.

\* **C. × powellii.** A very fine hybrid group varying in colour from pure white to deep rose-pink (Pl. **5**, 4), derived from *C. bulbispermum × C. moorei.* *Fl.* large, trumpet lily-shaped but opening wide on long pedicel and sometimes drooping, up to 4 in. long by 3 in. across. Stem 2–3 ft. with an umbel of up to 10 *fl.* opening in succession. Bulb large, ovoid with distinct neck, up to 5 in. across. *L.* strap-shaped, numerous, bright green. Bulbs increase freely once they are established but should be left unmoved in large groups and not be divided except at rare intervals. Spring planting is generally best. Hardier than its parents but in most counties flowering more freely if planted against a south wall, where it makes a fine complement to blue agapanthus. July–Sept., flowering at a time when there are few other bulbous plants of its stature or beauty in flower. In very cold areas the bulbs are best protected in winter with a pile of ashes or bracken.

Var. **album.** Pure white. (Pl. **5**, 2)

'HARLEMENSE' The finest pale shell-pink form and with a larger umbel than the type. (Pl. **5**, 3)

'KRELAGEI' Deeper pink, a very fine form.

# CROCOSMIA *Iridaceae*

A SMALL genus of S. African plants with corms, closely allied to *Tritonia* and containing the montbretia of gardens, a race of hardy hybrids between *C. aurea* and *C. pottsii.* The leaves are sword-like and the flowers orange, deep yellow or reddish-orange on stems 2–3 ft. high and quite conspicuous, the spike generally spreading over in a horizontal panicle towards the end. Except for the common montbretia they are not generally hardy and the corms should be lifted in late autumn and stored like a gladiolus but they will shrivel if dried out completely. They should be planted in a sunny position and increase rapidly by division of the clusters of corms.

**C. aurea.** Falling Stars. Stem up to 3 ft. with a large panicle of golden-orange or orange-red *fl.* about 2½ in. across with prominent stamens. *L.*

sword-like, light green and arranged in a fan. As a garden plant it has been largely superseded by the hybrid montbretias which are hardier and which in the best forms have larger *fl.* Syn. *Tritonia aurea*. Natal, Cape Districts. **C.** × **crocosmiiflora** (*C. aurea* × *C. pottsii*). This is the race of garden mont-bretias which as a generic name in the botanical sense is now restricted to a few sp. which do not closely resemble the garden montbretias. Stems 2–3 ft. with large, many-flowered panicle of yellow or orange *fl.* perianth funnel-shaped with long tube opening to a star of spreading segments 2–3 in. across. Aug.-Sept. The common montbretia is quite hardy in all except the very coldest areas and spreads very rapidly. The named selected forms with larger *fl.* are unfortunately less hardy and are only suitable for the milder areas unless they are lifted each autumn and housed in a frame. The original cross was made by M. Lemoine, the famous nurseryman of Nancy. Among these some of the finest are:

* * 'CITRONELLA' Lemon-yellow.
* * 'HIS MAJESTY' Orange-scarlet with dark crimson on outside of petals. A large *fl.*
* 'STAR OF THE EAST' Pale orange-yellow.
  EARLHAM HYBRIDS A good mixed group with larger *fl.* than the common form.

* **C. masonorum.** One of the most handsome members of the genus. Stem up to $2\frac{1}{2}$ ft. with a panicle of reddish-orange *fl.* arching over into the horizontal and all facing upwards. Probably hardy in a warm border, otherwise best grown in a cold frame. *L.* plicate and arranged like a fan around stem. July-August. (Pl. IV)

**C. pottsii.** Stem tall up to 4 ft. with an 8 in. flower-spike of handsome bright yellow *fl.* flushed with red outside or deep orange-red throughout except at base. Largely superseded as a garden plant by the montbretias of which it is one of the original parents. Fairly hardy. August. Syn. *Tritonia pottsii*.

# CROCUS *Iridaceae*

EACH AUTUMN, through the winter and up to the end of March the crocuses give a wonderful return to the gardener who has allowed them to become naturalised and spread over wide areas. It is possible to start with quite small numbers in the case of species such as the autumn flowering *C. speciosus* and the spring *C. tomasinianus*, since they spread rapidly by seeding. A number of the larger flowered hybrid crocuses, especially the 'Dutch Yellow' are sterile, but will spread freely by division of the corms.

Crocuses are plants of the Mediterranean regions where the summers are warm and dry and where the corms can get a thorough baking during the summer. These regions, however, for the most part have heavy rain in autumn, winter and early spring and there is no doubt that the crocus needs a good supply of moisture during its growing season. Good drainage, however, is the absolute necessity and in a water-logged situation they are very unlikely to succeed, while in a heavy clay soil some of the species may do better in beds raised slightly above the levels of the surrounding garden. A sunny position should always be chosen but some of them will also do well at the edge of woodland, where they will look especially lovely. Many of the very early flowering species and their varieties such as *C. laevigatus* and *C. chrysanthus* are delicate flowers with beautiful feathered markings, and while they can often be established in the garden, are specially suitable for pans in the alpine house or for planting in troughs or sinks. I find that each year one of the most rewarding features of my garden from December to early March is given by two troughs of early flowering crocuses and irises, the flowers opening wide at the first gleam of any warm sun. It is warmth rather than light which seems to cause crocuses to open and so a pan brought into a warm house will quickly open and will remain open throughout the evening, long after they would have closed outside. The more difficult species seem to maintain themselves well and even increase in a raised frame of John Innes Potting Compost covered from the end of May till mid-September.

The number both of crocus species and of varieties is very great, far more than it is possible to describe here. For an account of the species readers are referred to Mr. E. A. Bowles' excellent *Handbook of Crocus and Colchicum*. He was the widely acknowledged king of all crocus knowledge but yet in his wonderfully rich garden at Myddelton House, near Enfield, no specially favoured area, it was the blue carpets of *C. speciosus* that covered whole beds in the autumn and the lavender and purple masses of *C. tomasinianus* in February which covered his rock garden, that are among my most treasured memories. These were the results of fifty years' spreading, but he once told me that both had started as very small colonies.

In order to make the long lists easier to follow the crocuses are divided into (*a*) autumn flowering (late August to end of November), (*b*) winter flowering (December to mid-February), (*c*) spring flowering (mid-February to March) and (*d*) garden or large Dutch varieties. By the end of March the crocus season will be over but will begin again at the end of August, whenever it rains.

Crocuses will grow in a very wide range of soils and do well on chalk. The corms should not be planted deeply, just about their own depth, but they have a wonderful habit of adjusting themselves and retractile roots will pull down the young new corms to a suitable depth. They are best moved when dormant and not in full growth, as are many other bulbs such as snowdrops. With care, however, it is possible to move them even when in flower, but they may take a year to build up again before flowering after such a move. In dampish areas such as the West of England it is often advisable to lift many of the less vigorous species each year when the foliage dies down and dry them off in paper bags before replanting. They should not be given fresh manure, but a little bone meal or dried blood will help them to build up their corms for the following season.

Choice crocuses may be grown from seed sown in pans or frames but the process takes at least three or four years. A few species spread naturally by seed. Crocuses are classified into groups by the covering of their corms. One is smooth, *C. laevigatus*, a number are reticulate, that is, covered with a net-like outer tunic, while others have parallel fibres in the tunic. Yet others are annulate, that is, their old outer coverings split away in rings round the circumference of the corms. In a crocus frame it is often desirable to separate closely related species with very similar corms with rows of a commoner species with corms of a different group. In order to find the corms easily and also to assist drainage around them the actual corms may in heavy soils be set in a layer of sand.

Other important characters to help with the recognition of crocus species are the colours of the stigmas and anthers (see Fig. 6, p. 40). Crocus species are abundant in most of the countries bordering the north of the Mediterranean while choice forms may be often found endemic to particular Mediterranean islands. A little practice enables one to distinguish at a glance the long narrow leaves with their midrib of silver from the leaves of grass or sedges and then their collection adds a most rewarding hobby to one's holiday in these regions which range from Spain to S. and E. Turkey. The corms will generally be found growing much deeper, sometimes even up to 8 or 10 in., than they need to be planted in English gardens. A number of mountain species such as the wild forms of *C. vernus* of the Alps and the lovely and varying forms of *C. sieberi* in Greece and Crete come into flower just at the edge of the melting snow as does the soldanella, and as one climbs higher the crocus season may be extended even till the middle of June. In the markings and delicate featherings of these little flowers there is infinite variety. Hardly any two are quite the same.

## (a) Autumn flowering species

\* **C. speciosus.** This is the commonest and in my opinion most valuable of all the autumn flowering crocuses and it is also one of the easiest to grow satisfactorily, often spreading freely both by seed and division. The corms are surprisingly tolerant of a light forking over of their beds in summer when they are dormant and the small cormlets which form abundantly around the base of the parent corm may in this way be spread more freely about the bed.

# Crocus

This sp. may be allowed to spread in beds of shrubs or even of low growing herbaceous plants and in the rock garden except only among the most delicate and tender of alpines. It will do no harm and amply repay. (Pl. **6**, 3; **10***a*)

*Fl.* large, rather globose, up to 4 in. in height from the ground, varying in colour from deep blue-mauve to a light lavender-blue or white. They are generally prominently veined and the three outer petals are marked with deeper colour on the outside. The stigmata are deep reddish-orange and the anthers yellow. Flowers late August-October, appearing before the *l.* The corm is large and conspicuously annulate. When displayed dry in shops in late summer it is often seen with a long whitish shoot emerging from the corm and sometimes the *fl.* will even open on the dry shelf. When planted at that season the corms of this and of *C. kotschyanus* come into flower more quickly than any other plants I know, sometimes in a mere matter of a few days. Eastern Europe, Asia Minor, Caucasus, N.E. Persia. A number of forms have been selected from time to time and named and include the following :

    ' AITCHESONII ' Probably the largest form and having outer segments up to 3 in. in length, pale lavender-mauve, longer and more pointed *fl.* latish in *fl.*

    ' ARTABIR ' Pale lavender-blue with darker featherings.

    ' CASSIOPE ' Large flowered, bluish-lavender but with a pale creamy-yellow base, latish.

\* ' OXONIAN ' Probably the bluest of the many forms, though hardly a true Oxford blue. A beautiful *fl.* but not such a vigorous grower as most of the other forms. (Pl. **4**, 3)

    ' POLLUX ' Pale violet-blue, silvery-blue outside, *fl.* large.

## OTHER AUTUMN FLOWERING SPECIES

**C. asturicus.** Generally offered in its deep purple form var. *atropurpureus.* Medium in size, pale to deep lilac or purple, generally slightly striped at throat, occasionally white, young *l.* appearing with or very soon after the *fl.* Spain (Asturias). October. Closely related to *C. nudiflorus* whose range it overlaps, but with smaller and more pointed *fl.* A rarer plant in gardens and probably not such a desirable one. Corms roundish, tunic fibrous. (Pl. **6**, 11)

\* **C. byzantinus.** This is the very lovely sp. more often grown in gardens and offered in catalogues under the name *iridiflorus.* Easily distinguished from all other garden crocuses by the inner segments being considerably smaller than the outer, thus giving it something of the appearance of an iris. *Fl.* large, outer segments rich bluish-purple up to 2 in. in length, wide, inner segments pale silvery-mauve only up to 1 in. long, narrow and pointed; stigmata light purple, a feature also not found in any other commonly grown sp., but in a few forms whitish. Sept.-Oct. *L.* broad and without prominent silvery streak on upper surface. Corm small, tunic fibrous. E. Europe, Hungary, where it is recorded as a plant of light woodland. A very fine sp. best grown here in a slightly more shaded position according to Mr. Bowles. A plant that should be tried more often, but is now becoming rather rare. It is so different from other sp. that one authority at least has proposed for it a separate generic name *Crociris*, but this has not been generally adopted. (Pl. **6**, 7)

**C. cancellatus.** Large, varying from white, very pale silvery-lilac to deep mauve, often slightly feathered near base of flower on outer segments. (Pl. **6**, 1). Pale yellow at throat. Stigmata pale yellow, much branched. Sept.-Nov. Greece, Asia Minor. An attractive but variable sp., not seen as often as it should be. *L.* appearing with or soon after *fl.* Corm with a coarsely reticulated covering.

> Var. **cilicicus.** Distinguished by its white instead of yellow anthers, pale lilac-mauve. Sept. Asia Minor. (Pl. **6**, 5)

**C. clusii.** Small, pale mauve to deep purple with *l.*, throat white. Oct. W. Spain and Portugal where it is said to grow in open woodland. Probably more suited to the frame or alpine house than the rock garden. Corm reticulated.

**C. hadriaticus.** Medium in size, white but heavily veined purple towards base on outside segments, throat yellow, stigmata large, deep orange. Greece. Allied to *C. sativus*, the Saffron Crocus but not so large. (Pl. **6**, 12)

**C. hyemalis.** Small, starry, white, feathered purple, generally towards base, throat deep orange, sweet scented. Nov.-Jan. Palestine, Syria. Best in alpine house or frame owing to its late season of flowering. Flower with leaves. A variable sp. not very often seen in cultivation. Close to *C. ochroleucus* but distinguished by the more widely branched style and dark purple anthers. A variant with yellow-orange anthers has also been recorded.

**C. iridiflorus.** See under *C. byzantinus*.

* **C. kotschyanus.** This is one of the most valuable sp. commonly grown in gardens and is generally found in catalogues under the more appropriate name of *C. zonatus*. *Fl.* large, rosy-lilac and at base of each petal on inside are two bright orange spots joined together, which show prominently as the *fl.* opens; throat yellow. Generally the earliest sp. to flower, end of Aug.-Sept., the *fl.* appearing before the *l.* A robust grower spreading freely and suitable for naturalising, and second only to *C. speciosus* in this capacity. Asia Minor, Lebanon. Corm irregular in shape, often with protuberances and producing numerous cormlets which help to spread the colony. (Pl. **6**, 2)

> Var. **leucopharynx.** This is the crocus often offered as *C. karduchorum* and differs from the commoner *kotschyanus* by the white instead of yellow throat and absence of orange spots. *Fl.* pale bluish-lavender, less rosy than in the type. (Pl. **6**, 13). The true *C. karduchorum* of Maw is probably not in cultivation.

**C. longiflorus.** Large, globose rather than elongated, purplish-lilac outside, deep bluish-mauve inside, throat orange, stigmata deep orange, scented. Oct.-Nov. S. Italy, Sicily. A beautiful sp. and quite hardy. Corm medium in size and with a coarsely reticulated covering. (Pl. **6**, 8*a*)

> Var. **melitensis.** Distinguished by the prominent feathering on the outside of all its segments, sometimes seen against a buff ground on the three outer segments. Malta. (Pl. **6**, 8*b*)

* **C. medius.** Large, lilac outside, inside bright purplish-mauve, petals veined

94

with deeper purple towards base at inside, occasionally white, stigmata deep orange, finely branched and conspicuous, flowering before leaves develop. Oct.-Nov. S. France along the Riviera coast. Hardy and flowering outside later than *C. speciosus*, but should be given a sunny place, also good for the alpine house. (Pl. 6, 9)

\* **C. niveus.** Medium in size, white with rich yellow throat, stigmata deep orange, anthers yellow, thus distinguishing it from *C. boryi*, a white-flowered sp. also from Greece which has white anthers. Mr. Bowles has recorded his opinion that it is the most beautiful autumnal white sp. It is hardy but flowers in November and so is best protected with a cloche or grown in alpine house or frame. Corm medium in size with reticulate tunic. *L.* slightly developed at flowering time. (Pl. 6, 16)

\* **C. nudiflorus.** Large, deep purple, petals long, occasionally white, late Sept.-Nov. Stigmata bright orange, finely divided. *Fl.* appearing well before leaves. S.W. France, Pyrenees, N. Spain. A very handsome crocus which has the unusual character of spreading through underground stolons, for this reason it should be left undisturbed and will grow satisfactorily in grass and even in damp meadows. It is recorded that it has become naturalised in some districts of Yorkshire and the Midlands, but unfortunately some of these have now been built over. An interesting association has been traced between this distribution and that of property belonging to the Knights of St. John of Jerusalem and it is possible that they may have been the original distributing agents. Corm small. (Pl. 6, 10)

**C. ochroleucus.** Small to medium in size, petals rather long and narrow, white or pale cream, with deeper yellow blotches around throat, anthers creamy-white; style three-branched only. Lebanon, Northern Palestine. October. Not such a pure white or such a fine sp. as *C. niveus* or *C. hadriaticus* and although quite hardy needs the protection of a cloche or alpine house to mature its flowers satisfactorily. (Pl. 6, 18)

**C. pulchellus.** Large, pale lavender, slightly veined. Closely related to *C. speciosus* but flowering a little later and having a paler flower less blue in tone, also distinguished by the white anthers and more conspicuously marked deep yellow throat. October. Asia Minor, Turkey. Corm small, annulate. (Pl. 6, 4)

\* **C. salzmannii.** Large, lilac, almost self-coloured, petals pointed, deep yellow at throat. October. *Fl.* with *l.* S. Spain and N. Africa. Corms large. A strong growing sp. which seems quite hardy and able to maintain itself in the open rock garden without lifting. (Pl. 6, 6)

**C. sativus.** Saffron crocus. Large, rosy lilac-purple to deep purplish-mauve but variable in colour, distinguished by the very large orange-red stigmata which in the closed *fl.* often project even beyond the petals and when mature droop astride the *fl.*; petals generally deeper purple around throat. *L.* narrow, developed with *fl.* Sept.-Oct. S. Europe and Asia Minor ranging from Italy to E. Turkey. Saffron, a much prized drug and dye in the Middle Ages, is obtained from the large stigmata. (Pl. 6, 14)

It is a handsome *fl.* and the large corms are regularly on offer but somehow it is now rarely seen successfully established in English gardens although at one time there was a saffron industry in East Anglia, the name Saffron Walden being taken from it, and apparently the corms were grown by the acre. Mr. Bowles recommends for its culture frequent division and manuring an unusual recipe for a crocus, and kitchen-garden treatment in as warm and sunny a spot as possible.

* Var. **cartwrightianus.** Much smaller and with deeper mauve veining and feathering. Greece. This variety, however, seems to succeed much better in English gardens than the sp. and is well worth growing in the rock garden, flowering late Sept. or early Oct. By many authors it is treated as a separate sp.

**C. speciosus** (see p. 92).

**C. tournefortii.** Medium in size, bright lilac-blue, slightly veined purple on outside, stigmata orange, much branched, anthers creamy-white, flowering with the *l.* Oct.-Nov. and well worth the protection of a cloche at this time. Greek islands. Corm large, tunic membranous, soft. A handsome sp. but unfortunately only rarely seen. (Pl. **6, 15**)

**C. vallicola.** Medium in size, creamy-white, veined with pale lilac and with two golden spots at base of each petal. September-October. Corm small, *l.* narrow, four-angled. N.E. Turkey where it grows on damp alpine moorland of Pontic Range. Probably it does not require any summer baking.

**C. zonatus.** A syn. of *C. kotschyanus.*

# (b) Winter and very early flowering spring species

It is difficult to separate these both from the last of the autumnal species and from the earliest of the spring species, and their actual time of flowering will vary with each season although the succession will tend to be the same. *C. laevigatus* follows closely on to the autumnal species and in a few newly collected forms flowers may be seen in November. More often, however, especially in established clumps, they appear in late December and January. If the weather is not freezing we are generally able to pick a few of the lovely feathered mauve flowers on Christmas Day. Occasionally we can pick *C. imperati* at the same time. While all these species are absolutely hardy and the forms of *C. aureus*, *C. laevigatus*, *C. imperati* and *C. tomasinianus* are amongst the best of all species for naturalising and spreading, a few in pans or some protection from cloches will help to protect their flowers from damage. In general the species in this section will be likely to flower between the beginning of December and the middle of February, but others will follow close on, especially *C. sieberi* and its forms. The division I have chosen for convenience of presentation will not always be maintained in the garden.

Plate 11: ERYTHRONIUM. 1, *E. oregonum* subsp. *leucandrum*. 2, *E.* 'White Beauty'. 3, *E. revolutum* var. *johnsonii*. 4, *E. grandiflorum*. 5, *E. helenae*. 6, *E. hendersonii*. 7, *E. tuolumnense*. 8, *E. citrinum*. 9, *E. dens-canis*. 10, *E. howellii*. 11, *E. americanum* (without leaf)

*Plate* 12: Freesias. Some modern hybrids

*Plate* 13: FRITILLARIA. 1, *F. drenovskyi.* 2, *F. meleagris,* 2 forms. 3, *F. recurva.* 4, *F. liliacea.* 5, *F. obliqua.* 6, *F. pyrenaica.* 7, *F. tuntasia.* 8, *F. olivieri.* 9, *F. crassifolia.* 10, *F. pontica.* 11, *F. latifolia.* 12, *F. graeca* var. *thessala* 13, *F. pudica.* 14, *F. sibthorpiana* (below, style and stamens). 15. *F. armena.* 16, *F. graeca.* 17, *F. tubiformis* var. *moggridgei.* 18, *F. latifolia* var. *nobilis.* 19. *F. pinardii*

*Plate* 14: GALANTHUS (SNOWDROPS) AND LEUCOJUM (SNOWFLAKES). 1, *G. plicatus* ' Warham '.
2, *G. plicatus*. 3, *L. aestivum*. 4, *L. aestivum* var. *pulchellum*. 5, *G. nivalis* ' Atkinsii '. 6, *G. nivalis*
' Magnet '. 7, *G. nivalis* ' Merlin '. 8, *L. trichophyllum*. 9, *L. vernum* var. *carpathicum*. 10, *G.
elwesii*. 11, *G. fosteri*. 12, *G. byzantinus*. 13, *L. vernum* var. *vagneri*. 14, *G. nivalis* ' Scharlokii '.
15. *G. nivalis* double yellow form. 16, *G. nivalis* ' Viridapicis '. 17, *G. nivalis*. 18, *G. nivalis*
double form. 19, *G. ikariae* subsp. *latifolius*. 20, *L. nicaeënse*. 21, *L. vernum*. 22, *G. ikariae*
subsp. *ikariae*. 23, *G. nivalis* var. *flavescens*

# Crocus

In this section, particularly among the forms of *C. chrysanthus*, are some of the most lovely and most rewarding of all crocuses, and their season of flowering makes them doubly welcome.

\* **C. aureus.** This is the wild sp. from which the 'Dutch Yellow' has been derived but as a garden plant it has several additional merits. It is fertile rather than sterile, it flowers about a fortnight earlier, often at the same time or even earlier than the little " Tommies " with which it mingles beautifully to make a naturalised picture of great beauty, and it is a much richer deeper golden colour, a rich burning orange, almost crackling like a flame in the midst of winter.

*Fl.* large, taller and more slender than the 'Dutch Yellow', appearing before or with the first *l.*, but always from a distinct fibrous sheath which is more prominent than in most other sp. Late Jan. to mid-Feb. Greece to W. Asia Minor and Roumania. Corms large. There are also several varieties with paler *fl.* ranging from ivory-white to sulphur-yellow but they are all very rare in cultivation and are reported to be of much less vigour than the type of the sp. (Pl. **7**, 12; **10b**; **18b**)

**C. chrysanthus.** As a parent this sp. has given rise to a tremendous range of seedlings of almost infinite variability and a large number have been selected, given names and propagated as clones. Among them are a number of our most beautiful and useful crocuses, especially for cultivation in pans in the alpine house and in troughs. The late Mr. Bowles raised a large number of seedlings and named them after birds and some very fine ones have also been raised in Holland. The sp. as found in Greece and Asia Minor has medium-sized, rather globular *fl.*, varying from deep yellow to bright orange and generally flecked or feathered with deep purplish colouring on the outside of the three outer petals and with a golden throat, anthers orange with small black tips or barbs at the base. Early mid-Feb. Corms medium in size, round, tunic annulate, producing a number of *fl.* from each corm.

The colour of the seedlings ranges from creamy to deepest orange with mahogany markings and the *fl.* are generally larger than those of the wild sp. The petals usually have a silvery sheen. There is also a small range of blue-flowered seedlings, probably arising originally through hybridisation with another sp. such as *C. biflorus* var. *weldenii* or *C. aerius*, but unfortunately these varieties, which are a richer blue than any other crocus, are the least vigorous of all the forms and seem difficult to retain from year to year, while they divide slowly, hence their maintenance of a high price. Their *fl.* are also smaller but they include some of the most beautiful of all crocuses in colour and markings.

Out of a long range of named varieties the following may be selected:
'ADVANCE' Large, pale golden-yellow with prominent dark maroon streaks and feathering on outside of 3 outer petals. A striking variety,
'BLUE BEAUTY' Pale blue, darkening towards base.
\* 'BLUE BIRD' Dark purplish-blue with a white margin to petals, white inside.
'BLUE BONNET' Pale blue with a yellow throat.
'BLUE BUTTERFLY' Deep blue with a tinge of violet, darker towards base, a fine variety. (Pl. **7**, 29)

# *Crocus*

* ' BLUE PEARL ' A beautiful variety of pale blue with deep orange stigmata.

' BLUE GIANT ' Very large for this section, globular, pale mauvy-blue on outside with lavender colouring near tips of petals, deep yellow throat, outside a little dark grey-blue feathering. A promising new variety.

' BULLFINCH ' Globular, creamy-yellow and richly feathered outside with crimson-purple, pure white inside and orange at throat. Mr. Bowles regarded this as one of the best of his seedlings but it is unfortunately now very rare.

' CANARY BIRD ' Rather small flowers, bright orange-yellow, feathered with deep bronze on outside, petals rather pointed.

* ' CREAM BEAUTY ' Pale creamy-yellow, medium-large size, free-flowering.

* ' E. A. BOWLES ' Large globular *fl.* deep butter-yellow, heavily feathered with bronze towards base of petals. An outstanding and free-flowering variety fittingly named after Mr. Bowles by its Dutch raiser and still unsurpassed in its colour. (Pl. **7**, 18 and Pl. VI*a*)

' E. P. BOWLES ' Smaller than the preceeding, but slightly deeper in colour and with more prominent feathering.

' FUSCO-TINCTUS ' Probably a wild form of the sp. *Fl.* small, starry, but of a rich golden-yellow, heavily shaded outside with bronze feathering.

' GOLDILOCKS ' Large deep golden-yellow *fl.* feathered with bronze outside, a fine variety of great brilliance.

' JOHN HOOG ' Sulphur-yellow, marked with deep purple on outside, named by Mr. Bowles after Mr. Hoog of Messrs. van Tubergen in Holland who had raised so many good varieties. A fine form but now unfortunately rare.

* ' KITTIWAKE ' Slender, pale silvery-grey with blue-mauve markings almost covering outside of outer 3 petals, almost white inside, a beautiful variety.

* ' MOONLIGHT ' Large pale sulphur-yellow *fl.* fading to creamy-yellow, a very beautiful variety.

' PEACE ' White, outer 3 petals creamy on outside and feathered with bluish-grey. Closer to ' Snow Bunting ' but slightly paler.

* ' SNOW BUNTING ' An aptly named *fl.* white inside and on the outside of the 3 inner petals, the outer petals outside being creamy and feathered with dark lilac like the wings of the bird after which it is named. A free-flowering variety. (Pl. **7**, 20)

' SULTAN ' A very handsome large *fl.* deep purplish-mahogany on the outside of the 3 outer petals, margined with white, the inner petals whitish, deeply yellow towards the throat. (Pl. **7**, 16)

' SUNSHINE ' Orange-gold, darker at base, very slightly darker than ' Goldilocks ', large *fl.*, a fine variety.

* ' WARLEY WHITE ' *Fl.* large, outer petals pale cream and heavily suffused with deep bluish-purple, inner petals creamy-white with greyish-purple blotches outside at base, inside white with yellow throat, a very handsome *fl.* and one of the earliest to open, often in January. (Pl. **7**, 19)

* ' YELLOW HAMMER ' A beautiful deep buttercup-yellow, freely feathered on the outside, now unfortunately rarely seen.

* ' ZWANENBURG ' Sometimes called ' Zwanenburg Bronze ', named after the nurseries in Holland of Messrs. van Tubergen, a very spectacular large

# *Crocus*

*fl.*, deep orange heavily suffused on the outside of all outer petals with very deep purplish-mahogany giving the appearance when closed of a rich mahogany-coloured *fl.*, orange inside.

* **C. imperati,** named after a famous Italian botanist of the sixteenth century called Imperato, is always one of the earliest to flower and I have several times been able to pick flowers on Christmas or New Year's Day, although its more normal season is late January to early February. *Fl.* large, globular but tall in bud, up to 3 in. across when fully open, outer 3 petals which cover *fl.* when closed pale yellowish-buff veined prominently with deep purple, inner 3 petals and inside of *fl.* bright lilac-mauve veined deeper mauve, stigmata orange, throat yellow. Scent acrid. The flower illustrated in Pl. **7**, 3 is an unusually finely coloured one, that in bud (Pl. **7**, 4) being more typical. On a sunny day a patch of this crocus gives a striking effect. It maintains itself and increases freely in the open ground in rather dry situations and is much to be recommended both for its earliness of flowering, its vigour and its beauty. S. Italy.

* **C. laevigatus.** Another beauty and a real winter flowering plant with a season from late November till the end of January. *Fl.* medium in size, distinctly smaller than the preceding, petals pale lilac-mauve, outer three heavily and variously feathered with deep lilac-mauve, inner three only marked towards base, inside pale lavender, stigmata feathery, orange, anthers white, throat yellow. Greece. Var. *fontenayi* (Pl. **6**, 17) is often offered and has a slightly larger *fl.* with prominent feathering but in this variable sp. the forms really merge one into the other. Some are found with a whitish instead of lilac ground colour. *C. laevigatus* is a good garden plant in a dry situation and one patch with me has lasted a number of years and increased and flowered regularly. The corm is unlike that of any other crocus, the outer tunic being hard and smooth, giving the corm the appearance of a hazel nut.

* **C. tomasinianus.** This sp. occupies the place in early spring that *C. speciosus* has in autumn and once planted spreads very freely by seed and also by the dividing of its corms. I would certainly never wish to be without the little " Tommies " shooting up all over the place at the end of January or early February (Pl. V). *Fl.* medium in size, slender in bud, in the typical form very pale suede mauvish-blue on the outside of the outer 3 petals, but when opening in the slightest gleam of sun the 3 inner petals and the inside of the *fl.* are shown and these are a bright lilac-mauve (Pl. **7**, 7 and 10*b*). As might be expected from a plant which seeds so freely the *fl.* colour is very variable. In some the outer petals are just tipped with mauve or purple, and this form has been called *pictus*. The *fl.* is also richer in colour than the average and generally opening less widely. Occasionally one will find a seedling that is a reddish-purple, sometimes also a white one. Three specially fine forms have been selected and named.
* ' BARR'S PURPLE ' Rich purple-lilac inside, outside of three outer petals pale mauvish-grey as in the sp. Large *fl.*
* ' TAPLOW RUBY ' Dark rich reddish-purple, probably the deepest coloured form, the colour being darkest towards the tips. (Pl. **7**, 1)
* ' WHITEWELL PURPLE ' Named after the rectory where Rev. Joseph Jacob collected together so many unusual and good plants. *Fl.* purplish-mauve,

but not quite so deep in colour although bluer than the preceding form. Pale silvery-mauve inside. A very beautiful and free-flowering variety.

This sp. is native to Dalmatia and the eastern side of the Adriatic. The corms are generally small and roundish. Since it flowers early with the *l.* showing it may be planted under deciduous shrubs which do not make too dense a shade and then left to look after itself. The fine grass-like foliage will seldom be a nuisance but should always be left to mature.

## (c) Spring flowering crocuses

These follow hard on the flowers of those in the previous group and there will generally be some overlap. The season I have in mind for this group is generally from early February till nearly the end of March but of course will vary from year to year. In this group I have treated the species and varieties close to them but the garden-raised large forms of *C. vernus* I think are best dealt with in a separate section.

**C. aerius.** Pale lilac-blue with yellow throat marked with dark purplish-crimson on outside of outer segments, small-medium in size and variable in colour, globular in form. Feb.-March. *L.* appear with the *fl.* Asia Minor. Corm annulate. It hybridises freely with *C. chrysanthus*, a close relative, and possibly with *C. biflorus* and several fine forms or hybrids have been segregated.
  Var. **major.** *Fl.* larger than in the type.
* ' CELESTE ' Pale blue, larger than type and with heavy feathered markings on outside of outer three segments. A beautiful *fl.* raised in Ireland and possibly a hybrid between *C. aerius* and *C. biflorus* var. *weldenii*, which has distinct blue markings on the outer segments. (Pl. 7, 33)
  ' GREY LADY ' Slender, medium size, pale mauvish-grey, flushed heavily with deeper mauve on outside petals.

**C. ancyrensis.** *Fl.* small, petals narrow, but a brilliant orange in colour, sometimes feathered near base and forms have been found with a purple perianth tube, free-flowering. End of Jan. to mid-Feb. Asia Minor, Turkey. Corm with reticulate tunic thus distinguishing it from *C. chrysanthus*, the narrower petals and slenderer *fl.* distinguishing it from *C. susianus*. A good grower.

* **C. balansae.** One of the most brilliant of all orange *fl.*, rivalling *C. aureus* in this character. Small to medium in size, rich orange feathered with dark mahogany on outside of outer segments. Orange stigmata finely divided into threads. *L.* broad, appearing with the *fl.* Feb. to early March. W. Asia Minor. A good plant for the raised bed or sink or alpine house pan. (Pl. 7, 11)

* **C. biflorus.** Medium-large, ground colour generally whitish but varying to pale lilac, generally feathered or even striped purple on outside of outer segments, throat yellow. *L.* appear with the flowers. Mid-Feb. to early March. Corm with annulate tunic. Italy to Asia Minor, the forms from Dalmatia being among the finest. An unusually fine form is that sold as

100

# Crocus

' Scotch ' crocus with large striped *fl.* and a whitish ground. It is probably an old garden form arising in cultivation and is one usually supplied by nurserymen. It is also known as ' Cloth of Silver ' to distinguish it from *C. susianus* which is ' Cloth of Gold.'

Var. **parkinsonii.** *Fl.* smaller, globular, pale lilac and with outside of outer segments creamy-buff with purple feathering. This is closely related to var. *argenteus* (Pl. **7**, 30), which is sometimes interchanged with it.

* Var. **weldenii.** Probably the finest form of the sp. Large, white entirely (*weldenii albus*; Pl. **7**, 21) or pale blue or white speckled with blue; outer segments on outside almost entirely deep blue, with a white edge to petal, throat white (Pl. **7**, 28). Dalmatia.

Var. **alexandri** is very close to this but deep purplish outside. Both are hardy and good garden forms. Mid-Feb. to mid-March.

**C. cambessedesii.** *Fl.* small, often under 1 in. in length, outer segments buff on outside, feathered with deep purple, inner segments pale lilac-purple, the *fl.* being like a very miniature copy of *C. imperati.* However, with its orange-scarlet stigma it is attractive in the alpine house or frame where it is best grown. It has a long season of flowering in its native habitat of the Balearic Islands, from November till March. (Pl. **7**, 34)

**C. candidus.** Very variable in colour, white, cream, pale yellow to orange, often feathered with purple outside, medium-large. Late flowering. March-April. Asia Minor. Corm medium in size with strongly ribbed tunic. A good garden sp. but flowering late, it tends to get confused with the Dutch varieties. The deep orange form, often distributed as var. *mountainii* is a very fine crocus and well worth growing. The pale yellow forms are also attractive and may be distinguished as var. *subflavus.*

* **C. corsicus.** Small to medium in size but so beautifully marked as to be one of the finest of all crocus sp.; outer segments pale lilac or buff coloured and heavily feathered with deeper purple; inner segments lilac-mauve; throat white or pale lilac inside, tinged yellow on outside. Late flowering, March-April. Corsica, where it grows in the mountains up to 7,000 ft. Corm small with finely reticulated tunic. (Pl. **7**, 15)

* **C. dalmaticus.** Medium to large in size; outer three segments pale lilac or lavender-grey outside with deeper lilac markings towards base. Feb.-March. A good garden and alpine house plant. Dalmatia. Corm with reticulate tunic. (Pl. **7**, 9)

**C. danfordiae.** Small, pale to deep yellow, but white and pale lilac forms have been recorded, sometimes with brownish veining or suffusion on outside of outer segments. Feb.-March. Asia Minor. A plant for the alpine house or raised frame rather than the open garden and rarely seen. (Pl. **7**, 13)

* **C. etruscus.** Large, pale lilac or greyish-lavender often with buff colouring in outer segments and with deeper mauve feathering. Variable in colour and in its best forms a good sp. not seen nearly as often as it should be. Late Feb.-March. W. Italy. (Pl. **7**, 6)

**C. fleischeri.** Small to medium, white, striped with deep purple towards base, segments narrow, stigmata orange-scarlet and finely divided. Early flowering,

101

# Crocus

February. Asia Minor. Corm yellowish, very finely reticulate. *L.* very narrow. (Pl. **7**, 10)

**C. korolkowii.** Small, deep yellow, outer segments on outside heavily flushed and feathered with purplish-mahogany; segments rather narrow, starry, but inside glossy and shining like a celandine. Early flowering, Jan.-early Feb. (Pl. **7**, 2). Afghanistan and Turkestan. Corms large, rather flat with a tunic of fine parallel fibres. Hardy and free flowering but best in the alpine house and unfortunately now rarely seen.

\* **C. minimus.** Small to medium, hardly the smallest-flowered member of the genus but without doubt one of the most beautiful, the outer segments being very richly feathered and marked with deep purple on a buff background and the inner ones being deep mauvish-purple. The *fl.* are slightly smaller than those of *C. corsicus,* but the markings of the outer segments are much more pronounced and in some forms the deep purple almost covers the entire petal; stigmata orange-scarlet. March-April. Corsica and Sardinia, but growing at lower levels than *C. corsicus.* Hardy but perhaps best in the alpine house or frame where its fine markings can be clearly seen. (Pl. **7**, 23)

**C. olivieri.** Medium in size, rather globular, very brilliant deep orange in colour, in some forms marked on the outer segments and around throat with purplish-mahogany. Feb.-early March. *L.* very broad. Greece, Bulgaria, Roumania. A good sp. for the alpine house but quite hardy also in the rock garden. (Pl. **7**, 25)

\* **C. sieberi.** Medium-large and among the most beautiful of all crocuses. Several very distinct varieties have been named, but all are distinguished by the orange-yellow throat. The one usually sold as *C. sieberi* is var. *atticus* with deep mauve, rather globular *fl.* from the mountains of Attica and Mt. Parnassus. A good garden plant and a vigorous grower.

    ' VIOLET QUEEN ' is a smaller-flowered form of this with deeper coloured *fl.* (Pl. **7**, 27)

    Var. **tricolor,** a very beautiful form with a white band between the deep yellow of the throat and the mauve upper part of the petals; inside pale lilac-mauve; *fl.* large, globular. Mt. Chelmos and North Peloponnese only, where it flowers high on the mountains in April-May at the edge of the melting snow and is a lovely sight as the sun opens the *fl.* It grows with rich blue scillas and other dwarf bulbs. I have seen a single plant of a pure white form.

    \* Var. **versicolor,** also known as var. *heterochromus,* comes from similar situations in the White mountains of Crete. It is not such a vigorous plant but it is undoubtedly one of the most beautiful, if not indeed absolutely the most beautiful of all crocuses. *Fl.* white to very pale lilac-mauve, but feathered prominently on the outside of the three outer segments; always golden-yellow at base. (Pl. **7**, 22). The amount of feathering is very variable sometimes covering almost the whole petal with a deep purplish-mahogany, in other forms only just tipping the *fl.* with colour. Stigmata long, deep orange-scarlet. Late Jan. to mid-Feb. A superb plant for the alpine house but not one of the easiest

# Crocus

sp. to retain satisfactorily from year to year. It was to this plant that the name *C. sieberi* was originally given. *L.* much narrower than in the other varieties. Two very fine hybrid seedlings are also in cultivation:

* ' BOWLES'S WHITE ' Pure white with deep yellowish-gold base. This was considered by Mr. Bowles to be his best white spring flowering crocus and certainly it is a very beautiful *fl.* Early Feb.

' HUBERT EDELSTEN ' A very beautiful hybrid raised between var. *versicolor* and var. *atticus*, and having many of the qualities of both. *Fl.* large, outer segments feathered and marked with a wide central band of deep mauvish-purple, interrupted by a white band across the *fl.*; inner segments pale lilac-mauve; throat golden. (Pl. 7, 24)

**C. stellaris.** Medium in size, golden-yellow, heavily feathered on outside of outer three segments and at throat with mahogany. March. Although now rare this plant has long been known in gardens but has never been found wild. It has been suggested that it may be a hybrid between *C. aureus* and *C. susianus*. It is sterile. (Pl. 7, 5)

* **C. susianus.** The ' Cloth of Gold ' crocus and most aptly named. *Fl.* small to medium in size but brilliant deep orange in colour and the outside of the outer three segments and the base of the inside segments very prominently marked with mahogany. Feb.-March. Very dwarf and usually early to flower. S.W. Russia, Crimea. A good garden plant as well as an excellent one for the alpine house. The little *fl.* have a fiery intensity of colour that is only equalled by *C. aureus*, *C. balansae* and *C. olivieri*. (Pl. 7, 26)

**C. suterianus.** Small, globular, variable in colour from butter-yellow to deep golden-yellow. *Fl.* generally borne in a bunch. Distinguished from *C. olivieri* by the narrower *l.* and less brilliant orange *fl.* Asia Minor. Several forms have been distinguished among which ' Golden Bunch ' (Pl. 7, 31) and ' Jamie ' (Pl 7, 32) are two of the best.

**C. veluchensis.** Medium to large in size, resembling *C. sieberi* but without the yellow throat, that of this sp. being pale lilac or whitish; *fl.* lilac-purple. Mountains of N. Greece. Corm small. Not such a vigorous grower as *C. sieberi*.

**C. vernus.** This is the wild crocus of the Alps and the Pyrenees and is found in great drifts at the edge of the snows flowering with the soldanellas. It is very variable in colour and markings from pure white to deep purple, and often presents a most beautiful spectacle, but one that no gardener has succeeded in reproducing in this country. These variable forms have however given rise to a large race of garden hybrids sometimes known as Dutch hybrids, mostly of excellent constitution and with much larger *fl.* than in the wild sp. These are discussed in the next section.

* **C. versicolor.** Large, variable in colour from white to purple but generally pale lilac-grey prominently feathered on all segments outside with purple. March. S. France. A good garden plant which has long been in cultivation but the forms usually seen in gardens are larger than those commonly found in the wild. Some named varieties have been distinguished in the past but in such a variable sp. they tend to merge into one another; that most commonly

found is var. *picturatus*, in which the ground colour is white and the purple markings are prominent and make a good contrast. (Pl. 7, 8)

**C. vitellinus.** Small-medium in size, golden-yellow-orange, rather slender, with narrow segments, sometimes with slight feathering of deeper colour towards base, fragrant. Stigmata much divided. Early flowering: Jan. to mid-Feb., sometimes earlier. Asia Minor, Syria. Corm with smooth reddish-brown tunic. Best grown in the alpine house owing to its early flowering.

Var. **syriacus,** with fine feathering of five lines on the outer segments, has been distinguished.

## (*d*) Garden varieties

These large-flowered garden varieties, for the most part raised in Holland and so often known as Dutch varieties, follow closely on the season of the species and overlap it in parts. Their season begins with the brilliant orange globes of the ' Dutch Yellow ' and the pale mauve rather slender flowers of ' Vanguard,' the earliest of the mauve and purple forms, and these, more perhaps even than the species, serve as the first heralds of spring.

They are very vigorous and adaptable plants and may either be naturalised in grass in full sun or grown in clumps at the edges of borders or in drifts in the wild garden. In general they are not suited either to the formal or to the rock garden. The corms, which are considerably larger than those of the species, should be planted about 3 in. deep and about the same distance apart. They generally look best in drifts of informal outline rather than in more regularly shaped patches. Wherever they are planted it is important that their foliage should be allowed to die down naturally after the flowering and this will not be completed till about the beginning of June. Consequently, where they are planted in grass, it must be left long till then. This generally does not matter around the bases of trees and in rough paddock or on the edge of woodland. Many people consider that they obtain the best effects through planting in drifts of a single colour or variety, others like to mingle white and mauve and purple together. In general it seems best to avoid mingling the yellow and the mauve ones, and the yellow will be largely over before the others come out in most seasons. Their arrangement, however, is a matter of taste.

It is not necessary to lift the corms every season, but probably every third or fourth season it is desirable where they may have got congested. When growing in grass their vigour is generally diminished and it may not be necessary to lift them for a number of seasons but then it will often be found desirable to supplement the display by planting a few extra corms each year, especially on a light soil. They should be planted early in the autumn if possible and certainly before mid-November. The large-flowered varieties may be grown in pots or pans for the cool greenhouse, but in this case they must not be forced unduly and must be grown cool until the flower buds are showing, then they may be brought into some heat to bring them on before those outside. If desired they may be plunged outside in the earth or under a pile of ashes until late January when they may be brought into the house. They are generally better in pans of earth than in bulb fibre but can be grown in the latter if desired as long as care is taken not to give them too much water.

The following are a selection from the many good kinds available in catalogues arranged under colours.

*White*

> ' JOAN OF ARC ' One of the largest *fl.*, pure white, tinged violet towards base, orange stigmata.
> ' KATHLEEN PARLOW ' An old variety but still one of the best, of fine form and with large *fl.*, pure white with prominent orange stigmata.
> * ' SNOWSTORM ' A very fine variety with very large, pure white *fl.*; considered by many to be the best of the white varieties.

*Pale lilac-mauve without stripes*

> ' ENCHANTRESS ' Pale lilac-mauve, tinged deeper purple towards base. Early flowering.
> ' EXCELSIOR ' Lilac-mauve but deeper in colour than ' Enchantress.'
> ' HAARLEM GEM ' Small, pale lilac-mauve, pale silvery-lilac on outside, very early.
> ' JUBILEE ' Pale lilac-mauve, rather late flowering.
> ' LITTLE DORRIT ' Very pale silvery-lilac, large round globular flowers.
> ' QUEEN OF THE BLUES ' An old variety but still one of the best, large bluish-lavender flowers.
> * ' VANGUARD ' Very pale silvery-lilac, long slender flowers. The first to flower of this group and for this reason much to be recommended.

*Pale mauve with darker stripes*

> ' CINDERELLA ' Pale lilac-mauve but with outer petals striped with dark mauve.
> ' MIKADO ' Pale silvery-grey, finely striped with purple.
> ' MISS AINSWORTH ' Almost white with lilac-mauve stripes.
> ' PICKWICK ' Pale lilac, heavily striped, deep purple at base.
> ' STRIPED BEAUTY ' Pale silvery-grey with deep mauve stripes, base violet-purple.

*Deep purple*

> ' GLADSTONE ' Deep purple, large.

* 'NIGGER BOY' One of the deepest in colour, purplish-maroon, a very fine *fl.*; early.
'PAULUS POTTER' Reddish-purple, large *fl.*
* 'PURPUREUS GRANDIFLORUS' Large *fl.*, deep rich purple, an old variety but still unsurpassed in its colour and with a lovely satin sheen.
'REMEMBRANCE' Violet-purple, large *fl.* Early. Paler in colour than the others of this section.
* 'THE BISHOP' Large *fl.*, deep rich purple and with satin sheen to petals.

*Golden-yellow*

* 'DUTCH YELLOW' Sometimes called Large Yellow, or Yellow Giant; very early and very floriferous. Sterile but spreading by division of the corms.

# CURTONUS *Iridaceae*

A S. AFRICAN genus with only one species which was formerly included in *Antholyza*. It is distinguished by the bent or zigzag flower spike.

C. paniculata. Deep orange-red *fl.* on branching stems up to 4 ft.; conspicuous, like a larger montbretia. *L.* plicate and decorative. Aug.-Sept. S. Africa, Transvaal, Natal. Hardy and often seen as large clumps in old herbaceous borders. Syn. *Antholyza paniculata* and popularly known as " Aunt Eliza " and in S. Africa as " Pleated Leaves."

# CYCLAMEN *Primulaceae*

THIS GENUS includes some of the most delightful and beautiful tubers for naturalising in the woodland or rock garden, some of the finest alpine house plants and also, as a derivative of a wild species, a race of greenhouse tubers, easily raised from seed, which are perhaps the most popular of all flowers for Christmas and winter decoration in the house. So for a genus of only 14 or so species it is very rich and every one of its members desirable. Of cyclamen indeed it has been truly and frequently said: " No garden can have too many." Luckily they increase freely from seed. The cyclamen season is primarily the autumn, winter and early spring, but species can be found in flower from mid-August till mid-May. I propose to deal with them in three groups since their requirements are not uniform:

(*a*) The late summer and autumn flowering species such as *C. europaeum* and *C. neapolitanum.*

# Cyclamen

(b) The spring flowering species such as *C. orbiculatum* and *C. repandum* and the wild forms of *C. persicum*.

(c) The giant forms of *C. persicum*.

Unfortunately, the nomenclature of the hardy cyclamen has been much confused in the past, largely owing to earlier authors' lack of precision in describing the species to which they referred; in many cases it is probable that their descriptions covered one or more species as we now understand them. Consequently later authorities have interpreted their names in varying ways and some have had to be rejected as sources of confusion. The nomenclature in the following pages is probably that most generally accepted now and appears to be reasonably in accordance with the natural affinities of the species.

Several of the species, particularly *C. neapolitanum*, *C. europaeum*, *C. orbiculatum* with all its varieties and hybrids, and *C. repandum*, form excellent plants for naturalising in the wild woodland garden. They will even grow well under beech trees, where the growth of most plants is very much restricted. All species will grow equally in chalky soils, but they require good drainage and should not be planted in marshy or water-logged places. *C. europaeum* and *C. repandum*, while surviving in the shelter of woodland will only spread freely in the milder areas of the country. *C. neapolitanum* and *C. orbiculatum* grow well in all areas provided they have an adequate supply of leaf-mould and reasonable drainage and are absolutely hardy.

The tubers should not be planted too deeply: 2–3 in. is quite sufficient and all of these hardy species appreciate a mulch of fine leaf-mould or compost from time to time.

All cyclamen can be easily raised from seed. It should be sown as soon as possible after ripening and the seedlings should flower in three or four years. It is the only way of raising a large stock since the tubers do not increase by division. They only grow each year in stature.

The species mentioned above as good for naturalising will generally spread by themselves once they are established but the area of the patch can be increased by scattering the seed further afield and by transplanting the young seedlings. Seeds may also be raised in pots or boxes in a frame or cool greenhouse and the seedlings pricked out when in their first leaf. This is a more certain way of raising the more tender species. Directions for raising the large-flowered florists' forms of *C. persicum* will be found in the section dealing with them.

E. A. Bowles used to grow the more tender species of cyclamen in deep wooden boxes around the edge of a cool slightly heated house and in this position they flourished and required little care. In pans in the alpine house or greenhouse one should avoid watering over the leaves and either stand the pans in water or water carefully round, but not above, the corm and not too much in cold weather.

## (*a*) Late summer and autumn flowering species

In this group there is one species that is predominant and that should find a place in every garden and that is *C. neapolitanum* (Pl. 9, 4) from Southern Italy, Greece and the Mediterranean regions. As E. A. Bowles, a great authority on the genus, wrote in the R.H.S. Journal, "it pays rent for eleven months out of the twelve" and there are few plants that can equal this. The flowers have a delicate, an elfin grace all their own, like some beautiful ballet dancer pirouetting on one leg.

Like all cyclamen the petals are recurved and in this and several others of the autumn flowering group they have slightly bead-like auricles round the mouth of the flower and constricting it; in this species the mouth is not so much round as hexagonal. Each flower is about half an inch in height and an old-established tuber may bear 50 or more on 4–6 in. stems, clustering so thick as to jostle each other. The earliest flowers come before the leaves after a heavy shower, sometimes towards the end of July but more often during August, while their season of greatest flowering is generally the first half of September.

In colour they range from pure white through pale pink to deeper pink and mauvish-pink, often being deeper in colour round the auricles. About September the young leaves will begin to appear. These are the plants' second glory and form almost as good a background to the flowers as the bare brown earth. These leaves vary infinitely in form, in size and in markings, in fact hardly two plants seem to have leaves quite similar. Some are almost round, while others vary from oval to arrow- or even lance-shaped. Some have almost smooth edges while others are wavy or even crinkled; some are generously marbled with broad splashes of silver against the dark green while others are almost entirely green. It is well worth collecting forms for the fine markings of their leaves as well as for their flowers, especially as the leaves are with us for nine months in the year and form one of the most decorative and also most competent forms of ground cover for smothering weeds available to the gardener. In May the round seed-heads, like deep purplish-crimson marbles held on stalks closely coiled like a spring, ripen and disgorge the seeds, which are worth collecting and sowing either in the open on a bed of leaf-mould, preferably raked fine, or in a box in a frame. Owing to the peculiar coiling of the stalk of the seed-pod, common in cyclamen, many of the seeds tend to germinate on top of the old tuber and then die

out. Others may be distributed by ants or other insects and this is likely
to account for the many young seedlings often to be seen coming up at
quite a distance from the parent.

The tubers of *C. neapolitanum* are large and flat, roundish or saucer-
shaped and sometimes as large as quite a good-sized saucer; they have
the peculiarity of producing their roots from the upper surface only
of the tuber, from which they also produce short nobbly " branches "
from which the flowers grow. It is important not to break these branches
in all species since they may take several years to form again to the old
vigour. This is the reason why bought tubers often do not flower in the
first year when these branches have been broken off. It is very important
also to plant the tuber the right way up and it is easy enough to make
mistakes. Generally there is a slight indentation on the upper surface
as well as signs of these branches. The lower surface will be domed like
a mushroom and is devoid of roots. From this it follows that it is little
use burying a mass of compost well below the tubers. Rather should
they be mulched preferably in July and early August when they are
dormant with sifted or fine leaf-mould or compost. A sprinkling of bone
meal or dried blood will also help their vigour.

### OTHER AUTUMN FLOWERING SPECIES

† **C. africanum.** Very similar to *C. neapolitanum*, but larger in its *l.* and tubers
which may sometimes be as large as a small turnip. *Fl.* generally white,
whitish with a faint rose-purple tinge especially around mouth, or rosy-purple
in colour. Sept.-Oct. Distinguished from *C. neapolitanum* by the anthers
which are yellow instead of purple, by the number of chromosomes which
are twice the number of *C. neapolitanum* making the plant a tetraploid and,
according to the Botanical Magazine, by the more strongly toothed calyx.
Common in Algeria, especially in pine woods and maquis scrub around
Algiers, but not generally hardy in this country or in N. America, where it
should be grown in pans or boxes in a frame or cool greenhouse. (Pl. 9, 3)

\* **C. cilicium.** A smaller and more delicate flowering sp. than *C. neapolitanum*.
Reputed to be tender except in warm situations but grows well in alpine
house or scree frame and will in many areas also flower in the open, being
rather hardier than its reputation suggests. *Fl.* pale rose pink, constricted
at the mouth but without auricles and with a prominent red spot at the base
of each petal, fragrant. Oct.-Nov., usually appearing before or with first
*l.* *L.* roundish with silvery markings above, very slightly toothed. (Pl. 9, 1).
A form with smaller *fl.* and *l.* generally smaller than a halfpenny has been
separated as *C. cilicium* var. *alpinum* or *C. alpinum*, but is little known;
tubers flattened, becoming large in an old plant of typical *C. cilicium*, smaller
in var. *alpinum*, rooting from middle of underside. Asia Minor, Cilician
Taurus.

† **C. cyprium.** A tender, small, white or pinkish-flowered sp. with auricles
around the mouth of the *fl.*, flowering with the *l.*, fragrant, corolla lobes

# Cyclamen

generally twisted and with a crimson spot at the base of each petal. Oct. *L.* obcordate, broadly lobed and toothed, very dark velvety with yellowish-green markings, crimson below. Cyprus. (Pl. **9**, 8)

\* **C. europaeum.** One of the finest sp. and hardy in all except very cold gardens. The *l.* should remain throughout the year. The very fragrant deep carmine or pink *fl.* are about the same size as those of *C. neapolitanum* but without the auricles and so the mouth of the *fl.* is wider. July-Sept. *L.* round or kidney shaped with rather indistinct silvery markings on upper surface, occasionally without markings. Abundant in parts of Italy, particularly around Lake of Como and in sub-alpine woodlands. On the basis of this distribution one would expect it to be hardier than *C. neapolitanum* which comes from southern Italy and Greece but it is not so. In cold gardens it is sometimes beneficial to protect the tuber by putting part of it under a rock or large stone, though of course with soil between it and the rock. Tuber often large, corky and rooting all over. There is also a very beautiful and rather uncommon variety with white *fl.* (Pl. **9**, 7)

† **C. graecum.** Closely allied to and resembling *C. neapolitanum* and overlapping it in distribution, but the leaves are velvety and have a horny margin which can be felt distinctly if the finger is rubbed along it. *Fl.* auricled, carmine, pale pink with deeper carmine base, whitish with pink base, generally dark carmine inside throat. (Pl. **9**, 2). Sept. *L.* large, generally cordate but variable, often but not invariably red below. Tuber globose, large, turnip-like and in its native land often found very deep and hard to collect with frail " branches " connecting the leaves to the tuber. These should be collected unbroken if possible. Greece, Macedonia, Crete, Cyprus and Rhodes. Various island forms have at times been distinguished with separate names, the best-known being *C. pseudo-graecum* from Crete (Pl. **9**, 6) but the majority of modern authorities do not consider these differences sufficient to justify separate specific rank in such a variable plant and I agree.

**C. neapolitanum.** See above p. 108.

† **C. rohlfsianum.** An attractive sp. from Cyrenaica in N. Africa with pink or crimson *fl.*, slightly auricled, resembling those of *C. neapolitanum* in form but slightly stouter and differing from all sp. of cyclamen by having the anther cone projecting beyond the corolla tube. Sept.-Oct. *L.* handsome, large, variable in shape but generally kidney-shaped and broadly lobed, prominently marked on upper surface and with a crimson succulent petiole, appearing before and with the *fl.* Tuber very large, corky. The most tender of the cyclamen sp. and only suitable for a frost-free greenhouse. (Pl. **9**, 5)

## (b) Spring flowering species

**C. atkinsii.** See under *C. orbiculatum.*

† **C. balearicum.** A sp. restricted to the Balearic Islands. *Fl.* small, white or whitish generally with some pink colour at the mouth, slightly fragrant. Feb.-March. *L.* ovate or roundish with edge slightly sinuate and with small teeth, distinguished by the silvery mottled and speckled markings on the

# Cyclamen

upper surface. Tender and suitable for cool greenhouse or alpine house culture. Tubers small, rooting from centre of lower side. (Pl. **8,** 5)

**C. coum.** See under *C. orbiculatum.*

† **C. creticum.** Larger in *fl.* and *l.* than the previous sp.; as seen in the Cretan mountains it is a *fl.* of great charm and delicacy. *Fl.* white, petals rather narrow but long and waved, spicy fragrant, corolla tube rather narrow, generally white but a carmine form has been recorded; flowering in Feb.-March with the *l.* which are ivy-shaped or ovate and broadly toothed, deep green and only slightly marked with silver, crimson below. (Pl. **8,** 4). Tender. Tubers small, rooting from base in their native habitat generally 6–9 in. deep among the rocks and in the mountains flowering at end April and early May. This plant seems to be intolerant of strong sun or exposure in this country and those growers who have been most successful with it have planted it out *underneath* the greenhouse staging.

**C. ibericum.** See under *C. orbiculatum.*

†* **C. libanoticum.** One of the most beautiful of all the cyclamen sp. *Fl.* large, salmon-pink fading to very pale blush-pink at base, with deeper markings at base of each petal around the wide mouth of the corolla tube; petals up to 1 in. in length in a really well-grown specimen, broader than in the preceding sp., slightly fragrant. Feb.-March; *l.* developing before *fl.* in early winter, variable in shape, ivy-shaped or ovate or cordate, sharply dentate, sometimes crenulate, deep green but broadly marked with more yellow-green splotches. Tender and best grown as a cool greenhouse or alpine house plant, although occasional plants have been recorded as growing out of doors in various parts of the country. Tuber globose, corky. Native of the Lebanon. (Pl. **8,** 10)

* **C. orbiculatum.** This is the name now given to the large group of winter and early spring flowering cyclamen which in their season take the place of *C. neapolitanum* in the autumn. The varying varieties will naturalise almost as freely in many places and their dumpy little *fl.*, generally very strongly coloured, are seldom out of place appearing in the cold weather from December till the end of March from little pointed buds which first lie horizontally along the ground before coming erect. (Pl. **8,** 8 and Pl. VI*b*)

Under this sp. are included those known as *C. atkinsii, C. coum, C. hiemale* while *C. vernum* and *C. ibericum* are regarded as syns. of the sp. All forms are completely hardy and seem able to withstand, even when the buds are showing colour, the worst winter weather or hardest frosts. This makes it one of our most valuable winter flowering plants; as an underplanting to the yellow *Hamamelis mollis* it gives us a delightful picture often lasting for a month or more.

The *fl.* vary considerably in colour and in size but all have short broad petals and a wide throat to the mouth of the corolla tube. In colour they vary from white with crimson or purplish-magenta markings round the throat, through pink of all shades to a deep purplish-magenta, a colour which seems more welcome in the winter garden than at other seasons of the year. The *fl.* stalks are seldom more than 3 in. high, sometimes less as also befits the season of Dec.-March. The *l.* are rounded or cordate and

111

variously marbled on the upper surface, deep crimson below. Tubers globose, rooting from below only. Those sold as *C. atkinsii* are generally either good forms of *C. orbiculatum* or hybrids between it and its var. *coum* and their colour is equally various. The original published description of this hybrid states that it arose from *C. orbiculatum* var. *coum* × *C. persicum* wild form but neither the picture published then nor any forms now known in cultivation support this origin while the chromosomal differences would make it extremely unlikely. However, cyclamen under this label are nearly always worth having.

* Var. **coum**. A small, very dumpy flowered variety occurring both in white and in rather harsh purplish-magenta forms and distinguished by the rounded *l.* which are dull green above and quite without any silver markings. No-one has found this plant in recent years wild on the island of Kos its supposed home, although as a cultivated plant it has been known for several hundred years. (Pl. **8,** 9)

 Var. **hiemale**. Generally the earliest variety to flower, the *fl.* being a slightly larger, strong shade of magenta-carmine and each petal having a prominent dark spot at its base; *l.* roundish with silvery zones or markings above. This variety is native to the area of Turkey around Istanbul. (Pl. **8,** 6)

†* **C. persicum**. The wild forms of this sp. are regarded by many as the most beautiful of all cyclamen and certainly they have good grounds for being so praised. They have a grace and a charm which has been lost in the much larger florists' forms. They are distinct from all other sp. of cyclamen by having the stalk of the seed capsule straight instead of coiled. *Fl.* white, pale blush-pink and occasionally carmine-pink, borne on stems 6 in. or more high and raised well above the *l.*; petals are up to 1 in. long, rather narrow and twisted; very fragrant. March-April. *L.* ivy-shaped or rounded, very variable in size and markings and varying from deep green to a light yellowish-green particularly in the forms sometimes known as *C. latifolium* (Pl. **8,** 3) which in all other respects seem to come well within the limits of the specific variation; *l.* generally prominently marbled on upper surface, green below. This sp. is not native to Persia but is found in Cyprus, several of the Greek islands including Crete and Rhodes, Lebanon, Palestine and in North Africa around Tunis. Tubers large in old established plants. Tender, but a good plant for the cool greenhouse or the alpine house where an old tuber will produce a large number of *fl.* The pots may be plunged outside preferably in a shady place during the summer. (Pl. **8,** 2)

* **C. pseudibericum**. A very beautiful but still uncommon sp. whose origin was long considered rather mysterious. The stock was derived from one plant collected near Smyrna in 1897 and this was thought possibly to have been a natural hybrid with *C. orbiculatum*, to which it is most closely related, as one parent. Recently, however, fresh collectings of it have been made in the Amanus mountain of Turkey and the stocks introduced are quite variable both in *fl.* and *l.* but all are desirable. *Fl.* large, deep rich crimson-carmine, purplish or violet-carmine and generally pale pink or white around mouth of corolla, petals $\frac{3}{4}$–1 in. long by $\frac{1}{2}$ in. wide and with a deep crimson spot at base, *fl.* raised well above foliage on stems up to 6 in. fragrant. Jan.-March. *L.* cordate, broadly toothed around edge, marked on upper surface with

*Plate 15:* MODERN HYBRID GLADIOLI

*Plate* 16: HYACINTHS. 1, ' Princess Margaret '. 2, ' Myosotis '. 3, ' Ostara '

*Plate* 17: IRIS. 1, *I. reticulata* 'J. S. Dijt'. 2, *I. reticulata* 'Royal Blue'. 3, *I. winogradowii*. 4, *I. reticulata* 'Cantab'. 5, *I. reticulata*. 6, *I. histrio*. 7, *I. bakeriana*. 8, *I. histrioides major*. 9, 10, *I. histrio* var. *aintabensis*. 11, *I. reticulata* var. *cyanea*. 12, *I. danfordiae*. 13, *I. reticulata* 'Krelagei'

Plate 18: Above, *Narcissus bulbocodium* in the Alpine Meadow at Wisley. Below, *Iris histrioides, Crocus aureus, Cyclamen orbiculatum* and snowdrops in mid-February at Maidwell Hall, Northampton

light yellowish-green, deep crimson below. Tender and generally regarded as only suitable for cool greenhouse or alpine house, but some plantings of the recently collected forms have been established outside and seem quite vigorous. (Pl. **8**, 7)

†* **C. repandum.** Often called the Ivy-leaved Cyclamen. *Fl.* scented, pink, crimson or white, in pink forms generally deeper in colour around mouth, petals narrow, twisted, up to 1 in. in length, carried well above *l.* which are variable in shape and markings, generally handsome with wide open sinus at base, sinuate toothed edge and prominent silvery markings as in *C. neapolitanum*, deep crimson below. *Fl.* late spring, March-early May. Tender in cold districts where it is best grown in a frame or alpine house; in milder districts, however, it may be naturalised freely in open woodland where it will spread and make a delightful picture. It is native to S. Europe ranging from S. France to Greece and Crete and Aegean islands. Tubers globose, smaller than in *C. neapolitanum*, roots produced only from middle of lower surface. This sp. has been known in some works as *C. vernale* or *C. hederifolium*, which must now be regarded as syn. (Pl. **8**, 1)

**C. vernum.** See under *C. orbiculatum*. Probably the first name in this group to be identified with absolute certainty, since it is very well portrayed in Sweet's *The English Flower Garden*.

## (c) Giant forms of *C. persicum*

These giant forms, grown so frequently by florists for Christmas decoration, require a warm greenhouse to bring them into flower at that season, in a cool greenhouse they will flower later and be unlikely to be so large or fine. The majority of the plants sold are grown from seed sown in August or September and grown through the winter of that year and the succeeding summer without a resting period to flower the following winter, i.e. in 16 months from seed. It is important to keep them growing steadily during this period and not to let them get either very dry or sodden. Frequent ventilation is desirable.

Seeds should be sown in pans or boxes of which the bottom is covered with a layer of granulated peat or leaf-mould. John Innes Seed Compost is recommended and the temperature should be kept up to 55°F. The seed should be covered and the pans covered with a pane of glass or placed in a propagating case. Light should be excluded until germination which from fresh seed should not take more than 5–6 weeks. The seedlings should be placed near the roof of the greenhouse in order to ensure firm stocky growth. In January or February they will be ready for pricking out into other boxes, the seedlings being spaced about 2 in. apart. The small tubers should be just covered. About April the seedling, should be potted into $3\frac{1}{2}$ in. pots in potting compost. Care is required that the roots are damaged as little as possible and the plants should be shaded for a few days after planting. Final potting should take place in May or early June and the soil should come up near to the top of the tuber or lightly cover it but deeper planting should be avoided. The soil will tend to work down lower in respect of the tuber during the year. During the summer months the plants should be kept in a cool greenhouse or even a frame and given ample water and ventilation. From August the plants may be fed with diluted liquid manure, dried blood or weak soot water. Before the end of September all the plants must be housed in a medium warm greenhouse and kept at a temperature not below 55°F. Very high temperatures, however, should be avoided. The resulting plants should come into flower from late October onwards.

In the warm living-room cyclamen are often difficult to keep successfully. They will probably last longer in one of the cooler rooms. Any dying flower stalk or leaves should be pulled out from the tuber with a sharp twist. The plants should not be stood permanently in water but may be watered from the top, although not over the corm, whenever dry, possibly about once a week. They should as far as possible be kept out of draughts and away from gas fires.

After flowering the corms may be grown on in a cool or intermediate greenhouse until the leaves die down, after which they may be plunged in a frame or even outside and given little water until mid-August when they should be brought into the greenhouse again, top dressed or repotted and grown on as for seedlings. The finest and largest flowers are, however, generally obtained from seedlings and most growers raise new seedlings each year.

Apart from troubles due to over-watering or inadequate drainage or lack of water these cyclamen are very free of diseases and pests. Aphis and Thrips sometimes occur and may be dealt with by spraying with DDT, Lindane, HETP or one of the other numerous proprietary substances made up to kill these insects.

### STRAINS

A number of seedsmen and nurserymen who specialise in cyclamen have evolved their own strains and some of these now come true to colour with very little variation. Seed of mixed colours is often commonly grown, and some strains have fringed petals. The following named strains in simple colours are recommended:

'AFTERGLOW' Deep cherry-pink.   'BONFIRE' Scarlet-red.
'MAUVE QUEEN' Purplish-mauve.   'PINK PEARL' Deep salmon-pink.
'ROSE QUEEN' Deep salmon-pink.   'SALMON KING' Pale salmon-pink.

# †CYPELLA *Iridaceae*

A SMALL genus of bulbs from Tropical and S. America distinguished by the three large spreading petals, widely separate and very distinct from the three inner ones. They are not unlike smaller and more delicate tigridias and share the same brilliant colour and the short life of each flower. The spikes are often branched and the leaves rather narrow and plicate. Unfortunately none of the species are reliably hardy except in very warm areas, and are best suited to cool greenhouse or frame conditions, but the bulbs may be planted outside in a very sheltered position and taken up in the autumn and kept in dry sand.

C. **herbertii**. The most beautiful and best known member of the genus. Stem up to 1 ft., branched. *Fl.* about 2 in. across, outer petals waved, deep golden-yellow, contracted at centre, inner petals small, spotted with pale purple. July. Argentina, S. Brazil.

C. **peruviana**. Two or three fl. to a stem, with 3 large outer petals, deep yellow, spotted at base, inner segments small, spotted up to $3\frac{1}{2}$ in. across. Peru, Bolivia, Andes.

C. **plumbea**. Stem slender up to $2\frac{1}{2}$ ft. *Fl.* pale yellow in centre, outer petals dull mauvish-blue, said to resemble colour of lead, pale at base. *Fl.* very short lived. Late summer. S. Brazil, Argentina, Mexico.

# †CYRTANTIIUS *Amaryllidaceae*

A LARGE genus of African bulbous plants, mostly from S. Africa in the Eastern Cape Province and Transvaal and E. Africa, with loose umbels of mostly drooping, tubular flowers, in which the perianth tube is usually curved and distinctly longer than the lobes, thus distinguishing it from *Crinum* to which it is closely related. The flower heads, however, are considerably smaller and more slender and the stems generally hollow. None of the species are reliably hardy in this country and they are best suited to cool or intermediate greenhouse cultivation in pots. Unfortunately they are rarely seen in cultivation and are perhaps not sufficiently showy ever to become very popular. They require rather different treatment as to resting periods and watering, depending on their area of origin. Those from the higher regions of the Transvaal receive a higher summer rainfall when they flower and are dormant in winter and so might be treated like a gladiolus. None are native to very dry areas.

**C. angustifolius.** Stem up to 1 ft. with 2 or 3 or more orange-red *fl.*, horizontal or drooping, about 1½–2 in. long. W. Cape Districts on mountains, flowering in S. Africa Nov.-Feb. Bulb ovoid; *l.* linear, narrow and appearing with or very soon after the *fl.* Late summer flowering in this country.

**C. falcatus.** A very handsome sp. with long, pendulous *fl.* 2½ in. long and 1 in. across at mouth, pinkish-red, flushed outside along centre with yellowish-green and with deeper red margins to segments. Stem spotted purple, stout, up to 1½ ft. tall, distinctively arched over in a narrow bend at top. March. Bulb globose. *L.* broad strap-shaped with acute tip, falcate. Natal. Cool greenhouse.

**C. galpinii.** A dwarf plant with stem up to 9 in.; only 1 or 2 *fl.*, erect, 2 in. long, tubular ending in spreading lobes, 2 in. across, scarlet or pink. *L.* very narrow, appearing after *fl.* (usually only 1 per bulb). Transvaal, Zululand. Flowering July-August in S. Africa. Syn. *C. balenii.* A handsome plant.

**C. huttonii.** Stem about 1 ft., stout with an umbel of up to 20 drooping *fl.*, bright red outside, yellow inside, tubular, 2 in. long with spreading lobes. *L.* wide, 1 in. across. May. Cape Province where it blooms Dec.-Jan.

**C. mackenii.** Stem slender, 1 ft. with an umbel of up to 10 *fl.* each with a narrow curved tubular perianth 2 in. long with spreading lobes. Horizontal in growth or even upright and not pendulous. White, cream or pale yellow. Spring. Natal where it flowers in July-August. *L.* narrow.

**C. obliquus.** One of the most striking sp. with large ovoid bulb, 3 in. across. Stem stout 1–2 ft. with up to 12 large drooping tubular *fl.* 3 in. long, yellow at base, flushed orange, lobes only slightly spreading, tipped with bright green. May-June. Cape Province where it flowers Oct.-Dec. Natal.

# DIERAMA *Iridaceae*

A SMALL genus of very graceful S. African plants with a swollen rootstock resembling a large corm and fibrous roots. Stem slender, up to 5 ft., arching over near top like a fishing rod, with numerous bell-shaped, pendulous flowers in shades of purple, mauve or white. Leaves narrow, stiff, grass-like. Dieramas resent transplanting when mature and should either be planted out of pots or placed as young seedlings in their final position. Not very hardy in cold areas and unsuitable for hot dry positions. Only one species, D. *pulcherrimum*, is generally grown and numerous fine varieties have been raised in N. Ireland; the majority are named after birds such as ' Plover ' (Pl. VII); ' Heron ', wine-red; ' Skylark ', purplish-violet; ' Kingfisher ', pale pinkish-purple.

# DRACUNCULUS *Araceae*

A SMALL genus of two species very closely related to *Arum* and formerly included in it. It is separated from *Arum* by the arrangement of the ovules on the spadix and more obviously by the pedately divided leaves. Only one species is in common cultivation, *D. vulgaris*, but this is a most striking plant.

† **D. canariensis.** Spathe narrow, pale green, spadix yellow with a long tail. Madeira, Canary Islands. Not in general cultivation and likely to be tender.

**D. vulgaris.** The Dragon Arum. Stem fleshy, strikingly spotted, up to 2 ft., spathe very large, reddish-maroon inside, purplish-green outside, opening from a bulbous tubular base like a rather unseemly vase, glistening and velvety often 1 ft. long by 8 in. across. Spadix tapering; almost black, as long as spathe which turns back near tip to allow spadix to lean out. After it has been open for some time and has been visited by flies it develops a strong and rather disagreeable smell as of bad meat due partly to the dead flies. May-June. Tuber large, roundish. *L.* large, handsome, deeply divided. In this country it should be planted in a warm position, preferably under a south-facing wall. Mediterranean. The famous plate in Dr. Thornton's *Temple of Flora* depicts it well, although showing it against a dark thunderstorm rather than the brilliant June sun of its native habitat.

# ENDYMION *Liliaceae*

THIS GENUS includes the Spanish bluebell and also our own native bluebell both of which are magnificent garden plants. Unfortunately these two have been peculiarly subject to a nomenclatural and taxonomic game of musical chairs. In the older books they will be found under *Hyacinthus* while in much of gardening literature they are found under *Scilla*. However, they seem now to have come to an uneasy rest in *Endymion*, a genus of only about four species, although with a strong flutter towards *Hyacinthoides* on grounds of priority. They differ from *Scilla* in having the bulb formed afresh each year and in its being made up of tubular scales, though these are far from obvious on a cursory inspection. The bluebells are excellent plants for the open woodland, spreading very freely and few sights are more lovely than an English bluebell wood in May. The bulbs are large and fleshy and should be planted several inches deep and then left alone until the clumps are so thick that division is necessary. They seldom flower so well in deep shade as in open glades or semi-shade and

117

seem to do best on a mediumly heavy clay or good loam soil. The two species grown will hybridise together readily.

**E. hispanicus.** The Spanish bluebell with larger stouter spikes and heavier bells than in our native bluebell, up to ¾ in. long. An equally vigorous and hardy garden plant but almost scentless. Colour very variable from deep indigo-blue to pale China-blue, pale pink and white. Anthers blue as opposed to cream in our native bluebell. Spain and Portugal. May. Syns. *Scilla campanulata, Scilla hispanica, Endymion campanulatus.*

A number of selected and named varieties are available of which the following can be recommended:
' Excelsior ' Deep blue, very large.
' King of the Blues ' Deep sky-blue.
' Mount Everest ' White.
' Myosotis ' Sky-blue, very fine.
' Queen of the Blues ' Purplish-blue.
' Queen of the Pinks ' Deep lilac-pink.
' White Triumphator ' A good white, very tall spikes.

**E. non-scriptus.** Our common bluebell. Syns. *Scilla non-scripta, Scilla nutans.*

# ERANTHIS *Ranunculaceae*

OUR WINTER aconites are tuberous rather than bulbous, but still they are usually to be found in the same catalogues as our spring bulbs and should be treated in the garden in the same way so that they merit inclusion here. They are among the earliest of our hardy spring plants and also among the brightest in the pure yellow-gold of their cup-shaped flowers. Once planted they should be left undisturbed to naturalise, which in a favourable soil and position they will do freely through seeding. The best display of the ordinary winter aconites that I know is on a sloping bank under horse-chestnut trees in Hampshire. The best and most vigorous species is undoubtedly *E. hyemalis*, our common winter aconite, but the hybrid *E. × tubergenii* has even more striking flowers borne on taller stems. The tubers are knobbly and irregularly formed like those of an anemone and should be planted in late summer or early autumn, not too deep, or even better transplanted soon after flowering. The leaves are much divided and all radical. Leafy bracts form a rosette below the flower like a toby dog's ruff. The conspicuous part of the flower is actually made up of five to eight petal-like sepals. There are about seven species but only three are usually grown in gardens and the one hybrid.

**E. cilicica.** Closely related to *E. hyemalis* but with slightly taller stems but not nearly such an adaptable and freely growing plant in English gardens.

*Fl.* of similar bright yellow colour.   Feb.-March.   Greece and Asia Minor. Slightly later than *E. hyemalis* and with involucres more deeply segmented.

**E. hyemalis.**   Our common Winter Aconite.   Stem 2–4 in.   *Fl.* single, bright glistening lemon-gold, sessile on leaf.   Feb.-March.   W. Europe.

**E. pinnatifida.**   *Fl.* white on short stalks, otherwise very similar to *E. hyemalis* but not nearly so vigorous.   Japan.   Rarely seen in English gardens.   The *l.* are smaller than in *E. hyemalis* and bluish on the under-surface.

**E. × tubergenii.**   A hybrid between *E. cilicica* and *E. hyemalis* and larger than both its parents and lasting longer but usually sterile.   Deep, shining, golden-yellow globular *fl.* on stems 3–5 in. high.   One of the best forms is that known as ' Guinea Gold,' slightly deeper in colour and with bronze-tinted *l.* slightly later than the others.

# ERYTHRONIUM *Liliaceae*

THESE ARE among the loveliest and most graceful of all spring flowering bulbs with flowers like small reflexed-petal lilies in shades of cream, yellow, pink and mauve.   It is always surprising to me that the only one grown, or indeed known, in most gardens is the European Dog-tooth Violet, *E. dens-canis*.   The remainder are North American, ranging from the eastern states to the mountains by the Pacific coast where they reach their greatest and finest development, and are known by such attractive names as Trout Lily from their beautifully marbled and blotched leaves, Adder's Tongue from their bright green leaves or Avalanche Lily, the name given to *E. montanum* since it flowers as the snow melts.   Those from the lower mountain regions of the pine belt seem to settle down better in English gardens than those from the higher mountain areas.

While *E. dens-canis* is a very easy plant, flourishing in shade or sun, with or without lime, the American species should have a moister situation in semi-shade where they do not dry out during their growing season. The yellow *E. tuolumnense* and the creamy hybrid ' White Beauty ' will, however, succeed in most gardens and the bulbs will spread into clumps by the formation of offshoots.   Where they are doing well the stems may grow to 18 in. high with, in the case of some species, three or four flowers, the petals spreading outwards and then recurving like a small Turk's-Cap lily.   It is reported from America that the largest spikes are found where the ground has recently been burnt so it is possible that a top dressing of potash would have the same effect.   The bulbs should never be allowed to dry out and shrivel when they are out of the ground and so should always be carefully packed.   If they are to be divided and moved in the same garden this is probably best done when they are beginning to die down after flowering. Erythroniums can also be raised from seed but they are sometimes slow to germinate and may take up to five years to flower. The seed should be sown as soon as ripe and the pots plunged outside and never allowed to dry out. A good stock of them, however, is well worth the trouble. They are classified by the markings on the leaves, being divided easily into two main groups, those with plain green leaves and those with marbled leaves, and also by the shape of the stigmas, according to whether they are lobed or not. The colour in many of the species is rather variable. A useful key to the W. American species will be found in the *New Flora and Silva*, Vol. ix, p. 265. It is by Prof. Elmer Applegate, and was originally published in the American botanical journal *Madrono*. It is a monograph by an authority who has collected as many of the species in the wild as possible and so is able to give their distribution. Other useful information will be found in Lester Rowntree's *Hardy Californians* and in an article by Carl Purdy in Vol. ii of *The Flora and Silva*. Both of these also knew them well in the wild and to Carl Purdy most of the older gardeners owed their stocks. I am also indebted to Mr. E. B. Anderson's account of the genus prepared for the Lily Group of the R.H.S. and published in the R.H.S. Journal for March, 1958.

**E. albidum.** An E. American sp., very rare in cultivation in this country. *Fl.* white, sometimes slightly bluish outside and yellow at the base, drooping on stems up to 9 in. high. *L.* narrow, hence the name Adder's Tongue, only slightly mottled. Widespread from Eastern Canada down to Texas.

**E. americanum.** Another E. American sp. but with single pale or deep golden-yellow *fl.*, flushed with dull red on the outside at the base of the petals and speckled with red inside. Stem short, up to 4 or 5 in. but *fl.* large and handsome, 2¾ in. across when open, the segments being much reflexed and pointed. Stigma club-shaped with three furrows. *L.* thick, lanceolate-elliptic, slightly glaucous and with prominent liver-coloured blotches. April. A damp position and rather deep planting up to 4 in. seem best for this sp., which should if possible be left undisturbed to increase until it becomes crowded. It has flowered well on the rock garden at the Royal Botanic Garden, Edinburgh, and is perfectly hardy. It is certainly a fine plant worth some trouble to obtain and cultivate satisfactorily. The specimen illustrated is rather smaller and paler than many of the better forms recorded. It is shown without a leaf. (Pl. **11**, 11)

\* **E. californicum.** One of the best sp. which seems to settle down and flower well in English gardens, particularly in places which are not too dry. Stem not usually more than 1 ft. here, often branching above the *l.*, with 3 *fl.*, but recorded from its native habitat up to 2 ft. with 16 *fl. Fl.* creamy-white the segments being wide-spreading and reflexed at the tips. At the base of each is a rather faint ring of orange or orange-brown beady markings. *L.* very dark green, heavily mottled, broad, obovate-lanceolate with rather long petioles. Widespread in California where it grows on lower hillsides among bushes. Forma *praecox* is slightly earlier flowering.

# Erythronium

There is a group of closely related sp., also with white, creamy or yellow *fl.* which come from rather similar situations in California and Oregon and require similar treatment in the garden. Since there has been in the past much confusion between them it will probably be better to discuss them together here. They all have mottled *l.* and a lobed stigma. The local distribution of each appears however to be distinct.

*Distinguished by having the filaments of the stigma filiform, i.e. thread-like rather than dilated at the base*

**E. californicum.** Pale creamy-white *fl.* and white anthers. Described above.

**E. helenae.** Golden-yellow anthers. (Pl. **11**, 5). Syn. *E. californicum bicolor*, a very lovely sp. with large white *fl.* suffused yellow at base and very dark mottled *l.* Said to be fragrant and early flowering, requires good drainage.

**E. multiscapoideum.** Distinguished by the stem branching at the *l.* rather than above it and the longer stigma lobes and the strongly recurved perianth. *Fl.* up to 2¾ in. across when fully open, white with bright yellow marking at base both inside and out, generally only one to a stem. March. *L.* dark green, heavily mottled. Often known in older literature as *E. hartwegii*. It produces offsets freely.

*Distinguished by having the filaments of the anthers strongly dilated at base, the stigma longer and more protruding and golden-yellow anthers*

\* **E. oregonum.** *Fl.* white or cream on long drooping peduncles, up to 3 in. across when open. The inner markings at the base of the segments are a strong orange-brown and distinctly larger than those of *E. californicum*. A slightly more vigorous sp. than *E. californicum*, it sometimes produces up to 7 *fl.* and one of the largest members of the genus, spikes up to 2 ft. having been recorded. Undoubtedly many of the plants grown under the former name really belong to *E. oregonum*. There is also a form with white anthers distinguished as subsp. *leucandrum* (Pl. **11**, 1) which is the more common in cultivation.

\* ' WHITE BEAUTY ' is thought to be a natural hybrid of *E. oregonum* subsp. *leucandrum* and *E. citrinum*, but it may be no more than a fine selected form of *E. oregonum*. (Pl. **11**, 2). At any rate it is one of the best of the Trout Lilies and frequently establishes itself well and spreads into large clumps growing under slightly drier conditions than some of the other sp. It is also the one most readily obtainable and from seed it is said to show only slight variation. The *fl.* are about 2–2½ in. across when fully open, segments pointed and recurved at tips with prominent orange-brown markings at base and heavily mottled *l.*

**E. citrinum.** A rather misnamed sp. since the *fl.* are creamy-white but with deep lemon-yellow base, distinguished from *E. californicum* by the entire stigma and having auricles or appendages at the base of the segments. Stem short, purplish, not often over 6 in. with rarely more than 3 *fl.* *L.* mottled, dark purplish-green. (Pl. **11**, 8). Very closely related is *E. howellii*, distinguished by the absence of the auricles at the base of the segments and slightly more yellow *fl.* (Pl. **11**, 10). Both come from Oregon and California

121

and flower March-April. In *E. howellii* the basal markings are rather warmer in colour, ranging from dull orange to a terracotta.

\* **E. dens-canis.** Our European Dog's Tooth Violet, one of the most beautiful of the sp. even if not the most spectacular, easily grown in any garden, but preferring open woodland conditions either with or without lime as in its native habitats. The *fl.* are variable from white through pale pink to deep pinkish-mauve but always with a ring of orange-red markings round the base of the *fl.* and the lovely blue-green, heavily marbled *l.* (Pl. **11**, 9). In Northern Spain I have found particularly fine forms with dark, almost purple *fl.* and turquoise-blue anthers. The poise of the *fl.* is always the same, gently nodding with the perianth segments pointed and partly recurved, the *fl.* borne singly on peduncles up to 6 in. high. March-April. It extends right across Europe into Siberia and as far as Japan. Two geographical varieties have been distinguished, var. *japonicum* whose *fl.* are probably the largest of the sp., up to 3 in. across, violet-purple with a dark spot at the base on stems up to 8 in. and var. *sibiricum* whose *fl.* are also large and said to have a yellow eye at the base. Some fine selected forms have also been given cultivar names ' Franz Hals ', light reddish-violet, ' Pink Perfection ', bright clear pink, ' Rose Beauty ', a deeper pink, ' Snowflake ', a fine white. The corms are long and narrow supposedly like the canine tooth of a dog and they increase very rapidly by offsets and form quite thick clumps.

**E. giganteum.** This name has been used for several plants and is now usually regarded as invalid. Those without mottling on the *l.* are probably *E. grandiflorum* and those with mottling *E. oregonum*.

**E. grandiflorum.** One of the finest sp., but unfortunately rarely seen in cultivation; distinguished by the dark green unmottled *l.* and the large bright golden-yellow *fl.* with lobed stigmas. (Pl. **11**, 4). This last character distinguishes it from *E. tuolumnense* which it otherwise resembles. It is said to grow in masses on the mountain slopes of N. California, Oregon and Washington and is there known as the Glacier Lily. It has also been described as like a field of yellow daffodils. Several varieties have been distinguished on the colour of the anthers. The typical sp. has red anthers, var. *pallidum*, syn. var. *parviflorum*, has white or cream coloured, var. *chrysandrum* golden-yellow, the one usually seen in English gardens. Probably this sp. does best under moist conditions but it is generally reported as lacking vigour in this country.

**E. hartwegii.** A syn. of *E. multiscapoideum*. See under *E. californicum*.

**E. helenae.** See under *E. californicum*.

\* **E. hendersonii.** One of the most lovely and distinct of all the erythroniums, also fortunately one of the more vigorous and easy growers, distinguished by the heavily mottled dark *l.* in which the dark areas are divided by lighter green lines and the pale lilac *fl.* at the base of which are dark purple markings. *Fl.* large, several to a stem, up to 13 having been recorded, peduncles long, pale mauve, and anthers blue-mauve. (Pl. **11**, 6). Early flowering, April. If possible leave undisturbed once planted; in a moist situation it is likely to increase in height and size of corm as it becomes established. A plant of the lower valleys.

# Erythronium

**E. howellii.** See under *E. citrinum*.

**E. montanum.** The Avalanche Lily from the higher mountain slopes of Mt. Hood and Mt. Rainier. Photographs show it flowering in great masses as the snow melts as do the forms of *Crocus vernus* in the Alps. Unfortunately like these it is reluctant to adapt itself to cultivation in the lowlands. There is no record to my knowledge of its becoming established and flowering regularly in England; it has rarely flowered here at all. It is equally difficult to grow in the coastal and lower regions of the Pacific States. A distinct challenge to the grower of difficult alpine plants, but really only for him. *Fl.* white with anthers golden-yellow and stigma lobed. *L.* yellowish-green, unmottled, lanceolate with a cordate base.

**E. multiscapoideum.** See under *E. californicum*.

**E. oregonum.** See under *E. californicum*.

**E. purpurascens.** Distinguished by the unmottled, bright, almost metallic green *l.*, the entire stigma, the narrow petals without appendages and rather smaller *fl.* cream to pale yellow but becoming purplish as they age, hence the name, usually several to a stem. A high mountain sp.

\* **E. revolutum.** The rose-pink Trout Lily and undoubtedly one of the most beautiful of all the genus. Fortunately it is also one of the easiest and most successful in cultivation. It is a variable plant in colour, ranging from white to deep pink through lavender-white. A number of forms have been shown and probably one outstanding hybrid, namely ' Pink Beauty '. Apart from the colour of the *fl.* it is distinguished by the heavily mottled *l.*, the lobed stigma and long filiform style, the strong dilation of the filaments and the appendages to the perianth segments. *Fl.* large, 1–3 to a stem, strongly recurved with broad segments and stand up well above the foliage on stems of 5 in. or more. A plant of the damp coastal woodlands, ranging from N. California to British Columbia. *Fl.* up to 5 in. across have been recorded in Oregon but I have not seen them nearly so large in cultivation in this country. However 2½–3 in. is not unusual. April-May, one of the last to flower. Best in a damp semi-shaded position. The deeper pink forms have been sometimes distinguished as var. *johnsonii* or as *E. johnsonii* (Pl. **11**, 3) but this name is now usually relegated as a syn. of *E. revolutum*, as are also *E. smithii* and *E. grandiflorum smithii*. Those known under the names var. *bolanderi* and var. *watsonii* are forms of *E. oregonum* or *E. californicum*. \*' Pink Beauty ', a magnificent plant, is thought to be a hybrid between *E. revolutum* and *E. oregonum* or *E. californicum*.

**E. tuolumnense.** Distinguished by its light yellowy-green unmottled *l.* and golden-yellow *fl.*, separated from *E. grandiflorum* by the entire stigma and the often slightly smaller *fl.*, opening wide into a star on stems up to 1 ft. or more. It is one of the best garden plants in the genus and increases by offsets into large clumps if left alone in a suitable situation. It is said to grow on shady banks among deep, rich, damp leaf-mould and is probably an easier garden plant than *E. grandiflorum*. (Pl. **11**, 7). Recently a more vigorous and very promising hybrid from this sp. called ' Pagoda ' has appeared with stout stem up to 1½ ft. and *fl.* larger than in the sp.

123

The following three sp. have not yet been recorded in cultivation in this country: **E. idahoense** with white *fl.* and white anthers, lobed stigma and unmottled *l.* **E. klamathense** with creamy-white *fl.*, entire stigma, short style and unmottled *l.* **E. nudopetalum** with yellow *fl.*, entire stigma, long style and unmottled *l.*

# †EUCHARIS *Amaryllidaceae*

AN UNUSUAL and beautiful genus of bulbs from S. America with large white, sweet-scented flowers. Unfortunately they come from the warmer regions and in this country need to be grown in large pots in a warm greenhouse. A temperature of 65° to 70°F. is usually recommended for them when in growth and they then need plenty of water and feeding and a moist atmosphere and even after flowering they should not be dried off completely. The bulbs are large, ovoid with a long neck, the leaves elliptic, large and broad, and a bright yellow-green, the flower stems stout with an umbel of a few flowers to a stem. Flowers pure white, glistening, with a distinct perianth tube ending in six broad spreading lobes up to 3 in. across and in some species a central staminal cup or corona. The scent is often very strong. Among the eight or so species the following are the best known but even these are rarely seen owing to the heat required. *E. grandiflora* used to be grown much for market.

**E. amazonica.** A syn. of *E. grandiflora*.

**E. candida.** Stem up to 2 ft. with up to 10 drooping pure white *fl.* each about 3 in. across; centre of *fl.* shaped like a corona and flushed with yellow. Colombia.

**E. grandiflora.** The best known sp. and probably unsurpassed by any others. Stem up to 2 ft. with 4–6 large drooping *fl.* sometimes 5 in. across, glistening white with a prominent central corona or staminal cup slightly tinged with green. Scent very strong. *L.* broadly ovate, slightly waved at edges and plaited. Bulb roundish up to 3 in. across. Andes of Colombia. Winter flowering in warm greenhouse.

**E. sanderi.** Smaller than the preceding with *fl.* not more than 3 in. across and without the prominent corona or strong scent. Nov.-Dec. *L.* broad, ovate. Colombia.

# EUCOMIS *Liliaceae*

A SMALL genus of African bulbous plants with curious thick spikes of yellowish-green flowers distinguished by a small tuft of leaves at the top like a pineapple or a Crown Imperial. The genus is related to *Scilla* and *Ornithogalum*, having star-shaped flowers with six equal perianth seg-

# *Eucomis*

ments which are densely aggregated together. The plants grow up to 3 ft. in height and always attract attention in late summer because of their unusual colour and form. They remain in flower for a long period. They are not over-hardy and should be given a warm situation preferably sheltered by a wall in all except the warmest counties. Alternatively they can be grown easily as pot plants in a cool greenhouse. The bulbs are ovoid or globose, quite large and tunicated and should be planted rather deeply and protected for the first winter at least with a heap of ashes or litter and they do best with some feeding in not too light soil. Those in cultivation are S. African.

† **E. autumnalis.** Stem not often more than 1 ft. with 6 in. spike of green *fl.* each ½ in. across sometimes whitish, closely aggregated on short pedicels surmounted by large tuft of *l.* Aug.-Sept. *L.* wavy at edge, broad lorate. S. Africa. Syn. *E. undulata* under which name it is better known.

† **E. bicolor.** Stem about 1 ft. long, *fl.* less densely aggregated than in previous sp., white or pale green and edged with purple. In this it is distinct from other cultivated sp. *L.* oblong, clasping base of stem, slightly undulate at edge. Late summer flowering. Natal. Doubtfully hardy and perhaps better grown in a cool greenhouse.

**E. comosa.** The best known sp. Stem thick, spotted purple, fleshy, up to 2 ft. with a flower spike of 1 ft. *Fl.* yellowish-green each about ½ in. across. Scented. Sometimes tinged with pink or purple. Ovary violet-purple. Bulb large; *l.* lanceolate, up to 2 ft., spotted below with purple, rather bright green. S. Africa, Natal. July-August. Syn. *E. punctata.* Var. *striata* with *l.* striped with purple below instead of spotted. Stem rather similar.

† **E. pole-evansii.** The largest sp. with stems up to 5 or 6 ft. and a 2 ft. flower spike in S. Africa, rarely so much in this country. *Fl.* yellowish-green tinged with white on first opening. Probably not quite so hardy as *E. comosa* but a fine distinctive plant and with *fl.* which stay open for a long time. Late summer. Bulb large, up to 4 in. across. *L.* broad and shiny. S. Africa, Transvaal.

**E. punctata.** A syn. of *E. comosa.*

**E. undulata.** A syn. of *E. autumnalis.*

# †FREESIA *Iridaceae*

A S. AFRICAN genus containing a small number of very closely allied species which have been hybridised and selected to produce the many coloured race of florists' freesias which are so beautiful as cut flowers over a long season from October to May. (Pl. 12). Their grace and scent are combined with a considerable range of colour varying now from whites and creams to deep yellow, orange and even crimson and also to blue-mauves of considerable variety. These were originally derived from *F. refracta* which has creamy-yellow funnel-shaped flowers; its variety *leichtlinii* which has pale yellow flowers with a deeper yellow blotch at the base, var. *alba* with white flowers and *F. armstrongii* which is very similar in habit but has small pink flowers. The corms of freesias are round or ovoid and have a coarsely-netted tunic. The stems are up to 2 ft., often branched, usually with one branch much larger than the others, the flowers funnel-shaped, slightly irregular and opening in succession along the branch, which usually becomes bent over to the horizontal, enabling the flowers to face upwards.

A large number of named varieties have been selected and must be grown from corms planted in pots or boxes in the autumn. In Britain only in parts of the Scilly Isles and the Channel Islands are freesias sufficiently hardy to be left safely in the ground throughout the winter. The best scent is still found in the orange, white or creamy-yellow varieties and there is generally much less among the lavender-blues and blue-mauves and crimsons although recently some new varieties have been exhibited which had not only brighter coloured flowers but also stronger scent than anything previously raised in the red colour. The earliest flowers are derived from seedlings grown straight on from seed without any check and this is the technique used now by most market growers. Those grown from corms do not usually flower before February but generally have slightly bigger sprays of flower. The seeds are sown either by the big grower directly into the soil of the house in which they are to flower or by the amateur more often into pots or boxes—about five to seven seeds in a 5 in. pot and eight to twelve in a 7 in. one, or in boxes at 20 seeds to the sq. ft. Boxes should be deep, 6 in. if possible. Germination is not always very reliable but is helped by a process called " chitting " of the seeds in advance. This consists of either chipping the hard outer coat with a knife or a file or mixing the seeds in a jar or box of damp peat and keeping them in warmth for a few days or a week until there are signs of germination, and then planting them in the compost. John Innes

# Freesia

Potting Compost No. 1 is very satisfactory. Alternatively the hard outer coat of the seed may be softened by scalding in fairly warm water for 24 hours before sowing. The earlier the seeds are sown, the earlier will be the flowers, but they germinate best in the warm temperature of a propagating frame at about 65° to 70°F. If this is not available it is better to delay sowing until the outside temperature is higher at the end of April or early May. If sown too thickly the seedlings can be transplanted if this is done when they are quite small but better plants are grown without it. Once started the seedlings do not require artificial heat during the summer and are best grown slowly with plenty of ventilation, or the pots or boxes may be stood outside for the summer in an open position or placed in a cold frame. They must never be allowed to dry out and in warm weather will require watering every day. In the early autumn during September or in August if very early flowers are required they should be brought into the greenhouse again. Some heat will now be required on cold nights and the time of flowering will depend to some extent on how much is given but artificial heat should never be used to raise the temperature above 55°F.; 45°F. is quite safe. Plenty of ventilation will still be required. Small twigs can be used for support. The treatment of freesias grown from corms in the autumn follows the same pattern as those raised from seeds. They should not be planted later than September and preferably in August and may be stood for the first month in a cool frame. After flowering they must be kept growing and watered until the foliage dies down if good corms are required for the next year.

Recently, pre-treated freesia corms have been put on the market which will flower outdoors if planted in April or early May and these succeed quite well but probably their flowers are not valued so highly then as they would be in the winter. The strain most freely offered is known as Paradise Freesias and contains a good variety of colours including some blues. The named varieties are numerous now and only a small selection is given here.


*White*

　　' SNOW QUEEN ' Large *fl.* and good for cutting.
　　' WHITE MADONNA ' Large *fl.* with yellow throat.
　　' WHITE SWAN '


*Cream and pale yellow*

　　' CARO ' Creamy-yellow with gold blotch at base.
　　' FANTASY ' Double, a very large *fl.* New and not yet readily available but very promising.

127

# Fritillaria

### Deep yellow and pale orange

' BUTTERCUP ' Deep yellow with golden blotch at throat, an old variety.
' EL DORADO ' Buttercup-yellow, deeper in colour round edges of petals.
' ORANGE FAVOURITE ' Vigorous, deep yellow with some orange towards edge.
* ' ORANGE SUN ' Deep golden-yellow, orange at throat and bronze towards edges of petals.
' PRINCESS MARIJKE ' Lemon-bronze with orange tinting and yellow throat and some purplish-red or violet.

### Pinks and crimsons

' CARNIVAL ' Orange-scarlet with deep golden-yellow throat.
' MARGOT FONTEYN ' A lovely crimson-red. New and not yet readily available.
' PINK GIANT ' Deep mauvish-pink with deeper orange flush.
' RED CHIEF ' One of the deepest crimson varieties now marketed.
' ROSAMUNDE ' Soft pink with white centre.

### Blues and mauves

' APOTHEOSE ' Deep mauvish-lilac with some bright pink colour developing as *fl.* matures. White throat.
' ROYAL PRESENT ' Lavender-violet with yellow blotch, throat white, quite a good scent.
' SAPPHIRE ' Pale lavender-blue.
' VANGUARD ' Rosy-lavender, large *fl.* New and not yet readily available.

# FRITILLARIA *Liliaceae*

ALTHOUGH lacking the brilliant colours of many of the other flowers described in this book, the fritillaries have a peculiar distinction and interest of their own with their nodding bell-like flowers of green and maroon, splashed or chequered with dull reds and ochres. The Snake's Head fritillary or 'Guiné Flower' (*F. meleagris*) is one of our most beautiful native wild flowers and is an equally good garden plant in most areas while the Crown Imperial (*F. imperialis*) is one of the favourites of many old cottage gardens and has more colour and vigour than many of the other species.

*Fritillaria* is a large genus, mainly centred on the Mediterranean part of Europe and the middle east, but extending to China in the east and to the Pacific states of N. America in the west. Systematically the species present unusual difficulty and, like the tulips, seem to grade into one another in a number of cases and probably a number of so-called species may be merged when a new revision of the genus is published. Mean-

*Plate* 19: LILIES. 1, *L.* Bellingham Hybrid. 2, *L. davidi* var. *macranthum.* 3, *L. auratum.* 4, *L. aurelianense.* 5, *L. henryi.* 6, *L. speciosum*

*Plate* 20: LILIES. 1, *L. martagon* var. *album*. 2, *L. martagon* var. *cattaniae*. 3, *L. wilsoni*. 4, *L.* 'Enchantment'. 5, *L.* 'Dunkirk'. 6, *L.* 'Yellow Maid'

*Plate* 21: Lilies. 1, *L. regale.* 2, *L. candidum.* 3, *L. japonicum.* 4, *L. testaceum.* 5, *L. szovitsianum.*
The flower of *L. testaceum* is not quite typical and is only just opening. Later the segments
recurve more in the Turkscap style

*Plate 22.* LILIUM 'LIMELIGHT'

while in this book only a small proportion of the species can be included and even some of these are still rare as garden plants and not easy to obtain. Probably a number of further species are grown by the small band of fritillaria enthusiasts. Unfortunately many of these species are undoubtedly intolerant of cultivation in this country and tend to be short-lived in our gardens. In their native habitats they are generally found either as solitary plants or in small groups, although both *F. meleagris* and *F. pyrenaica* are exceptions to this statement. The majority, but by no means all, grow in areas where they are well ripened during a long and hot summer. In this country good drainage is essential. One successful grower grew many of his fritillaries in a raised scree bed in the open. The most successful growers at present seem to live on rather heavy clay soils rather than on light sandy soils, but this may be chance.

For many species cultivation in pots or deep pans in the alpine house offers the best chance of success. The compost should either be the John Innes Potting Compost with an extra amount of drainage material at the base or else a compost made up with extra grit or coarse sand as might be suitable for the higher alpines. For many growers the uncertainty and difficulty of growing fritillaries adds to their attraction. It is a challenge like that of the Oncocyclus irises or the higher androsaces and few gardeners are totally immune from such a challenge. Again there is a difference of opinion over the thoroughness of the ripening that should be given to bulbs in such pans in the summer. Probably it should not be as complete as that required by tulips.

As far as is known all the European and Asiatic species are tolerant of lime in the soil, of the American species there are not sufficient in cultivation for me to venture an opinion.

The flower of a fritillary is made up of six equal or nearly equal perianth segments arranged in two whorls and forming a bell. These segments are often prominently chequered, hence the name fritillary from the Latin for a dice box, while at the base is generally a conspicuous nectary like a dark maroon or green drop. The bulb is made up of two or three large fleshy scales, in the majority of the European and Asiatic species, but in the American species the inner scales are smaller and surrounded by a number of small scales like rice grains, which easily break away and can be grown on to form new plants. The bulbs of all fritillaries are fleshy and fragile and if left out of the ground for any time or sent by post should be carefully wrapped and also prevented from drying out. The basal leaves produced singly from young bulbs are generally broad, and differ widely from the narrower stem leaves. Fritillaries can be easily grown from seeds sown either in the early autumn as soon as they are ripe, or in the spring. They are, however, unlikely to flower under four years and many may take longer.

For further information on the genus readers should consult Miss Christabel Beck's useful little book entitled *Fritillaries* which has been compiled after many years' study and cultivation of the genus. I acknowedge my debt to it and also to her for the many specimens which she has exhibited from time to time at the Shows of The Royal Horticultural Society, in my compilation of the following notes. I emphasise again that it is by no means intended to be a full account of the genus but rather to cover only those most likely to be found in cultivation.

The European and Asiatic ones are described first and then the few North American ones in cultivation in this country. They are, however, for the most part more difficult of cultivation than the first group. *Korolkowia* has here been accepted as a separate genus. There are at present no known hybrids in the genus and the few named varieties of *F. meleagris* and *F. imperialis* are easily treated under these two species.

## (*a*) European and Asiatic species

\* **F. acmopetala.** One of the most amenable sp., even spreading freely in a few gardens. Stem slender, up to 18 in. and bearing 1–3 nodding bells on long curved pedicels, about 1–1¼ in. deep and about the same across, with segments only slightly recurved at edge, three outer segments pale jade-green, inner largely brownish-maroon on outside, inside pale yellowish-green, veined with dark brown, nectaries green. *L.* glaucous, narrow on stem and with an involucre of three arising from top of stem at base of pedicels of *fl.* Basal *l.* of non-flowering bulb wider up to 1½ in., glaucous. Bulb with two or three large fleshy scales. Early April. Asia Minor and according to Miss Beck in Cyprus also.

**F. armena.** A rather dwarf sp. from northern and central Turkey, the Caucasus and W. Persia, with rather broad glaucous *l.* and single pendant *fl.* with rather narrow bell of mauvish-maroon with a slight grey bloom overlaying ochrish-yellow. (Pl. **13**, **15**). A rare plant in cultivation of which further introductions would be valuable. In its native habitat it is apparently a mountain plant growing up to 7,000 ft. and reported there as forming large clumps up to 8 in. high. Bulb rather small, said to be cup-shaped. Probably should be grown in pans in the alpine house. Very closely allied to *F. caucasica* and *F. pinardii.*

**F. aurea.** See under *F. latifolia.*

**F. bithynica.** A small yellow-flowered sp. from N.W. and W. Asia Minor. The plants attributed to this sp. from Greece which are said to flower earlier in gardens are doubtful. *Fl.* nodding, 1–3 on slender stem up to 6 in. segments up to 1 in. long, outside of bell citron or greenish-yellow, generally overlaid with a pale silvery green, glaucescent, outer tepals margined faintly with red, inner with green. Inside citron-yellow with some green markings. Nectaries

# Fritillaria

lanceolate, scent pungent, stem *l.* linear-lanceolate, glaucous, but basal *l.* where solitary is broadly oblanceolate. Bulb small. April. Syns. *F. citrina, F. dasyphylla, F. pineticola.*

    *F. dasyphylla.* More purplish *fl.* outside; from Asia Minor and *F. pineticola* from Samos have now been merged in this sp. having been doubtfully distinguished on the colour of the bells and the relative shapes of the stigmas but these three are very rare in cultivation. All this group are more suited to cultivation in pans in the alpine house than in the open garden.

**F. camschatcensis.** An interesting sp. which appears to bridge the gap between those of the Asiatic and the North American, being found in Japan as well as Camschatica but also extending through Alaska and British Columbia down to Washington State and Oregon. In Alaska it is said to be very abundant and to colour some of the meadows with its dark blooms. *Fl.* very dark maroon-purple, often appearing almost black, wide bell-shaped, pendant on short pedicels, generally one but sometimes up to three on a stem up to 15 in. high. *L.* glaucous, narrowly lanceolate; bulb with a large central conical scale like *F. imperialis* but with numerous small bulblets or rice grains around it, thus resembling more the structure of the bulbs of the American sp. Late flowering, mid-May to early June. It is one of the easier grown fritillaries and in some gardens has persisted outside and become well established. In hot gardens it is generally best grown in semi-shade and with some moisture in the soil as it must experience in its native lands.

**F. canaliculata.** From S. and S.E. Asia Minor is very close also to *F. bithynica* but has unequal tepals, glaucous-green on the outside, yellowish-green inside. Syn. *F. glaucoviridis.*

**F. caucasica.** From N.E. Turkey and Caucasus is a mountain plant with very dark but slender maroon bells, yellowish inside and covered with a silvery-blue bloom outside. *L.* glaucous, narrow. March-April but later in the wild, mid-May among bushes in alpine zone of Pontic Range of Turkey. A lovely plant.

**F. citrina.** A syn. of *F. bithynica.*

**F. cirrhosa.** A widespread Central and Eastern Himalayan sp. extending also into Western China. *Fl.* generally one but sometimes up to three, variable in colour, generally purplish-brown but sometimes with more greenish or even creamy-yellow colouring, chequered inside, bells widely campanulate; stem also variable in length, recorded up to 3 ft. but rarely as much. Its name is derived from the uppermost leaflets which are cirrhose or having a tendril-like top, other *l.* linear, shiny, dark green, up to 4 in. long. April-May. Bulb small. Rarely seen in cultivation though apparently often found in its native habitat. The bulbs are said to be eaten by Sherpas as a preventitive against goitre.

    **F. roylei,** from Western Himalayas is very similar and closely allied, but is without the tendril-like tips to the top linear *l.*

**F. crassifolia.** A very handsome sp. as the plate shows with long bells, purple, heavily overlaid with jade green and chequered. *Fl.* 1–2 on a stoutish stem up to 15 in., bells up to 2 in. long by 1 in. wide. *L.* broad, green.

# Fritillaria

(Pl. **13**, 9). Asia Minor including Lebanon, Syria, Iraq and N. Persia, generally from the mountains. Bulb large, of two fleshy scales up to 1½ in. through. May. Unfortunately rare in cultivation and further collections would be welcome.

**F. dasyphylla.** A syn. of *F. bithynica.*

**F. drenovskyi.** A pretty, slender sp. from Bulgaria with dark maroon *fl.* with a thin yellow line along centre of outside of each segment, lemon-yellow inside, slightly veined with purple. Rare. (Pl. **13**, 1)

**F. glaucoviridis.** A syn. of *F. canaliculata.*

**F. gracilis.** A fairly slender growing sp. as its name implies, coming from Southern Yugoslavia and said to be variable in the wild. Very close to *F. nigra* which would be the prior name if the sp. should later be merged. Stem up to 1 ft., *fl.* 1–3, narrowly campanulate but wider at mouth, up to 1 in. long by ⅔ in. across at mouth, outer tepals heavily blotched or tessellated with dark red on a background of light yellowish-green, inside brighter, yellowish-green, usually with a medium band of brighter green. Inner tepals dark red, nectaries green. *L.* linear, acute, glaucous-green.

**F. graeca.** A small-flowered sp. widely spread on the Greek mountains and from a few neighbouring countries, but always solitary or in small groups, often in the shade of spruce woods but on Mt. Hymettus in the open. *Fl.* 1 or 2 on rather slender stem, 6 in. or sometimes slightly taller, variable in colour, chocolate-brown to dull reddish-brown overlying a green colour and generally with a definite green stripe down centre of the tepals, unchequered or very slightly so; perianth segments up to 1 in. in length, often less, and about ½ in. broad. (Pl. **13**, 12 and 16). *L.* glaucous, lanceolate; bulb small, generally with two scales only. April. *F. guicciardii* is very close indeed to this sp., sometimes being distinguished by a dwarfer habit and stouter stem, but these may well be merely environmental characters.

**F. hispanica.** A dark chocolate-brown sp. from the Spanish mountains, where it appears to be wide-spread, although nearly always solitary. I have seen it both in the Picos de Europa in the north and in the Sierra Nevada in the south, in the latter generally growing in the middle of a prickly shrublet, well protected from all animals and collectors. *Fl.* generally single on a stem up to 12 in., dark brown-maroon, sometimes with slight green markings and without any obvious chequering, yellowish-green inside. *L.* narrow, linear, glaucous. In appearance not unlike a rather more slender *F. pyrenaica*. April-June. *F. lusitanica*, from Portugal, is very closely related to this and very similar, but generally not so tall and with rather more colour in the *fl.*, but these are two which may well be merged.

\* **F. imperialis.** Probably the most handsome sp. that can be grown in gardens and a well-known plant under the name Crown Imperial, a favourite of the old Dutch flower painters. Stem up to 4 ft., thick with numerous green, slightly fleshy *l.* up the stem, ending in a close whorl below which hang the clusters of pendant bells, deep lemon-yellow to brick-red or reddish-orange in colour and up to 2½ in. deep by nearly as much across. Nectaries prominent, generally white. Bulb large, up to 4 in. in diameter, usually with a

132

conical hollow at top, for this reason many gardeners prefer to plant it on its side; when damaged it gives out a strong, foxy and most unpleasant smell. Early flowering, April; Western Himalayas. A good border plant or suitable for the edge of a shrubbery where it can receive almost full sun. A group of the lemon-yellow variety is particularly effective. It grows best in heavy clay soils or in the better loams and is often difficult in light sandy soils. In some soils the bulbs increase rapidly and probably should be lifted and divided from time to time, but they are likely to take at least a year to settle down again. Any lifting should be done as soon as they have died down. The following varieties have been distinguished: ' Aurora ', deep reddish-orange, vigorous; *lutea* and ' Lutea maxima ', deep lemon-yellow, very handsome; ' Orange Brilliant ', orange-brown ; ' Rubra maxima ', rich burnt-orange, shaded with red, vigorous; *chitralensis*, butter-yellow and smaller than the type; *raddeana*, straw-yellow, dwarfer, sometimes regarded as a separate sp.; *inodora*, said to be almost without the scent of the type in both bulbs and flowers. Less vigorous than the type. Bokhara. The Crown Imperial is said to be the *fl.* associated with the legend of Calvary, the one *fl.* which would not bow its head as Jesus passed, and ever afterwards bowed its head in repentance with unshed tears in the form of its nectaries. (Pl. VIII)

**F. involucrata.** A slender sp. from the Maritime Alps and the Riviera foothills both of France and Italy in a few parts of which it grows plentifully. One to three *fl.* but generally one only on a foot-high stem, tepals 1–1¼ in. long, palish green with purple markings but only slight chequering; variable. The three prominent bracts out of which the *fl.* grows are narrow and spread out horizontally. *L.* glaucous, narrowly linear, bulb globose, slightly flattened, up to 1 in. across. April-May. A plant chiefly for the alpine house. Resembling *F. pontica* but more slender and taller in growth and with a lighter coloured *fl.*

**F. ionica.** See *F. pontica.*

**F. latifolia.** A very variable sp. found in the Caucasus, N.E. Turkey and Cilicia. Closely allied to *F. meleagris*, but with *fl.* on much shorter stems and more tubby and squat in form, generally solitary. Colour very variable, to some extent depending on geographical situation. Most forms are fairly easily cultivated either as alpine house plants or in the open garden. The type of the sp. is the Caucasian plant with deep purple-maroon chequered *fl.* up to 2 in. in diameter. (Pl. **13**, 11). The following varieties have also been distinguished sometimes being regarded as separate sp. all flower April-May:

Var. **aurea.** Deep yellow, marked with chocolate; dwarf, generally not more than 4 in. high. Turkey, Cilicia.

Var. **lutea.** Yellow; dwarf, generally not more than 4 in. high. Caucasus, 7–16,000 ft.

Var. **nobilis.** Pale purple, chequered, yellowish-green inside and slightly spotted there, stem 4–6 in. (Pl. **13**, 18). Caucasus and Turkish Armenia. Bulb small and globose. A mountain plant growing under nearly fine scree conditions in the Pontic Range of N.E. Turkey.

**F. libanotica.** A syn. of *F. persica.*

# Fritillaria

**F. lusitanica.** See under *F. hispanica.*

**F. lutea.** See under *F. latifolia.*

\* **F. meleagris.** One of the most beautiful and unusual of our native wild *fl.*
but also found in most other European countries. The slender stems bear
1 or 2 pendulous bells in varying shades of purple and chequered all
over, thus earning it the name of Snake's Head, or Guinea Flower from the
resemblance to a guinea fowl. The *fl.* are broadly campanulate, as broad
as an egg but not so long, up to 1½ in. long by 1¼ in. across the mouth;
(Pl. **13**, 2) *l.* narrow, linear up the stem, slightly glaucous. April. The white
form with green veins and chequering is also common and also represents a
large proportion of seedlings. In the wild it is found in damp meadows but
it will grow adequately in any reasonably moist soil or in open woodland,
though probably it will only naturalise and become permanent in a really
damp place. Some especially fine forms have been selected and named.

\* ' APHRODITE ' White, strong-growing.

' ARTEMIS ' Dusky purple with prominent chequering.

' CHARON ' Dark purple, probably the darkest of the named forms.

' CONTORTA ' Bells narrow, with perianth segments joined, a botanical
curiosity.

' POSEIDON ' Large flower, soft purplish-rose.

' SATURNUS ' Light reddish-purple, large flowered.

**F. messanensis.** A variable sp. from Crete, Sicily whence the name is derived,
Greece and the Balkans, usually with a single pendant and wide bell about
1¼ in. long and nearly as much wide, tessellated, chocolate or purplish-brown
with maroon and green markings and generally well marked green stripe on
the back of each perianth segment, *l.* slightly glaucous, linear, the uppermost
in whorls of 3. April. A rare sp. in cultivation, probably best suited to the
alpine house, related to *F. gracilis* and *F. oranensis.* In Crete grows in open
woodland of evergreen oak or light pine.

**F. nigra.** Allied to the better known *F. pyrenaica* but with a much wider,
although very local, distribution extending from S. France through Italy and
eastwards to the Caucasus. *Fl.* dark purple, chequered, variable in colour,
generally greenish-yellow inside, rarely seen in cultivation and probably not
such a good garden plant as *F. pyrenaica.*

**F. obliqua.** A Greek sp. but probably extending eastwards also in its distribution. Stem recorded up to 2 ft. with 12 *fl.* but 18 in. with 3–5 *fl.* is more usual,
bells widely campanulate and perianth segments rather pointed, dark purplish-
maroon overlaid with a silvery-blue sheen, as dark inside as out. Distinguished
by its trifid style and glaucous slightly twisted leaves. (Pl. **13**, 5)

**F. olivieri.** An attractive and apparently absolutely hardy sp. from the
mountains of Western Persia, where it flowers in June near the melting snows
at 6,000 ft. Here it flowers in April and May in the open, slightly earlier
in an alpine house. Stem rather stout, up to 1 ft. *Fl.* solitary, nodding,
1¼ in. long, widely campanulate with tips of perianth segments recurved,
bright green on the outside with purplish-brown margins, yellowish-green
inside, tessellated, nectary dark brown. (Pl. **13**, 8). Close to *F. pontica* but

differing in the light green, not glaucous *l.*, narrowly lanceolate and slightly twisted. Probably one of the best fritillaries for the rock garden.

**F. oranensis.** Probably the only N. African sp., the distribution extending from the Atlas Mts. in N.W. Morocco through Algeria to Tunisia, found in Cedar forests. Allied to *F. messanensis* and *F. hispanicus*, but distinguished from the former by being a slenderer plant with scattered, not whorled *l.*, rather broad and with comparatively wide and squat-shaped bells with perianth segment tips recurved, dark livid purple on the outside, usually with a dull medium green band down the centre, the bells being covered with a glaucous bloom, no chequering. A handsome and striking sp. Said to grow best in moist ground.

**F. pallidiflora.** A stout sp. with stem 18 in. to 2 ft. and large bulbs, *fl.* in groups in axils of the upper whorls of *l.*, up to 12, but generally about 6 in 2 whorls; pedicels short, *fl.* pale greenish or creamy-white, broadly campanulate, up to 1¾ in. long and 1¼ in. wide, inside flecked with very small crimson dots. The form illustrated in the Botanical Magazine is a much stronger green in colour than those at present seen in English gardens, but this was derived direct from Dr. Regel in Russia so that the re-introduction of more stock from the mountains of Siberia, where it grows at altitudes of up to 9,000 ft., would be desirable. *L.* wide, glaucous. Quite hardy and one of the easiest grown sp. in most gardens, coming freely from seed.

**F. persica,** from the eastern mediterranean extending through Palestine, Syria and Transjordan, Iraq and N.W. Persia, forms a very distinct section in the genus with large egg-shaped bulbs up to 2 in. in height and stout stems up to 2½ ft. with a grey bloom, with pale green, slightly glaucous *l.* often twisted, and up to 25 medium-sized *fl.* in a loose raceme. Each *fl.* a wide open bell shaped like a low cone with a wide base, greenish flushed with dull purple or deep purple-maroon with a slight sheen of grey bloom or deep rose, nectaries green. March-April. Hardy, but since it starts into growth early in the season may then be the better for some protection. However it has been recorded as flowering regularly in some gardens. *F. libunotica* which was formerly regarded as a separate sp. has now been merged in it. Long known in Europe, having been described by Parkinson and figured by Redouté. A handsome plant of bizarre colouring.

**F. pinardii.** A small-flowered sp. from the Cilician Taurus and other mountains of Turkey and also from Chios, with drooping campanulate *fl.* about ¾ in. long by ½ in. broad, dusky purplish-brown, flushed green with perianth segments recurved at ends, olive-green veined with brown inside. (Pl. **13**, 19). *L.* dark green, not glaucous and comparatively broad; bulb a flattened globe, unusual in the genus in producing stoloniferous growths which produce new bulbils at the end. Rare in cultivation and probably best suited to the alpine house.

**F. pontica.** A widely distributed sp. from Turkey and Thrace and extending north into Bulgaria and possibly westwards into N. Greece, said to be frequent on the wooded hills along the north of the Bosphorus up to 3,000 ft. Stem up to 18 in. but generally less, 1–3 bells, colour variable but without tessellation, up to 1½ in. long by 1 in. across, yellowish-green overlying a brownish-purple,

# Fritillaria

which is more prominent on inner segments, always with a broad median greenish stripe, nectary black. (Pl. 13, 10). April. One of the easiest sp. for both alpine house and rock garden. Distinguished easily by its ribbed seed head from var. *ionica* from N. Greece and Corfu which is very closely allied. *Fl.* dull purple and slightly tessellated, variable in colour and with slight bloom. *L.* broad, deep green. Alpine house.

\* **F. pyrenaica.** One of the best garden plants in the genus, often establishing and spreading freely. A very variable sp. from the Pyrenees and Northern Spain. Stem 8 in. to 1½ ft., rather slender with one or occasionally two bells, hanging on long curved pedicels, narrowly-widely campanulate, dark purplish-mahogany variously marked and chequered with darker crimson-purple and yellow and in some forms yellow entirely inside; very variable in colour. (Pl. 13, 6). I have seen a great variety both in colour and form of bell growing closely together among rocks and short grass in the passes of the Western Pyrenees. *L.* scattered, linear, only slightly glaucous. April. Quite hardy.

**F. raddeana.** See under *F. imperialis*.

**F. rhodokanakis.** A small sp. only found in the Island of Hydra off the east coast of Greece, but one of the more easily grown plants for the alpine house or very warm border. Stem up to 6 in. with single narrowly campanulate bell of dark maroon, slightly tipped with gold, yellowish inside, ¾–1 in. long by ¾ in. wide; *l.* lanceolate, green. April-May.

**F. roylei.** See under *F. cirrhosa*.

**F. sibthorpiana.** A dainty sp. with slender stem 4–6 in. and bright yellow, widely campanulate bells, one to a stem, ½ in. to ¾ in. long. *L.* linear, slightly glaucous. April. Greece, S.W. and Central Asia Minor, Chios. A beautiful little plant for the alpine house but generally not very permanent outside. (Pl. 13, 14)

**F. tubiformis.** A dwarf plant with a surprisingly and disproportionate large bell, one of the biggest in the genus. Stem stout, 3–6 in., *fl.* nodding, sometimes almost resting on the ground, 1½ in. long by 1½ in. wide, deep reddish-purple, heavily chequered, *l.* lanceolate, glaucous. S. France in Maritime Alps, lower slopes of mountains in N. Italy and S. Tyrol but up to 5,000 ft. on limestone. April. Syn. *F. delphinensis*.

> Var. **moggridgei** is bright yellow lightly speckled with deep crimson or brown, otherwise similar in form and stature. (Pl. 13, 17). Maritime Alps. Alpine house.

**F. tuntasia.** Closely allied to *F. obliqua* but with an entire instead of a trifid style and a rather more vigorous plant. *Fl.* 1–4, dark purple, rather small, widely campanulate, nodding on stem up to 1 ft. *L.* linear, often twisted. The Greek islands particularly Kythnos. A rare plant, probably best suited to the alpine house. (Pl. 13, 7)

**F. verticillata.** A taller plant up to 2 ft. with 1–6 tepals, whitish-green or cream, lightly tipped with green sometimes spotted crimson inside near base, pendant, bells 1 in. long and as much across, easily distinguished by the prominent curl at the ends of the *l.* *L.* crowded together, slightly

136

# *Fritillaria*

glaucous. China, Japan and Central Asia (Altai mountains) up to 10,000 ft. Quite hardy and one of the easier sp. in many gardens, may be grown in half shade. April-May.

## (*b*) American species

These are numerous, mostly inhabitants of the higher slopes of the Pacific Coast ranges, damp in spring and hot in summer. Unfortunately with only a very few exceptions they have proved very difficult and unsatisfactory in English gardens and few of them are seen. The bulbs of many of these are made up of a large conglomeration of small bulblets like rice grains adhering to the main scales and the species can be propagated from these usually taking about 3 years to flower. The following, mostly from the lower regions, are the best species for English gardens, but owing to lack of opportunity to grow them our knowledge is still very inadequate and fresh importations of these and others would be well worth while.

**F. liliacea.** *Fl.* 1–3, widely expanded bells on a stout stem up to 9 in. Whitish-green or creamy with pale green streaks and some purple dots. A very distinctive plant with its broad leaves mostly growing in a basal rosette. Said to be fragrant and not too difficult in the alpine house. April-May. California, where it grows in open fields on heavy clay soils. (Pl. **13**, 4)

**F. pudica.** A small graceful yellow-flowered sp., not unlike *F. citrina* and *F. sibthorpiana* but stouter. Stems up to 8 in., *fl.* 1–2, widely campanulate, a good golden-yellow, up to 1 in. long but generally less. April. Western N. America, where it is known as " Johnny-Jump-Up " from its early flowering. Generally best in the alpine house but will sometimes survive and even multiply in well-drained positions outside. (Pl. **13**, 13)

**F. recurva.** The scarlet fritillary and probably the glory of the genus where it can be grown and certainly worth every effort. Stems slender and graceful up to 2 ft., *fl.* usually 1–9 but there is a record of up to 35 on one stem, rather narrowly campanulate with tips of perianth segments recurving, up to 1 in. long, scarlet, flecked with orange or yellow, especially inside. *L.* linear-lanceolate mostly around centre of stem in whorls. Bulb large. Said to grow best in damp positions but should be kept dry in winter. April. California (Sierra Nevada) and S. Oregon up to 5,000 ft., recorded from dry hillsides. (Pl. **13**, 3)

Var. **coccinea,** without yellow markings and said to be an even brighter scarlet. Mt. Hood.

# GALANTHUS *Amaryllidaceae*

IT IS not often realised how much variety there is among the snowdrops and that the season of flowering can range from October till April. For this reason it is well worth while to grow some of the less common species in addition to the well-known *G. nivalis*. There are also a number of hybrids and selected forms which are excellent garden plants.

In view of Sir Frederick Stern's excellent study on this genus and the Leucojums, *Snowdrops and Snowflakes*, published by The Royal Horticultural Society, I do not think it is necessary here to give very detailed descriptions of each species and so I have grouped them into the three series used by him and I acknowledge my debt to him and his work as well as to the late Mr. E. A. Bowles for so much of my experience and information on this genus. There is some quality in the various snowdrops which arouses the greatest and nearly always lifelong enthusiasm in its devotees.

In all snowdrops the flowers are white, globular or bell-shaped and pendulous, the three inner segments of the perianth being considerably smaller than the three outer ones and forming a kind of inverted cup around the stigma and stamens. Each of the inner segments has a broad notch at its lower end and round the notch is a green blotch or marking; sometimes there is also a green blotch at its base (top end). In a few species and varieties they run together to form a green band. The bulbs are generally rounded, fleshy, covered with a dark outer membrane which easily rubs off, the leaves linear or strap-shaped, all radical, bright apple-green or glaucous. Flowering through the winter months and being resolutely hardy, in fact almost impervious to all the frosts and storms of winter, the bowed heads rising again as the ground thaws. Being also very easy to grow, they flourish both on the chalk and on the heaviest clay. In fact, they seem to do best on the heavier soils where there is plenty of body and moisture in the soil. On hot and dry sandy soils a mixture of peat and loam should be dug in for them. They are intolerant of fresh animal manure but may be fed with dried blood or bone meal, or both. Those species and varieties which flower from October till the end of January seem to do best in more open conditions either of full sun or semi-shade, but the later flowering species and especially our common *G. nivalis* like open woodland conditions and will grow well in quite a degree of shade. The finest masses of naturalised snowdrops are generally to be seen to best effect in Scottish and in some northern and western gardens, where they are a wonderful sight. Probably a few of the named seedlings of vigour, such as ' Atkinsii ' and ' S. Arnott ' would do equally well if they were available in sufficient quantity to make an extensive start.

All snowdrops are best moved and divided while they are making growth or just after they have flowered. But they seem to come to no harm at all by being taken up and divided or moved when in full flower, as long as their roots are not then allowed to become dry. If planted as dry bulbs they may take a season to establish and this method is not so satisfactory. They are easily increased by division while the majority also set seed and will spread by this means, the seedlings flowering in three to four years.

The snowdrops are best classified by the vegetative characters of the leaves and their position relative one to the other on emerging from the ground; this is called their vernation and there are three different types, some being pressed flat and face to face, others being wrapped round each other or convolute. Some snowdrops, particularly those of the *plicatus* group, have the edges of their leaves folded back, i.e. reduplicate. The position of the green markings on the inner segments of the perianth is also a useful and fairly, though not absolutely, constant character in the division of some of the species. Some of the garden varieties that have been named are so close to one another that it is extremely difficult and probably rather fruitless to distinguish them. Those mentioned here are, however, reasonably distinct.

## (a) Nivales

These are the species which resemble and can be grouped around our common English snowdrop, *G. nivalis*. They are distinguished by the emerging leaves being pressed flat against each other in their vernation, by the comparatively narrow, strap-shaped and generally slightly glaucous leaves of almost equal width throughout their length and, except in the case of *G. graecus*, by the lack of green markings at the base of the inner segments of the flower. In all snowdrops there is a green marking round the sinus at the tip of the inner segment.

* **G. nivalis.** The most widespread sp. As well as being naturalised in many parts of this country it is found in woods all over Europe as far west as Spain and as far east as Kiev in Russia. It is consequently very variable. Late Jan.-Feb. (Pl. **14**, 17)

  Subsp. **cilicicus,** from Turkey and the Lebanon; distinguished by the more glaucous *l.* which are further developed at time of flowering, by the short pedicel which is shorter than the spathe and by its earlier flowering, Dec. to early Jan. A rare plant and generally without the vigour of the type. Should be grown in a more open position.

  * Subsp. **reginae-olgae,** from the mountains of S. Greece is the earliest (or

latest!) snowdrop to flower, generally in October, sometimes even in September. The *fl.* appear before the *l.* and in this character it is distinct from all other snowdrops. (Pl. **32**, 11). Otherwise it very closely resembles *G. nivalis*; the *l.* however, which appear as soon as the *fl.* fades are distinguished by a rather prominent silvery glaucous band along centre. It is quite a strong grower in an open situation and should be kept dry in summer. It has persisted and increased even in a light Surrey sandy soil with me for several years and always excited interest at its time of flowering. Another form of autumn flowering snowdrop obviously very close to this, if not synonymous with it, has been given the name *rachelae* but it is very rare in cultivation.

## *G. nivalis* VARIANTS

Var. **flavescens** (Pl. **14**, 23) and var. **lutescens,** distinguished by the yellow instead of green markings on the inner segments. Almost indistinguishable one from the other and always weak growers. There are also double forms of these varieties with yellow markings (Pl. **14**, 15), as there are also double forms of those with green markings. (Pl. **14**, 18)

' SCHARLOKII ' A very unusual form distinguished by the two spathes of the *fl.* which are elongated and stand up like asses' ears. It grows quite easily in most gardens and is a curiosity rather than a particular beauty. *Fl.* tends to be small. (Pl. **14**, 14)

' VIRIDAPICIS ' A form with a green spot at the tip of each outer segment of the perianth, very distinct in this character. (Pl. **14**, 16)

Garden selected variants of particular merit:

* ' ATKINSII ' A very vigorous and strong growing form which seems to do equally well in the open as in woodland; *fl.* large, globular, usually distinguished by one malformed segment. Early flowering, usually by mid-Jan., setting no seed it increases freely, however, by division of the bulb. One of the best of all snowdrops for any garden. One of the tallest and placed first by E. A. Bowles among the garden varieties. Formerly known as *G. imperati* var. *atkinsii*. (Pl. **14**, 5)

' MAGNET ' A beautiful variety distinguished by the very long slender pedicels on which the *fl.* hang as on a fishing cast. (Pl. **14**, 6)

* ' S. ARNOTT ' Sometimes known as ' Arnotts' Seedling ', a very strong and vigorous variety with large perfectly formed *fl.* and regarded by some as the finest garden variety generally available.

* ' STRAFFAN ' A very vigorous and freely spreading variety with large *fl.* selected in the garden at Straffan House in Ireland. Late flowering. (Pl. IX)

**G. corcyrensis.** Distinguished from *G. nivalis* by the much broader green marking around the sinus on the inner segment, by the short pedicel, by the earlier flowering season, generally late Nov. to early Dec., and by the *l.* which are only about 1 in. long generally at the time of flowering but develop later. In this respect it is intermediate between subsp. *reginae-olgae* and *G. nivalis*. Corfu and Sicily. Best grown in a sunny position.

**G. graecus.** Distinguished from all other snowdrops by the narrow glaucous

# Galanthus

*l.* having a twist, and from other members of this series by the basal green marking on the inner segment. Variable in size of *fl.* Early flowering, Jan. to early Feb. Best in an open situation. Greece and Balkans.

**G. rhizehensis.** Distinguished by its narrow, green, not glaucous *l.*, recurving after flowering, early flowering, generally mid-Dec. to Jan. Turkey, around Trebizond only. It is also unusual in having both diploid and triploid forms. A rare plant, not so vigorous as typical *G. nivalis* and with rather smaller *fl.* but surviving adequately with me in Surrey, although without any appreciable increase.

## (b) Plicati

These species are close to *G. plicatus* and distinguished by the leaves being flat in vernation, i.e. not folded round each other at the base on emerging and with the margins rolled or folded back, broader than those of the *Nivales*, glaucous in the two species described.

* **G. byzantinus.** A vigorous sp. from Turkey along the shores of the Bosphorus, spreading freely by division and seed in most gardens and early flowering, mid-Jan. to early Feb. *L.* broad, glaucous, margins folded back. *Fl.* easily recognised by the deep green marking at the base of the inner segment, thus easily distinguishing it from *G. plicatus.* It has sometimes been suggested that *byzantinus* could be a natural hybrid between *G. elwesii* and *G. plicatus* since it combines some of the characters of each sp. A variable plant in size, but the larger forms are among the finest snowdrops. Grows equally well in full sun as in shade. (Pl. **14,** 12)

**G. plicatus.** One of the largest *fl.* Easily recognised by the broad glaucous *l.* with the margins folded back and the large, rather solid *fl.* with prominent green marking round the sinus of the inner segment, but without any marking at the base. (Pl. **14,** 2). Later flowering than *byzantinus* and in most gardens best grown in open woodland.

* ' WARHAM ' A specially fine form collected during the Crimean War and the only snowdrop to have received a First Class Certificate (the highest award) from The Royal Horticultural Society. (Pl. **14,** 1). The double form of *plicatus* is also a very handsome and distinctive plant and probably the finest of the double snowdrops. Russia around the Crimea and Roumania.

Probably closely allied is *G. woronowii* from the Caucasus, which is said to be distinguished by the lighter green of the *l.* and the smaller *fl.*, but although my experience with this sp. only relates to one season it seems very doubtfully distinct from *G. ikariae* subsp. *latifolius* and also hardly worth growing.

Some of the finest garden varieties have been raised with *G. plicatus* as one parent but they tend to be shorter lived than the *nivalis* seedlings.

# Galanthus

## (c) Latifolii

These species centring round *G. ikariae* and *G. elwesii* and distinguished by the emerging leaves being convolute in vernation, that is, wrapped round each other, broad, either green or glaucous.

**G. allenii.** An uncommon sp. described from a garden plant and unknown so far in the wild although it is probable that *G. alpinus* of the Caucasus is synonymous with this. Distinguished by the broad green, not glaucous *l.*, the tall stem with long pedicel, and the comparatively large *fl.* in which the inner segment has a broad apical marking round the sinus but none at the base. Late flowering and in most gardens rather slow to increase.

**G. caucasicus.** A variable snowdrop with several forms differing chiefly in their size and time of flowering. The earliest is often in flower in early January while the latest spreads into mid-February. It is distinguished from *G. nivalis* by the broad glaucous *l.* and from *G. elwesii* by the less upright, more recurved *l.* and by the absence of any green markings at the base of the inner segments. A valuable garden plant well worth obtaining for its varying forms, growing equally both in full exposure or semi-shade. Russia, Caucasus and Transcaucasia.

\* **G. elwesii.** One of the finest sp. with broad, glaucous and erect *l.* and large *fl.* on stout stems, late flowering. Distinguished by the broad dark-green marking at the base of the inner segment. Variable. Turkey around Smyrna and the Greek islands of Samos and Thasos. (Pl. **14**, 10)
\* Var. **whittallii.** Has been distinguished as a specially large form. Early flowering.
   Var. **maximus,** from N. Greece, Bulgaria and S. Yugoslovia, a fine large form distinguished also by the twisting of the *l.*
   ' COLESBORNE ' A rather dwarf snowdrop but with large *fl.*, found in the grass at Colesborne by Mr. Elwes and distinguished also by the green markings on the inner segments extending the full length, possibly a hybrid between *G. elwesii* and *G. caucasicus.*
   ' MERLIN ' Tall and with a large *fl.* in which the inner segment is completely green, probably a hybrid of *G. elwesii* × *G. plicatus.* One of the finest garden varieties but not a very strong grower. (Pl. **14**, 7)

**G. fosteri.** A tall growing sp. from mature bulbs but variable, and small bulbs tend to produce very small and poor *fl.* Distinguished from *G. elwesii* by the deep apple-green, not glaucous *l.* and from *G. ikariae* by the taller habit of growth and the broad basal green marking on the inner segment. Jan. to early Feb. S. Turkey and the Lebanon. This snowdrop has the reputation of being less easy to grow and maintain than all the other sp. Recent importations, however, seem to be more vigorous. It is possible that in cold areas it may be slightly tender and at any rate should be grown where it can get a good summer ripening. (Pl. **14**, 11)

**G. ikariae.** This includes the snowdrops commonly known as *ikariae* and *latifolius* which are now treated as subsp. Distinguished by the recurved

142

deep green, not glaucous *l.* and by the absence of any basal green marking on the inner segment. As the prior published epithet the name *ikariae* has now been given to the whole sp.

Subsp. **ikariae.** Probably finer in its size of *fl.* with outer long claw-shaped petals than the various forms of subsp. *latifolius* but in most gardens not such a vigorous grower. These outer segments are half as long as broad. Generally a rather dwarf plant. Only collected on the island of Nikaria, south-west of Samos in the E. Mediterranean. (Pl. **14,** 22)

Subsp. **latifolius.** A widespread plant from Turkey and S. Russia, including the Caucasus. Rather variable in its size of *fl.* Distinguished by the recurved and bright green lorate *l.* Although less effective as regards size of *fl.* than *G. elwesii* or *G. plicatus* or many garden varieties, in my dry Surrey garden it increases in semi-shade much more freely than any other snowdrop. The green markings around the sinus of the inner segment are usually rather broad and distinct. Syns. *G. latifolius, G. platyphyllus.* (Pl. **14,** 19)

# GALTONIA *Liliaceae*

A GENUS of four species of handsome summer flowering bulbs with white pendulous bells on tall spikes, closely allied to *Hyacinthus* but distinguished by the much more numerous and angular seeds and by the much longer flower stems. The one commonly grown is *G. candicans* and it is probably the best as well as the hardiest. It is best planted in spring in a sunny position or in the border and the bulbs should be not less than 5 in. deep. Once established they should not be disturbed.

\* **G. candicans.** Stem up to 4 ft. with a loose raceme of large drooping white bells on long pedicels. *Fl.* faintly tinged with green towards the base and often also tipped with green, 1½ in. long and 1 in. across. Bulb large, round. *L.* glaucous, long and strap-shaped. Slightly scented. Aug.-Sept. Mountains in S. Africa from Cape Province to Natal. It is not suitable for very dry positions. Known in S. Africa as the 'Berg Lily,' where it flowers in mid-December.

**G. clavata.** Smaller than the preceding; *fl.* greenish-white with darker green longitudinal bands on long drooping pedicels and short perianth segments. S. Africa. Rarely grown and not nearly so fine a plant as *G. candicans.*

**G. princeps.** Closely allied to *G. candicans,* but rather smaller. Late summer. Rarely grown, Eastern Regions of S. Africa.

**G. viridiflora.** *Fl.* greenish-white. Probably not in cultivation at present.

# GLADIOLUS *Iridaceae*

THIS IS a very large genus, mainly of S. African corms but also extending through Tropical Africa and Asia Minor into S. Europe. By gladiolus the average gardener understands only the large-flowered hybrids which are so extensively grown for summer flowering and as cut flowers; the varieties of these are now very numerous indeed. The species of *Gladiolus* are, however, equally beautiful, although much quieter and smaller in flower and without the flamboyance of the larger hybrids. Many of them, however, flower in the spring or early summer after making their growth in the winter and so are only suitable for cool greenhouse treatment. It is sad that out of a genus of 150 or more species, so few are in cultivation and there is a great need of a modern and authoritative monograph of the genus. In these circumstances and since I have also no knowledge of them growing in S. Africa I have confined my account of the species to only a very small proportion of those which might be cultivated in this country if they could be obtained. Their popularity was greater at the end of the eighteenth century when S. African plants were being introduced for conservatories in great quantities and many are portrayed in the early issues of the Botanical Magazine.

The cultivation of the species and of the hybrids is very different and so it is proposed to treat them here separately, dealing first with the hybrids and then with the species. The origin of the hybrids is by now so mixed and they have developed so far from their original parent species that there would be little help to the gardener in trying to trace them back here although it is one of the great success stories of the horticultural world comparable with the development of the dahlia or the chrysanthemum.

The flowers of gladioli are funnel-shaped and slightly irregular, borne on a spike which is often one-sided so that the flowers all face in one direction. The corms are flattened and the leaves sword-like and plaited. The range of colours covered is very wide although among the hybrids there is not yet a good blue.

## (*a*) Hybrid gladioli

These are usually planted as mature corms in April or early May and the time of flowering will depend to some extent on the season of planting. The corms should be planted about 4 in. deep and an open sunny position is best. They are rarely successful in the shade. A sandy soil or a loam

144

*Plate 23:* Peacock Moraeas. Top and bottom, *M. pavonia* var. *magnifica*. Left, *M. villosa* hybrid. Right, *M. villosa*, an unusually fine purple form

*Plate* 24: Muscari, Chionodoxa, Scilla and other Spring Bulbs. 1, *Hyacinthus amethystinus.*
blue and white forms. 2, *M. tubergenianum.* 3, *M. paradoxum.* 4, *M. moschatum.* 5, *Hyacinthus
dalmaticus.* 6, *C. luciliae,* blue, white and pink forms. 7, *S. sibirica* var. *atrocoerulea.* 8, *C.
gigantea,* blue and white forms. 9, *S. sibirica* var. *taurica.* 10, *S. sibirica* var. *alba.* 11, *M.
latifolium.* 12,13, *S. bifolia* (blue, white and pink forms). 14, *S. sibirica.* 15, *M. neglectum.* 16, *C.
tmoli.* 17, *S. tubergeniana.* 18, *C. sardensis.* 19, *Puschkinia scilloides.* 20, *Hyacinthus azureus.*
21, *C. nana*

*Plate* 25: DWARF NARCISSUS. 1, *N. triandrus* var. *albus*. 2, *N. ' Hawera '*. 3, *N. obvallaris*. 4, *N. pseudonarcissus*, the Lent Lily. 5, *N. ' Minicycla '*. 6, *N. bulbocodium* var. *conspicuus*. 7, *N. canaliculatus*. 8, *N. bulbocodium* var. *obesus*. 9, *N. cyclamineus*. 10, *N. watieri*. 11, *N. rupicola*. 12, *N. asturiensis*. 13, *N. cantabricus* var. *monophyllus*

*Plate* 26: SOME MODERN DAFFODILS. 1, 'Spellbinder'. 2, 'Ceylon'. 3, 'Kingscourt'. 4, 'Hunter's Moon'. 5, 'Cantatrice'. 6, 'Jenny'. 7, 'Preamble'. 8, 'Amberley'

suits them best provided it has in the previous autumn been well enriched with old manure or compost. The hybrid gladioli need to be treated generously in this respect to ensure good spikes. It is important also not to allow them to become very dry during the growing season. A dressing of bone meal or a complete fertiliser at planting time will also help to develop the spikes. Good drainage, as in the case of practically all the S. African bulbs and corms is important and so a heavy clay soil needs to be well worked and lightened with compost or even sand before planting. Early staking is necessary in nearly all cases of the hybrid gladioli since even with the miniatures the spikes are so heavy, that after a storm they will not stand up securely on their own. If grown in rows for cutting they can be easily supported with stakes at intervals joined by twine. All corms should be taken up by early November at latest and dried off. Then the stems should be cut off and the mature corms, which have formed on top of the old ones, should be separated and stored in a dry place. Generally numerous cormlets develop round the old corm and these can be grown on separately and will form mature corms for flowering in two or three years. If the cormlets have become very dry and hard in the winter, they can be soaked in water before planting with advantage. Gladioli can also be raised from seed and will flower in three to five years but the hybrids are so mixed in parentage that it is hardly worth growing them in this way.

The hybrid gladioli are usually classified for convenience and Show purposes according to size of flower, the early flowering *nanus* or *colvillei* group being treated separately. Here the scheme of the British Gladiolus Society is following although I have amalgamated together some of their classes. Since a large number of new varieties appear each year and the catalogues of the suppliers list with descriptions a large and very varied number only a comparatively small selection under each colour is given here. The majority of these are ones which have gained awards in the Wisley Trials or have been outstanding in the R.H.S. Shows at Vincent Square but undoubtedly there are many other good ones and the best of these, which are new and rare, will in a very few years become the standard varieties.

### EARLY FLOWERING NANUS GROUP

These were originally raised from a cross between the pale yellow *G. tristis* and the red *G. cardinalis* and are still often called *G. × colvillei* after the nurseryman at Chelsea who first introduced them to popularity and some of the original varieties are still grown. They have retained a delicacy which otherwise is only found in the species and their near hybrids. They flower much earlier than the larger hybrids, generally from April to early June and so should be treated quite differently. They should be planted in autumn in pots for the cool greenhouse, about 5 corms in a 6 in. pot or in the soil of a cool frame. The pots may be plunged outside until there is a good root development or until the beginning of December when they should be brought into the house. They do not require much heat. In warm areas they can be grown in a border under a wall with some protection from ashes or bracken and will survive all but the most severe winters. They may also be planted in early spring for flowering in June. They rarely grow more than 2 ft. high and are excellent as cut flowers since many varieties have darker blotches and other markings around the throat.

'ACKERMAN' Bright orange-scarlet with darker flaking around throat. One of the original varieties.

'AMANDA MAHY' Deep salmon-pink with small violet flaking. A vigorous variety.

'BLUSHING BRIDE' White with bright carmine flaking.

'NYMPH' White with crimson flakes, vigorous.

* 'PEACH BLOSSOM' A shell-pink. One of the oldest but still one of the most beautiful.

* 'SPITFIRE' Deep salmon-orange with small violet flakes. One of the most striking varieties.

'THE BRIDE' Pure white, one of the original varieties but still vigorous and excellent for cutting. Early flowering.


## MINIATURE- AND SMALL-FLOWERED HYBRID GLADIOLI

These include the British Gladiolus Society's classes:

(1*a*) Midget-flowered with florets not exceeding 1½ in. across.
(1*b*) Miniature-flowered with florets over 1½ in. but not exceeding 2½ in. across.
(1*c*) Small-flowered with florets over 2½ in. and not exceeding 4 in. across.

These have become very popular in recent years and many attractive varieties have been raised, some with ruffled edges to the flowers. They are particularly suitable for cutting. In the garden they vary in height from 2–4 ft., and height is not necessarily related to size of flower. Unfortunately many of them do not build up large corms so vigorously as the larger-flowered varieties and so they have remained relatively more expensive. Their cultivation is similar to that of the large-flowered ones. The Butterfly gladioli are included in this group.

### Creamy-white and pale yellow

'ARES' (1*c*) Butterfly. Pale creamy-yellow with bright reddish blotch. Early flowering.

'WHITE CITY' Creamy-white, with green marking on lower petal, mauvish-purple throat.

### Pale pink and salmon-pink

'BO-PEEP' (1*c*) Pale terracotta with yellow throat and ruffled edge.

'ELF' (1*c*) Butterfly, widely spaced and delicate *fl.* but sometimes large

# Gladiolus

enough to be classified as (1*d*). Salmon with yellow blotch at throat, petals lightly overlaid with shrimp-red.

'KATHLEEN FERRIER' Salmon-pink, overlaid with orange, throat crimson.

### Deep pink

'FEMINA' (1*c*) Butterfly. Pale carmine and rose with dutch vermilion blotches at throat and a band of white outside.

* 'MELODIE' (1*c*) Butterfly, but sometimes large enough to be (1*d*). Deep pink with orange-scarlet blotches banded with cream. A striking colour.

'PICCOLO' Carmine Rose with red throat.

### Orange-scarlet and scarlet and crimson

* 'APEX' (1*c*) Crimson-red with creamy-white edge. A seedling from 'Atom' but generally of better constitution.

'ATOM' Scarlet-red with creamy-white edge. *Fl.* well spaced. A primulinus hybrid. Lovely for flower decorations.

'URANUS' Deep crimson with cream throat.

* 'VIVALDI' (1*c*) Butterfly. Orange-scarlet, with deeper scarlet blotch and pale throat. A popular and conspicuous variety, sometimes reaching (1*d*) in size.

### Pale yellow to light orange

'BONANZA' (1*c*) Straw-yellow with deeper yellow blotch at throat and light scarlet markings.

'CITRONELLA' Pale yellow. Slender. Primulinus hybrid.

'CRINKLETTE' Salmon-orange, heavily frilled and ruffled at edge.

'DONALD DUCK' (1*c*) Butterfly. Mimosa-yellow with red blotch.

* 'GREEN WOODPECKER' (1*c*) Deep yellowish lime-green with crimson blotch. A most unusual colour. Outstanding for flower decoration.

'GREENLAND' (1*c*) Pale creamy-yellow with green flush. An unusual colour.

'PEGASUS' A primulinus hybrid. Creamy-white with red tips to petals and red markings.

* 'TOPOLINO' (1*c*) Butterfly. Primrose-yellow with orange-scarlet blotch.

## LARGE-FLOWERED HYBRIDS

These include those classified by the British Gladiolus Society as:

(1*d*) Medium-flowered with florets over 4 in. and not exceeding 5 in. across.
(1*e*) Large-flowered with florets over 5 in. and not exceeding 6 in. across.
(1*f*) Giant-flowered with florets over 6 in. across.

The majority of these will reach 4 ft. in height if well cultivated.

'ANTARCTIC' (1*e*) Tall, white with pale cream throat with a touch of purple at the base, frilled edges.

147

# Gladiolus

'BALLERINA' (1*d*) Ivory-white with rose-pink blotch at throat. Large spike.

'ICE FOLLIES' (1*d*) Tall, white with cream at throat. Classified by some growers as a Butterfly type.

'LEIF ERICSSON' (1*e*) Tall, large-flowered, cream or very pale yellow, tinged green at the throat.

'SNOW PRINCESS' Tall, milk-white, tinged green at throat, large-flowered. A vigorous grower.

## Pale yellow to light orange

'ACCA LAURENTIA' (1*d*) Orange-red. Early flowering.

'ARANJUEZ' (1*d*) Deep yellow overlaid with orange-red. An older variety of medium size.

'HANS VAN MEEGEREN' (1*d*) Deep yellow.

'HOKUS POCUS' (1*d*) Deep lemon-yellow with prominent blotch of deep red. An old variety but early and free flowering.

'HOPMAN'S GLORY' (1*d*) Deep yellow, an old variety and not as large in *fl.* as some, but of good substance and form. Early flowering.

'PACTOLUS' (1*d*) Deep yellow flushed with orange-red, lower petals pale yellow with a blotch of vermilion-orange. Early flowering. An older variety.

## Pale pink and salmon

'BENARES' (1*e*) Pale salmon-pink with crimson markings.

'BERMUDA' Light salmon-pink with white throat, heavily ruffled.

\* 'EVANGELINE' (1*f*) Very large-flowered and a magnificent exhibition variety with a large well-formed spike. Pale salmon-pink.

'HOLLAND'S GLORY' (1*e*) Apricot-pink, sulphur-yellow throat and yellow blotch.

\* 'KOSMOS' (1*e*) Very large-flowered, deep salmon-pink with outer splashing of orange-red, with pale yellow blotch.

'LEEWENHOORST' (1*f*) Salmon-pink, very large *fl.* An effective variety.

'PICARDY' (1*f*) An old favourite, salmon-pink and with large *fl.*

'POLYNESIA' (1*e*) Outer petals pale pinkish-red, flecked with deeper colour, inner petals cream flushed with red, throat deep yellow with red blotch. A striking colour combination.

## Deep pink and orange-pink

\* 'ALFRED NOBEL' (1*e*) Deep rose with flush of scarlet, with large cream blotch at throat.

'DR. FLEMING' (1*e*) Medium pink with white throat. Vigorous and tall

'GENERAL EISENHOWER' Very large-flowered. Deep pink.

'PALET' (1*e*) Deep pink with mauve blotch and throat. An unusual colour combination.

'ROSA VAN LIMA' (Rose of Lima) Rose-pink.

148

# Gladiolus

### Orange-scarlet, scarlet and blood-red

* ' ATLANTIC ' (1e) Bright mandarin-red, shading to vermilion in inner petals. An unusually fine variety with tall spikes of Show standard.

' CIRCE ' (1e) Poppy-red with cream blotch and crimson feathering. Early flowering.

' JO WAGENAAR ' (1e) Bright blood-red, slightly hooded. An unusually fine variety.

' JOHAN VAN KONYNENBURG ' (1e) Orange-scarlet. Very bright colour.

' NEW EUROPE ' (1e) Mandarin-red, very brilliant colour.

' OSCAR ' (1f) Very large-flowered. Signal-red. Brilliant in colour.

* ' VOLCANO ' (1d) Dutch vermilion, very brilliant colour.

### Deep crimson and maroon

' ARABIAN NIGHT ' (1d) Very dark maroon-red, especially at edges of petals.

' ATATURK ' Very dark maroon-purple. Flower of medium size.

' CASWALLOWN ' (1e) Late flowering. Deep crimson-scarlet.

' HARRY HOPKINS ' (1e) Deep wine-red.

' HAWAII ' Deep mahogany-red, lighter towards edge.

* ' MANSOER ' (1e) Deep blood-red overlaid with maroon, velvety. A beautiful variety.

' TOBRUK ' (1d) Ruby-red, becoming deep maroon near edges of petals, velvety texture. An old variety but still worth growing.

### Violet-blue and pale mauvish-blue

' ABU HASSAN ' (1d) Deep violet-blue. Early flowering.

* ' BLUE CONQUEROR ' (1d) Violet-blue, deepening towards margin to royal purple, throat silvery-blue. A very rich deep colour, deep crimson blotch.

' BLUE LOU ' (1e) Light violet-blue, veined with royal purple. A promising newer variety, better than its name suggests.

' MAJOLICA ' (1e) Light lavender-blue with deep purple blotch, deeper blue colour on outside.

* ' OBERBAYERN ' (1d) Deep violet-blue with large creamy-white throat. A striking colour combination.

' PFITZER'S SENSATION ' (1e) Deep violet-blue becoming royal purple at tips, throat white. One of the finest deep violet-blue varieties yet raised.

* ' RAVEL ' (1d) Light violet-blue with deep blotch and streaks of deep crimson. An older variety but still one of the best in its colour.

' SALMAN'S SENSATION ' (1e) Dark violet-blue with deeper mauve markings and light throat.

### Smoky-pinks and shades of dusky-purples

' KEUKENHOF ' (1e) Pale fuchsine-purple with cream blotch and white mid-rib, colour deepest towards edge. Outer petals overlaid with pink.

' UHU ' Dusky-pink overlaid with pale mottling of bluish grey, yellow throat, marked with red.

## (*b*) Gladiolus species and a few hybrids of them

The species of gladiolus from the Cape District of S. Africa flower for the most part during our winter or early spring and so are only suitable for greenhouse treatment. They do not, however, require much heat and can be grown either in boxes, pots or planted out in a bed made up on the bench. The majority start into growth during our autumn or early winter and should then be watered in moderation but never allowed to become sodden. Good drainage is most necessary. Winter damp is probably their greatest difficulty in this country and any heat given is required more to keep the atmosphere from being too damp especially in foggy weather than to force them on.

For grace and quiet charm of flower a number of them, however, have very high claims on a place in our house, particularly as several are also quite strongly scented. After they have died down the corms should either be lifted and replanted in the autumn or else kept quite dry.

The S. African species described and chiefly grown in this country are those from the winter rainfall area of the Cape districts. In regions of S. Africa a little further north and in some of the mountain ranges, however, there are areas with summer rainfall where the bulbs rest in winter and flower in summer such as *G. psittacinus* and *G. primulinus*. The species from these areas have so far been little grown in this country but might prove more amenable to cultivation, being taken up and dried off in winter like the large-flowered hybrids. Coming from warmer districts they tend, however, to be more tender.

In recent years a number of very lovely hybrids retaining the grace and delicacy of the species and many with fine scent but slightly larger flowers have been raised and shown by Mr. T. T. Barnard. Their parentage is in most cases complicated and the species used include *G. carinatus*, *G. grandis*, *G. caryophyllaceus*, *G. tristis* and its var. *concolor*. Probably ' Christabel,' a primrose-yellow variety with the upper petals shaded and veined with purple, is so far the best established but a number of others have been named and received awards and we hope may become more plentiful.

The three S. European species are hardy in warm places and sometimes spread and seed freely. *G. byzantinus* is probably the best and most striking of these but in all the colour is a rather fierce deep pinkish-magenta.

**G. alatus.** Wing-flowered Cornflag or Kalkoentjie. Little Turkey. Dwarf, up to 1 ft., generally less. Stem slender with 5–10 tawny-orange *fl.* 1½ in.

# *Gladiolus*

across, veined with deeper orange-red and with prominent yellow markings on lower petals and with yellow throat. Lateral petals considerably wider than others. Scented. S.W. District of Cape Province, S. Africa, flowering in spring there (Sept.-Oct.). A rose-pink variety is also recorded.

**G. atroviolaceus.** Stem up to 2 ft. slender and wiry. *Fl.* 3–5, dark purple or violet-purple rather variable in colour, marked at throat with lighter colour. Corm small; *l.* linear, grasslike. Turkey, May-July. We found this sp. densely colouring a very damp grass meadow in N.E. Turkey and flowering in early July. An attractive graceful plant, worthy of more trial in English gardens and probably as hardy as *G. byzantinus.*

**G. blandus.** Broad leaved Painted Lady or Bergpijpie. Stem slender up to 2 ft. but variable with 3–10 *fl.* 2 in. across, blush pink outside, very pale, almost white inside with conspicuous small deeper pink blotches on lower petals. Petals waved at edge. Scentless. Corms small. Cape Peninsula where it flowers Sept.-Jan. on mountain slopes. Paler forms of *G. colvillei* resemble this but are larger and stouter. A number of varieties have been described.

Var. **albidus.** Pure white inside, almost white outside.

Var. **carneus.** Pale mauvish-pink.

Var. **erubescens.** Much larger and stouter up to 3 ft. and with 8–10 *fl.* 2½ in. across and all opening together. Rich rosy-pink with deeper median streaks of crimson on lower petals, but no blotch. Conspicuous in flower but not known in the wild. Late flowering, in England in October.

Var. **mortonius.** Very pale blush-pink.

**G. byzantinus.** Stem up to 2½ ft. with 6–10 *fl.* of strong magenta-crimson. June-July. E. Mediterranean regions where it is often common and hardy in Southern and Western areas in well-drained sunny positions and sometimes naturalising and spreading freely. Conspicuous for its colour. There is also a good white form but it is usually shy to flower.

**G. cardinalis.** Waterfall Gladiolus. Stem up to 2 ft. with large bright crimson *fl.* up to 3 in. across, spike usually curved. July-Aug. in England; Nov.-Dec. in S. Africa. Cape districts, where it grows in semi-shade. One of parents of modern hybrids. This is a winter grower with a very long growing season and so is likely to need some winter protection in most areas. Its resting period is immediately after flowering till October.

**G. carinatus.** Blue Afrikander. Stem slender up to 2 ft. with 3 or 4 rather small dainty *fl.* pale mauve with yellow markings on lower petals and deeper mauve central stripe. Variable in colour, strongly scented. S.W. districts of Cape in sandy places.

**G. caryophyllaceus.** Sand Veld Lelie or Lily, Pink Afrikander. Stem up to 2 ft. with up to 6 medium sized rose-pink *fl.* about 2 in. across. Lower petals are marked with deep colour. Sweetly scented. Cape. Syn. *G. hirsutus.*

**G. cruentus.** Stem up to 3 ft. with a few large scarlet *fl.* up to 4 in. across with white patches on lower petals and yellow around throat. A very handsome sp. Basutoland, Natal. Flowering Dec.-Feb. in S. Africa; September in England. One of parents of modern hybrids. Reported now as rare in wild.

**G. gracilis.** Slender Cornflag. Stem very slender but wiry. *Fl.* 2–6 to stem, blue generally in the wild but less attractive colour forms sometimes arise from seed in pale pink or mauve, spotted at base on lower petals. S.W. Cape districts where it flowers in spring, in England April. Scented. *L.* very narrow, rushlike.

**G. grandis.** Large Brown Afrikander. *Fl.* pale reddish-brown, shaded with yellow but variable. Stem 2 ft. with 3 or 4 quite large *fl.* Distinguished for its strong carnation scent in the evening. Petals rather narrow, pointed, undulating at edge. S.W. Cape district.

**G. hirsutus.** A syn. of *G. caryophyllaceus.*

**G. illyricus.** Stem slender up to 1½ ft. with 3–6 loosely spaced *fl.* of bright magenta-purple. Mediterranean regions. Hardy in warmer areas but not so free spreading or vigorous as *G. byzantinus*, and recorded as wild in Britain in a very few places. June-July.

**G. orchidiflorus.** Green Kalkoentjie, *fl.* small, greenish-yellow and white with a reddish-brown centre. Scented. An unusual and delicate *fl.* that is worth growing as a cool house plant, rather tender outside. S.W. Cape districts where it flowers in spring.

**G. primulinus.** The gladiolus of the Victoria Falls where it is said to grow in the spray cloud. Stem up to 2½ ft. *Fl.* pale yellow, hooded, widely spaced. Also found in drier districts of Tanganyika and it has been suggested that there are two separate sp. under this name, the plant from Victoria Falls being renamed *G. nebulicola*, a fitting name but one not yet generally adopted. Renowned as a parent of so many modern hybrids.

**G. psittacinus.** Parrot Gladiolus. Stem quite short up to 3 or even 4 ft. Up to 12 *fl.*, yellow heavily flushed and spotted with orange-red, sometimes almost scarlet. A vigorous plant. Widely distributed in S. Africa and in Rhodesia. One of sp. which have contributed to modern hybrids.

**G. quartinianus.** A handsome plant from the mountains of Equatorial Africa. *Fl.* yellow, heavily flushed and spotted with scarlet. Strong growing in wild and a parent of some modern hybrids.

**G. segetum.** A rosy-purple or rosy-magenta sp. from the cornfields of S. Europe, resembling *G. illyricus*, but rather stouter. Almost hardy. May-June.

**G. tristis.** Yellow Marsh Afrikander. Stem slender up to 1½ ft. with only 3–4 *fl.* but these are quite large, up to 3 in. across. Pale sulphur-yellow, tinged dull red on outside. Distinguished for its sweet scent. May. *L.* narrow, rushlike. Cape districts. Natal. This is the hardiest of the winter growing Cape sp. and has been established successfully in sheltered places in the South and West of England.

## Gloriosa

Var. **concolor.** Very pale sulphur-yellow without red colouring. Tends to be slightly deeper in colour and larger in *fl.* and slightly hardier. Has been in cultivation in Europe since the 18th century.

**G. viperatus.** A syn. of *G. orchidiflorus.*


# †GLORIOSA *Liliaceae*

CLIMBING, scrambling or prostrate trailing plants with very conspicuous flowers in which the segments are bent backwards and upwards like those on a Turk's-Cap Lily but are long and narrow with undulating edges while the stigma and stamens project downwards. The flower in general looks like some very exotic insect, floating at the end of long pedicels. Coming from Central Africa, N. Rhodesia and the Transvaal it is not generally hardy in this country and is usually grown as an Intermediate greenhouse plant, although *G. superba* has been successfully planted out during warm summers and flowered well in this country. The leaves are narrow and have tendrils at their tips by which they climb or scramble. The root is a thick rather brittle tuber which may fork and will grow up to nine inches in length. In winter it should be rested in dry soil. The flowers are so striking that they are worth a definite effort to grow them satisfactorily. Plenty of moisture and feeding and a rather humid atmosphere in summer seem to suit them best and they need sticks or other support, sometimes being grown on a small trellis.

**G. abyssinica.** *Fl.* deep yellow, 2–3 in. across, perianth segments reflexed but not crisped as in other sp. Less tall than *G. rothschildiana* or *G. superba.* Abyssinia, tropical Africa. Summer, depending on the amount of heat given.

\* **G. rothschildiana.** Probably the finest sp. *Fl.* bright crimson-red with long segments, waved and crisped at edge, up to 3½ in. long, yellow at base on first opening, borne on long pedicels up to 4 in. Tropical Africa, Uganda where it sprawls over the ground in dry sandy places and is very conspicuous. Up to 6 ft. Needs warm greenhouse treatment in this country.
Var. **citrina,** with yellow *fl.* marked with deep purple.

**G. simplex.** Better known as *G. virescens.* *Fl.* deep reddish-orange with yellow at base and on underneath of segments, with broader segments only slightly undulating at edge. Stems up to 4 ft. Summer. Tropical Africa, south to Natal and Rhodesia. Syn. *G. virescens.*
Var. **grandiflora,** larger in *fl.* and bright yellow but with narrower segments. Tropical Africa.

\* **G. superba.** *Fl.* deep orange and red or deep clear yellow, very conspicuous, segments much crisped at edge all along, undulating at edge. Up to 6 ft.

Summer. Tropical Africa south to N. Transvaal; India. The best known sp. in cultivation and probably the hardiest.

**G. virescens.** A syn. of *G. simplex.*

# GYNANDRIRIS *Iridaceae*

A MONOTYPIC genus formerly included in *Iris* and containing only one sp. *G. sisyrinchium*, which is still better known under *Iris*. Its small bright lilac-blue flowers with golden and white markings are very abundant in S. Europe, particularly by the seaside and in sandy places by the Mediterranean in spring and early summer. They are borne on short stems rarely more than 8 in. high and open in succession but each only lasts a day. Rootstock is a corm, not a bulb as in *Iris*, but it is netted like a reticulate iris. Leaves are narrow and filiform. Unfortunately it is rarely successful for long in English gardens where it is usually very shy-flowering. A good summer baking is certainly required.

# †HABRANTHUS *Amaryllidaceae*

A SMALL genus of beautiful bulbous plants from S. America with flowers slightly larger than those of *Zephyranthes* but rather smaller than those of *Hippeastrum*, to both of which genera it is closely related and with which its species have frequently played musical chairs. It is also distinguished by having stamens of unequal lengths, generally of four different lengths. Unfortunately none of the species are very hardy and can only be grown outside in really warm situations in this country such as a sunny border beneath a wall, but they are excellent in the cool greenhouse. The flowers are funnel-shaped and usually solitary or occasionally two and distinguished from *Hippeastrum* by the spathe which sheathes the base of the pedicel. The best-known species *H. pratensis* has been recently lost to *Hippeastrum*.

**H. advenus.** See under *Hippeastrum advenum.*

**H. andersonii.** *Fl.* golden-yellow, flushed coppery-brown outside and with dull red streaks towards base, but variable in colour, about $1\frac{1}{2}$ in. long, erect, single on stems of 4–6 in. Bulb globose with dark tunic; *l.* narrow, linear, slightly glaucous and only just appearing at time of flowering. May-June but sometimes in early autumn as well. S. America, Argentina, Uruguay, S. Chile. Hardy in a warm situation with a little winter protection. Syn. *Zephyranthes andersonii.*

# Habranthus

Var. **texanus.** *Fl.* yellow with more rounded segments and slightly less copper flush on outside. Southern U.S.A. Texas, but there is some doubt as to whether it is native there or introduced.

**H. brachyandrus.** *Fl.* large, solitary, erect on long peduncle up to 1 ft. with a pedicel of 2 in. and long spathe, funnel-shaped, large, pale rose-pink, much veined and deepening to claret at base both inside and out, 3½ in. long and nearly as much across. July–Sept. Bulb ovoid; *l.* linear up to 1 ft. developed before *fl.* S. America, Argentina. A very beautiful but unfortunately also rare sp. There are records of its having flowered outside in a warm border but it would probably be safer in a cool greenhouse.

**H. cardinalis.** *Fl.* large, funnel-shaped, opening widely, pale scarlet, 3 in. long by 3 in. across. Spathe rose-pink. June. *L.* strap-shaped with the *fl.* The exact native habitat of this rare and beautiful plant is unknown but almost certainly it is S. American. Probably nearly hardy but safest in a cool greenhouse.

**H. gracilifolius.** Several *fl.* to a stem, small, pale pink with deeper veins, campanulate, 1 in. long and as much across, appearing before the *l.*, spathe pale green; *fl.* said only to open in the sun, base of *fl.* green. Sept.–Nov. *L.* slender, filiform. S. America, Uruguay. Very rare in cultivation. Probably best cultivated in a cool greenhouse.

**H. pratensis.** See under *Hippeastrum pratense.*

**H. robustus.** Large, single, funnel-shaped, opening widely, 3 in. across by 3 in. long, pale pink with deeper veining and green throat, almost white near base but with slightly deeper flushes of pink near tips of segments, stem rather stout and *fl.* with long pedicel. Early Autumn. Bulb globose with dark brown tunic; *l.* linear, slightly glaucous, channelled. S. America, probably Uruguay, but plants in cultivation appear to derive from bulbs sent through the Argentine. Nearly hardy and has been grown successfully outside in this country but in most areas best grown as a cool greenhouse plant. It resembles *Zephyranthes grandiflora* in many characters, but with larger *fl.* more green at base and longer pedicel. Syn. *Zephyranthes robusta, Z. brachyandrus* (in part only), *Hippeastrum tubispathum* (in part only).

**H. texanus.** See under *H. andersonii.*

**H. versicolor.** Known as the " Changeable Habranthus." *Fl.* single, red in bud, but as it opens fading to white with pink tinge at tip of petal and deep pink base; *fl.* 2 in. long by 2 in. across. Stem 5–6 in. with pedicel of 1½ in. and rose-pink spathe. Bulb oblong with dark tunic; *l.* linear, up to 1 ft. long. Flowering usually in winter after summer rest and so best grown in a cool greenhouse. S. America, probably Uruguay and Brazil.

# †HAEMANTHUS *Amaryllidaceae*

A LARGE genus of S. African and Central African bulbous plants with flowers like brilliantly coloured shaving brushes and leaves like green leathery razor-strops. Unfortunately none of the species are really hardy but they are good plants for a cool or intermediate greenhouse where they can be planted out in a bed or given really large pots. In S. Africa they are known under various names such as " Paint Brush," " April Fools " and " Torch Lilies." The flower-heads are undoubtedly more peculiar than beautiful, consisting of dense umbels of many small flowers with long cylindrical perianth segments joined in a tube and prominently protruding stamens. These are framed at the base with two or more large and brightly coloured bracts which take the place of petals. Some of the S. African species such as *H. coccineus* need a very definite period of resting and even baking after the leaves have died down and before they flower and all species need some such rest although the leaves may not completely die away. After flowering they need to be kept growing and watered until the leaves begin to show signs of dying off. Once potted they should be left unshifted as long as possible even though potbound and the large fleshy bulb may with advantage be encouraged with weak liquid manure when in growth. They should not be planted deeply but with the neck of the bulb just covered. The stems are thick and fleshy and often spotted and the leaves thick and leathery in the case of the Cape species. Unfortunately only a few are in cultivation.

**H. albiflos.** Stem up to 1 ft. *Fl.* white or greenish-white with upright and protruding stamens in umbels about 1 in. across, bracts pale greenish-white. *Fl.* borne with the *l.* which are oblong, strap-shaped and leathery with ciliate margins. Summer flowering. S. Africa.

**H. coccineus.** One of the most striking both in *l.* and *fl.* *Fl.* produced without the *l.* on short thick fleshy and spotted stems, generally not more than 9 in. high. *Fl.* heads large, coral red with prominent upright stamens, umbel up to 3 in. across and subtended by thick, fleshy, scarlet bracts larger than the umbel. September. *L.* 2 to a bulb, very large, broadly strap-shaped and up to 2 ft. in length by 6 in. wide, lying flat on the ground, only developing after the *fl.* and dying away in the summer. Bulb large, up to 3 in. across. S. Africa, where it flowers in March or April after the summer. Flowering in this country fairly regularly provided that bulbs are mature and are given a really good summer ripening.

**H. katharinae.** The " Blood Flower." Stem tall, 1–2 ft. with large round umbels up to 6 in. across, packed with bright scarlet, stalked *fl.* with prominent stamens. July-August. *L.* large, oblong but not so leathery as in two

156

previous sp. and borne on a separate stem which does not die away at time of flowering. Bulb very large, globular. Natal, E. Transvaal, S. Rhodesia. Best grown in tubs or planted out in an intermediate greenhouse and requiring plenty of space and some warmth while growing, but a very handsome plant.

**H. magnificus.** "Royal Paint Brush." Flower stem up to 15 in. with large umbel up to 5 or 6 in. across of orange-scarlet *fl.* with obtruding golden stamens. Bracts dull red. A pink-flowered variety is also known and one (var. *insignis*) in which the bracts develop so much that they overtop the *fl.* Summer flowering. *L.* large, oblong with a wavy edge and borne on a separate stem. Bulb very large. Only suited to an intermediate or warm house. Natal and Transvaal where it *fl.* in October.

# † HERBERTIA *Iridaceae*

A SMALL genus, native of Southern N. America and S. America and named in honour of Dean William Herbert who was one of our leading authorities on bulbous plants in the first half of the last century. Probably only one sp. *H. pulchella* is now grown in English collections and even that is very rare. It is only hardy in very warm situations and is usually best grown as a cool greenhouse plant in pots.

**H. pulchella.** *Fl.* pale blue-purple, with 6 segments and a short tube, 6 in.–1 ft. white at base and with some hairs and flecked with lilac. The three outer segments are much larger than the inner ones and open flat. They are much narrower at their base than on the blades giving the *fl.* a slightly spidery appearance rather like that of a *Cypella*. Corm rounded, small; *l.* narrow, slightly pleated.

# HERMODACTYLUS *Iridaceae*

A MONOTYPIC genus closely related to *Iris* under which its only species *H. tuberosus* is often found. Distinguished from *Iris* by its unilocular ovary.

**H. tuberosus.** A peculiar *fl.* of sombre colouring, sometimes known as the "Snake's Head." Stem rather weak, up to 1 ft. with a single *fl.* about 2 in. across. Falls dark purplish-black with orbicular blade, claw and standards rather bright yellowish-green. April-May. Bulb irregular, rather narrow, almost tuberous. *L.* linear or narrowly lanceolate, long, having four sides. Common in Greece where it grows on the mountains and E. Mediterranean regions. Hardy but should be planted in a warm sunny position. Syn. *Iris tuberosa.*

# †HIPPEASTRUM *Amaryllidaceae*

THE GENUS *Hippeastrum* is best known for the magnificent series of greenhouse hybrids which are so often described as ' Amaryllis.' They are, however, quite separate from that genus which contains only one species, the Belladonna lily. In addition to the large-flowered hybrids there are also several species of much smaller-flowering bulbs from S. America which are suitable for a cool greenhouse. None, unfortunately, can be described as generally hardy although two, *H. advenum* and *H. pratense*, have been grown outside successfully in some very warm places in this country.

The hybrid hippeastrums are some of the most striking and imposing of all bulbous flowers and especially so since they bloom in late winter or early spring depending on the amount of heat given. It is possible to grow and flower them successfully in a cool greenhouse or even on a warm window ledge but undoubtedly they do much better in a rather warmer and more moist house where the minimum temperature does not go below 55°F. In order to bring them into flower during the winter the bulbs will need to be plunged in a bed with bottom heat giving a temperature of 60°F. or higher. The large bulbs should not be over-potted and need not be fully covered with soil. They are usually potted or re-potted during the winter after their rest, but this need not be done each year. They should not be given much water until the buds begin to show. After they have flowered the bulbs should be kept growing through the summer until the foliage begins to show signs of dying down, when they should be rested on their sides for two or three months before being started again into growth. During growth feeding with liquid manure is desirable and in order to get really good flowers it is necessary to grow them generously. Numerous strains have been selected for self-coloured flowers ranging in colour from pure white to deep blood-red and the trumpets reach nearly six inches across. For those who like rather smaller flowers with more in a head on stems not quite so stout, the older hybrids such as *H. × ackermannii* and *H. × johnsonii* are still available and are excellent plants for the intermediate or even the cool greenhouse while strains derived from *H. rutilum* and *H. rutilum* var. *fulgidum* have scarlet flowers distinctly smaller and more graceful than those of the great trumpet hybrids.

**H. × ackermannii.** An old hybrid, sometimes and perhaps more correctly known as *H. acramannii*, with deep crimson-red trumpet-shaped *fl.* in late summer. Probably derived from *H. aulicum* as one parent. Summer flowering. Almost hardy and excellent for a cool greenhouse.

# *Hippeastrum*

**H. advenum.** *Fl.* stem up to 1 ft. with several *fl.* on pedicels up to 2 in. long. *Fl.* funnel-shaped, borne horizontally, bright crimson-scarlet with yellowish-green venation, petals rather narrow, 1½ to 1¾ in. long. Bulb ovoid to globular about the size of a small hen's egg, tunic very dark; *l.* strap-shaped, narrow, slightly glaucous, growing after *fl.* S. America, Chile. Almost hardy and has been flowered successfully outside in a very warm border beneath a greenhouse wall but in most areas better as a cool greenhouse plant. Late summer flowering. Syn. *Habranthus advenus.* A pale yellow form has also been recorded.

**H. aulicum.** Stem up to 1½ ft. with *fl.* large, 5–6 in. long, trumpet-shaped, scarlet-red, striped with deeper crimson inside and greenish at base. *L.* not glaucous, strap-shaped. Winter flowering. Central Brazil. A fine plant for the intermediate or even cool greenhouse.

**H. equestre.** *Fl.* bright scarlet-red, like a slightly smaller but otherwise typical ' Amaryllis ' hybrid. Known often as Barbados Lily although really native of Mexico, Tropical America and West Indies. Widely grown in tropical gardens and even naturalised where it seems to be almost perpetually in *fl.* Cool greenhouse but largely superseded in this country by larger flowering hybrids.

**H. × johnsonii.** One of the finest hybrids for cool or intermediate greenhouse, not so large as the modern hybrids but with much more grace. First raised by Mr. Johnson of Prescot near Liverpool from *H. vittatum × H. reginae* about 1798 but by inter-pollination and back crossing with seedlings and the parents it quickly became a hybrid group but with a fair degree of uniformity. Stem up to 2 ft. with up to 4 *fl.* Bright scarlet, green at base inside with narrow white streaks part way up each petal. Outside streaked with green near the base. *Fl.* funnel-shaped up to 5 in. long and 4 in. across when open. Spring. Bulb large up to 3 in. across; *l.* strap-shaped up to 2½ ft. long and 1½ in. across. This handsome plant was well portrayed both in Mrs. Bury's *Hexandrian Plants* and by Redouté. It is probably one of the easiest hippeastrums to grow.

**H. pratense.** More commonly known in gardens under *Habranthus pratensis.* Stem up to 1 ft.; *fl.* bright scarlet with yellow veined base, funnel-shaped, up to 3 in. across and up to 3 *fl.* to a stem. Spring and early summer. *L.* narrow, strap-shaped up to 1½ ft. and produced with the *fl.* S. America, S. Chile. Hardy in very favoured warm situations and a very attractive plant of brilliant colouring and not too large. Excellent also for the cool greenhouse.

**H. procerum.** See under *Worsleya rayneri.*

**H. reginae.** The " Mexican Lily." *Fl.* large, trumpet-shaped, bright scarlet-red with greenish-white star-like base, up to 5 in. across. Summer. *L.* long up to 2–3 ft., broadly strap-shaped, developed after *fl.* Intermediate greenhouse. Also found in Brazil, Peru and W. Indies.

**H. rutilum.** *Fl.* bright scarlet-crimson, open funnel-shaped, with green base and central streak, up to 4 in. across several to a stem. Petals pointed and

159

narrower than in *H. equestre.* Spring to early summer. *L.* strap-shaped, rather narrow, up to 1 ft. long. Venezuela, Brazil.

Var. **citrinum** with yellow *fl.* rare.

Var. **fulgidum** probably the finest crimson form, like a smaller and more graceful ' Amaryllis ' hybrid with more pointed petals. Intermediate or even cool greenhouse.

**H. vittatum.** *Fl.* large, white with scarlet stripes, up to 5 in. across. Stem up to 3 ft. with several *fl.* Andes of Peru. Cool greenhouse.

# † HOMERIA *Iridaceae*

A SMALL genus of S. African plants with corms, closely allied to *Moraea,* in which genus several have been placed in the past. The flowers are conspicuous, cup-shaped at first, then opening nearly flat, orange or yellow with segments unconnected right to the base. Only one species *H. collina* is in cultivation and several varieties of it have been named. Summer flowering, it should be treated as a cool greenhouse plant although if the corms are taken up and kept dry in the winter they can be planted outside for the summer in a warm sunny border with a reasonable chance of success in the same way as an *Ixia.* In S. Africa they are called " Tulps."

**H. collina.** Stem slender up to 1½ ft. sheathed by a single *l.* for lower half. *Fl.* numerous, borne singly on long erect peduncles, following each other in quick succession, 2½ in. across when open, yellow at base usually dull orange-red but variable in colour from bright scarlet to pale creamy-white. Early summer; in S. Africa Aug.-Oct. Corm slightly flattened with dark coarse fibrous tunic; *l.* single, narrow, linear. Cape districts. Common.

Var. **aurantiaca,** with brighter orange-red *fl.* with a yellow centre. Sometimes treated as a separate sp.

Var. **ochroleuca,** with yellow *fl.* Taller. Probably the plant shown and given an award as *H. comptoni* is only a fine form of this sp.

# HYACINTHUS *Liliaceae*

A GENUS of about 30 species, mostly native to the Mediterranean regions. Only a few species are in cultivation but from one of them, *H. orientalis,* has been raised the great race of florists' hyacinths which are so valuable for indoor growing and forcing in pots and bowls. A few species are also native to Tropical and S. Africa but these are not in cultivation in this country.

*Plate* 27: Some Modern Daffodils. 1, ' Polindra '. 2, ' Binkie '. 3, ' Ataturk '. 4, ' Green
Island '. 5, ' Mahmoud '. 6, ' Fermoy '. 7, ' Blarney's Daughter '. 8, ' Red Goblet '

*Plate* 28: Tigridia pavonia Varieties

*Plate* 29: DWARF TULIP SPECIES. 1, *T. clusiana.* 2, *T. orphanidea.* 3, *T. stellata.* 4, *T. sylvestris.* 5, *T. australis.* 6, *T. hageri.* 7, *T. ostrowskyana.* 8, *T. primulina.* 9, *T. batalini.* 10, *T. linifolia* x *batalini.* 11, *T. aitchisonii.* 12, *T. linifolia.* 13, *T. kolpakowskiana.* 14, *T. chrysantha.* 15, *T. celsiana.* 16, *T. biflora.* 17, *T. violacea.* 18, *T. urumiensis.* 19, *T. humilis.* 20, *T. tarda.* 21, *T. aucheriana*

*Plate* 30: EARLY-FLOWERING TULIPS. 1, *T. eichleri.* 2*a*, *T. kaufmanniana.* 2*b*, 'Cesar Frank'.
2*c*, 'Lady Rose'. 2*d*, 'Gluck'. 2*e*, 'Fritz Kreisler'

# Hyacinthus

The Mediterranean species are best grown in full sun and are delightful plants for the rock garden.

*Hyacinthus* is close to *Muscari* and *Scilla* as a genus but is distinguished from the former by the absence of any constriction at the mouth of the cylindrical tube and from *Scilla* by the perianth segments being joined in a tube for part of their length. By some botanists it has recently been divided into a number of genera of which *Bellevalia* and *Hyacinthella* are the most used, leaving only *H. orientalis* in *Hyacinthus*, but in view of the fact that the differentiations are not very strongly defined and have been little adopted by horticulturists it seems better to describe the few species grown under *Hyacinthus* even if it does not represent a very uniform genus. The bulbs are uniformly globose and fleshy.

* **H. amethystinus.** *Fl.* tubular, drooping, a delicate shade of Cambridge porcelain-blue, not amethyst, and one of the most beautiful and delicate of all early spring flowering bulbs. Stem up to 8 in. *l.* narrow-linear. March-April. Pyrenees, where it flowers in May and early June in the alpine meadows. A white form is also available. (Pl. **24**, 1). Syn. *Brimeura amethystina*.

* **H. azureus.** *Fl.* in densely clustered heads like a *Muscari* but the bells unconstricted at the mouth, a brilliant deep azure-blue. Stem up to 8 in. *L.* broadly linear, broader than in the preceding sp., strongly keeled. March-April. Mountains of Asia Minor. E. A. Bowles recommended growing it with *Crocus aureus* for contrast and the two will flower together. Syn. *Hyacinthella azurea*. (Pl. **24**, 20)

**H. candicans.** See under *Galtonia candicans*.

**H. dalmaticus.** Dwarf, up to 8 in. with a rather dense raceme of numerous pale blue *fl.*, small or medium in size. Late spring. Yugoslavia in sub-alpine woodlands. Rare in cultivation. (Pl. **24**, 5)

**H. fastigiatus.** See under *H. pouzolzii*.

**H. orientalis.** The sp. from which all the florists' hyacinths have been derived, but in itself a delightful and delicate plant for the rock garden. Stem up to 1 ft. with up to 15 bell-shaped *fl.*, loosely spaced on the stem and with the upper half of the perianth segments spreading out flat in a star-like form. Varying in colour from white to pale mauve or deep mauvish-purple. Very fragrant. April. Central and Eastern Mediterranean.
    Var. **albulus.** *Fl.* white, the variety from which the Roman hyacinth has been derived. S. France.

**H. pouzolzii.** Better known as *H. fastigiatus*. A delicate little plant with whitish *fl.* from the mountains of Corsica and Sardinia. Stem up to 6 in. with up to 7 star-shaped *fl.* *L.* filiform. Bulb small, ovoid. Rarely seen in cultivation and superficially more like a *Scilla* than a hyacinth, but the segments of the perianth are united into a cup. April. Syn. *Brimeura fastigiata*.

**H. romanus.** A rather distinct plant often in literature described under *Bellevalia romana*. Stem up to 1 ft. with a dense raceme of small greenish-white or greenish-yellow, rather globular bells. Not a very conspicuous plant but with a good scent. Widespread in S. Europe and Mediterranean regions. April-May.

## Florists' hyacinths

These have been derived from *H. orientalis* by a long process of cross-breeding and selection and have increased gigantically in stature, becoming waxy, fat and stout, but luckily they have not lost their scent, though much of the grace of the wild species has been lost. They are very widely grown in pots and in bowls of fibre for decorating the house in winter and early spring. They are very suitable for forcing and for this the specially prepared bulb should be chosen. These bulbs are subjected in the dormant period during the summer before the flowers are required to a period of about five weeks' warmth of 68° to 78°F. which favours flower-bud formation and tends to retard foliage formation so that the spike will stand up well above the leaves. They do not require so much subsequent cooling as narcissi. The bulbs for the house should be planted either in August or September, the earlier the better, and kept cool either in a cellar or standing outside on a bed of ashes and covered with ashes or peatmoss, but they must not be allowed to become dry. They should not be brought into the warmth of a greenhouse or living-room until they are well-rooted and the flower spikes are beginning to show. This will not be before mid-November usually and may even be later. Unprepared bulbs will usually flower a fortnight to three weeks after the specially prepared ones. The Roman Hyacinths tend to flower among the earliest and the spikes are rather looser and more delicate. The double hyacinths which were much fancied by the Dutch in the 18th century are now very rarely seen and not readily obtainable although their pictures show striking spikes.

In recent years the breeding has tended to produce more massive uniform spikes and clearer, stronger colours particularly among the reds. The following is only a small selection of varieties in each colour.

For planting in the garden and for bedding, smaller bulbs than those supplied for the house will usually suffice and they will flower in April, but for park-like displays they need to be replaced with fresh bulbs each year.

*White*

    ' CARNEGIE ' Large rather congested spikes. Late.
    ' EDELWEISS ' A good variety for early forcing.
\* ' HOAR FROST ' Ivory-white. A large spike. One of the best varieties in this colour.
    ' L'INNOCENCE ' An older variety with very pure white *fl.*

# *Hyacinthus*

'QUEEN OF THE WHITES' A less massive spike with more widely spaced *fl.* A good white.

## Yellow

'CITY OF HAARLEM' Primrose-yellow. A large spike.
'PRINCE HENRY' Pale creamy yellow. A large spike.
'YELLOW HAMMER' A deeper yellow.

## Pale blue

'DELFT BLUE' Early flowering. Porcelain-blue, flushed pale mauve outside.
* 'MYOSOTIS' One of the finest, pale sky-blue. (Pl. **16**, 2)
'PERLE BRILLIANTE' Paler than the preceding with large bells.
'QUEEN OF THE BLUES' Brighter blue, late flowering, unsuitable for early forcing.
'WINSTON CHURCHILL' Deep porcelain-blue, flushed with Prussian blue outside. A very fine *fl.* Later.

## Deep blue

'KING OF THE BLUES' Indigo-blue. Rather late flowering.
* 'OSTARA' An outstanding variety with very large spikes of bright blue with a deeper blue band down centre of each segment of the bell. (Pl. **16**, 3)

## Pale pink

'FLUSHING' Pale shell pink. A large spike.
'GIPSY QUEEN' Salmon pink. A promising newer variety.
'LADY DERBY' Shell-pink. Large bells in a rather loose spike.
* 'PRINCESS IRENE' Deeper pink than the preceding. A very fine variety.
* 'PRINCESS MARGARET' Pale pink, flushed with deeper rose. (Pl. **16**, 1)
'QUEEN OF THE PINKS' Late flowering. Rose-pink.
'SALMONETTA' Salmon pink. A rather loose spike.

## Deep pink and scarlet

'CYCLOP' Bright crimson red. A large spike.
'JEAN BOS' Bright crimson-red. Early flowering but not so large or tall as some.
'PINK PEARL' Deep pink. Good for forcing.
'ROSALIE' Bright pink. A delicate spike with loosely spaced bells, often several spikes produced from one bulb. Almost a Roman hyacinth in form. Early flowering.
'TUBERGEN'S SCARLET' Bright crimson-scarlet.

163

# † HYMENOCALLIS *Amaryllidaceae*

A LARGE genus of S. American bulbous plants named from the cup-shaped membrane which joins together the base of the stamens superficially like the corona of a narcissus. They are closely allied to *Pancratium* with which in the past some of the species have been confused. *Pancratium* is, however, native to the Mediterranean regions though outlying species extend to the Canary Islands, Ceylon and the West Indies and some are nearly hardy. *Ismene* has in the past been sometimes regarded as a separate genus but is now more often regarded as a subgenus and included in *Hymenocallis*. It contains *H. amancaes* and *H. narcissiflora*, two of the best known species. Unfortunately none of the species can be regarded as completely hardy although the two just mentioned are nearly so. The majority of the species are most suitable for the stove or warm greenhouse and are now so rare in cultivation that they are not discussed here. The hardier species can be grown outside during the summer in a warm border but should be lifted before the winter and kept in a heated house. They can, however, be left fairly dormant during this time and should be given little water. The stove species are mostly evergreen and need large pots and generous treatment with regard to feeding and watering. There is one greenhouse species *H. harrisiana*, however, which can be kept dormant during the winter and can be grown in an intermediate or even a cool house.

The flowers are white or in the case of *H. amancaes* bright yellow, somewhat spidery from the long and narrow outer segments and borne in loose umbels of two or more on long pedicels. The perianth tube is usually long also. The bulbs are large, ovoid, with a neck like a larger narcissus bulb and the leaves bright green, strap-shaped, and sheathing the scape at the base. Sometimes they give the appearance of forming a false stem.

H. amancaes. *Fl.* large bright yellow, 2 to 5 to the umbel on stems up to 1½ ft., perianth tube up to 3 in. and outer segments narrow spreading, 3 in. long, staminal cup funnel-shaped, fimbriated at edge, streaked with green towards base inside. Scented. June. Peru, on hills around Lima. A beautiful plant which is unfortunately now rare in cultivation. Almost hardy, but in most areas best grown as a cool greenhouse plant. It may, however, be planted outside for the summer and lifted and kept dry in winter.

H. calathina. A syn. of *H. narcissiflora*.

H. harrisiana. *Fl.* large, white, spider-like since the staminal cup is small, the perianth tube long, up to 5 in. green and the outer segments wavy, linear, narrow, 2½ in. long by ¼ in. wide. Stem rather short, up to 9 in. with 2–4 *fl.* to a stem. Summer. Bulb large. *L.* oblanceolate. Mexico. Intermediate greenhouse but since the *l.* die away in winter it can be kept dry and cool and rested then.

**H. narcissiflora.** Better known under its syn. of *H. calathina* or even *Pancratium calathinum* and known by our ancestors by the delightful name " Chalice-crowned sea Daffodil," although it does not grow by the sea and the name should more properly belong to a sp. of *Pancratium*, which does grow on the sea shore. *Fl.* white, perianth tube long, staminal cup large, funnel-shaped with fimbriated edge. Outer segments long, up to 3 in. but rather narrow, often reflexed. Stem up to 1½ ft. with up to 5 *fl.* Very fragrant. Bulb large; *l.* rather broad. Summer. Peru, Andes. Almost hardy.

**H. × spofforthiae.** A hybrid group between *H. narcissiflora* and *H. amancaes* first raised by Dean Herbert. *Fl.* pale sulphur-yellow with narrow green bands on the staminal cup. Outer segments 2½ in. long and cup about the same depth. The best known variety is ' Sulphur Queen ', raised by Messrs. Van Tubergen in Holland. Summer. Intermediate greenhouse.

# IPHEION *Amaryllidaceae*

A SMALL genus of which only one species is in general cultivation in this country. *Ipheion uniflorum* is one of the most attractive and also one of the easiest to grow of our early-flowering spring bulbs. Unfortunately it is one of those plants which has never been settled in its generic name and at times it has been fitted into *Brodiaea, Milla* and *Triteleia* and several others. As defined *Ipheion* differs from all of these in having a bivalved spathe and a membranous tunic to the bulb.

✱ **I. uniflorum.** *Fl.* single on 6 in stalk, white, pale mauve or even bright lilac-blue, up to 1½ in. long, segments joined at base into a funnel-shaped tube and opening in upper half into a star-shaped *fl.* of which a number are usually borne on one bulb; slight odour of garlic. *L.* narrow, linear, rather grass-like, all basal. March-April. S. America, Peru, Argentina. Quite hardy and does best in a sunny well-drained border, increasing rapidly into large clumps, when it should be divided.

# IRIS *Iridaceae*

IRIS IS one of the largest and most important horticultural genera to come within the scope of this book. Its flowers are among the most lovely to be described. They are also some of the most difficult owing to their subtle variations in colour. Irises are easily divided into two main groups, the bulbous and the rhizomatous. The latter include all the magnificent bearded irises and also the superb but difficult *Oncocyclus* and *Regelia* sections. They are not considered to come within the scope of this book. This leaves us with three sections which have true bulbs: the *Reticulata*, the small species of very early spring; the *Xiphium* which include the Dutch and the Spanish irises; and finally the *Juno*, a large, wholly fascinating, but unfortunately for the most part rather difficult section for the gardener. Still, they are not as fugitive as the more renowned and spectacular *Oncocyclus*. These three sections are very divergent from each other both in their appearance and to some extent in their requirements under cultivation. All irises, however, are plants of open sunny positions and it is one of the few genera in which the majority of species—probably all those discussed here—appear to grow and flower better where there is a small amount of lime present. This can always easily be added in the form of lime rubble. Good drainage is a prerequisite for those we shall discuss; while they require plenty of moisture during their rather short flowering and growing season, they come from countries where they are well baked after growth has died down, usually for several months. Often a glass over them between June and September will be of more benefit than winter protection.

The Iris flower is made up of six perianth segments joined together by a short tube above the ovary; the outer three are called the falls and grow out horizontally or half-vertically along their haft and then turn downwards towards their tips along the blade, the three inner are vertical except in the June section, generally rather smaller, and are called the standards. Above the falls and protected to some extent by the standards are the three styles which are often wide and almost petaloid in appearance with a pronounced crest like a cockatoo, the stigmatic surface being like a lip below this. These closely shield the three stamens which are below them and are generally rather shorter.

The late W. R. Dykes, a schoolmaster at Charterhouse and then Secretary of the R.H.S., was for many years the leading authority on the genus and it is still to his magnificent book *The Genus Iris* that the majority of us turn. I readily acknowledge my debt to him in the compilation of the following pages as well as for the interest and enthusiasm which his work has helped to kindle in me for his favourite genus.

## (*a*) *Reticulata*

These include the dwarf and early flowering bulbous species from Asia Minor and the Caucasus which are some of our best bulbs for late January to March. They are distinguished easily from the *Xiphium* group by the reticulate coat to the bulb, by the single flower on a short stem and also by their leaves which are almost rounded or rush-like in outline, although when examined closely they will be seen to have either four or eight small ribs. They are distinguished from the *Juno* group by the net-like or reticulate coat to the bulb, which is usually quite small, and also by the fact that the roots are not fleshy and die away annually during the resting period.

All these species, with the possible exception of *I. vartani*, are quite hardy but owing to their early flowering should be planted in a warm sunny place where they can be well ripened after flowering. Good drainage is certainly important if the bulbs are to persist and some authorities recommend a light sandy loam as being the best. It is necessary to record, however, that the largest and most persistent clumps of *I. histrioides* I have ever seen are growing in a garden in the Midlands of England with a fairly heavy clay soil, although below is broken sandstone. All this section are excellent plants for growing in pans in the alpine house and the slight protection brings them out a little earlier and ensures that the flowers are undamaged. The bulbs should be planted in early autumn not more than 3 in. deep, and in areas where the drainage is not good or the summer rainfall high they should either be protected in summer with a glass to ensure ripening or lifted annually as soon as the leaves die off, which probably will be early in June. With me they persist and increase well in a raised frame of John Innes Compost with a layer below the bulbs of old mushroom compost. In their own habitat in N.E. Turkey and N.W. Persia, where I have seen them growing, *I. reticulata* at least seems to have plenty of moisture in its flowering season. It was nearly always found on quite steeply sloping ground where the drainage would be particularly good.

Unfortunately the bulbs of this section suffer badly from Ink Disease or Bulb Scab caused by a fungus. It is easily recognised by the black blotches on the outside of the bulbs, but the rot very quickly spreads through them. Such bulbs should be discarded and burnt. Mr. Dykes used to lift all his bulbs of this section every other year and when dry soaked them for two hours in a weak solution of formalin (one part in 300). It is important that they should be dry. He claimed that this, combined with discarding any badly infected bulbs, kept his stocks clean. The bulbs were then stored until replanting time.

Although the Dutch nurserymen produce unfailingly large quantities of bulbs of this section every year, it is surprising and sad how few large and persistent colonies one sees in English gardens. Many of them tend after flowering to split up into a number of little rice grain bulblets which need separating and then growing for two or three years to flowering size.

This is particularly prevalent in the yellow *I. danfordiae*. They may be grown easily from seed and will then flower in three or four years.

**I. bakeriana.** One of the most lovely members of the section, easily recognised by the 8 ribs to the *l.* and by the very conspicuous deep violet, almost black, blotch on the ovate blade of the fall where it recurves downwards. A slender plant with *fl.* slightly smaller than those of *I. reticulata*, height 4–6 in., standards pale mauve, falls horizontal except at tip, white along centre with deeper mauve veining and some dark mauve spots near tip of blade, in some forms with some golden markings as well, but this character is variable, styles pale lilac covering falls and crest curving upwards away from blade of fall. On a warm day the *fl.* give out a noticeable fragrance as of violets. Early flowering, Jan. to mid-Feb. Iraq, E. Turkey and N. Persia. Unfortunately this lovely *fl.* is not usually a very robust or vigorous grower nor in most gardens do the bulbs persist long. It is, however, well worth growing whereever possible. (Pl. **17**, 7)

**I. danfordiae.** Very distinct for its rather squat, bright lemon-yellow *fl.* in which the standards are reduced almost to large bristles. A stout little plant rarely exceeding 4 in. high when in *fl.* and with the *l.* at this time only just appearing and shorter than the *fl.* *Fl.* up to 2 in. across, the haft of the falls stout, lemon-yellow and spotted with bright yellowish-green with some orange markings along centre, the blade of the fall lemon-yellow with green markings, standards much reduced, not more than ¾ in. long, style almost erect over haft of falls, lemon-yellow. Early flowering, late Jan.-early Feb. E. Turkey. Quite hardy but also a good plant for the alpine house. It flowers strongly from Dutch-grown bulbs but then tends to divide up into many little bulblets which take several years to grow on again. Persistent flowering colonies are very rare in English gardens. (Pl. **17**, 12)

**I. histrio.** This and *I. histrioides* are obviously very closely related and are both found over a large area of Asia Minor. *I. histrio* is a variable plant, early flowering, but not such a strong or robust grower as *histrioides*. Height 4–6 in. *Fl.* 2½–3 in., across to the tip of the falls, rather like a shorter and more delicate *reticulata*, variable in colour from lilac-blue to reddish-purple, generally with a white band along centre of fall but not going to the tip, often marked with gold and also with dark mauve or dark purple, standards slender nearly as long as the falls. Late Jan.-early Feb. Asia Minor, Turkey, Syria, Lebanon. *I. histrio* is distinct from *reticulata* in that after flowering the bulb tends to form a large number of small bulblets like *danfordiae* rather than several larger bulbs of near flowering size. (Pl. **17**, 6)

\* Var. **aintabensis.** A smaller form with pale blue falls and standards, the fall having a central orange ridge and a few black markings. Very early flowering when the *l.* are only slightly developed, and seemingly more persistent and even increasing more in English gardens than the larger forms. N. Syria. The plants are said to last a month in flower and are very weather-resistant. (Pl. **17**, 9 and 10)

\* **I. histrioides.** The stoutest and best garden plant in this section. *Fl.* bright royal blue with white centre to fall and golden ridge, generally only 3 or 4 in. high but as much across, falls stout and haft horizontal, the blades being wider than in any of the other sp. of this section, styles and standards large and of the same colour. The whole effect is like a sturdy little blue oak. The colour is a much stronger blue also than in other members of the section. By mid-Jan. often the stout buds are appearing and the *fl.* quickly open if the weather is not too cold. They are extremely resistant of bad weather and even of frost when in flower. They should, however, be protected from slugs if possible. The bulbs divide freely and seem to grow well in a wider range of gardens than other members of this section, probably they are best, however, where the soil is not too light. The *fl.* appear before the foliage is much developed. This is undoubtedly one of the most valuable winter flowering bulbs that we have and a patch seldom fails to attract attention. It also sometimes sets seed, the capsules being half buried in the ground and the seeds should be collected, dried and then sown. Asia Minor, Turkey, N.W. Persia.

Var. **major,** the form usually grown and probably the best. (Pl. **17,** 8 and **18***b*)

Var. **sophenensis,** a rather smaller form sometimes referred to *I. histrio,* with paler *fl.,* narrow falls and standards and pale sea-green styles. Rare in cultivation. Early flowering.

Hybrids between *histrioides* and *reticulata* are described under *I. reticulata* since they are usually catalogued under that sp.

**I. kolpakowskiana.** Distinguished from other members of the section by the more coarse and darker brown tunic of the bulb and the linear, rather crocus-like *l.,* channelled along centre and with a thicker edge. *Fl.* very dwarf, stemless but with a 2 in. tube, under surface of falls pale greenish-yellow, blade narrow, upper surface creamy-white with yellow central ridge and prominent tip to blade with bright purple markings, style and standards light mauvish-purple. Said to flower in April. A very rare plant from Turkestan and as far as I know no longer in cultivation in this country. Reputed to be more difficult and less persistent than other members of the section but would probably be worth a new collection. The two available coloured plates of this *fl.,* one in *The Garden* for 1888, the other in *The Botanical Magazine* for 1880, differ widely in colour, particularly of the blade of the falls, so it may be a variable plant.

\* **I. reticulata.** The best known and probably the favourite member of this section for its ease of cultivation as a pot plant and its beautiful and graceful, scented, velvety *fl.,* deep blue-mauve with gold markings, which appear in early February. Height 6–8 in. at flowering time with narrow four-ribbed *l.* often slightly taller than the *fl.* and later elongating to 15 in. *Fl.* deep blue-mauve, the haft of the falls being inclined upwards towards the vertical and making a sharp angle with the blade to display the central bright orange-gold and white markings, 2 in. high and 2½ in. across. Russia, Caucasus and N. Persia. Curiously the blue-mauve form, which is the common one in cultivation, has never been collected from its native habitat and may prove to be a hybrid. (Pl. **17,** 5). Those in the wild and also the larger proportion of any batch of seedlings are like the reddish-purple forms known as ' Krelagei ' (Pl. **17,** 13) or ' J. S. Dijt ' (Pl. **17,** 1) and these usually flower slightly earlier. Several of these have been named as has also the pale blue form appropriately known as ' Cantab ' (Pl. **17**, 4) of which *cyanea*, (Pl. **17**, 11) an almost indistinguishable type, has also been found wild. Hybrids with *I. histrioides* have also been raised and it is sometimes difficult to tell whether they are forms of *reticulata* or hybrids. Those with *histrioides*, however, usually show their origin in the larger *fl.* with more horizontal falls and in the deep sky-blue or royal-blue colour. They are among the most lovely and satisfactory of spring bulbs and are especially to be recommended.

FORMS OF I. reticulata

(*a*) *Reddish-purple*

'Hercules' Reddish-purple with a prominent orange blotch on blade and falls.
'J. S. Dijt' Reddish-purple, reputed to be a stronger grower than ' Hercules.' (Pl. **17**, 1)
'Krelagei' Reddish-purple, very closely resembling the previous plant. (Pl. **17**, 13)

(*b*) *Pale blue with orange blotch on the blade of the falls, rather smaller than the type and generally less vigorous*

'Cantab' (Pl. **17**, 4) and var. *cyanea* (Pl. **17**, 11) almost indistinguishable; probably hybrids with *I. histrioides*.
* 'Harmony' Deep sky blue with prominent golden markings.
* 'Joyce' Very similar to ' Harmony '.
* 'Royal Blue' Dark royal blue, darker than *histrioides* and with broad falls with conspicuous yellow blotch on the blade. (Pl. **17**, 2)
'Wentworth' Deep purplish-blue.

**I. vartani.** A very slender dwarf iris from Palestine, tender and flowering very early, often in December or even before. *Fl.* pale slaty lavender or white with a pale yellow central ridge to the haft of the falls. Not a very robust or vigorous grower tending to fade away after flowering. In a warm room the *fl.* gives off a noticeable scent of almonds. The white form is that usually supplied by nurserymen.

**I. winogradowii.** A pale dwarf yellow sp. from Central Georgia, resembling a slightly less sturdy and rather looser yellow version of *I. histrioides*. *Fl.* lemon-yellow, the falls with an orange central ridge and also some small dark markings the blades broad, up to ¾ in. across, standards and styles pale yellow. *L.* slightly channelled, dull green, not glaucous and developing in length after flowering, bulb with pale brown tunic. Rare in cultivation but apparently quite hardy and doing well on a very chalky soil with good drainage. A beautiful plant well worth making an effort to obtain and grow. Feb. to early March. (Pl. **17**, 3)

## (*b*) *Xiphium*

These parents of the race of Spanish and Dutch and English irises belong to the Atlantic and Western Mediterranean regions, the Pyrenees, Spain, Portugal and N.W. Africa and are in their distribution very distinct from the *Reticulata* of Asia Minor and S. Russia. They are all larger plants, reaching 1 ft. or 18 in. and summer flowering.

*I. xiphioides*, a parent of the English irises, grows in damp alpine and sub-alpine meadows on both sides of the Pyrenees and consequently may be allowed to remain moist throughout the year. The other members of the section all grow in dryer, more sandy places and require a dry resting period after flowering. In many gardens they are better lifted in late July when the foliage has almost died down and replanted in October. *I. tingitana* and its var. *fontanesii* have proved most suitable for forcing and have been developed considerably for the florists' trade. The remaining sp. *boissieri, filifolia, juncea* and *linifolia* remain rare in cultivation, generally lacking in vigour and although of undeniable beauty are hardly ever seen.

The bulbs are easily distinguished by their smooth outer coats from those of the *Reticulata* section and from the *Juno* irises by their lack of persistent fleshy roots as well as of a considerable difference in habit. They should be planted in autumn 4–6 in. deep and mostly increase freely by division. In *fl.* they are close to the members of the *Spuria* section of the *Apogon* group which are rhizomatous.

† **I. boissieri.** A very rare sp. restricted to the Sierra de Gerez mountains in the North of Portugal and the area just over the Spanish border. It is a handsome plant, stem up to 12 in. with 1 or 2 *fl.* up to 3 in. across, with rich blue-purple falls and standards, veined with red-purple and with a conspicuous central ridge of yellow on the haft and blade of the falls, but not reaching to the tip. Tender and unfortunately rather difficult in cultivation if indeed now it is to be found at all other than in its own mountains. The *fl.* is distinct also from all other members of this section in having a slight beard of bright yellow hairs down the keel of the lower part of the falls. Probably best in large pots or a very well-drained mixture and kept dry from late July to October.

**I. filifolia.** A conspicuous iris with very rich red-purple *fl.* On the blade of the falls is a conspicuous orange patch, edged on the outside with an irregular band of deep blue. Stem up to 1½ ft. with one or two *fl.* *L.* narrowly-linear, but not quite so narrow as its name suggests. June. S. Spain and Gibraltar, N.W. Africa around Tangiers. Hardy but rare in cultivation.

**I. juncea.** A very beautiful deep golden-yellow sp. like a Spanish iris, but even richer in colour from N.W. Africa and the Atlas Mountains. I remember finding it in early spring during the Tunisian campaign in clearings in the cork oak woods near the border of Algeria and Tunisia and have remembered its glowing colour. Stem 12 in. or slightly more, slender with 1 or 2 *fl.* of which the falls hang down vertically, blade of fall nearly round but rather flimsy. *L.* narrow, rushlike; bulb with thick outer tunic bristly at top, rather globose. Slightly tender. Scented. June.

† **I. tingitana.** A great favourite for slight forcing in the cool greenhouse where it will flower in late January, tender in all except the warmest gardens otherwise it should be as popular outside as it is in. Close to *I. xiphium*

but distinguished by the longer perianth tube and by the rather narrow, pointed standards and also by its early flowering, generally in April but earlier with forcing to which it is very amenable. A native of N.W. Africa around Tangier and in Morocco where it is said to be magnificent in flower. Stems up to 2 ft. with 2 or even 3 large *fl.* These are pale bluish-purple with pale blue central band on the haft of the falls and a light yellow patch on the blade of the fall which is broad and rounded. *I. tingitana* is reputed to flower better with a very rich soil, the bulbs being planted above a layer of old and very well-rotted manure. Often a cloche placed over them in winter and early spring will enable the foliage to survive undamaged and the *fl.* to be produced satisfactorily.

\* Var. **fontanesii** – deeper violet-blue, probably the finest form. Mid-May.
  Probably some of the fine varieties usually listed as Dutch Irises such as ' Wedgwood ' are hybrids of *I. tingitana* with forms of *I. xiphioides.*

\* **I. xiphioides.** Often called the English iris, although not a native of this country, but of the Central and Western Pyrenees and N.W. Spain where it grows in damp alpine meadows and is a wonderful sight when in flower in late June or early July. The chief parent of the group known as English irises, and one of the parents of the Dutch Irises which are widely grown both for garden decoration and as florists' flowers. Height up to 2 ft. with 2 or 3 large *fl.* opening in succession, up to 5 in. across with an almost orbicular blade to the fall, rich deep blue with a large golden blotch on the blade. The wild plants are nearly always of this colour but garden raised forms are very variable in colour ranging through pale lilac to reddish-purple and also white. It is distinct from other irises of this section in that the leaves do not appear above ground till the early spring. The bulbs do not need to be lifted after flowering and do best in a moist and rich soil. Seedlings flower in about four years. An explanation of how the name English Iris became attached to it will be found in Dykes's *The Genus Iris.*

**I. xiphium,** the Spanish Iris is a native of S. Spain, Portugal, S. France and N.W. Africa. It is the main parent of our largest group of garden bulbous irises. A more slender plant than *I. xiphioides* and usually flowering about a fortnight earlier. Stem up to 2 ft. with 1 or 2 large *fl.* sometimes up to 5 in. across, variable in colour in the wild from deep to light purple, and with a prominent central band of deep yellow along fall, running almost to the tip, rather variable in outline. The standards are usually of a deeper purple than the falls. Yellow forms also occur and at one time were distinguished under the name *lusitanica.* Var. *praecox* is an early flowering form, generally late April to mid-May.

### DUTCH IRISES

A hardy race of excellent bulbous irises raised from *I. xiphium* var. *praecox* and and *I. tingitana* flowering mid-June to early July about a fortnight earlier than the Spanish irises and following the large bearded rhizomatous irises. In most areas they may safely be left in the ground from year to year. The bulbs should be planted in early autumn about 3 to 4 in. deep in an open sunny position. They may also be forced into flower rather earlier in pots or boxes in a cool greenhouse. The range of colours of the modern varieties is considerable, new ones are constantly being introduced and those given below are only a small selection from the ones available.

*White*

'JEANNE D'ARC' Creamy-white.
'PRINCESS IRENE' Creamy-white standards with deep orange falls.
'WHITE PEARL' Good white.
'WHITE SUPERIOR' Very large with small golden blotch on falls.

*Yellow and bronze*

'ALASKA' Orange-yellow, self colour.
\* 'BELLE JAUNE' Pale yellow with orange-yellow falls, large flowers.
'BRONZE QUEEN' Bronze with some blue on standards, orange blotch on falls, a striking combination of colour.
'GOLDEN HARVEST' Deep yellow, large flowers, a very popular variety.
\* 'LEMON QUEEN' Citron-yellow, falls slightly paler than standards, a striking flower in the garden.
'ORANGE KING' Self-coloured deep orange.
'PRINCESS BEATRIX' Orange-yellow, falls being slightly deeper than standards.
'YELLOW QUEEN' Bright golden-yellow, a strong grower and good for forcing.

*Blue, mauve and purple*

'BLUE CHAMPION' Bright blue with yellow blotch on falls. A strong grower with large *fl.*
'IMPERATOR' Deep blue, good for forcing.
'KING MAUVE' Deep mauve.
'SAXE BLUE' Light blue with large yellow blotch, a vigorous variety.
\* 'WEDGWOOD' Light blue with yellow blotch, early flowering and very good for forcing. Falls lighter in colour than standards. A large proportion of the Dutch Irises sold commercially in florists' shops are of this variety. Probably a hybrid with *I. tingitana.*

## ENGLISH IRISES

Forms and hybrids of *I. xiphioides*, generally flowering rather later than the Dutch irises and with rather more solid *fl.* in shades of white, blue, mauve and purple.

'ALMONA' Pale lavender-purple standards, falls pale blue, a large flower.
'BLUE GIANT' Standards deep bluish-purple with darker flaking, falls deep blue with a white eye.
'KING OF THE BLUES' Dark blue with darker flaking.
'LA NUIT' Deep reddish-purple with darker markings as well as some white markings.
'MONTBLANC' Pure white.
'THE GIANT' Deep blue, large *fl.*

# Iris

## SPANISH IRISES

The earliest to flower in this group, derived chiefly from *I. xiphium*. In most areas they are better lifted in July after flowering and re-planted in September. In shades of white, blue, purple and yellow.

'BLUE ANGEL' Bright cornflower blue with yellow blotch.

'CAJANUS' A good yellow.

'HERCULES' Purplish-blue with bronze shading and large orange blotch on falls.

'KING OF THE BLUES' Deep blue with small yellow blotch.

'KING OF THE WHITES' 'L'INNOCENCE' 'QUEEN WILHELMINA' Good white varieties, 'Queen Wilhelmina' being the earliest to flower and 'L'Innocence' the latest.

'RECONNAISSANCE' A bicolor with pale purple standards and bronze falls with an orange blotch.

## (c) Juno

The centre of distribution of this interesting group of irises lies in the foothills of the great ranges of the Pamir, Alai and Tien-Shan to the south and east of the cities of Bokhara and Samarkand. These cities have a reputation of fabulous unapproachability and some of this group of irises seem to have something of the same reputation for difficulty of cultivation away from their own mountains. This they share with the *Oncocyclus* group and with them also they share a strange beauty, ranging from the dwarf *I. persica* with its fascinating and strange range of colour combinations to the soft blues of *I. graeberiana* and *I. magnifica* and the creams and yellows of *I. orchioides* and *I. bucharica*. The distribution of the group extends westwards through the Caucasus, Persia, Iraq and Turkey to an outlier (*I. planifolia*) in Sicily, Spain and N. Africa.

Although bulbous like the Reticulata and Xiphium sections, a large part of their growth is maintained by a series of plump and fleshy roots which grow down below the bulb and persist throughout the year. It is most important not to break these roots either in collection or in cultivation. It is from these fleshy roots that the small lateral rootlets grow during the growing and flowering season and through these the bulbs absorb their water and mineral salts. The leaves are distinct in being deeply channelled or keeled and at their base folded round the stem. In flower members of this section are easily recognised since the part of the flower which we usually call the standard is reduced in size and grows out horizontally often below the falls or else actually hangs down.

All the species seem to do best in a heavy soil and require a thorough dry baking period in the summer but should not be left long out of the ground. The easiest to grow are the cream and yellow *I. bucharica* and *I. orchioides* and probably the most difficult is *I. persica*.

174

They are usually slow to increase. Imported bulbs usually flower well for the first year but it has always proved difficult to build up enough strength in the bulb to keep it going for a succeeding year. Although dried well after they die down they must most certainly not be starved or kept too dry while they are growing. A number of additional species are described in the *Flora USSR* but since these have not been in cultivation in this country and are little known they are not described here.

**I. aitchisonii.** A very rare sp. from the northern borders of Pakistan and possibly also from Afghanistan around Peshawar and Rawalpindi, probably not now in cultivation. Stem up to 2 ft. with lilac-purple *fl.* with a conspicuous yellow central ridge to the fall and with blade of a darker purple. A yellow form is also recorded. Early flowering, probably March-April.

**I. alata.** A syn. of *I. planifolia*.

**I. albo-marginata.** Much confusion appears to attend this sp. and probably many of the plants referred to as *I. coerulea* now regarded as a syn. of it, because of previous use of name for another sp., should be referred to *I. magnifica*. The true plant should have a very short stem, described as only 2 in. high in its native habitat in the Tien-Shan mountains of Turkestan. *Fl.* rather small, bluish-mauve. The plant described in Dykes, *The Genus Iris* under the name *I. coerulea* is now thought to be *I. vicaria*. Syn. *I. caucasica coerulea*.

† **I. aucheri.** This is the iris usually known as *I. sindjarensis* and one of the most beautiful of the section. The change of name is due to a description by the famous botanist J. G. Baker of a Xiphium iris under the name *aucheri* a few years before Boissier's description of *I. sindjarensis* and it seems most likely that it was the same sp. that they were describing. *I. aucheri* is a native of Iraq and N.E. Syria where it comes from the lower levels. It is consequently an early flowering sp. in England from February to April. In all except the warmest gardens it should be regarded as slightly tender and given the protection of a glass or alpine house. In cultivation it is generally lacking in vigour and persistence, but not quite to such an extent as is *I. persica*, its closest relative. Stem 6–9 in. with distichous, channelled *l.* and up to 6 but usually fewer large *fl.*, up to 2½ in. across, borne sessile in the axils of the *l.* Haft of falls and blade pale bluish-mauve with darker veining and a central yellowish-green median band or crest, styles bluish-lilac, deeper in colour than the rest of *fl.* and with pale blue wavy crests, standards growing out horizontally or drooping below falls, pale bluish, about 1 in. long by ¼ in. broad. The general *fl.* colour is, however, very variable and in some cases the greenish-yellow colour predominates.

\* ' SINDPERS ' is a hybrid between *I. aucheri* and *I. persica*, raised in Holland by Messrs. Van Tubergen and has usually a better constitution than either of its parents. Unfortunately it has now become rare in cultivation. Early flowering. *Fl.* pale azure-blue with yellowish-green and orange markings on the fall.

' WARLSIND ' is a hybrid of *I. warleyensis* and *I. aucheri*, later flowering and taller, falls yellow edged with blue and standards deep blue.

**I. baldschuanica.** Dwarf with *fl.* variable in colour, pale lilac to deeper purple with orange crest to fall. A yellow form is also recorded. Turkestan. Rare and probably not now in cultivation. In stature and form close to *I. rosenbachiana* but flowering late in early March. Syn. *I. rosenbachiana* var. *baldschuanica.*

* **I. bucharica.** One of the easier sp. in cultivation of this section and hardy in most gardens, but best in a slightly protected and sunny situation. Stem up to 1½ ft. with deeply channelled green, not glaucous, rather broad *l.* and up to 7 *fl.* on a long perianth tube in the axils of the *l.* *Fl.* creamy-white with conspicuous deep yellow wide blade to the fall. Styles creamy-white with conspicuous erect crests, standards almost rudimentary, horizontal below falls, creamy-white, *fl.* 2 in. across by 2½ in. deep. A vigorous grower and in some gardens increasing freely. April-early May.

**I. caucasica.** A dwarf sp. with pale yellow *fl.* from the Caucasus, N.E. Turkey and N. Persia. Stem short with 1–4 *fl.*, up to 3 in. across, pale greenish-yellow, almost translucent but with a brighter yellow ridge. Standards very small, deflexed below the horizontal. *L.* distichous, glaucous below and with a white horny margin; bulb ovoid with fleshy roots. Rare in cultivation and probably not very vigorous although Col. Grey describes it as " presenting no difficulty in full sun and light, well-drained soil." In N.E. Turkey and N.W. Persia it grows near the tops of the mountains, always on steep slopes and in semi-scree conditions. A number of plants in two varying forms flowered from our recent collecting. March. Sir Michael Foster also described two varieties which were apparently slightly larger than the type:

Var. **major.** Up to 5 *fl.* Larger than type. Syn. var. *turkestanica.* This variety has also been referred to *I. orchioides.*

Var. **kharput.** Origin uncertain. Stem up to 1 ft. Up to 5 *fl.*; sessile in the axils of the upper leaves, greenish-yellow except for orange ridge on fall. More compact than in the type.

**I. fosteriana.** A striking sp. from the borders of Afghanistan and Russian Turkmenia where it grows in dry soil on low hills up to 4,000 ft., easily distinguished among the Juno Irises by the yellow and purple bicolor *fl.* and by a dark olive-green outer coat to the bulb. Stem short up to 1 ft. almost hidden by the long distichous *l.* One or two *fl.*, haft and fall pale creamy-yellow with a broad, wavy-edged blade of deeper yellow and with some dark purple linear markings; styles with broad wavy crests, pale yellow. Standards horizontal or slightly pendulous, bright mauve with broad blade 1 in. long by ¾ in. across. *L.* ribbed and with a thickened horny border narrow, almost linear. Rare in cultivation and probably not very vigorous, requiring alpine house treatment. Bulb slender with the fleshy roots only slightly developed. This sp. appears to be intermediate between the Juno and the Xiphium section.

* **I. graeberiana.** One of the finest members of this section and also one of the easiest in cultivation. Stem when mature up to 1½ ft. but generally not so much at flowering time, bearing 4–6 medium-sized *fl.* up to 2½ in. across, pale silvery-mauve with the blade of the fall pale cobalt-blue marked

*Plate* 31: Tulips, Darwin and other Late-Flowering Hybrids. 1, ' Prunus '. 2, ' Mariette '. 3, ' Sebastian '. 4, ' G. W. Leak '. 5, ' The Bishop '. 6, ' Therese '. 7, ' Golden Hind '. 8, ' Queen of Bartigons '

Plate 32: ZEPHYRANTHES AND OTHER AUTUMN-FLOWERING BULBS. 1, *Narcissus viridiflorus*. 2
*Schizostylis coccinea* ' Mrs. Hegarty '. 3, *Schizostylis coccinea*. 4, *Narcissus elegans*. 5, *Leucojum
autumnale*. 6, *Zephyranthes grandiflora*. 7, *Narcissus serotinus*. 8, *Zephyranthes candida*. 9,
*Leucojum roseum*. 10, *Sternbergia lutea*. 11, *Galanthus nivalis* subsp. *reginae-olgae*

with whitish centre and blue veins. Depth of colour variable. Styles up to 1½ in. long, pale bluish-mauve, deepening in colour towards base, crests broad with wavy margin. Standards horizontal, up to 1 in. long, pale bluish-mauve. *L.* distichous, broad, deeply keeled, slightly glaucous below. Late March-April. Turkestan. Hardy in a warm sunny position and often quite free flowering. In damp districts it is recommended to lift the bulbs in August and replant in November.

**I. linifolia.** A little known sp. from N. Bokhara in Turkestan, probably not now in cultivation. Stem short, up to 6 in. falls greenish-white with a yellow patch on blade. *L.* linear. Two other unusual features are the bilobed stigma and the white aril on the seeds. Reputed to be difficult in cultivation.

\* **I. magnifica.** One of the tallest and largest members of this section sometimes grown under name *I. vicaria.* Stem up to 2 ft. with up to 7 *fl.* in the leaf axils; pale lavender-blue, sometimes whitish, falls with an orange blotch on the blade. Turkestan. April. When better known this may well prove one of the best for garden purposes of the Juno irises. Probably a number of the latter plants grown under the name *I. coerulea* should be referred to this sp. \* Var. *alba*, tall, white.

\* **I. orchioides.** One of the easier members of this section in cultivation. Stem up to 1 ft. with broad distichous green *l.* with a horny border. Up to 4 *fl.* on a stem, deep golden-yellow falls in the best forms with broad blade to the falls with an orange crest; styles large, pale yellow; standards small, horizontal, pale yellow. Colour variable, some forms with lilac colouring have been recorded. Bulb large, ovoid. Turkestan, mountains up to 7,000 ft. April. Syn. *I. caucasica* var. *oculata.* Col. Grey records a pure white style for this sp. but I have not seen it. In habit rather similar to *I. bucharica* and requiring similar conditions. (Pl. XI)

**I. palaestina.** See under *I. planifolia.*

**I. persica.** One of the most fascinating and most elusive of all irises, described by Parkinson in 1629, featured as the first plate of the Botanical Magazine in 1787 it is still a very rare and difficult plant and we do not seem yet to have mastered the continued successful cultivation of it from year to year although, from a new importation, flowers may frequently be seen in the first year. Although widely distributed in Asia Minor from Turkey to Persia, yet it is never recorded as being abundant, always local and occasional. It is extremely variable and a number of separate varieties have been named. The typical form is about 6–8 in. high, sometimes less, with 1 or 2 *fl.* to a stem. *Fl.* about 3 in. across, rather stouter than those of *I. reticulata*, pale greenish-blue in colour with a dark purple blotch near the tip of the blade of the fall and with a golden median ridge dotted with black along the fall. Standards small, horizontal. *L.* narrow, ribbed, linear. Bulb ovoid with a dark parchment-like outer tunic and thick fleshy roots below. It is particularly important in this sp. not to break the roots. Flowering January-March, it needs some protection from the weather, preferably that of an alpine house or cool greenhouse, and when it has died down it certainly requires thorough ripening though again it probably should not be allowed to become so desiccated that the fleshy roots or the bulbs shrivel. Some authorities have considered that it is likely to do better in a stiff clay soil than in a lighter sandy one.

For the description of the varieties I have had to rely chiefly on Mr. Dykes in *The Genus Iris* since the majority have not been seen in cultivation for a long time; they were mostly originally collected and sent by Herr Siehe of S. Turkey. It is probable that if a long series were collected from different localities there would be much grading into one another of these varieties.

Var. **bolleana,** pale yellow with a purple or violet patch on the falls. Turkey, Cilician Taurus up to 700 m.

Var. **galatica.** Apparently variable from dull grey through purplish-yellow to light blue or yellow with red-purple blotch on blade of fall. Turkey, Galatia and Northern Cappadocia.

Var. **isaacsonii.** Creamy-white tinged with green, with deep violet veins but without dark blotch on blade of fall. S. Persia.

Var. **issica.** Straw-yellow without any markings except for a few black dots on the orange crest. *L.* said to be ciliate along the edge. Turkey, Eastern Cilicia.

Var. **purpurea.** *Fl.* reddish-purple with central orange ridge from falls and a darker purple blotch on tip of blade. One of the parents of ' Sindpers.' Turkey, Armenia.

Var. **sieheana.** *Fl.* reddish-purple with a silvery-grey or greenish-yellow background, slightly larger than var. *purpurea.* Turkey, Cilician Taurus, S. Cappadocia.

Var. **stenophylla.** *Fl.* pale grey-blue with deeper colouring on blade of dark velvety blue-black and central ridge of dull brownish-white; style crests unusually large. Turkey, Cilician Taurus.

Var. **tauri.** *Fl.* dark violet-purple veined with white; central ridge to the fall deep orange dotted with purple. Dykes records this as one of the easiest varieties to grow. Turkey, Cilician Taurus.

**I. planifolia.** This is the iris much better known under its syn. *I. alata,* a real winter flowering beauty from N. Africa, Sicily, and the slopes of Mt. Etna, Sardinia and S. Spain; magnificent bunches of it are sold about Christmas time in the streets of such Algerian cities as Constantine. Stem 1 ft. with up to 3 large *fl.*, pale silvery-mauve or lilac, $3\frac{1}{2}$ in. across, with a broad undulating blade to the fall, a conspicuous golden ridge down the centre of the fall and styles with large fringed crests; standards small, pale lilac, horizontal below haft of fall. *L.* broad, distichous. Bulb large, oblong-ovoid, with reddish-brown tunic. Unfortunately in this country it usually starts to grow too early and the foliage becomes damaged. The bulbs usually flower well the first season after being collected, about Dec. to early Jan., but it is very rare to see either in the garden, alpine house or cool greenhouse plants which have become established and flower regularly from year to year. It requires a good baking after the growth has died down. (Pl. X)

Var. **alba.** *Fl.* white. Dykes records that this and *I. palaestina* are distinct from all other irises by the possession of very small spines on the pollen grains. *I. palaestina* is probably an eastern variety of this sp. distinguished by the smaller more greenish *fl.*, Syria, Israel, close to the coast, variable in colour and including a greenish-yellow form. Rare in cultivation and reported difficult.

# *Iris*

**I. pseudocaucasica.** Very close to *I. caucasica*, but *fl.* blue with a yellow ridge to the fall. Dwarf. Late April.

**I. rosenbachiana.** A striking dwarf sp. from the mountains of Turkestan and Bokhara at 6,000–9,000 ft. Very variable in colour. Stem very short— usually under 6 in. at flowering time, bearing 1–3 *fl.* about 2¼ in. across with long perianth tube up to 3 in. The more usual colour is pale mauve with a prominent dark purple wide blade to the fall and marked with a central deep yellow or orange ridge as well as some irregular white markings; styles pale lilac with large crests and some yellow colouring on upper side; standards small, horizontal or drooping. Three to five *l.*, slightly falcate, short at flowering time, deep green. Bulb ovoid with large fleshy roots. Early flowering, Jan.-March, probably later in its native mountains. Probably best suited to alpine house culture here, although apparently quite hardy but unfortunately now very rare in cultivation. Dykes reported that seedlings showed great variety of colouring and also writes of an early white form with a deep crimson tip to the falls.

**I. tubergeniana.** A dwarf sp. with deep yellow *fl.* and prominent golden crest to the falls which are about 2 in. long, styles large, greenish-yellow with prominent crests, standards v. small. Bulb slender. *L.* broad, green. The *fl.* almost nestles among the *l.* Early flowering, Feb.-March, at same time as *I. reticulata.* Rare and probably no longer in cultivation but well worth another introduction from Turkestan. Closely allied to *I. caucasica* but more dwarf, and with *fl.* of a deeper yellow and *l.* more glaucous.

**I. vicaria.** Close to *I. magnifica.* Stem well developed with violet-blue *fl.* and deep yellow markings on falls. Turkestan. Probably not now in cultivation and imperfectly known.

**I. warleyensis,** a taller sp. from Bokhara of the same habit as *I. orchioides* but with 3–5 pale, mauve-violet *fl.* on stem 1½ ft. high. Haft of fall pale violet with deeper parallel veining; fall has prominent deep violet patch on blade, edged round the tip with a narrow band of white; crest bright orange. Said to be variable in colour. Bulb rather slender. *L.* has a distinct horny margin. Rare now in cultivation but reported to be quite hardy and easy in a light sandy soil in a sunny position. March.

**I. willmottiana.** A small plant with the habit of *I. caucasica*, stem short with 4–6 *fl.* almost sessile, lavender or whitish flecked with lavender-blue, said to be variable, rather small. *L.* with a thick horny edge, flowering earlier than *I. caucasica.* Bulb stout, globose. E. Turkestan, said to come from " mountains of a considerable height." Difficult and probably not now in cultivation in this country, although originally described by van Tubergen as exceedingly free flowering.

A white form or hybrid was also collected at the same time and is still in cultivation.

### OTHER BULBOUS IRISES

**I. sisyrinchium.** See under *Gynandriris sisyrinchium.*

**I. tuberosa.** See under *Hermodactylus tuberosus.*

179

# IXIA *Iridaceae*

A GENUS of about 30 species of S. African corms distinguished for the bright colours of its flowers and the slender wiry stem and narrow leaves which give an appearance of grace to the flower. Unfortunately they are not really hardy in the majority of gardens and are best treated as pot plants for the cool greenhouse, five or seven of the small corms being planted to a pot in October. In warm areas they may be tried outside and are best planted rather late in October or November and given a covering of ashes or bracken as protection from severe frost. This should be removed in late March or early April or it will harbour slugs. They usually flower about midsummer and since each spike carries a number of flowers their season is quite long. They only open, however, in bright sunlight and not generally very early in the morning. The flowers open flat and the centre is usually dark. The species are rarely grown now except the striking *I. viridiflora* with its most unusual electric greenish-blue flowers. Usually ixias are offered by nurserymen as a mixed strain or as named hybrids of which the following would give one a good range.

'AFTERGLOW' Orange-buff with a dark centre and bronzy outside.
'AZUREA' Bright violet-blue with a darker centre and a greenish tinge.
'BRIDESMAID' White with a red centre.
'BUCEPHALUS MAJOR' Carmine-red, large *fl.*
'CONQUEROR' Orange-red outside, inside deep yellow.
'HOGARTH' Creamy-yellow with a purple eye, large *fl.*
'URANUS' Dark lemon-yellow with a deep red centre.
'VULCAN' Scarlet, shaded orange, a striking *fl.*

**I. viridiflora.** This is a plant which most connoisseurs will try at one time or another. The *fl.* are 1½ in. across, star-shaped with a dark centre and of a most startling shade of electric greenish-blue, the kind of tone sometimes seen at the base of a sunset before the sun sets. May-June. The common description of green *fl.* does scant justice to this most unusual plant. The sp. does not appear to be as vigorous or as long-lived as the hybrids but is well worth renewing from time to time. Rare in the wild.

# IXIOLIRION *Amaryllidaceae*

A SMALL genus of bulbous plants from Central Asia of which only one species is usually found in gardens. They are allied to *Alstroemeria* and the flowers are trumpet-like with spreading lobes in a loose umbel,

# Korolkowia

generally in shade of blue or violet-blue. The six petals are divided to the base.

*I. montanum* is a desirable garden plant, especially in its deeper blue forms, but needs to be grown in a warm border such as that under a greenhouse wall and to have good drainage. The leaves appear early in spring and may be damaged by late frosts. In pans in the cool greenhouse they should present no difficulty but may be considered scarcely showy enough to be worth the space. In superficial appearance they rather resemble a small *Brodiaea*.

**I. kolpakowskianum.** Stem up to 1 ft. slender. *Fl.* pale blue or white with a long narrow tube; *l.* narrow, grass-like. April-May. Central Asia, Turkestan. Very rare in cultivation.

**I. ledebourii.** A syn. of *I. montanum*.

**I. montanum.** Stem 1–1½ ft. *Fl.* pale lavender-blue to deeper blue, 2 in. across, *l.* narrow, grass-like. Bulb ovoid with a long neck. May-June. Central Asia, Turkey, N.W. Persia in the Elburz mountains, Afghanistan.
    Var. **macranthum.** Probably the best variety; deeper blue *fl.*, slightly larger than the type variety and shaded with purple.
    Var. **pallasii.** *Fl.* rose-purple, later flowering. Caspian regions.
    Var. **sintenisii.** *Fl.* pale blue. Caspian regions.
**I. tataricum.** A syn. of *I. montanum*.

# KOROLKOWIA *Liliaceae*

A MONOTYPIC genus, closely allied to *Fritillaria*, in which its species *K. sewerzowii* was formerly placed. It also shares some characters with *Lilium*. The bulb apparently consists of a single fleshy scale and is without tunic and the flowers are campanulate. They differ from *Fritillaria*, however, in having the nectary as a slender furrow and not as a pit.

† **K. sewerzowii.** Stem up to 1½ ft. with up to 12 but generally fewer drooping *fl.*, purplish or greenish-yellow, sometimes flushed deep lemon yellow, campanulate, rather variable in colour, segments rather narrow and pointed. *L.* glaucous, rather broad. March. Central Asia, Russian Turkestan. Rare in cultivation and not a very striking plant. Not very hardy and needing good drainage and the same conditions as a *Fritillaria* but not very vigorous nor usually very long lived. Probably best as an alpine house plant. There are two very varying plates in the Botanical Magazine, one deep purple, a form not now in cultivation, the other larger greenish-yellow, lemon-yellow inside, flushed with purple at the base.

# †LACHENALIA *Liliaceae*

A LARGE genus of S. African bulbous plants with attractive pendulous, rather waxy-orange or yellow tubular or bell-shaped flowers on rather stiff spikes. White and purple species are also known. The segments are of different lengths, in this case the outer three being much the shorter. They flower in spring or early summer but unfortunately none are hardy. They are, however, easy to grow in a cool greenhouse from which the frost is excluded. The bulbs increase rapidly and so need frequent division and repotting. A rather rich compost is desirable and air should be given freely when the weather is not too cold. If possible they should be potted early in August or the first half of September, and given little water until growth shows. Usually at least seven and often more can be grown together in the same pot.

The flowers are long-lasting, sometimes up to two months in a cool greenhouse and a good-sized bulb will produce several spikes. They need good ripening after the growth has died down. The foliage is slightly succulent and often pleasantly mottled, but also very attractive to aphids and they need watching and spraying frequently. Many hybrids and named forms have been raised of which * ' Burnham Gold ' is both one of the best known and most to be recommended.

**L. aloides.** More often known as *L. tricolor*, very variable and a number of varieties and hybrids have been named. Stem up to 1 ft. with up to 20 pendulous *fl.*, green at base, then with a red band and yellow in lower part, 1 in. long, tubular. March-April. *L.* mottled with purple blotches. Bulb globular.

Var. **aurea.** Bright golden-yellow.

Var. **lutea.** Deep yellow without green and red bands.

' NELSONII ' Bright golden-yellow, slightly tinged green, probably a hybrid and one of the best.

Var. **quadricolor.** *Fl.* green at base, then deep orange with reddish lower end and purplish margin, outer segments tipped with green.

**L. bulbifera.** Better known as *L. pendula*. A stout plant with larger *fl.* nodding rather than pendulous, purple and green at top of inner segments, then with a coral-red band and yellow at lower ends; outer segments nearly as long as inner ones, yellow and green near tips; *l.* broad. April-May. Early flowering from December; in S. Africa, May-Sept.

**L. glaucina.** *Fl.* pale, either whitish or pale blue or pale lilac-mauve, rather small but numerous, borne horizontally, inner segments opening wide at tips, twice as long as outer. Stem and *l.* both usually spotted and striated but forms without spotting have been recorded. Bulb small globose. *L.* 2, oblong. An unusual plant of peculiar colouring.

**L. mutabilis.** Stem slender, up to 8 in. *Fl.* numerous, pale, slightly iridescent bluish-mauve, ½ in. long with reddish-yellow tips to inner perianth tube segments. The top buds do not usually open. Closely allied to this but rather smaller is *L. orchioides* with whitish *fl.* tipped with green.


# LAPEIROUSIA *Iridaceae*

QUITE A LARGE genus of S. African plants with corms but only one, the little scarlet-crimson *L. cruenta*, often known as *Anomatheca cruenta*, is grown in English gardens, and is probably the only one that is likely to be at all hardy here and then only in warm positions in sheltered sunny gardens in the South and West. In the Scilly Islands and in Riviera gardens it has become naturalised and springs up all over the place. Probably best planted in spring and treated like an *Ixia*, but will also do well in semi-shade.

**L. cruenta.** Stem up to 1 ft. or more in S. Africa with up to 12 carmine-scarlet *fl.* with a straight perianth tube about 1 in. long and segments opening to a star-like *fl.* the lower ones having a rather indistinct blotch at the base. Corm small, flat at base and with a matted tunic; *l.* narrow, linear, sword-like resembling those of a freesia but smaller. A white form has also been recorded. Summer flowering. Syn. *L. laxa.*

**L. grandiflora.** Closely allied to the preceding but larger in all its parts and less deep in colour. Very rare in cultivation. Central Africa, Zambesi country.


# LEUCOCORYNE *Liliaceae*

A SMALL genus of bulbous plants from Chile, allied to *Brodiaea*. Unfortunately only one species, *L. ixioides*, is in cultivation and that is not reliably hardy. Generally it is grown in pans in a cool greenhouse or alpine house where its strong scent early in the year is delightful. Its introduction to our gardens we owe to Mr. Clarence Elliott who collected the fine form sometimes distinguished as *odorata*. This is entirely without the smell of garlic found in some other species of the genus. It requires similar treatment to *Freesia*. In its native habitat its local name is said to mean " Glory of the Sun " and by this name it has become widely known.

† **L. ixioides.** Stem slender, up to 1½ ft. with a loose umbel of 6–9 *fl.*, pale blue, about 1½ in. across with narrow tube and spreading perianth segments,

divided to the base. Sweetly scented at least in the form *odorata*. March-April or earlier if slightly brought on in a warm house but much heat must not be used. Bulb small, ovoid with dark brown tunic; *l.* narrow, linear.

# LEUCOJUM *Amaryllidaceae*

THE LEUCOJUMS (snowflakes) are easily separated from the *Galanthus* (snowdrops) since the six segments of the perianth are all equal in length while in the snowdrop the three inner ones are considerably smaller than the outer ones. The name was originally Leucoeion, white eye, and this describes well the snowy-white flower of *L. vernum,* the commonest and most widely grown species.

There is great variety of form in the genus, which for purposes of botanical classification is usually divided into four sub-genera. The chromosome pattern also shows considerable variation in number, but can be arranged as an ascending series. Since Sir Frederick Stern's fine book *Snowdrops and Snowflakes* describes the species in detail it will not be necessary to discuss them in such detail but merely to acknowledge again our debt to this work. Three species, *L. vernum, L. aestivum* and *L. autumnale* are good and hardy garden plants, the remainder are rather tender and best grown as pot plants in the cool greenhouse or alpine house. All grow either with or without lime in the soil. The flowering season of the genus as a whole is very long, extending from the early spring to the early autumn.

It is easiest to divide them into two groups. The first, including the sub-genera *Aerosperma* and *Leucojum*, is distinguished by the large white pendulous flower with a hollow scape and the broad strap-shaped leaf. The first sub-genus includes *L. aestivum* and the second *L. vernum*. The second group has smaller flowers, white or white tinged with pink, a solid scape and leaves which are filiform or narrowly linear. This includes the sub-genera *Acis* to which *L. autumnale* belongs and *Ruminia*, which contains *L. nicaeënse*. Altogether these are much slenderer and more delicate plants. The bulbs of the first group should be planted 3-4 in. deep and are best moved soon after flowering, those of the second group rather more shallowly and given good drainage.

## (*a*) Sub-genera *Aerosperma* and *Leucojum*

**L. aestivum.** The Summer Snowflake is a popular native of Britain still recorded as growing by the banks of the river Loddon in Berkshire and probably also in other sites. It is much the largest sp. in the genus, reaching

2 ft. or more with several *fl.* in a terminal umbel, bell-like, pendulous, white with green markings just above the tips of the segments, ¾ in. deep and across. The *l.* are long, strap-shaped and bright green; the bulb large and ovoid with a brown tunic, rather narcissus-like, generally dividing freely to form large clumps. Flowering from mid-April to early May its name may be regarded as something of a misnomer. In most gardens it grows and increases freely, doing best in rather dampish places or even by a streamside. It will grow in shade or in the open but is rarely good in hot dry places. The finest form is one known as *'Gravetye var.' which has larger *fl.* than the type, up to 1 in. in length and across. It was distinguished by Wm. Robinson from his garden at Gravetye. This sp. is very widely distributed, being found from the West of Ireland to the Caucasus and south into Asia Minor. (Pl. **14**, 3)

Var. **pulchellum,** the form from the Balearic Islands and Sardinia, has smaller *fl.* two or three weeks earlier. Rare in cultivation. Syn. *L. hernandesii.* (Pl. **14**, 4)

* **L. vernum** has the largest *fl.* of any member of the genus and is one of the most valuable of our late winter and early spring *fl.*, being quite hardy and increasing freely in any reasonable moisture-retentive soil. In very hot dry soils it is generally less good. *Fl.* usually single, occasionally 2 on short stout scapes up to 8 in., perianth segments broad, overlapping, up to 1 in. long, white with a green spot near the tip on the outside; *l.* strap-shaped, broad, deep green; bulb fleshy, globose, with a thin brown tunic. Feb.-March. Europe from France to Poland and N. Italy, prob. naturalised in England. (Pl. **14**, 21)

Var. **capathicum.** Distinguished by the yellow or yellowish-green, instead of green, markings near the tips of the perianth segments. Poland and Roumania. (Pl. **14**, 9)

Var. **vagneri.** A very fine robust form generally with 2 *fl.* to a stem. Hungary. This is undoubtedly the best form but is unfortunately rather rare in cultivation. (Pl. **14**, 13)

## (b) Sub-genera *Acis* and *Ruminia*

**L. autumnale.** A beautiful slender sp. flowering in Sept. *Fl.* white, tinged with pink, appearing before the *l.* usually single, occasionally 2, small, bell-like on their stems, up to 8 in. high. This differs from all other sp. of this group of *Leucojum* by having generally only one spathe instead of two. *L.* narrow, filiform, produced after the *fl.* Portugal, Spain, to Sicily and N.W. Africa. (Pl. **32**, 5). It grows freely under the wall just inside the main gate of the R.H.S. Gardens at Wisley and has spread into a thick border. It is a beautiful sight when in flower in September. It is probably best planted in a warm and sunny position.

Var. **oporanthum.** A strong growing form from Morocco, up to 10 in.

Var. **pulchellum.** Distinguished by the *l.* appearing at the same time as the *fl.* Morocco and S. Spain.

**L. longifolium.** Distinguished by the narrow *l.* which are longer than the scape at flowering time. *Fl.* white, rather small, 1–3 on long pedicels and subtended by 2 upright spathes. Stem up to 8 in. Late spring, April-early May. Corsica, always on sloping shady banks up to 1,500 ft. Probably tender and rare in cultivation in this country.

**L. nicaeënse.** Better known as *L. hiemale,* which at any rate was a misnomer since in its native habitat, a small area only of the Alpes Maritimes and along the French Mediterranean coast from Nice to Monaco, it flowers from the end of March till late May. *Fl.* white, usually single, sometimes 2, pendulous on short stem from 2–5 in. high, *l.* narrowly linear and produced with the *fl.* Distinguished from all other Leucojums except the very rare *L. valentinum* by the ovary being disc-like in form and with six small lobes. Tender and best suited to the alpine house. In spite of their Mediterranean habitat these small flowered snowflakes are better not dried off completely in the summer. (Pl. **14,** 20)

**L. roseum.** Autumn flowering, but distinguished from *L. autumnale* by the short pedicel which is shorter than the twin spathes, by the shorter stature, generally not more than 4 in., and by the pinker colour of the *fl.* (Pl. **32,** 9). Sept.-Oct. Corsica and Sardinia. An attractive and dainty sp. for the alpine house. Sir Frederick Stern describes it as " one of the easiest of the small Leucojums to grow " and practises what he preaches, but others have found it a more difficult and unsatisfactory plant.

**L. tingitanum.** A spring flowering sp. from N.W. Africa, distinguished by the much broader *l.* and stouter stem. *Fl.* white, on stem up to 1½ ft. A very rare plant and not known to be in cultivation in this country.

**L. trichophyllum.** Early flowering from Jan.-April. *Fl.* white, stem up to 10 in., up to 4 to a stem, perianth segments ¾ in. long; *l.* filiform, bulb small. S.W. Spain, S. Portugal and Morocco. Probably only suitable in this country for growing in pots in the cool greenhouse or alpine house and interesting for its early season. (Pl. **14,** 8)

**L. valentinum.** A very rare sp. from Central Spain, closest to *L. nicaeënse* because of the lobed disc to the ovary. *Fl.* 1–3 on short stems up to 4 in. said to be " milk-white," small. Aug.-Sept. Not known to be in cultivation in this country.

# LILIUM *Liliaceae*

LILIES ARE the aristocrats of the bulb world. They form a large and diversified genus of 80 or more species extending throughout Europe, Northern Asia and N. America. None of them lack natural distinction, and the finest are among the outstanding plants that can be grown in any garden. Their cultivation in most cases also presents a certain spice of difficulty and a few of them are notoriously fickle, coy and hard to please. Some, however, such as *L. regale* and *L. hansonii*, should grow well in nearly all gardens.

Their flowers are arranged in six parts, six petals, six stamens and six rows of seeds in a tri-locular capsule. They are often divided into trumpet lilies with narrow funnel-shaped flowers or even broad open trumpets and Turk's-cap or Martagon-type flowers in which the petals are reflexed, turning upwards and backwards. The name Martagon is an old one and may have been derived from a similar Turkish word for a special kind of turban, hence the name Turk's-cap. However, when the genus is considered over its range both of species and hybrids there is every kind of intermediate shape of flower between these two; it has therefore not seemed to me that any useful purpose can be gained for gardeners by dividing the genus in this book either into these two groups or into the four botanical sections sometimes used which are largely based on these characters. An alternative classification has been proposed based on the way of germination of the seedlings whether direct or epigeal, as in most normal seedlings, or hypogeal, in which the cotyledon remains below ground while a small bulb is formed from which a true leaf is thrown up, the whole process taking much longer. This differentiation is of some importance to gardeners growing their lilies from seed, which is indeed the best method of building up stocks. However this germination difference is not easily or clearly correlated with any morphological distinctions either in the flowers or leaves and so has not been adopted here for purposes of dividing up the genus.

Instead a purely artificial division has been chosen. Space does not permit a description of each species on the lines of the descriptions in the rest of this book nor is this necessary, since very full accounts with practically all that is known about the rarer lilies will be found in *Lilies of the World*, the present standard horticultural book on the genus by the late Judge H. B. Drysdale Woodcock and W. T. Stearn. I acknowledge freely my debt to it in compiling this account and recommend it to all lily growers.

I have divided my account into three groups. Firstly the species which are generally not too difficult for the average gardener willing to take care and trouble; these are described in full and included among these are a few hybrid groups which have been clearly differentiated and are widely grown. Secondly, the species which are either unduly difficult in cultivation or so rare that the majority of gardeners are never likely to see them; these are only very briefly described. Thirdly, a small selection of hybrids which I personally can recommend. The names of Lily hybrids are recorded in the *International Lily Register* published by The Royal Horticultural Society and it is a very long list. No useful purpose would be served by trying to describe more than a very small proportion here.

Apart from the flowers the clearly defined characters of lilies rest in the shape of the bulb and the arrangement of the leaves. The bulbs are distinct from practically all other genera described in this book in that they are made up of a number of overlapping fleshy scales not contained in any outer skin or tunic. In the closely related genera *Cardiocrinum*, *Nomocharis* and *Fritillaria* the number of scales is very limited, often only two or three, and so they can be usually distinguished from *Lilium* although the dividing lines between each of them and also from *Lilium* are sometimes difficult to draw. The consequence for gardeners of this is that lily bulbs must never be allowed to become really dry. If they are lifted and cannot be replanted immediately they should be covered with fairly dry peat moss or some other substance. It is important also to avoid damaging the basal plate from which the roots grow and the rather fleshy roots if possible. While lilies, however, are doing well it is generally better to leave them where they are. Clumps, especially of the more vigorous hybrids such as Bellingham Hybrids, which are becoming congested and less strong should, however, be lifted and divided carefully in late summer or early autumn when they have finished flowering and begun to die down. Mid-September is not too early in most cases. It is better to avoid dividing and replanting lilies in midwinter between the end of November and the end of March, but it can safely be done again in April when they have just begun to grow. Lily bulbs received during these months are generally best planted in pots and plunged in a cold frame and then carefully planted out again in April or early May.

In some species, particularly of N. American lilies, the scales are clustered round a short thick, horizontal rootstock like a rhizome and along this other bulbs form so that the division is easy. These are called rhizomatous and *L. pardalinum* is a good example. A few other lilies such as *L. wardii* make definite stolons creeping underground and producing new bulbs along their length. *L. superbum* will increase in this way also.

The leaves are generally narrow and linear and may be arranged either in whorls at intervals up the stem as in *L. martagon* or they may be arranged irregularly up the stem. Combinations of whorled leaves and single irregular leaves are found in a few species.

The European and Asiatic lilies mostly come from the mountainous parts of these regions, although only rarely from the very high alpine slopes. They are found, however, chiefly on sloping ground where the natural drainage is very good. Many are plants of the woodland zones where they grow in open glades, rarely in very deep shade. Many are protected during the resting winter season by a covering of snow. A few grow in places which become hot and dry in the later summer but the majority are found in places which are kept moist throughout the summer and where in the spring there is an ample supply of moving water. Some of the N. American species grow in boggy or marshy places but in this country they are best kept away from places where there is any stagnant water.

Although often solitary in their own growth they are naturally gregarious as regards growing with other plants, being frequently found growing through low bushes and in places where there is plenty of root competition from other plants. This probably serves to keep the ground from ever getting too sodden by removing surplus water while the bulbs are shaded from hot sun in summer and protected when the young growths first emerge. To a certain extent this is a good counsel for their placing in gardens also, but the competition must not be too fierce nor must they become too shaded nor overgrown. In groups near the edge of a shrubbery with perhaps a few very low shrubs in front lilies look well and generally do well. In general the European lilies grow better in more sun than the Asiatic ones. In all cases though the drainage is the most important factor and where this is bad such as in heavy clay soils it will be desirable to prepare special beds which may even be raised, mixing the soil well with compost, leaf-mould, very coarse sand and even ashes. It is better to trench and mix thoroughly the soil in the whole bed or in the area where the lilies are to be planted rather than to dig a hole and fill its base with drainage material since this may easily become a sump into which the water from the surrounding ground will drain and not be able to get away again. In light sandy soils, peat moss, leaf-mould and compost are needed in generous quantities. Lilies do not generally do well in hot dry, sandy situations, while certain lilies such as *L. auratum* will not succeed on lime soils. These will be indicated in their descriptions. Lilies have a high potash requirement from the time of flowering till the leaves begin to die down and a dressing of sulphate of potash then will help to form a good bulb for next year.

The placing of lilies in the garden is worth considerable care and will of course depend on individual tastes. In general they do not show their best in close association with other flowers of strong colour and for this as well as for other reasons they are not really suitable plants for the herbaceous border, nor to my mind should the various kinds be mixed indiscriminately. The ideal is to grow each group of lilies in a place to itself with a background of green and this applies both to the light coloured ones and the stronger coloured oranges. The scarlets such as *L. chalcedonicum* look well in a border in front of a white wall and this particular species from Greece, as well as *L. candidum* and *L. pomponium* from the Maritime Alps, do best in a warmer situation than the woodland species. Warm summers seem to suit most lilies as long as there is plenty of moisture in spring, particularly *L. auratum*, *L. speciosum* and *L. sulphureum* and their hybrids. This is one of the reasons why they do so well in New Zealand and in the more North Western parts of U.S.A. such as Oregon.

## LILIES IN POTS AND TUBS

The majority of lilies may be grown successfully in pots and tubs and young seedlings can be grown on either to flowering size or to a size fit to plant out in small pots as well as in boxes. In the case of pots there is the advantage of having practically no root disturbance if they are planted out carefully.

For flowering size bulbs it is desirable to plant them in deep pots especially in the case of stem rooting species such as *L. auratum*. These pots, known as Long Toms, which are deeper in proportion to their top size than the normal pots are ideal if they can be obtained. Good drainage with plenty of crocks is desirable and for the majority of species a John Innes Potting Compost will prove satisfactory. For a few such as *L. rubellum* and *L. japonicum* probably an additional proportion of sifted leaf-mould would be desirable. In the cases of lilies in small- or medium-sized pots repotting each year is desirable. For those in large pots or tubs, and where several bulbs are to be planted together the tubs are preferable, repotting every second or even third year will be sufficient provided the top soil is scraped away each year and they are top dressed with fresh compost. It is always advisable when potting mature bulbs of lilies to leave sufficient space at the top of the pot for some additional top dressing with compost or peat moss to cover any stem roots when they are growing and some growers even insert pieces of extra tile around the top of the pots to hold this. Lilies in pots should be kept dry during the winter either plunged in a frame or in a cool greenhouse. They do not then require heat but it is a good practice to cover the top of the pots with peat moss or even ashes. This will also help to keep out mice. When the young stems appear they should be watered well and after that at intervals, but except in the case of very quick-growing lilies such as *L. longiflorum*, they should be allowed to become almost dry between waterings and the compost in the pots must never become sodden. Many more lilies in pots are rotted by over-watering than suffer from under-watering.

In pots the lilies require a certain amount of extra feeding; dried blood and bone meal are excellent for them and even very well-rotted manure as a top dressing may be used, but *never* hot fresh manure. Liquid manure may also be used but again in moderation.

# *Lilium*

A supply of lily bulbs can be built up either by (*a*) division of the bulbs, (*b*) in some cases by growing on the bulbils which form up the stem, (*c*) by taking off a few of the outer scales from the bulb and placing these in a warm moist environment where they will form bulbils at their base which can then be detached and grown on or (*d*) from seed.

(*a*) *Division*. This should be done carefully so that the bulbs and roots are damaged as little as possible. A few scales will inevitably become detached and fall off. Division of bulbs should only be done when a further colony is required or if they are becoming overcrowded. In general once established lilies are best left alone. The best months for transplanting are September-October or April. Some lily growers even begin in August but this is not advisable if it should perchance be hot and dry.

(*b*) *Bulbils*. This is one of the easiest methods. The bulbils should be detached in late summer and planted on the surface of pots or pans to grow on. They should not be planted deeply or even covered more than very superficially until they have made roots and begun to grow away. From bulbils flowering-sized bulbs can generally be produced in three to four years. Some lilies such as *L. auratum* and *L. speciosum* will sometimes produce bulbils at the base of the stem while not producing them up the stem and these need to be detached with care. Sometimes a lily which does not usually produce bulbils can be stimulated to do so by wrenching the stem partly out from the bulb and laying it down flat on the ground and partly covering with soil. This cannot, however, be beneficial to the main bulb.

(*c*) *Scales*. This can be done at almost any time of the year although it will be much slower in mid-winter. The scales should be detached carefully and then placed, tip upwards, with the bases just pressed into a propagating mixture. Coarse sand and peat is good, or vermiculite. They may then be covered with sphagnum moss and the pot, box or pan placed in a warm propagating frame if this is available. In summer this method will be successful in the open under a cloche provided the mixture is never allowed to dry out but it will take longer. An alternative which has proved quite successful is to place the scales in a polythene bag with damp peat moss and sand, tie the bag tightly and put in a warm place such as a hot kitchen cupboard or on the mantelpiece. Light is not necessary. One must, however, inspect the bags regularly and take out and pot up the young plants as soon as the bulblets are formed and a leaf begins to grow. In this way if the young plants are grown on in pots or boxes in a frame of a cool greenhouse a flowering-sized bulb will be obtained in three to four years, sometimes even less.

(*d*) *Seed.* For raising a large stock of the species this is undoubtedly the best method, since one raises them free of the virus diseases which can be transmitted through the previous three methods if the parent bulb has been diseased. So far I do not know of any authenticated cases of the transmission of viruses through seeds in lilies, although it is not impossible. Seed propagation is slow, however, particularly in some species such as *L. martagon* and *Cardiocrinum giganteum* which may take up to seven years. On the other hand *L. regale* and *L. philipinense* will generally flower in two years from seed and sometimes in one. Authorities differ in their opinions as to the best time of sowing seed. Many say that one should sow it as fresh as possible whenever it is ripe, others retain it till spring. At any rate it is best sown thinly either in pots or boxes or even direct in a cold frame and a John Innes seed mixture would seem to be suitable in all cases.

Some species such as *L. auratum* and *L. rubellum* may take a year or even longer to germinate. Species such as these require first a warm period in which the new bulblet forms under the ground, then a cold period of at least several weeks in which they can be safely frozen, followed by a warm period in which the first leaf will appear above the ground. The period can be shortened sometimes by placing the seed in a small polythene bag of sand and peat moss or vermiculite and placing it first in a warm cupboard for six weeks then in a refrigerator for the same period and then back to the warm cupboard. A close watch must, however, be kept on it at this stage and the seedlings with their young bulbils removed from the bag as soon as they are apparent. Young lily seedlings always need specially careful transplanting as they seem to recover slowly from breaking of the roots. It is always worth while teasing these apart carefully. In the case of some species known to be difficult in transplanting and also most of the nomocharis it is often best to take the whole pot or box and either plunge the seedlings in a block without disturbance of the soil in a larger pot or plant the whole block out. But to do this successfully it is necessary to sow one's seed thinly. Then later they may be divided when there is more strength in the bulb.

### LILY DISEASES

*Viruses.* These are the worst diseases from which lilies suffer. It is not known at present to how many different viruses lilies are susceptible but it is probable that there is more than one and lilies vary greatly in their susceptibility. The symptoms show in yellow mottling of the leaves, in

*Plate I. Allium karataviense,* showing its decorative combination of foliage and flower head

*Plate II. Arisaema candidissimum*, an attractive and hardy Chinese species.
This group was growing in a London garden

twisting of the leaves, in narrowing and twisting of the petals and finally in general collapse with the stems turning over. The leaf discoloration is not always quite a clear sign since a similar yellowing can be caused by overwatering or even lack of iron salts in a strongly alkaline soil while some twisting and curling of the leaves may be caused by aphids. However, such plants should be segregated away from the others. In the more advanced stages any bulbs with virus should be burnt. No case is known at present of complete recovery from virus, although it is possible that some lilies such as *L. tigrinum* may live and flower, not too unsuccessfully, with a mild degree of virus in the garden for a number of years. For this reason they are best planted well away from other lilies.

Viruses are spread by aphids and so it is most important to keep lilies clear of these pests by spraying at regular intervals. There are many suitable sprays such as Malathion or Lindane.

*Fungus diseases.* *Botrytis elliptica* is the commonest of these and particularly affects the basal leaves of *L. candidum* in early spring. It is particularly prevalent in damp, close weather and shows as reddish-brown spots on the leaves and later a withering away of the entire leaves, while the spores sometimes show as a grey mould on the surface. These are highly infectious to other lilies being wind carried and badly diseased leaves should be taken off and burnt. The disease can be much ameliorated and often prevented by spraying with a copper mixture such as Bordeaux mixture or a sulphur one such as Sybol. The plants can equally be dusted with copper lime dust, but either spraying or dusting should take place once a fortnight at least in early summer. Bulbs whose foliage is badly infected are not killed but are considerably weakened in their build up for the following year.

*Basal Rot.* This is caused by a fungus, *Fusarium oxysporum* forma *lilii*, and rots the basal plate so that the roots are no longer joined to the scales which fall apart in a bad case. By then the plant is practically defunct. Lilies are variable in their susceptibility to basal rot. Some dusting of the basal plate of new bulbs with a fungicide such as Arasan will probably help to prevent infection. In established bulbs the best prevention lies in good cultivation with plenty of drainage. In sour soil infection is very likely as well as general rot of the roots.

*Lily Rust* is fortunately much less common than the previous three diseases. It shows as small reddish-brown spots on the leaves and the cure for a mild infection is spraying with a colloidal copper solution. Badly infected stems should be cut and burnt since it can spread very quickly through the airborne spores.

## LILY PESTS

The worst of these are the aphids which not only spread very quickly and cause twisting of the leaves and general weakening of the plant but also spread virus diseases through their sucking mouth parts. Luckily they are easily controlled by regular spraying with Malathion or Lindane or in greenhouses almost complete control can be obtained by a regular emanation of insecticide from an aerovap heated by electricity. White Fly and Red Spider also attack lilies in greenhouses and provided they are treated before the infection is really thick can be cured by fumigating cone such as Azobenzene for Red Spider and D.D.T. with Lindex for White Fly.

On young lily shoots slugs can do much damage and lilies seem among their favourite subjects of diet. These are best controlled in spring by various proprietary slug dusts etc. which mostly contain Meta and attract the slugs to them. In the soil wireworm and leather jackets can be troublesome and at present there is little practical cure for these under garden conditions, although various soil sterilisers have been tried.

## LITERATURE

Lilies are such beautiful flowers and the genus is so large and varied that an ample literature has sprung up around them. The original H. J. Elwes' *Monograph of the Genus Lilium* was published in 1880 and is now a rare and expensive volume. The plates are large and hand-coloured from paintings by William Fitch. An even more sumptuous and much more beautiful volume is the Supplement to this work by A. Grove and A. D. Cotton, with hand-coloured plates by Lilian Snelling, published in parts between 1933 and 1939. This is still available and contains plates of many of our best garden lilies such as *L. regale* which have been discovered since Elwes' Monograph was published and further parts of the supplement are being published by The Royal Horticultural Society. The last pre-war part deals with Notholirions. Two illustrated year books dealing with lilies are published annually, one by The Royal Horticultural Society and one by the North American Lily Society and both contain many valuable articles, pictures and discussions. It is surprising what a large amount of interesting information on the subject there is each year. Probably with these and the handbook *Lilies of the World* by Woodcock and Stearn the genus is better covered than any other group of bulbous plants.

A subject of perennial difficulty to beginners in gardening is the large number of plants which have been popularly called lilies but which really belong to other genera under which they will be found. A short list of these is given below:

African Lily. Agapanthus; not bulbous and so not included in this volume.
African Corn Lily. See under *Ixia*.
Arum Lily. See under *Zantedeschia*.
Belladonna Lily. See under *Amaryllis belladonna*.
Bugle Lily. See under *Watsonia*.
Caffre Lily. See under *Schizostylis*.
Day Lily. Hemerocallis. Not bulbous.
Glory Lily. See under *Gloriosa*.
Guernsey Lily. See under *Nerine sarniensis*.
Kaffir Lily. See under *Schizostylis*.
Lily of the Valley. *Convallaria majalis*. Not bulbous.
Peruvian Lily. Alstroemeria. Not bulbous.
Plantain Lily. Hosta. Not bulbous.
St. Bernard's Lily. See under *Anthericum*.
St. Bruno's Lily. See under *Paradisea*.
Scarborough Lily. See under *Vallota purpurea*.
Torch Lily. Kniphofia, not bulbous.
Water Lily. Nuphar or Nymphaea. Not bulbous.
Wood Lily. See under *Trillium*.
Lilies of the Field. In the biblical sense the attribution is debatable and may actually refer to the white Madonna lilies. It is more likely, however, to refer to the yellow *Sternbergia lutea*.

There are many other attributions to lily in popular names while many plants, such as crinums, which superficially resemble lilies, are often confused with them.

## LILY CLONES AND GROUPS

Lily seedlings have been raised in very large quantities in recent years and marketed in two different ways so that it is important to distinguish between the two categories. When a raiser produces a large group of seedlings he tends after some years of trial to select a few from the group and build a stock of each of these by vegetative propagation (division, scales or bulbils). These are called *clones* and each bulb is literally a piece of the original plant which was selected and given a separate name and which may have received an award. If one buys a clone one can justifiably expect to have exactly the same flower as one has seen on the Show bench. The names of such clones are usually written with fancy names other than Latin ones and the names placed in single quotation marks. The disadvantage of this system lies in that it takes a number of years to build up a large stock and in this time the stock, often kept all together, may become infected with virus. The bulbs are also inevitably expensive since they have needed care over a long period and are a very small selection probably from a large number of seedlings.

From the bulk of seedlings the really poor ones are generally discarded and burnt straightaway and this practice of selecting the outstanding ones and discarding the poor ones may continue over a number of generations. This leaves a large bulk of good flowering bulbs which do not merit a separate name but which are good garden plants of reasonable vigour, often an advance on many earlier selected clones, and which are probably free from disease, having been grown only a few years from seed. These can of course be marketed much more cheaply than the clones and are sold under a group hybrid name such as Bellingham Hybrids or Backhouse Hybrids or even under a Latin name such as *L.* ×*parkmannii*, a term covering all the hybrids between the particular parents. Such names should be now written without quotation marks. As long as the differentiation is clearly made and the buyer realises that the stock he buys may show considerable variations, a kind of much cheaper lucky dip in lilies, the system has advantages in providing lilies for those who cannot afford the high prices charged maybe justifiably for newer clones and generally unjustifiably for many of the species.

## (*a*) Lilies commonly found in cultivation

**L. amabile.** Martagon. Stem hairy, 2 to 3 ft., with up to 8 or more grenadine-red or orange-red *fl.* of medium size with strongly reflexed petals, heavily spotted with black. Anthers dark chocolate-brown. Scent rather pungent and often considered unpleasant. July. Korea. Bulb rather small with whitish tight scales flushed with pale yellow, ovoid, stem rooting. *L.* narrowly lanceolate, scattered up stem. One of the easier lilies to grow and suitable for light woodland, tolerant of lime and easily raised from seed. Nevertheless this has never become a very popular lily, probably because of the scent. It is certainly not one of the more conspicuous or most beautiful members of the genus and suffers in comparison with other members of the same section with orange or reddish *fl.* such as *L. davidii.*

Var. **luteum,** *fl.* clear orange-yellow.

**L. aurantiacum.** See under *L. bulbiferum.*

\* **L. auratum,** the golden-rayed lily of Japan, justly described as the Queen of lilies and undoubtedly one of the most magnificent sp. Stem purplish-green, up to 8 ft. but generally less with up to 30 or even more *fl.* per stem but generally fewer. 6–8 are a good average and make a very handsome spike. *Fl.* very large, 8 in. or more across, open funnel-shaped or even saucer-shaped, but petals not reflexed, thick, waxy, white with yellow or crimson spots and rays, very variable indeed in markings, especially when raised from seed, opening horizontally (Pl. **19**, 3). Bulb large, up to 6 in. across, sub-globose, scales numerous, yellowish, sometimes flushed with crimson. The largest monster bulbs do not generally establish themselves

# *Lilium*

so well in the open as rather smaller and firmer ones 3–4 in. across. Stem rooting. Aug.-Sept., but imported bulbs, especially those from New Zealand, may flower much earlier as will bulbs grown in a greenhouse. *L.* narrowly lanceolate but in var. *platyphyllum* wider and narrowly ovate, dark green, scattered on stem. Japan, where it grows abundantly on volcanic ash on the lower mountain slopes. This lily is particularly suited for planting in open woodland, but it should be given a position where the heads will at least grow through into full sunlight. It appreciates damp growing conditions in spring and warm summers, hence its great success in New Zealand where fields of it are grown from seed for the export of bulbs. Good drainage is essential, and the bulbs should be planted 4–6 in. deep depending on their size. When the shoots appear in spring they may be mounded up slightly with compost to provide good growing conditions for the stem roots. It is also excellent in large pots and tubs for decoration of the house or verandah. Not suitable for gardens with lime. Numerous and very variable hybrids have been raised with *L. speciosum* and tend to follow *L. auratum* chiefly in form, although often opening flatter and more saucer-shaped, being even larger in *fl.* and often with deeper crimson colouring.

It is often difficult to distinguish these hybrids with certainty from the natural varieties of *L. auratum*. They are grouped under the name *L. × parkmannii*, although the original hybrid raised by Francis Parkman in Boston and first flowered in 1869 has probably long died out; fortunately it was painted by Fitch for the Elwes Monograph.

Groups of hybrids have also been raised between *L. auratum × L. japonicum* and *L. auratum × L. rubellum*, particularly by Dr. Norma Pfeiffer of New York. These are charming and quite attractive *fl.* but so far have not shown the peculiar distinction of any of their parents. Unfortunately *L. auratum* and its hybrids are very susceptible to virus diseases and it was largely for this reason and from basal rot arising from damage to the roots and basal plate that the hundreds of thousands of bulbs of this lily imported previously from Japan and sold by the crate have almost entirely disappeared. Better and cleaner stocks are now available from bulbs raised from seed in this country or from New Zealand, Australia, western Canada or U.S.A. and it has been shown that such can be established satisfactorily in English gardens and flourish for many years.

The main varieties of *L. auratum* commonly distinguished are as follows but it is doubtful whether they accord with any particular areas in the wild distribution of the sp.

Var. **pictum.** *Fl.* heavily spotted with crimson and with a broad coloured band to each petal changing from yellow at the base to crimson near tip.

Var. **platyphyllum.** *Fl.* slightly larger, enormous and often less heavily spotted. *L.* broader. Stem generally not so tall. Said to occupy the more southern areas of the distribution in Japan.

* Var. **rubro-vittatum.** Heavily spotted and with deep crimson band along centre of petal, often yellow at base. Anthers red.

Var. **rubrum.** Band deep crimson and heavily spotted. It is often difficult to distinguish this and var. *pictum* and var. *rubro-vittatum* apart and their garden value is very similar.

Var. **virginale**. Almost an albino form with pale yellow band and spots instead of golden and crimson. Not very vigorous but a beautiful *fl.*

The names given to the *parkmannii* hybrids are becoming very numerous and only a few of the best so far shown can be described here. In general the *fl.* are very large and very conspicuous, opening flat to a large crimson soup-plate in form, but with less distinction and charm than *L. auratum*. However opinions will differ on this point. In constitution they are mostly vigorous but generally not bearing more than 4 or 5 *fl.* to a stem, often fewer.

\* ' CRIMSON QUEEN ' In this the central broad crimson streak tends to flush the petals with crimson all over. (Pl. XV*a*)

' EXCELSIOR ' Similar to the preceding in colouring but a slightly smaller and more delicate *fl.*, up to 8 in. across.

\* ' JILLIAN WALLACE ' *Fl.* very large, almost flat with petals slightly undulating at margin, Tyrian Rose in colour with narrow white margin to petals, spotted with deeper crimson, but the form of the central ray is almost lost. Raised in Victoria, Australia, by Mr. Roy Wallace from *L. speciosum* ' Gilrey ' × *L. parkmannii* ' Crimson Queen '.

' LAVENDER LADY ' Much paler than the other hybrids of this group but with the crimson markings replaced with pinkish-lavender flush and spottings. Opening more like *L. auratum*.

\* **L. × aurelianense**. One of the most successful groups of lily hybrids raised in this century and now the parent of numerous fine hybrids (Pl. **19**, 4). (*L. henryi* × *L. sargentiae*). This hybrid was originally raised twice, first by M. Debras near Orleans, France, and then by Mr. Stookes of Hereford, England. The forms differ a little, that of Mr. Stookes having slightly larger *fl.* Stem up to 7 ft., green flecked with purple. *Fl.* numerous, borne horizontally or slightly pendulous, petals rather narrow, yellowish-orange near base and paler yellow near tip, slightly tinged purple on outside. Bulb globose with yellowish scale. *L.* lanceolate, numerous, irregularly arranged, dark green. Late June-July. Vigorous and doing especially well on chalk.

Many back-crosses have been made between this lily and its parents producing a great variety of seedlings. With more than one half *L. sargentiae* in their parentage they do not flourish on lime soils. Among the best is ' Highdown Sunset ', a very vigorous plant with more reflexed petals than in *aurelianense* and paler *fl.* The Aurelian group of hybrids raised at the Oregon Bulb Farms by Mr. Jan de Graaf combines characters from *L. aurelianense* and its parents as well as from *L. sulphureum* and *L.* ' T. A. Havemeyer ' and show great variation between trumpet-shaped *fl.* and completely Turk's-Cap ones in colour from creamy-white to deep golden-yellow. They are mostly vigorous growers. This group has been split into various sections known as Hearts Desire with bowl-shaped *fl.*, \*Golden Clarion, with fine golden-yellow trumpets flushed with deep maroon on outside and Sunburst which have reflexed petals like *L. henryi* but are slightly larger in *fl.* \*Golden Clarion is among the best group of lilies for cultivation either in a sunny border or in pots.

*L.* Backhouse Hybrids. See under *L. martagon*.

*L.* Bellingham Hybrids. See under *L. humboldtii ocellatum*.

\* **L. brownii**. Undoubtedly one of the most distinguished and beautiful of all lilies, a large trumpet of perfect form, with a smooth waxy glistening quality of petal, white inside and rich purplish-mahogany outside, anthers chocolate-brown; faintly scented. Stem purplish-brown, seldom more than 3 ft. with up to 4 *fl*. *L*. deep glossy green, narrowly lanceolate, scattered on stem, bulb whitish, becoming darker on exposure, flattened on top with the scales tightly packed. Stem rooting. July. China.

This is probably the earliest Chinese lily to have been introduced to England and there is some mystery as to exactly where it came from. It was probably a cultivated plant and was introduced here about 1835. No exact complement to this plant has been discovered wild in China although the two other varieties have been. It is generally sterile although by the use of growth promoting hormones at the base of the stigma a few seeds have been produced recently. Since this was the plant first described and is the type of the sp. this form, or clone as it probably is, should correctly be called *L. brownii* var. *brownii*. However, it is the plant that gardeners know under the name *L. brownii* and distinctly the finest. Unfortunately it is not a very vigorous grower and not hardy in all gardens, but colonies have been established generally in open woodland: Pl. XII shows it perfectly placed in the garden of the late Mr. Scrase-Dickens at Coolhurst.

It is probably not suitable for gardens with lime. Owing to its flattish top it is advisable to plant the bulbs slightly inclined. As a pot lily a number of growers have flowered it satisfactorily and it is certainly worth every trouble. Small bulblets are generally produced at the base of the stem and may be grown on.

Var. **australe** is the narrow-leaved race of this lily from Hongkong and S. China. The trumpet is much less wide open than in var. *brownii* and has much less dark colouring on the outside. Too tender for outside cultivation in most British gardens.

Var. **viridulum**. Better known to gardeners as var. *colchesteri*. From Central China, where it appears to have a wide range extending up to 5,000 ft. Distinguished from the type by the narrower trumpet, by the rose-purple rather than mahogany-purple colouring outside, by a yellow base to the petals inside when they first open, by reddish-brown anthers, by a stronger scent and by a grey-green stem. Unfortunately it is no easier to grow satisfactorily in English gardens, although equally lovely.

**L. bulbiferum.** This comprises the group of orange lilies with upright *fl*. from the mountains of Western and Central Europe and more often known as *L. croceum* or *L. aurantiacum*. Unfortunately not all of them carry bulbils. Linnaeus listed seven varieties and there is still confusion in their nomenclature. However, they are very handsome in the wild either hanging over some rocky ledge or at the edge of woodland and their colour is as strong and intense as that of any member of the genus. As long ago as 1543 Fuchs, the famous herbalist described them as fire-red and it is hard to better this description. It has been shown that the bulbil producing habit is not certainly uniform from year to year. All the varieties should be grown in full sun in the garden and provided virus free stocks are obtained, they generally grow well, up to 3 ft. with a cluster of *fl*., in fact rather larger than in the wild. The following varieties are commonly distinguished.

Var. **chaixii**. From the Maritime Alps. Generally dwarf and with few

# Lilium

*fl.* and generally without bulbils up the stem. *Fl.* orange-yellow tipped with reddish-orange and spotted towards the base with reddish-purple spots and papillae. Sulphur-yellow outside.

* **Var. croceum.** From Western and Central Alps, this is the plant usually grown in gardens where it more than doubles its height and number of *fl.* as compared with wild plants. *Fl.* light orange, tipped with deeper orange, up to 5 in. across when fully open. Stem 1–4 ft. with numerous scattered linear-lanceolate *l.*; bulb globose, generally rather small, whitish; often found up to a foot in depth in the wild. Stem rooting and best grown in full sun; where happy increasing rapidly. June-July.

**L. × burbankii.** A variable group of hybrids from the parentage *L. pardalinum × L. parryi*, named in honour of the American Luther Burbank who raised many thousands of lily seedlings and hybrids. *Fl.* usually horizontal, saffron-yellow with darker chocolate spots and often flushed with crimson, petals recurving. Fragrant. Stem up to 6 ft.; *l.* in whorls. The best clone is probably 'Peter Puget' raised at the Bellingham Research Station in Washington, U.S.A. *Fl.* numerous up to 15, yellow, black spotted. Best in partial shade.

* **L. canadense.** One of the most graceful and beautiful of all lilies, the pale orange or butter-yellow *fl.* with petals slightly recurving at the tip being carried on long pedicels which arch over and downwards away from the stem like the sprays of a fountain or the branches of a well-designed candelabrum. Stem up to 5 ft., smooth, green with numerous *fl.* when well-grown. *Fl.* of medium size up to 4 in. across, variable in colour from pale butter-yellow to light orange. Bulb ovoid with whitish or pale yellow scales. *L.* narrow, lanceolate and in whorls. The photograph Pl. XIII is a well-grown specimen and gives some idea of the grace and beauty of this lily. June-July. Eastern N. America where it is apparently quite common and widespread. It should be grown in open woodland or semi-shade and associates very well with low ferns or dwarf azaleas. It does not generally do well in a very dry situation and will not grow on lime. It may be raised from seed in four years but the seedlings often take a year to appear above ground.

   Var. **coccineum.** *Fl.* dark brick-red, yellow at the base inside and heavily spotted. Rare in cultivation in this country.

   Var. **editorum.** *Fl.* red with narrow perianth segments. From the Appalachian Mts. and the southern part of the range of the sp., even as far south as Northern Alabama.

* **L. candidum.** The white Madonna lily and probably the best known and best loved of all lilies, cultivated since the days of the Cretan civilisations at Knossos and so now widespread but only rarely found wild. In mediaeval and Renaissance religious painting it is usually associated with the Virgin Mary and was very especially her flower. Stem up to 6 ft. but generally less. with numerous wide open, pure white *fl.* with golden anthers, heavily scented (Pl. **21**, 2). Bulb broadly ovoid with pale yellow scales. *L.* lanceolate, scattered on stem, the upper ones quite short. Basal *l.* produced in September and over wintering. For this reason the bulbs are best transplanted early after flowering in late July or August and they should be planted shallowly with the tops only just below the level of the soil. They often work up so

that the tops of the scales show above ground and this seems to cause no damage. Madonna lilies usually grow well on lime soils and it is an advantage to give them some shelter from the wind, as long as the flower spike is in full sun. While not difficult to grow in many gardens, the Madonna lily is undoubtedly one of those capricious plants whose requirements have never quite been settled. The tradition that they do best in small mixed cottage gardens is very deep seated. This may be partly due to the extra feeding which they are likely to get there and also the shelter round the base. The basal leaves are very susceptible to Botrytis and dusting or spraying at intervals is well worth while.

*L. candidum* appears to be indigenous to the Balkan peninsula and has also been found, apparently wild, both in Macedonia, Lebanon and N. Palestine. Normally Madonna lilies do not set seed but the variety known as var. *salonikae* from Macedonia will often do so and if its pollen is used on other varieties these may also set seed in a warm summer. This variety also flowers earlier than the type and has more open *fl.* and green stems. ' Charles X ' is a named clone of fine form and size and was raised in France.

**L. centifolium.** See under *L. leucanthum* var. *centifolium*.

**L. cernuum.** A graceful, delicate little Turk's-Cap lily from Korea and Manchuria with rosy-lilac *fl.* spotted with deeper purple. Stem slender, up to 3 ft., generally less, with up to 12 pendent *fl.* Fragrant. Bulb ovoid, whitish, rather small. *L.* numerous, narrow, linear. June-July. Stem rooting. This lily is not generally long lived in English gardens but can be raised from seed, blooming in three years. It looks well in the larger rock garden or among low growing shrubs, occupying the same kind of position as *L. pumilum* which it closely resembles in all except colour.

**L. chalcedonicum.** The brilliant scarlet Martagon lily from Greece, perhaps the brightest colour in any lily. Stem up to 4 ft., sparsely hairy, with up to 10 pendulous Mandarin red *fl.* of which the thick waxy petals are strongly reflexed, unspotted. Bulb ovoid with yellow scales. *L.* linear, silver-edged and crowded on lower part of stems, reduced in length and growing adjacent to stem. This lily seems to do best in calcareous soils in hot situations and may be almost dried out in late summer. Unfortunately a good clump is a rare sight in English gardens. The bulbs take time to recover after disturbance and good drainage is essential.

The plant often known as *L. heldreichii* or subsp. *heldreichii* is probably only a rather more vigorous local form of *L. chalcedonicum*, meriting at the most varietal rank. It is indigenous to the Peloponnese and Central Greece. *Fl.* bright tomato-red with broad waxy petals.

Var. **maculatum.** A variety of *L. chalcedonicum* heavily spotted, reputed to be easier to establish than the type.

**L. columbianum.** A slender growing lily from Oregon, N. California and Southern British Columbia with smallish, yellowish-orange *fl.* with strongly reflexed petals, heavily spotted. In appearance it is not unlike a smaller and more slender *L. humboldtii*, although it has been recorded as growing up to 6 ft. in its native habitat. Bulb small, ovoid with whitish scales. This is a fairly easy lily for cultivation in a not too dry situation and can be grown

# Lilium

in partial shade. It is rarely seen, however, since it is not one of the more conspicuous lilies.

Var. **ingramii** is a slightly larger and more vigorous form, with deeper orange *fl.*

**L. × dalhansonii.** See under *L. martagon*.

**L. dauricum.** Dwarf lilies from eastern U.S.S.R. and N.E. Asia with upright cup or vase-shaped *fl.* on short stems generally under 2 ft. *Fl.* orange-red and spotted. Bulb globose with loose white scales. Stoloniferous. This lily should be planted in a warm sunny position and is suitable for the front of a border or for the rock garden. June-July. Unfortunately it is very susceptible to virus and is now largely replaced in gardens by the hybrid groups *L. × hollandicum* and *L. × maculatum*. It is closely allied to *L. wilsonii* and var. *pardinum* is probably synonymous with this.

Var. **luteum.** A fine form with deep yellow, broad-petalled *fl.* Alternative spellings " davuricum " and " dahuricum " can be discarded.

* **L. davidii.** One of the finest Chinese lilies and a fitting memorial to the intrepid white father Père David who first collected so many good plants for us from Western China. Stem up to 5 ft., strong, scabrid, with up to 20 nodding or horizontal Turk's-Cap, orange or reddish-orange *fl.* with darker spots on quite long pedicels. Buds hairy. Bulb globose, of medium size with white or pinkish scales. *L.* narrow, linear, numerous, usually with a small tuft of white hairs towards base. July-August. This is usually regarded as one of the easier lilies to grow and is a vigorous plant which can be success-fully established in most gardens. It should be planted where the base is shielded and the top grows into full sun.

Var. **macranthum.** An unusually vigorous form with *fl.* slightly larger and more strongly coloured than the type. (Pl. **19**, 2)

* ' MAXWILL ' A very fine hybrid raised in Canada from crossing *L. davidii* with *L. davidii* var. *willmottiae*. Pedicels long, giving drooping *fl.*, bright orange-red on stem up to 7 ft. July-August. One of the best garden lilies and stronger in stem than var. *willmottiae*.

' ORIOLE ' A very lovely paler yellow or yellowish-apricot form, also raised in Canada. Unfortunately not so robust in growth as the type or ' Maxwill.'

Var. **unicolor.** Spotting either absent or very much reduced; *fl.* paler than the type and stem shorter. Syn. *L. biondii* and in part *L. sutchuenense*.

* Var. **willmottiae.** Stem more slender than in the type and often creeping underground before ascending, spotted purple and without hairs at base of petioles, up to 7 ft. with up to 40 *fl.* on long drooping pedicels, deep orange or Saturn red, darkly spotted. The stems tend to arch over and generally require staking. It is, however, more graceful than the type and an excellent garden lily, easily raised from seed, but often not long-lived. Syn. *L. sutchuenense* in part, *L. willmottiae*, *L. warleyense*. The botanical and nomenclatural status of *L. davidii* and its varieties is discussed in full both in the R.H.S. Lily Year Book for 1938 and in the Supplement to Elwes' Monograph.

* **L. duchartrei.** Farrer's white ' Marbled Martagon,' one of the most graceful, delicate and charming of all lilies, it was collected first by Père David and

# *Lilium*

then by E. H. Wilson but we probably owe our garden stock to Reginald Farrer. Stem rather slender and needing support, stoloniferous at base, purplish-black, up to 4 ft. with up to 12 small to medium sized, white, pendulous or nodding, Turk's-Cap *fl.* spotted with deep purple and scented. Bulb ovoid, rather small with whitish scales. *L.* dark green, narrow, scattered. This lily is best planted in semi-shade with plenty of leaf-mould in a position rather damp. It appears to be tolerant of lime in the soil, and when once established it forms large clumps spreading through the stoloniform stem. Stem rooting. Closely related to the pink spotted *L. lankongense* which is, however, a stouter plant. Western China in mountainous regions above 8,000 ft. July. Syn. *L. farreri* and *L. duchartrei* var. *farreri*.

**L. elegans.** See under *L.* × *hollandicum*.

† **L. formosanum.** Usually a plant for the cool greenhouse, flowering very rapidly from seed, in fact it is often treated as a greenhouse annual flowering in nine months from seed. Stem green, usually 3–4 ft. but occasionally up to 7 ft. with 3 or 4 but sometimes more, long, white, scented, trumpet-shaped *fl.* borne horizontally. Trumpets often 6 in. in length but not so long as in *L. philippinense* and open wider at the mouth. Outside of trumpet flushed with crimson-purple, more so with the forms from higher altitudes. Bulbs rather small, almost globose, scales whitish or pale yellow, sometimes tinged with purple, stem-rooting. *L.* narrow, almost linear, dark green and numerous up the stem. Aug.-Sept. This lily appears to be restricted to the Island of Formosa but there apparently grows in a very unusually wide range of altitudes from the coastal plains up to 12,000 ft. The higher forms are much more dwarf, generally not more than 2 ft. and bearing only 1 or 2 *fl.* with rather stronger purplish colouring on the outside and often a definite pinkish-purple streak down the centre of the petal outside. These are distinguished as var. *pricei* after W. R. Price who collected the bulbs in 1912 and investigated this lily thoroughly in its native habitat. These higher forms are reasonably hardy in most sheltered gardens and will often persist for several years, although the number of *fl.* per stem and the height do not seem to increase. They also flower slightly earlier in late July-August and this probably gives the bulbs a better chance to ripen. The bulbs should be planted 4–6 in. deep among low shrubs.

This lily is unfortunately very susceptible to virus diseases and for this reason frequent fresh stocks are usually raised from seed. It is often used among other lilies as an indicator to tell whether virus is present. In the past it has been confused both with *L. longiflorum* and *L. philippinense* and the name var. *formosanum* attached to these sp. should be treated as a syn.

**L. giganteum.** See under *Cardiocrinum giganteum*.

* **L. hansonii.** A fine martagon-type lily with yellowish-orange *fl.* with very thick reflexed petals. Stem up to 5 ft., dark green with up to 12 rather nodding *fl.* up to 3 in. across. The petals are slightly spotted with a deeper brown, pollen yellow. Bulb ovoid with yellowish scales. *L.* in whorls. Late June-July. Korea. This lily is one of the most satisfactory garden plants among the lilies if not one of the most beautiful. Clumps have been known to persist for many years and it is tolerant of lime. It does best in open woodland

# Lilium

situations and shows well where the sun can be seen through the petals. It needs sun to light up the colour which in shade may appear rather dull.

**L. heldreichii.** See under *L. chalcedonicum.*

\* **L. henryi.** One of the easiest sp. to grow in the genus and doing particularly well on lime soils; sometimes known as the "orange speciosum lily." Stem usually very tall, purplish-brown, up to 8 ft., generally needing support, with a very large number of deep yellow or pale orange martagon-type *fl.* on long pedicels spreading horizontally. A usual number is 15–20 but up to 70 have been recorded on one stem. *Fl.* slightly spotted with darker colour and with prominent papillae near the centre (Pl. **19**, 5). Often 2 *fl.* to a pedicel. Bulb large, up to 8 in. across, nearly globose, creamy-white with purplish tips, becoming deep reddish-brown on exposure, stem rooting. *L.* numerous, lanceolate in lower and middle but changing near the inflorescence to short and broad, almost ovate. This is a distinguishing character. Late flowering —Aug.-Sept. China, found by Prof. A. Henry in Hupeh in the Ichang gorges on ledges, where it does not apparently grow nearly so tall or with so many *fl.* It was introduced by him. The bulb should be planted 6–8 in. deep in a rather open situation and not in peaty soil. It does well, however, in leaf-mould, and often spreads into large congested clumps from the many bulblets which form at the base. These need dividing every third or fourth year.

Var. **citrinum.** Pale lemon-yellow. Rare and not very vigorous.

**L. × hollandicum.** This is the group of orange lilies with upright *fl.*, more often described and found in catalogues as *L. umbellatum* and thought to have arisen as hybrids between *L. bulbiferum* and *L. maculatum* (*L. elegans*). Stems stout and rather short, rarely more than 2½ ft. *Fl.* of varying colours and a number of separate clones have been named varying from clear yellow 'Moonlight' and 'Golden Fleece' to orange-red 'Erectum' and 'Vermilion Brilliant,' always erect and cup-shaped, of brilliant colour. Bulb of medium size with numerous closely aggregated scales, stem rooting. *L.* numerous up stem. June-July. These lilies are very showy and are best grown in an open sunny situation although they may be used in the front of a shrub border. Unfortunately a number of the clones as often supplied have been infected with virus disease and the plants are therefore not always either very long lived or as vigorous as they should be.

**L. humboldtii.** A vigorous Turk's-Cap lily of rather brilliant, even garish colouring from the Sierra Nevada range of California where it grows in open woodland. Stem up to 6 ft. with up to 15 or more large pendulous *fl.* of orange-red prominently spotted with dark purple or maroon. Very variable in colour and markings. Bulb large, with pale yellowish scales. *L.* numerous generally borne in whorls up the stem. July. This is primarily a woodland plant and grows equally well on lime. In gardens in this country, however, the true sp. is more often replaced by its even more conspicuously coloured var. *ocellatum* or by the *Bellingham Hybrids which have proved such wonderful and vigorous garden plants and are to be seen in great abundance both on Battleston Hill at the R.H.S. Gardens at Wisley and in the Savill gardens in Windsor Great Park. (Pl. **19**, 1). These have been derived from crosses between *L. humboldtii* var. *ocellatum* × *L. pardalinum* and *L. humboldtii* var. *ocellatum* × *L. parryi* and show great variation of colour and size of flower. The basic colour is a rather hot orange and they are heavily spotted with dark red. There are, however, some such as the lovely *'Royal Favourite' where the basic colour is deep lemon-yellow. They grow as strongly as any lily, often reaching 7 or 8 ft. while the bulbs increase rapidly forming large clumps. 'Shuksan' with heavily spotted yellowish-orange *fl.* is generally regarded as one of the best clones.

Var. **bloomerianum,** a rather dwarf variety.

* **L. × imperiale.** This is the prior name for the hybrid group of white trumpet lilies derived from *L. regale* × *L. sargentiae* and more often known in gardens as *L. × princeps.* They are close in character to *L. regale,* which was the seed parent of the first strain developed but later strains have been raised with *L. sargentiae* as the seed parent and these are probably the ones usually grown today. They tend to flower about a fortnight later than *L. regale* and often grow slightly taller and are generally slightly larger in *fl.* As garden plants they have a good constitution unless infected with virus which is unfortunately rather prevalent in this group.

Among the best clones are 'George C. Creelman' and 'Pride of Charlotte' the latter bearing bulbils up the stem. A group known as Crow's Hybrids have been developed from 'George C. Creelman' × (*L. sulphureum* × *L. regale*) and these are excellent garden plants while in America the Olympic Hybrids, the Green Mountain Hybrids and various other groups have been developed in large quantities from similar parentage and while very variable in form and colour produce many good garden plants. They are easily raised from seed.

†*L. **japonicum.** This pale pink trumpet lily is one of the great beauties of the genus and one that never ages, but unfortunately is coy and hard, though not impossible, to please. As a pot plant it can be grown with reasonable success. In Japan it is known as 'Sasa-yuri,' the bamboo lily from its slender habit of growth and from its wild location among bamboos. Stems up to 3 ft. with up to 5, but generally fewer trumpet *fl.* of good form and waxy substance, pale shell-pink or white in colour with orange-brown anthers (Pl. 21, 3). Trumpets 4 to 5 in. long and as much across, when open the tips of the petals reflexing slightly. Mildly fragrant. July. Bulb small to medium in size, white, ovoid, stem rooting. *L.* not very numerous, dark green and with short petioles, narrowly-lanceolate, up to 6 in. This lily should be planted 5 or 6 in. deep in open woodland in rich but well-drained soil with plenty of leaf-mould or old pine needles. Its native habitat in Japan is a region with heavy snowfall in winter and heavy rainfall in spring and early summer, but with dry weather and abundant sunshine in late summer and early autumn. Some colonies are recorded as having persisted in the open in this country for a number of years, but such are rare. More often it is grown here as a cool greenhouse plant.

A group of hybrids between *L. auratum* × *L. japonicum* has been raised in America and are variable in colour and form. Those I have seen tended to be somewhat spidery with rather narrow petals and smaller than *L. auratum* but better ones may well appear.

# *Lilium*

**L. lankongense.** A pale pink spotted martagon-type lily from Western China. Stem up to 4 ft., generally less, sometimes stoloniform at base, *fl.* up to 15, pendulous or nodding, rose pink, spotted with purple, the segments pointed, opening wide and recurving at tips but not so much as in *L. duchartrei* to which it is closely related. July-August. Bulb small, ovoid, white turning pale pinkish on exposure. *L.* narrow, oblong-lanceolate, scattered, numerous. *L. lankongense* differs from *L. duchartrei* in the pink *fl.*, in having a racemose inflorescence, in the pointed petals and the later season of flowering as well as having a more southerly area of distribution in Western China. Although not often seen it is not unduly difficult of cultivation in an open situation and is tolerant of a very limy soil as long as there is good drainage.

**L. leichtlinii.** A beautiful Turk's-Cap lily from Japan with nodding lemon-yellow *fl.*, heavily spotted with deep purplish-brown. Stem up to 4 ft. with up to 5 *fl.*, buds hairy. August. Bulb small with white broad scales, stem stoloniferous at base and often wandering underground for some distance. Unfortunately this sp. cannot be considered an easy or a good garden plant in this country, lacking vigour and resistance to disease and being somewhat tender except in the milder areas. As a pot plant for the cool greenhouse it is easier to grow successfully but the stoloniferous stem tends to resent restriction in a pot. Unfortunately it is now a very rare lily in this country and for most garden purposes its place as a lemon-yellow Turk's-Cap has been filled with the yellow form of *L. tigrinum* called *flaviflorum* or incorrectly ' A. M. Vollmer '.

Fortunately the bright orange-red variety of this lily known as var. *maximowiczii* is much more amenable to cultivation. It is also apparently commoner in its native habitat and it is possible that the yellow form, although prior-named, may be an albino sport of it, thus accounting in part for the lack of vigour. Stem up to 8 ft., generally less, with up to 12 pendulous *fl.* with petals strongly recurved, orange-red and heavily spotted with purplish-brown. August. Quite hardy, although probably best in semi-shade. In general effect and garden value it is like a slightly more slender and graceful tiger lily. Bulb small but slightly larger than in the type, stem stoloniferous; *l.* numerous, linear-lanceolate. August.

**L. leucanthum.** One of the finest and tallest trumpet lilies, in its best forms only comparable with *L. sulphureum*, but less tender. It is variable both in size and colour and the variety usually grown in this country is var. *centifolium*. The type of this sp. collected by Augustine Henry in the Ichang gorges of Hupeh and sent to Kew grew 3–4 ft. and had up to 5 long funnel-shaped trumpets up to 5 in. long, milky-white, tinged with pale yellow outside towards the base and with a narrow greenish band on the outside of each petal. Fragrant. This form appears to have been lost to cultivation although forms subsequently introduced come near to it.

\* Var. **centifolium** is an even finer plant and was found only once by Reginald Farrer in a cottage garden in S. Kansu, just two spikes, in 1914. The account of it can be found in his book *On the Eaves of the World*. Stem up to 9 ft. with up to 18 *fl.*, large narrow funnel-shaped trumpets, white inside flushed yellow at throat but outside suffused with pale green and rosy-purple, anthers and pollen reddish-brown, petals recurved

# Lilium

slightly at tips. Bulb globose, dull yellow or reddish-brown, stem rooting. *L.* very numerous, narrow, linear-lanceolate. This lily has grown very well in the chalk of Sir Frederick Stern's garden at Highdown, near Worthing, but in other gardens it has proved rather more difficult to establish and keep satisfactorily and has now unfortunately become a rare lily. It should probably be given a warm and sunny position with some shade over the roots only. It is certainly worth every effort.

† **L. longiflorum.** This is the white trumpet lily grown widely for the florists' trade. It is an excellent cool greenhouse plant and can be forced for spring *fl.* It can also be grown outside in warm, sunny and sheltered positions but seldom persists for many years. It is easily raised from seed and flowers quickly, sometimes within the year. The bulbs however, are very susceptible to virus diseases and this has caused rapid deterioration of many stocks. Stem up to 3 ft. with up to 5 but generally fewer, large, pure white, glistening trumpet *fl.*, up to 6 in. long. Pollen yellow. Bulbs globose, whitish. *L.* numerous, lanceolate, scattered. A number of named varieties have been separated and among the best are ' Croft ', ' Estate ', *eximium*, ' Holland's Glory ', ' Slocum's Ace', and ' White Queen '. Tetraploid forms have also been raised with large substantial *fl.*

\* **L. mackliniae.** Although the most recent of the important lily discoveries in Asia, Kingdon-Ward's lily from Sirhoi peak in Manipur on the Indo-Burmese frontier has already shown its capacities as a good garden plant. It first flowered in this country in 1948. Stem up to 2½ ft., generally less, with up to 5 drooping bell-shaped white *fl.* lightly flushed with pink or pale carmine on outside and up to 3 in. across. Bulb small. *L.* numerous, narrowly lanceolate, scattered. This lily appears to develop best in a cool, semi-shaded position but it may be grown also in a large rock garden. Botanically it is on the border line between *Nomocharis* and *Lilium*, two very closely allied genera and was first allotted by its discoverer to the former genus, but luckily it does not appear to have the fastidiousness to successful cultivation of *Nomocharis*, particularly in southern gardens.

**L. × maculatum.** This is the hybrid group of yellow, orange and orange-red lilies with upright *fl.* often found in catalogues under *L. elegans* or *L. thunbergianum.* They are excellent garden plants, doing well in sunny positions. Unfortunately, however, many of the best clones have become infected with virus diseases. The parentage is uncertain, possibly *L. dauricum × L. concolor*, but they have been cultivated in Japanese gardens for a long time, whence, they were collected first by Thunberg and later introduced by von Siebold. Most of the forms are dwarf, not over 2 ft. in height with large cup-shaped *fl.* either singly or clustered in a tight umbel. When open they are up to 6 in. across, the perianth segments being clawed towards the base. Their colour variation is considerable from pale clear yellow to deep mahogany red and there are both spotted and unspotted forms. Among the best are ' Alice Wilson,' clear lemon-yellow, lightly spotted with dark red.

> Var. **alutaceum.** A very dwarf form with deep apricot-yellow *fl.* dark spotted not often over 9 in. Syn. ' Kirkak.'
>
> Var. **astrosanguineum.** Dark red, spotted with black.
>
> Var. **bicolor.** Bright orange, margined with strong red. 1 ft.

' MAHOGANY ' Deep mahogany-crimson. One of the finest.
' ORANGE QUEEN ' Bright orange-yellow.
Var. **sanguineum.** Deep crimson-red.
' WALLACEI ' Apricot-yellow with maroon spots. Stem stoloniform. One of the tallest up to 2½ ft.

**L.** × **marhan.** See under *L. martagon.*

**L. martagon.** This is the largest and most widespread group of European lilies and the only one which can really claim to have been naturalised, so much as to become a native sp. in this country. The type is variable in colour from light pinkish-purple to a wine-purple, while among the varieties are both these with pure white and deep maroon coloured *fl.* It ranges from the Spanish peninsula to the Caucasus in the S. East and to Siberia and Northern Turkestan and Mongolia. It is generally a plant of the lower wooded slopes of mountains but is also found in open grassy glades or meadows up to 7,000 ft. and grows well on lime soils. In cultivation it rarely exceeds 5 ft. in height and in the wild is generally 2–3 ft., stem stout, purplish, bearing a large number of pendulous waxy medium-sized Turk's-Cap *fl.*, varying shades of purple and spotted, scent strong and unpleasing to most people. June-July. Mrs. Maxwell in her excellent book *Lilies in their homes* suggests that this can be masked in vases by adding a little honeysuckle. Bulb ovoid, yellow with pointed scales. *L.* in whorls, oblanceolate. As a garden plant the typical sp. is considerably exceeded by its varieties *album* and *cattaniae* and by some of its hybrids with *L. hansoni.* It is, however, very suitable for naturalising in the woodland garden and requires less attention than other sp. The finest example of this is at Cambridge in the garden of St. John's College. Unfortunately it is rather slow to mature from seed, often taking seven years to reach flowering size. Recently I have seen some martagon seedlings of a cleaner shade of pink than usual and with the petals less reflexed and these seemed to me more attractive than the type.

* Var. **album.** A lovely lily with very clean white *fl.* and yellow anthers. It looks particularly well in groups on its own against a dark green background of evergreens or among ferns. Stems up to 5 ft. with 30 *fl.* (Pl. **20**, 1). The finest form is *album superbum*, but unfortunately it is rare and is considered to be the albino form of var. *cattaniae.* These white forms come true from seed although it is curious that there are no hybrids between the white and the purple forms in gardens, nor have I heard of them in the wild.

* Var. **cattaniae.** Taller than the type, up to 7 ft. in fine spikes and with *fl.* deep wine-purple or maroon and unspotted. (Pl. **20**, 2). This is probably the finest form and is as often in catalogues and the older literature under the name var. *dalmaticum* which must unfortunately be discarded both owing to priority and as a source of confusion. However, its origin is in Dalmatia and neighbouring areas of the Balkans.

Var. **dalmaticum.** A syn. of var. *cattaniae* but also sometimes misapplied to var. *sanguineo-purpureum.*

Var. **hirsutum.** Purplish-pink, spotted, chiefly distinguished by the hairy buds, stem and undersides of the *l.*

Var. **sanguineo-purpureum.** A very fine form with spotted *fl.*, otherwise corresponding to var. *cattaniae* and also from the Balkans.

*Plate III. Cardiocrinum giganteum*, an unusually fine group of this great white lily, still better known to gardeners as *Lilium giganteum*

*Plate IV. Crocosmia masonorum,* a slightly tender plant with bright orange flowers

*Plate V*. A naturalised mass of *Crocus tomasinianus* during a sunny day in February

*Plate VI.* Above, *Crocus chrysanthus* 'E. A. Bowles', one of the finest early-flowering varieties with deep butter-yellow, globular flowers
Below, *Cyclamen orbiculatum* in early spring

## *Lilium*

The best known hybrid group is known as *L.* × *marhan* (*L. martagon* × *L. hansonii*). *Fl.* dull orange-yellow, very thick petalled, but variable in colour, generally spotted reddish-brown. Vigorous and of good constitution. The finest named clone is *\* St. Nicholas ' raised by the Hon. Robert James with *L. martagon album* as one parent, *fl.* buttercup-yellow and only very slightly spotted. The petals of the *fl.* in these hybrids are less recurved than in typical martagons.

* BACKHOUSE HYBRIDS. A variable group of crosses between *L. hansonii* and the various varieties and forms of *L. martagon*, very floriferous and of good constitution, many yellow or tawny-orange flushed with pink. *\*' Brocade ', ' Sceptre' and ' Mrs. R. O. Backhouse ' are probably the best named ones up to date.

  **L.** × **dalhansonii** has one of the dark martagon varieties for one parent and the *fl.* are deep reddish-maroon, heavily spotted; of good constitution.

**L. michiganense**, a graceful Turk's-Cap lily from eastern and central N. America with medium-sized orange-red *fl.*, heavily spotted with deeper red or maroon. Stem up to 5 ft. with up to 8 *fl.* on long arching pedicels. June-July. Bulb of medium size, stoloniferous; *l.* narrow, numerous, in whorls. In the wild this lily grows in open grassy meadows rather than in woodland and in this country it should probably have more sun than shade. It is not, however, a suitable lily for a hot dry situation, thriving in the same kind of conditions as *L. canadense.*

* **L. monadelphum**, a very handsome lily with thick waxy pale yellow *fl.* from the Caucasus and N.E. Turkey, growing in open woodland and subalpine meadows. Stem up to 5 ft. with up to 30 but generally many fewer, large pale creamy-yellow, campanulate *fl.* sometimes spotted in varying amounts with purple, in other cases completely unspotted, petals tinged with purplish-red towards base, thick and reflexed near tips, borne on long pedicels giving a fountain appearance to a large spike. Stamens united in a tube around the ovary to a varying degree are a particular character of this lily. June-July. Bulb ovoid, yellowish, with many tightly packed scales. *L.* numerous, scattered, lanceolate. This lily seems to do best in heavier soils than the majority of lilies and also on soils containing lime It is best planted in half shade and left undisturbed as much as possible since it often takes a year or more to settle down satisfactorily after a move.

  Closely allied is *\*L. szovitsianum*, also from the S. Caucasus and N.E. Turkey, which has been distinguished by the absence of fusion of the stamens around the ovary and by the orange-brown instead of yellow pollen. (Pl. **21**, 5). Seedlings from both named plants, however, are very variable in these characters and it seems to me doubtful if the specific distinction could be well maintained if there were further collections from the wild. In cultivation there is little difference between the two. Also probably related and rather similar is *L. kesselringianum* with smaller and paler *fl.* from the same region but this is not at present in cultivation in this country. W. Kesselring, however, who had the opportunity of seeing a large number of *fl.* grown from collected bulbs firmly expressed. the opinion in the first issue of the R.H.S. Lily Year Book that the three should be treated as separate sp.

# *Lilium*

†* **L. nepalense.** A peculiar and strangely beautiful lily with large yellowish-green and purple *fl.*, but unfortunately rather difficult and a bit tender in cultivation and there are few records of its being grown successfully outside in this country. Stem rarely more than 3 ft. with 1–3 large funnel-shaped *fl.*, the petals strongly recurved from the tips and along a third of their length, up to 6 in. across and the same in length, texture of petals rather thin and papery in contrast to the thicker fleshy petals of *L. primulinum*; greenish-yellow or pale yellow, heavily flushed with purplish-crimson towards base and up much of the segments. Late May-early July. Bulb globose, white when young then becoming purplish, made up of rather few scales. Stem stoloniform at base. *L.* long, dark green, scattered, lanceolate.

Usually grown in a cool greenhouse and owing to the stoloniform habit of the lower part of the stem, it needs to be grown either in large pots or in boxes or even planted out in a greenhouse bed. In the latter case care must be taken that it does not get too wet during the winter months. In the spring growth is rapid and flowering time depends on the warmth given. If attempted outside it should be covered in winter with a mulch of dry peat and preferably a cloche as well. Its native habitat is the Himalayan ranges of Nepal and Bhutan between 6,000 and 8,000 ft.

Var. **concolor.** *Fl.* pale greenish-yellow and without any purple colouring. Very rare.

**L. nevadense.** This small-flowered Turk's-Cap lily from the Sierra Nevada range of California is closely related to *L. pardalinum* and is indeed not unlike a smaller version of it. Stem up to 6 ft. but generally much less with up to 20 *fl.*, orange-yellow, spotted with orange-red and with red tips to the segments, fragrant, borne on rather long pedicels. It is said to be very variable in its native habitat. Bulb rather small and rhizomatous, but not splitting into separate colonies. *L.* numerous in whorls, oblong, lanceolate. This lily is suitable for groups in the open woodland and appears to be quite hardy.

Var. **fresnense.** *Fl.* drooping on long slender pedicels and rather smaller, from Fresno County of California.

Var. **shastense.** See under *L. shastense* (p. 221).

**L. ochraceum.** See under *L. primulinum*.

* **L. pardalinum.** The Panther or Leopard Lily from its abundant spots, one of the easiest of western N. American lilies for a damp position where it usually increases rapidly. Stem up to 8 ft. with numerous nodding, Turk's-Cap *fl.*, light reddish-orange, usually crimson near tips of segments, heavily spotted with deep crimson-brown, 3–4 in. across but variable both in size and colour. July. Bulb of numerous small whitish scales forming clusters of bulbs on a horizontal rhizome. Dividing very freely. *L.* linear or lanceolate and in whorls. Coast ranges of California. It can be grown in semi-shade or full exposure and revels in a damp but not waterlogged position. In the latter case the bulb should be planted in small mounds, where the roots can reach down to the water. It can be seen abundantly in the old wild garden at Wisley. Every three years or so the clumps are likely to need division.

Var. **giganteum.** This is the lily more often found in catalogues as *L. pardalinum* ' Sunset '. Strong growing. *Fl.* reddish-crimson with yellowish-orange at base. Larger than in *L. pardalinum*. A desirable plant for the damper woodland garden. Probably California. Syn. *L. harrisianum.*

**L. pardinum.** See under *L. wilsonii.*

**L. ×parkmannii.** See under *L. auratum.*

\* **L. parryi.** A very beautiful lily with clear lemon-yellow or aureolin-yellow, funnel-shaped *fl.* recurved at the tips, from the mountains of California and S. Arizona. Stem up to 6 ft. but generally less, rather slender, with up to 25 *fl.* The colour—unusually clear and attractive and the *fl.* are borne on long pedicels which gives them unusual grace and lily growers have always rated this lily very highly for beauty. Bulb of numerous scales, rather small, often lengthened on a short horizontal rhizome. *L.* oblanceolate, in whorls. Unfortunately this lily does not have the reputation of growing easily or persisting long in gardens but in some it has been successful. It is certainly not a lily for a hot dry situation and is probably best planted in semi-shade in light woodland with plenty of leaf-mould or peat. It seems to do well in dampish places but not to the same extent as *L. pardalinum.*

† **L. philippinense.** A slender trumpet lily with pure white *fl.* tender and so usually grown only as a cool greenhouse plant. Stem up to 3 ft. with 1 or 2 very long narrow trumpets, often 6 in. in length, pure glistening white inside, outside white but flushed with green and a few streaks of red towards the base. Very fragrant. Bulb sub-globose, whitish. *L.* rather small and linear, bright green, scattered up stem. As a cool greenhouse plant this lily should not present any great difficulties and in summer the pots may be plunged outside. It flowers late July-September and comes from the Luzon Mountains in the Philippine Islands, well within the tropics. It has sometimes been regarded as a variety of *L. formosanum* but now is more usually classed as a separate sp.

**L. pomponium.** Dwarf, strong martagon-type *fl.*, waxy, glistening scarlet-red. From the Maritime Alps behind the French and Italian Riviera coasts. Stem up to 2½ ft. but generally less with up to 10 nodding *fl.* on long pedicels, lightly spotted with black. Its brilliance of colour makes it stand out at a distance. Scent rather pungent, slightly disagreeable to many. Bulb small, white, ovoid. *L.* narrow, linear and with silver margins crowded up the purplish stem. This lily should be planted in a warm well-drained position in full sun and does well on chalk. A position in a narrow south border under a greenhouse wall would be ideal.

†\***L. primulinum.** This is the lily more often known as *L. ochraceum* and one of the most beautiful of Western China and North Burma species. It has often been confused with *L. nepalense*, having somewhat similar colouring but is in reality quite distinct both in form of *fl.* and in distribution and can be considered as slightly less tender but still too tender to grow outside except in warm and very well-drained gardens except in its most northern forms. Generally divided into three varieties and since these differ somewhat both in size of *fl.*, colouring, distribution and hardiness it seems best to describe each separately.

    Var. **burmanicum.** This is the finest form of the sp. and the one usually seen in cultivation. Stem purplish, up to 8 ft. but generally much less with up to 7 quite large nodding *fl.* of greenish-yellow, heavily marked with reddish-purple towards the throat and base inside the outer half of the segments which are recurved and spotted with reddish-purple outside the zone of that colour but not right up to the tips. Yellowish-green outside. The segments are thick and fleshy and much more recurved than in *L. nepalense.* Rather pungently fragrant. Late flowering, August but it may flower as late as December in the case of newly imported bulbs. Bulb broadly ovoid, of medium size, whitish, becoming purple after exposure to light, stem rooting. *L.* dark green, rather broad, lanceolate, scattered. This variety is the more tender and is usually grown in large pots as a cool greenhouse plant but in some warm gardens has survived outside. Tolerant of lime.

Var. **ochraceum.** This is the smaller flowered form from Yunnan and Western China. It is much dwarfer growing and has smaller *fl.* recurved like a martagon lily, stem rarely over 3 ft. but often running underground before emerging. Hardier than var. *burmanicum.* July.

Var. **primulinum.** A self-coloured form of var. *burmanicum* but without any purple colouring in the throat and forming the original type of the sp. Very rare in cultivation. Should be treated as var. *burmanicum.*

**L. × princeps.** A syn. of *L. × imperiale.*

**L. pyrenaicum.** The yellow Turk's-Cap lily of the Pyrenees and Northern Spain. It is one of the most easily cultivated of lilies though unfortunately it is not one of the more beautiful ones while the foxy scent is regarded as unpleasing by most growers. As a plant for the wild garden it is, however, useful and distinctive and unlike most lilies will generally persist and even increase on its own. Stem up to 4 ft. but generally much less with up to 12 pendulous *fl.,* yellow or greenish-yellow, with many dark spots and with the segments tightly reflexed, small-medium in size, pollen orange-red and conspicuous. May-June. Bulb broadly ovoid, of medium size, whitish or pale yellow becoming tinged with pink on exposure. *L.* numerous, narrowly lanceolate, scattered.

Var. **rubrum,** a more handsome form of this lily with orange-red *fl.,* spotted with maroon, distinctly preferable to the type but rare in the wild.

\* **L. regale.** One of the finest trumpet lilies and distinguished by its ease of cultivation and the short time in which it can be raised from seed to flowering size. Often it will flower in the second year. The common remark of catalogues " should be grown in every garden " is very true in this case. Although one of the more recent lilies to be introduced it has already become nearly as well known as the white Madonna lily and is infinitely easier to grow satisfactorily in a wide range of gardens. It appears completely tolerant of lime in the soil and does well in full sun although for additional safety some root protection from small shrubs is often desirable in areas where spring frosts are bad since the young shoots emerge early. It should not, however, be planted in deep shade. Stem up to 6 ft. with up to 30 large funnel-shaped trumpet *fl.,* up to 5 in. long, glistening white inside with a yellow throat, flushed with maroon and deep pink towards the base outside and varying in the amount and depth of colour there. Segments slightly reflexed towards tip and trumpet opening wide. (Pl. **21,** 1 and Pl. XIV). Fragrant. July. Bulb large, broadly ovoid, yellowish-brown but becoming deep crimson-purple after exposure;

stem rooting. *L.* linear, numerous, scattered. Western China where it was discovered by Dr. E. H. Wilson in western Szechwan.

Recently a bright yellow group with purplish-maroon colouring outside has been placed on the market under the name *Royal Gold and it promises to become as valuable and fine a garden plant as the type. It is claimed to be a true breeding mutation.

\* **L. rubellum.** This is one of the most attractive of the smaller growing lilies, bearing graceful rosy-pink trumpets of fine form on short stems. Unfortunately it is not very easy to establish and is rarely seen in English gardens although small colonies have been reported as persisting for many years. In form and shape it resembles *L. japonicum* but is smaller in all its parts while the *fl.* are of a deeper pink. Stem slender, up to 2 ft. with up to 6 *fl.* but generally fewer, trumpet about 3 in. long, opening wide and with segments slightly recurved towards tips. Fragrant. June. Bulb small, white, globose, not more than 2 in. across, stem rooting. *L.* lanceolate, scattered. Japan, mountains of Northern Hondo between 2,500 and 6,000 ft. Wilson, who saw this lily in its native habitat reported that it was under heavy snow from November till the end of April but that thereafter the ground had plenty of moisture. In this country bulbs are very apt to rot away during the winter, especially newly imported ones and it seems to be established best where shrub or tree roots take much of the moisture out of the soil. On the other hand it is not a lily for hot dry places or very light sandy soils nor does it appear to grow satisfactorily on lime soils. However, it is so beautiful that it is well worth repeated efforts to establish it and to raise a stock from seed. A very rare white form has been observed also.

**L. sargentiae.** A large white trumpet lily from Western China, resembling *L. regale* and also introduced to cultivation by E. H. Wilson, but differing in the wider open trumpets, the darker, almost purplish-mahogany, colouring of the outside of the trumpets and by the bulbils produced up the stem and the broader *l.* Stem up to 6 ft. generally less with up to 10 large trumpet *fl.*, glistening white inside and flushed pale green towards throat, outside flushed with dark purplish-mahogany and green in varying degrees, fragrant. Stigma large with conical purple tip. Bulb dark red, broadly ovoid, large, stem rooting. *L.* lanceolate or linear-oblong, dark green, numerous, scattered. Unfortunately this lily has not proved nearly so easy in cultivation as *L. regale*, nor is it lime tolerant. It also tends to be tender except in the warmer gardens but it is a very fine cool greenhouse plant. It flowers in July or August, a little later than *L. regale*.

\* **L. speciosum.** Also from Japan and sometimes described as the Queen of Lilies and after *longiflorum* probably the most popular lily now for the florist trade since it can also be easily forced. Stem up to 6 ft. with often many large *fl.* on long pedicels, the segments are strongly recurved and slightly waved at the edges, making it often almost a Turk's-Cap lily in appearance, thick and waxy in texture and with prominent papillae, white with pink or crimson markings and spots and suffused crimson towards the base, but very variable in these characters. (Pl. **19**, 6). July-September. Bulb large, globose, purplish-brown, stem rooting. *L.* broadly lanceolate, deep green, rather broader than in most sp. Closely allied to *L. auratum*, this lily is, however, slightly more tender and generally only a success out of doors in the warmer areas. It should be planted in a sunny position. As a cool greenhouse plant it is excellent. Like *L. auratum* it does not do well on lime soils. A number of separate varieties and clones have been named of which the following can be recommended. The pure white forms are unusually beautiful but in general of a weaker constitution than the coloured ones.

\* Var. **album-novum.** A very lovely pure white form with yellow anthers. Probably the best of the white forms.

Var. **gloriosoides.** Spots scarlet rather than crimson and very richly coloured. Formosa and Central China. Very rare in cultivation.

Var. **kraetzeri.** A fine white form with orange-brown pollen.

Var. **magnificum.** One of the best coloured and most handsome. Segments suffused rose and spots deep crimson.

\* ‘ Melpomene ’ Very highly coloured, only the margins of the segments being white. One of the most vigorous varieties.

\* ‘ Namazu Beauty ’ Richly coloured and slightly larger than var. *rubrum.* One of the best to grow.

Var. **punctatum.** Rather pale with orange pollen. Early flowering.

Var. **rubrum.** Richly coloured.

†\*L. **sulphureum.** Often described in books under *L. myriophyllum,* but the name *sulphureum* has prior publication though only by two months. It is well described as one of the noblest of all lilies, although unfortunately it has now become a rare plant indeed in cultivation. Stem up to 8 ft., stout, with up to 15 large, narrowly funnel-shaped trumpets, with segments only slightly recurving at tips. Inside pale creamy-yellow or creamy-white, with deep yellow at throat but variable in the depth of yellow, outside flushed pinkish and chocolate-brown or pinkish and green, trumpets up to 11 in. long and 8 in. across mouth, among the largest in the genus. Heavily scented. August-September. Bulb globose, reddish-purple, stem rooting. *L.* numerous, up to 8 in. long, linear-lanceolate and bearing in their axils numerous bulbils from which the sp. can be propagated. W. China, Yunnan and N. Burma, Shan States. This handsome lily should be planted in a sunny, warm and sheltered position, such as the border in front of a greenhouse wall or near a house. The bulb probably needs to be planted deeply. It grew in many gardens in this country prior to the last war but since then seems to have died out almost completely and further stocks are much required. It appears tolerant of lime in the soil. On the continent where summers are warmer it has been recorded as flourishing in a number of places. As a cool greenhouse plant it also does well and should be so grown in all except the warmer areas of the country. As a parent it has yielded a number of notable hybrids. One of the finest is \* ‘ Sulphur Queen,’ the other parent being *L. aurelianense.* In this the trumpets are nearly white inside but heavily flushed yellow at the throat and deeply coloured outside with crimson and chocolate-brown. It appears to have a good constitution. ‘ T. A. Havemeyer ’ is a cross with *L. henryi* and carries large orange-buff *fl.* with heavily reflexed petals, but is very susceptible to virus diseases.

**L. superbum.** A lily indeed worthy of its proud name. Probably the tallest and finest of the deep yellow and orange-red Turk's-Cap lilies of the Eastern and Central States of N. America and curiously one of the earliest lilies to be introduced into this country, being known to Linnaeus and portrayed by Ehret and Redouté. In its native home it has many names, Swamp Lily, Wild Tiger Lily, American Turk's-Cap Lily, etc. It is closely allied to *L. canadense* but is generally a taller and stouter plant and the *fl.* are larger and the segments more recurved. Stem up to 8 ft. with up to 40 *fl.* up to 4 in. across on long curved pedicels which grow out horizontally and then curve gracefully downwards to give a nodding poise to the blooms. Colour of *fl.* variable from deep yellow to Cadmium Orange with crimson at tips of segments, and heavily spotted with crimson-maroon towards the base which is green from the large nectary furrows. July-August. Bulb white, almost globose and produced on a stolon. *L.* linear or lanceolate and in whorls up the stem. This lily succeeds best in a damp situation but in really boggy ground should be planted in a mound where the bulb is above the water level but can send its roots down into the damper soil. It should be planted with the base in semi-shade but where the sun can reach the upper part and needs a stake in most cases. Although not quite such an easy or vigorous increaser as *L. pardalinum* it is still a good garden plant where there is no lime in the soil and it can get sufficient moisture and it has certainly a better *fl.* both in colour and in poise than *L. pardalinum*. A particularly lovely clear deep yellow form has been named ' Norman Henry '.

**L. sutchuenense.** See under *L. davidii* var. *willmottiae*.

**L. szovitsianum.** See under *L. monadelphum*.

**L. taliense.** An attractive martagon-type lily from Yunnan with white *fl.* heavily spotted with reddish-purple. It resembles *L. duchartrei* to which it is closely related but can be distinguished by the racemose rather than umbellate head of *fl.* and the smooth purplish instead of green papillose nectary furrow. It has not unfortunately proved even as good a garden plant as *L. duchartrei* and is now very rare. Stem of 4 ft. though more has been recorded in the wild, stiff, stoloniferous at base with up to 12 *fl.* on short horizontal pedicels. *Fl.* white and with numerous small reddish-purple or mauvish-purple spots, segments tightly recurved, rather thick and fleshy, *fl.* about 2 in. across. Scented. Bulb small, cream coloured with some purple spots becoming yellow after exposure, stem rooting. *L.* scattered, linear-lanceolate. It is a plant of the higher mountain zones between 8,000 and 11,000 ft. and is completely hardy.

\* **L. ×testaceum.** The Nankeen Lily. This is probably the oldest recorded lily hybrid, the parents being *L. candidum* ×*L. chalcedonicum* and it has long been a favourite with gardeners, having *fl.* of a peculiar warm soft apricot colour which is not quite equalled elsewhere in the genus. (Pl. **21**, 4). As a hybrid it is very distinct from both its parents. The cross has been repeated several times and has shown some, but not an extensive variation. Stem purplish up to 6 ft. with a greyish bloom, with up to 12 large *fl.* with segments opening flat and then recurving on upper half, apricot-yellow with a few red spots. *Fl.* about 4 in. across, pollen reddish-orange. June-July. Bulb large, pale yellow. *L.* thick, rather small, lanceolate, numerous, margined but not so conspicuously as in *L. chalcedonicum*. This lily should not be planted deeply, 3–4 in. being sufficient, and should be given a sunny position with some shelter from cold winds. It seems to do best in a fat, rather kitchen garden type of soil and like its parents does well on lime soil. It sets no seed normally and must be multiplied vegetatively. By backcrossing with *L. candidum* a beautiful pure white form was obtained, the elusive ' White Knight,' but unfortunately it appears to have died out now and more experiments with this cross would be well worth making.

**L. tigrinum.** The Tiger Lily. After *L. candidum* probably the best known lily. Good patches of it are only rarely seen in this country; many strains are infected with virus diseases, so that it should always be planted well away from other lilies, which might be infected. It also does well on an enriched kitchen garden soil and in a warm sunny position. It seems to do better in those countries such as Canada which have a warmer summer than ours. Stem stout, dark and with numerous white cobweb-like hairs and bearing numerous bulblets in the axils of the *l*. Up to 6 ft. and with up to 25 *fl.* to a stem, nodding and with segments strongly recurved, bright orange-red with numerous deep reddish-purple or almost black spots, towards the base are two papillose ridges. Pollen purplish-brown. July–September. Bulb white, ovoid. *L.* linear-lanceolate, numerous. Japan and E. China. Tiger lilies do not do well on lime soils. Also they do not usually set any seed, being triploid in chromosome numbers. The basic diploid variety is known but is not nearly so large in *fl.*

Var. **flaviflorum.** Lemon-yellow with dark purple spots. A beautiful variety sometimes sold under the name ' A. M. Vollmer '. In general not so vigorous as the var. *fortunei* or *splendens*.

\* Var. **fortunei.** Larger and more floriferous than the type and with a very woolly stem. *Fl.* of similar colour to type. Dagelet Island, off coast of Korea.

\* Var. **splendens.** Deeper reddish-orange than type and more vigorous. Late flowering.

**L. wardii.** A martagon-type lily with pinkish-purple *fl.* from S.E. Tibet. Stem up to 5 ft., dark green suffused with purple, generally stoloniform at base and often running along for 1 ft. before ascending and producing small bulblets on the stolon. *Fl.* nodding, up to 3 in. across, segments pinkish-purple, varying in depth of colour, spotted with deeper maroon-purple, strongly recurved; fragrant, inflorescence racemose with up to 37 *fl.* and with broad leaf-like bracts, in this respect resembling *L. henryi*. July–August. Bulb rather small, becoming purple after exposure, stem rooting. *L.* dark green, narrowly lanceolate. Upper Tsangpo valley and S.E. Tibet between 5,000 and 10,000 ft. This fine lily was collected by Frank Kingdon-Ward in 1924 and first flowered in 1927. It was quickly acclaimed and was soon awarded an F.C.C. In cultivation individual bulbs have not appeared to be very long-lived but it is easily raised from seed or increased by bulblets. It should be planted in a semi-shaded position but preferably where the *fl.* can be in the open. It does not appear to be tolerant of lime. It is closely allied to *L. duchartrei* but the *fl.* are larger and the stem stouter and it is also distinguished by its smooth nectary. Its collector stated that it was " abundant in one region of pine and bracken clad slopes, scenting the forest."

**L. willmottiae.** See under *L. davidii* var. *willmottiae*.

**L. wilsonii.**   A Japanese sp. with upright orange-red *fl.* so prominently spotted that it has been described as the Panther Lily and is often found under its syn. *L. pardinum.*   Stem up to 3 ft. with large *fl.* often 5 in. across, borne erect, several to a stem, and opening wide, the segments recurving at tips, conspicuously clawed at base.   July-August.   Bulb yellowish-white with rather loose scales.   *L.* lanceolate, scattered.   This lily should be grown in an open sunny position and provided it is virus free should not prove a difficult lily in most gardens.   (Pl. **20**, 3)

Var. **flavum.**   A beautiful lemon-yellow from, also heavily spotted. Probably the lily ' Marlyn Ross,' first described as a hybrid, is really a form of this variety.   (Pl. XV*b*)

## (*b*) Lilies difficult or rare in cultivation

In most cases the rareness of these lilies is a measure of their difficulty in cultivation.   Great care has to be taken with them, especially in respect of drainage.   After flowering every opportunity should be taken to secure seed, since in most gardens the mortality rate among seedlings is apt to be high.   Of course, sometimes there is the exception and one of these species will settle down happily and remain for many years in a garden, but this is no guarantee that the success can be repeated elsewhere.   Their absence from gardens is occasionally due to a single introduction dying out and not being repeated.   In most cases the flowers are less conspicuous in size and form than those in the section previously described and it is safe to say that the best garden lilies are dealt with there.   Specific cultural directions cannot be given for the lilies of this section since we just do not yet have enough experience of them.

**L. albanicum.**   See under *L. carniolicum* var. *albanicum.*

**L. alexandrae.**   See under *L. nobilissimum.*

**L. amoenum.**   Dwarf, *fl.* pink, trumpet.   Yunnan, China.

† **L. arboricola.**   An absolutely unique lily recently discovered by Frank Kingdon-Ward in N. Burma, unique in that it is epiphytic and also in the colour of its *fl.* which are a delicate and luminous Nile-green contrasting with vermilion anthers.   The bulb is flattened and with very few scales, the stem weak, the *fl.* of martagon type with rather narrow pointed segments and of medium size; the *l.* wide.   Unfortunately this lily appears to be unusually difficult in cultivation and is likely to require warm greenhouse treatment.   The difficulty seems to be in keeping it through a short resting period after flowering.   It flowered once in England but then practically all the stock died out and a further collection is much needed.

† **L. bakerianum.**   *Fl.* creamy-white, very heavily spotted with dark maroon, especially near base, short trumpet- or bell-shaped.   Probably slightly tender and best suited for cool greenhouse.   N. Burma, Shan States, Yunnan.

Variable in colour and the following rather distinct varieties have been named. Syn. *L. lowii.*

> Var. **aureum.** Golden-yellow with deep purplish-maroon spots. N.W. Yunnan, China.
>
> Var. **delavayi.** Olive-green or greenish-yellow suffused with pink or pale purplish-red and with deep purple spots. N. Yunnan, China.
>
> Var. **rubrum.** Reddish with darker red spots. Yunnan and Kweichow, China.
>
> Var. **yunnanense.** White or pale pink, only slightly speckled with maroon. Yunnan, China.

**L. bolanderi.** Usually rather dwarf. Inflorescence and *l.* whorled. *Fl.* scarlet-red to deep brick-red, small, bell-shaped and opening wide, heavily spotted with maroon-purple, green at throat. Stem and *l.* rather glaucous. N. America, S. Oregon and N. California.

**L. callosum.** *Fl.* Turk's-Cap, rather small, orange-red with darker markings towards base, segments strongly recurved. 1–3 ft. China, Hupeh, Manchuria, Korea, Japan and Formosa. Related to *L. pumilum* but a larger plant.

**L. carniolicum.** Bright red Turk's-Cap lily from N. Yugoslavia, particularly the Julian Alps where it grows in coarse limestone scree. It is a strong clear colour and a handsome lily in its own habitat. Height up to 4 ft. with up to 6 *fl.* Not quite so vivid in colour as *L. chalcedonicum,* but the *fl.* are slightly larger.

> Var. **albanicum.** Pale orange-yellow. Usually rather dwarf. S. Yugoslavia and Macedonia.
>
> Var. **jankae.** Bright lemon-yellow with dark spots but anthers red. Yugoslavia and Balkans.

**L. catesbaei.** Rather dwarf. *Fl.* upright, red and yellow with darker spots, segments with conspicuous claw at base. N. America, Florida, Louisiana and Carolina in damp pinewoods and in swamps. Rather tender and best in a cool greenhouse. Rather more bizarre than beautiful.

**L. cathayanum.** See under *Cardiocrinum.*

**L. cernuum.** A delicate and dainty lily from Korea, but also known from Manchuria and eastern provinces of U.S.S.R. *Fl.* Turk's-Cap, rather small, rosy-lilac with darker purple spots. Fragrant. Rather dwarf.

**L. concolor.** A variable lily from Central China and Manchuria with upright rather narrow-petalled *fl.* giving it a star-like shape. Scarlet to orange-scarlet, unspotted. Numerous varieties have been named of which the best are probably ' Dropmore ' and var. *pulchellum.*

**L. cordatum.** See under *Cardiocrinum.*

**L. distichum.** Rather pale, orange-red martagon-type *fl.* but smaller and arranged in a compact raceme. Not very tall. Korea and Manchuria.

**L. fairchildii.** Imperfectly known in this country. Probably a variant of *L. humboldtii* var. *bloomerianum.*

# *Lilium*

**L. fargesii.** Rather dwarf, slender; *fl.* of martagon-type, greenish-white with small rose-pink spots. Never recorded in cultivation as far as I can find.

**L. fresnense.** A Turk's-Cap lily allied to *L. pardalinum* from California. *Fl.* yellowish-orange. Said to be very fragrant.

**L. georgicum.** See under *L. ponticum.*

**L. grayi.** An attractive lily with rather small, drooping funnel-shaped *fl.* deep crimson outside and inside red paling to orange in throat, heavily spotted. N. America from mountains of N. Carolina, Tennessee and Virginia. Allied to *L. canadense* but smaller in *fl.* and distinct in colour.

**L. henrici.** A delicate and beautiful white-flowered lily, rather resembling a *Nomocharis* and formerly placed in that genus. *Fl.* drooping with rather narrow segments, white with red markings at base. Requires similar conditions to *Nomocharis.* China. W. Yunnan.

**L. inyoense.** A Turk's-Cap lily with yellowish-orange spotted *fl.* smaller in *fl.* and habit than *L. pardalinum* but of this group. S.W. California.

**L. iridollae.** A beautiful and rare lily from N. America, S. Alabama and N.W. Florida with bright golden-yellow martagon-type *fl.* but segments not so tightly recurved, spotted not very freely with darker orange-brown. Only recently discovered by Mrs. J. Norman Henry who called it her ' Pot of Gold.' Allied to *L. canadense* and *L. superbum* but probably not so tall, likely to require similar conditions.

**L. kelleyanum.** A rhizomatous lily with yellow Turk's-Cap *fl.*, slightly spotted. Mountains of California by banks of streams. Probably requiring similar conditions to *L. pardalinum.*

**L. kelloggii.** A lilac-pink lily with martagon-type *fl.* but with segments often not so much or so tightly recurved. Tall and recorded in the wild as bearing very large spike of *fl.* The waxy *fl.* deepen in colour as they age and are finely spotted with deeper purple, fragrant. N.W. California and S. Oregon.

**L. kesselringianum.** See under *L. monadelphum.*

**L. lophophorum.** Formerly included in *Nomocharis* and requiring similar conditions. Dwarf with solitary bell-shaped drooping *fl.* of greenish-yellow of medium size, the segments being long and narrow. Western China.

**L. maritimum.** An unusual lily with tall stems in the wild and several rather small reddish-orange bell-shaped *fl.* heavily speckled inside with darker colour; segments recurved in the upper part. Coastal regions of California. Closely related to *L. bolanderi* and *L. occidentale* but taller and not so conspicuous in colouring. From its area of origin it may prove tender in cultivation in this country.

**L. medeoloides.** A martagon-type lily from Japan with apricot or orange-scarlet *fl.* usually heavily spotted but unspotted forms have been recorded. Distinct in that it has usually one, occasionally 2 whorls of *l.* with above scattered *l.* and so called " The Wheel Lily " in Japan.

219

# Lilium

**L. michauxii.** A Turk's-Cap lily from the southern states of N. America with orange-red or deep yellow *fl.*, heavily spotted. Sometimes described as the southern counterpart of *L. superbum* but more tender and without the long pedicels and magnificent poise of the *fl.* of that lily. *L.* in whorls, rather broad.

**L. nanum.** A dwarf plant formerly included in *Nomocharis* and apparently requiring similar conditions. It has also in the past been included in *Fritillaria. Fl.* generally solitary, pendulous, bell-shaped or with a wide open trumpet, deep purplish in colour overlaying greenish-yellow, speckled inside with deeper reddish-purple.

† **L. neilgherrense.** A beautiful pure white trumpet lily from S. India but too tender for planting outside in this country. Good for the cool greenhouse. *Fl.* up to 8 in. long, occasional *fl.* exceeding 1 ft. have been recorded, flushed with yellow towards throat inside. Trumpet rather narrow but tips of segments widely recurved.

† **L. nobilissimum.** A very beautiful cool greenhouse lily with pure white, wide-opening, trumpet *fl.* from the Ryukyu Islands of S. Japan. Fragrant. It is possible that there are two distinct lilies under this name, (1) the fine greenhouse trumpet described above which may need to be renamed *L. alexandrae* and (2) a much dwarfer plant from the mountains with smaller white trumpets recommended by Japanese growers for rock garden use.

**L. occidentale.** A small-flowered Turk's-Cap lily from the coast of N. California and S. Oregon. *Fl.* unusual in colouring, being orange or reddish-orange in the throat and crimson on the recurved tip of the segments while being green at the throat which is almost tubular, green and glaucous outside. In its native home known as the Eureka Lily. It is closely related to *L. maritimum*, which grows to the south of its area. In the wild, specimens have been recorded up to 9 ft. high with 25 *fl.*

**L. ocellatum.** See under *L. humboldtii* var. *ocellatum.*

**L. oxypetalum.** Formerly placed in *Nomocharis* and requiring similar conditions. Allied to *L. nanum. Fl.* usually solitary, bell-shaped, drooping, greenish or bronzy-yellow. Plant dwarf. N.W. Himalaya.

Var. **insigne.** *Fl.* mauvish-purple with a greenish midrib to each petal.

**L. papilliferum.** Slender growing. Small, deep maroon Turk's-Cap *fl.* Scented. China, Yunnan. *Fl.* seem to be amongst the smallest in the genus relative to the length of stem.

**L. parvum.** Small-flowered. Tall slender stems. Yellow or orange *fl.*, trumpet-shaped but opening wide, spotted towards base with deep purple. Mountains of California.

Var. **crocatum.** *Fl.* orange-yellow and almost without spots.

**L. philadelphicum.** A perpetual challenge to keen growers. An attractive little lily with upright cup-shaped *fl.* of very bright colouring, orange-scarlet with orange throat and heavily spotted with maroon. Segments narrowed at base into a distinct claw. Very widespread and variable in colour in the

220

eastern states of N. America but in American gardens apparently little easier than in English ones.

**L. pitkinense.** A very rare lily of the *pardalinum* group. *Fl.* orange-scarlet with rather narrow pointed segments and with a well-defined zone of yellow near base, lightly spotted at base, pedicels long. California. Without stem roots.

**L. poilanei.** A very rare lily from Indo-China allied to *L. primulinum* but with pale yellow bell-shaped *fl.* with a longitudinal stripe of bright red. As far as I know it has never been in cultivation but would be likely to require cool or even warm greenhouse treatment.

**L. polyphyllum.** An unusual sp. from the Western Himalaya, half way between a trumpet and a Turk's-Cap lily. Tube of *fl.* long and narrow but upper third of segments much reflexed. *Fl.* creamy-white inside and spotted with pale purple in throat, but pale pinkish forms have been recorded. Stem up to 8 ft. with 40 *fl.* in the wild, but in cultivation usually much less. Not an easy lily to keep and establish.

**L. ponticum.** *Fl.* primrose-yellow with heavy very dark purple markings at bese and with segments strongly recurved. Scent strong, pungent. Dwarf up to 2 ft. Related to *L. monadelphum* but smaller in *fl.* and not of such a good colour. Very rare in cultivation. N.E. Turkey and lower slopes of Southern Caucasus. Probably *L. artvinense* and *L. georgicum* are syn. of this.

**L. pumilum.** Dwarf. Small, martagon-type *fl.* of bright red from N. China, Mongolia and Manchuria. Often listed under name *L. tenuifolium.* ' Golden Gleam ' is an attractive golden-yellow form.

**L. roezlii.** See under *L. vollmeri* and *L. wigginsii.*

**L. rubescens.** One of the beauties of the genus. Curious upright-facing, waxy, white *fl.* changing to pink and then to pale purple as they age, so that all three colours may sometimes be seen on the plant together. *Fl.* tubular at base, the segments opening into a flat, broadly star-like *fl.* *L.* in whorls. Seems to do best planted among conifer needles near the foot of such a tree, but very rare in cultivation and always regarded as difficult. California and S. Oregon. Allied to *L. washingtonianum* but distinct in the wholly upright poise of the *fl.*

**L. sempervivoideum.** Very rare dwarf lily from Yunnan. *Fl.* white spotted with red inside. Not known in cultivation.

**L. shastense.** Often known as a variety of *L. nevadense*, to which it is closely related. A member of the *pardalinum* group with rhizomatous bulbs and rather small *fl.* with dark yellowish-orange segments spotted with purple towards base and much recurved. California.

**L. souliei.** Formerly included in *Nomocharis* and probably requiring similar treatment. A dwarf plant with deep purplish-crimson drooping *fl.*

**L. stewartianum.** Very rare Chinese lily from Yunnan. Rather small drooping *fl.* of deep olive-yellow very heavily spotted with deep maroon. Not known in cultivation.

**L. tenuifolium.** See under *L. pumilum.*

**L. tsingtauense.** Striking, with clusters of upright brilliant fiery orange star-shaped *fl.* from E. China and Korea. Rare in cultivation but in a few gardens has maintained itself well among dwarf shrubs almost in full sun.

**L. vollmeri.** A small-flowered lily of the *pardalinum* group. Tightly reflexed segments, orange-red *fl.* heavily spotted. Sometimes found in gardens under name *L. roezlii* but separate from *L. wigginsii.*

**L. wallichianum.** A beautiful white lily with long narrow trumpets from the Central and Eastern Himalaya. *Fl.* borne horizontally, thus distinguishing it from *L. neilgherrense,* and are wider open at the mouth and not so long. The trumpets are flushed with green outside and inside are creamy-white. Rather tender and usually grown as a cool greenhouse plant. Late flowering.

**L. washingtonianum.** A very variable lily from California where it attains considerable magnificence. *Fl.* tubular with segments opening flat in upper third, carried horizontally, white with purple markings and in the wild borne in very large heads on tall stems. Difficult and very rare in cultivation.

> Var. **purpurascens.** A more vigorous form with pinkish-purple *fl.* Commonest variety in its native country. There is also a pure white-flowered variety.

**L. wigginsii.** A rather small-flowered Turk's-Cap lily with clear yellow *fl.* spotted with purple from N.W. California and S. Oregon. It belongs to the *pardalinum* group and appears to be the lily, in part at least, formerly distributed as *L. roezlii* which must now be rejected as a name. Bulbs rhizomatous. It is close to *L. vollmeri* but larger in *fl.* and a clear yellow instead of orange-red.

## (c) Lily hybrids

\* ' AFRICAN QUEEN ' One of the finest trumpet lilies yet selected out of the Aurelian Hybrids raised at the Oregon Bulb Farms. Tall. Large *fl.,* warm mahogany-brown, suffused with deep yellow on outside, inside deep orange. A very spectacular plant. Sold both as a clone and a group.

' A. M. VOLLMER ' See under *L. tigrinum* var. *flaviflorum.*

' APOLLO ' *L. chalcedonicum* × *L. testaceum,* orange-red Turk's-Cap *fl.* Raised by Mr. Oliver Wyatt of Maidwell Hall, Northampton; ' Hephaestus ' and ' Zeus ' are seedlings from the same cross.

*aurelianense.* See p. 198.

AURELIAN HYBRIDS The name used by Mr. de Graaf of the Oregon Bulb Farms for the very varied group based on crosses between *L. henryi* and a trumpet lily. Out of this three distinct groups have been separated:

\* GOLDEN CLARION Deep yellow or orange-yellow trumpet *fl.* flushed with purplish-mahogany on outside. A variable group.

HEART'S DESIRE Lilies with shallow bowl-shaped *fl.* and outward flaring segments, very variable in colour.

SUNBURST A group of lilies with upright *fl.* and very variable in colour.

# Lilium

'BATEMANNII' A form of *L.* × *maculatum* with unspotted apricot-orange *fl.*

BELLINGHAM HYBRIDS See under *L. humboldtii* (p. 204).

\* 'BLACK DRAGON' A very fine trumpet lily, resembling *L. brownii*, inside pure white, outside dark brownish-red. Raised at the Oregon Bulb Farms where they are stated to grow up to 6 ft. with 12 large *fl.* Sold both as a clone and a group.

'BRENDA WATTS' See under Preston Hybrids.

\* 'COOLHURST' One of the finest of the hybrids. Brilliant orange erect *fl. L. bulbiferum croceum* × *L.* × *maculatum.* Raised by Mr. C. Scrase-Dickens of Coolhurst, Sussex.

CROW'S HYBRIDS See under *L.* × *imperiale* (p.205).

*dalhansonii* See under *L. martagon* (p. 209).

\* 'DESTINY' *L. amabile luteum* × *L.* 'Valencia'. *Fl.* erect on long pedicels and stout stems, deep lemon-yellow, heavily spotted with purplish-brown segments reflexed in outer third. A handsome lily raised at the Oregon Bulb Farms.

\* 'DUNKIRK' Glowing mahogany-red *fl.* borne horizontally in a well-spaced raceme, open trumpet- or bowl-shaped. A striking and unusual colour of great richness. A hybrid from *L. davidii* var. *willmottiae*, raised by F. L. Skinner of Manitoba, Canada. (Pl. **20**, 5)

\* 'ENCHANTMENT' One of the most outstanding of recent hybrids. The *fl.* are erect or horizontal, wide open or bowl-shaped, bright nasturtium-red, a very brilliant and striking colour in full sun; increasing from bulblets. Raised at the Oregon Bulb Farms. (Pl. **20**, 4)

'GEORGE C. CREELMAN' See under *L.* × *imperiale* (p. 205).

GOLDEN CLARION group. See under Aurelian Hybrids.

'GRACE MARSHALL' See under Preston Hybrids.

\* 'GREEN DRAGON' An unusually fine trumpet lily resembling *L. brownii* and almost as fine in form and substance of petal. The trumpet opens wide and is glistening white inside, outside deep purplish-brown. Selected from the Olympic Hybrids raised at the Oregon Bulb Farms who suggest that it has *L. sulphureum* and *L. sargentiae* among its parents. Sold both as a clone and as a group. The clone is probably one of the finest lilies raised in recent years.

'JILLIAN WALLACE' A *parkmannii* hybrid. See under *L. auratum* (p. 197).

'JOAN EVANS' One of the best of the upright flowering group, bright yellow, spotted maroon. Selected at the Oregon Bulb Farms from the Mid-Century Hybrids.

\* 'LIMELIGHT' A trumpet lily, opening wide, of a soft greenish-yellow that is most attractive. Selected from the Aurelian Hybrids and raised at the Oregon Bulb Farms. Sold both as a clone (Pl. **22**) and as a group.

'MARLYN ROSS' See under *L. wilsonii* var. *flavum* (p. 217).

\* 'MAXWILL' See under *L. davidii* (p. 202).

OLYMPIC HYBRIDS. A very mixed group of trumpet lilies, blooming later than *L. regale*, mostly white or pale pink inside and varying in colour outside. Raised from *L. brownii*, *L. leucanthum* var. *centifolium*, *L. sargentiae* and *L. sulphureum* at the Oregon Bulb Farms.

'PAGODA' A rather short-growing lily with stout stems and erect or horizontal bowl- or saucer-shaped *fl.*, large when open, orange-red, spotted with dark purplish-brown. Raised at the Oregon Bulb Farms. ' PARADE ' Rather similar to the preceding but *fl.* more orange.

PRESTON HYBRIDS. A large group raised by Miss Isabella Preston at the Ottawa Central Experimental Farm from *L. davidii* var. *willmottiae* × an unnamed hybrid of *L. dauricum* × *L.* × *maculatum*. They are good growers with horizontal or slightly drooping *fl.* with reflexed segments, orange or bright orange-red, generally heavily spotted. Some very brilliant in colour. They are named in two series (*a*) Stenographer Series, including ' Brenda Watts ', ' Edna Keen ', ' Grace Marshall ', ' Lilian Cummings ', ' Lyla McCann ', ' Muriel Condie ' and ' Phyllis Cox '. Probably *' Grace Marshall ' and *' Lilian Cummings ' are the two best of the group. (*b*) Fighter Series, including ' Corsair ', ' Hurricane ', ' Lysander ', ' Mosquito ', ' Spitfire ' and ' Typhoon '. On the whole these have proved less successful than the Stenographer Series. Both groups are suitable for rather open positions either in full sun or at the most semi-shade.

STOOKE'S HYBRIDS. A group of yellow Turk's-Cap lilies derived from crosses with *L. davidii*. These should be treated as *L.* ' Maxwill,' but are not generally not so tall.

' SULPHUR QUEEN ' The best of a fine group of trumpet lilies sometimes known as × *sulianense*. Hybrids of *L. sulphureum* with *L.* × *aurelianense*. Spikes tall, trumpets nodding, large, heavily coloured outside with deep purplish-maroon, inside creamy-white. *Fl.* heavy and waxy in substance.

' T. A. HAVEMEYER ' *L. henryi* × *L. sulphureum*. Tall with deep yellow, partially reflexed *fl.* but more closely resembling *L. henryi* than *L. sulphureum*. A fine lily but unfortunately very susceptible to virus.

' VALENCIA ' *Fl.* deep orange-yellow, borne horizontally and facing outwards. Raised at the Oregon Bulb Farms.

' YELLOW MAID ' One of the best of the deep yellow *parryi* hybrids raised by Mr. Oliver Wyatt of Maidwell Hall. A beautiful and graceful lily with slightly larger *fl.* than *L. parryi*. (Pl. 20, 6)

# LITTONIA *Liliaceae*

A VERY small genus of S. African tuberous plants allied to *Gloriosa* and *Sandersonia* and requiring rather similar treatment, but with smaller and much less conspicuous flowers. The stems are slender and need support and the plants are suitable for the Intermediate greenhouse.

**L. modesta.** Stem up to 6 ft., scrambling or climbing by their tendrils produced at the ends of the *l.* *Fl.* produced in the axils of the *l.* on short stems, bell-shaped, orange-red, up to 2 in. across, often pendulous, segments rather acute at tips. Tuber small, often with three branches. *L.* lanceolate, bright green; seeds red. Summer *fl.* Natal and N. Transvaal where it *fl.* Nov.-Jan. Tubers may be kept dry in winter and started in early spring, preferably in some heat.

*Plate VII.* The delicate fishing rods of *Dierama pulcherrimum* ‘Plover’, one of the finest varieties of the Wandflowers

*Plate VIII. Fritillaria imperialis* 'Aurora', one of the finest of the Crown Imperials

*Plate IX.* Naturalised snowdrops. A beautiful mass of galanthus 'Straffan' in the late Mr. E. A. Bowles's garden at Myddelton House, near Enfield

*Plate X. Iris planifolia*, better known to gardeners as *I. alata*,
a very early-flowering Juno iris

# LYCORIS *Amaryllidaceae*

A SMALL genus of bulbs from China and Japan, related to *Amaryllis* but also somewhat resembling *Nerine* both in appearance and in cultivation. Unfortunately none are reliably hardy in this country and they require to be grown in a cool or intermediate greenhouse. The nearest to hardiness are *L. radiata* and *L. squamigera* and there are records of their successful cultivation for a time in very warm positions. There are also records of their being naturalised in Glenn Dale, Maryland, U.S.A., where zero temperatures are experienced at intervals. They flower in the autumn and the flowers are in rounded umbels, usually before the leaves appear and are funnel-shaped, usually red, terracotta or yellow in colour, the segments being strap-shaped and divided to the base. The bulbs are ovoid with a short neck and the leaves linear or strap-shaped. They probably merit to be more widely grown than they are, having been largely superseded in most gardens by nerines. After the leaves have died down in the early summer they should be kept dry until the flower buds show from the top of the bulb. They need shallow planting with the neck appearing above the soil and should not be lifted too frequently.

**L. aurea.** Golden Spider Lily. Stem up to 1 ft. with an umbel of golden-yellow upright *fl.* with rather narrow wavy segments on medium-lengthed stalks. Aug.-Sept. China. Syn. *Amaryllis aurea.*

**L. incarnata.** *Fl.* pale rose-pink, slightly scented, large in an umbel of 6–10. China. Nearly hardy.

**L. radiata.** *Fl.* bright red or deep orange-pink. Segments spreading, waved at the edge and reflexing backwards. Aug.-Sept. China.
Var. **alba.** *Fl.* creamy-white with a yellow flush at base. Syn. *L. albiflora.*

**L. sanguinea.** *Fl.* bright red, up to $2\frac{1}{2}$ in. across, stem rather slender. July-Sept. Japan.

**L. sprengeri.** *Fl.* purplish-rose. Japan. Closely allied to *L. squamigera.*

**L. squamigera.** *Fl.* funnel-shaped, pink tinged with lilac and with partial yellow, central ray on inside of each segment, yellow at base, 3 in. across, scented. Aug. Bulb large, globose. *L.* strap-shaped, generally not produced till spring, hence this sp. is practically hardy in warm positions. Syn. *Amaryllis hallii.* Superficially this sp. looks not unlike *Amaryllis belladonna*, but is generally not so tall nor such a good pink colour.

# MERENDERA *Liliaceae*

A SMALL genus of dwarf plants with swollen corms, allied to *Colchicum* but separated from it by a narrow constriction at the base of each segment which gives it the appearance of a claw and by the absence of a perianth tube. The segments are free of each other to the base and tend to fall apart as the flowers mature. It is distinguished from *Bulbocodium* by the three styles which are also free to the base. The genus is native to S. Europe around the Mediterranean but extends eastwards to Persia and the Caucasus. The flowers are erect, funnel-shaped, rosy-lilac or occasionally white and are either autumnal or spring. All the species except *M. filifolia* are reasonably hardy but being small and very easily demolished by slugs are more often grown as alpine house plants in pans. None have exhibited any great freedom or vigour in cultivation and they are rarely seen. Good drainage is important for them. The commonest species is *M. montana*, more frequently known as *M. bulbocodium* which is quite common on the mountains of Spain and Portugal and in the Pyrenees in the lower pastures; flowering when the autumn rains come and giving a signal for the taking down of cattle to the lower zones. The corms are one-sided generally with a pronounced foot like a *Colchicum* and the flowers appear from the flatter side.

**M. aitchisonii.** A syn. of *M. robusta*.

**M. bulbocodium.** A syn. of *M. montana*.

**M. caucasica.** A syn. of *M. trigyna*.

**M. filifolia.** *Fl.* small with narrow petals, rose-pink, up to 1½ in. long. Late autumn. Corm small, dark brown with long neck. *L.* narrow, linear or filiform with *fl.* Balearic Islands, S. France near mouth of Rhône, Algeria. Rather tender.

**M. hissarica.** *Fl.* small, purplish-pink, rather globular, up to ¾ in. long. March-April. N. Persia.

**M. montana.** *Fl.* 1 or 2, almost sessile on the ground, rose-lilac, rarely white, petals lanceolate, rather narrow 1½–2 in. long. July-Oct. Corm small with a dark tunic, irregular in shape. *L.* linear, appearing in Oct. after *fl.* Pyrenees, Spain, Portugal. Syn. *M. bulbocodium, Colchicum montanum* in part. There is also a Greek form which has sometimes been regarded as a separate sp. *M. attica* and has slightly larger *fl.* It is said to be common by the sea shore.

**M. robusta.** *Fl.* 1–4, very pale reddish-lilac or white, 1½–2 in. long and as much across, anthers green, a distinguishing character. Spring, Feb.-May. *L.* narrow, just appearing with *fl.* and later lengthening. Persia, India, Punjab.

**M. sobolifera.** *Fl.* very small, pale rosy-lilac or white with very narrow strap-shaped petals 1 in. long, falling apart as *fl.* opens. Corm grows out into stout lateral horizontal stem at the end of which there is a swelling form which *fl.* and *l.* arise. This is a distinctive character. Feb.-March. *L.* narrow, linear, appearing with *fl.* Bulgaria, Asia Minor, Persia, Afghanistan.

**M. trigyna.** Better known as *M. caucasica. Fl.* 1–3, mauve-pink or white, small, petals narrow but wider than in preceding sp. March-April. *L.* narrow, appearing with *fl.* Caucasus, Persia. Syns., as above and *Bulbocodium trigynum, Colchicum trigynum* and *Colchicum caucasicum.*

# MONTBRETIA *Iridaceae*

NOW A VERY small genus of S. African plants with corms, closely allied to *Crocosmia* and *Tritonia*, to which genera many of the plants often known by gardeners as montbretias have been transferred. The hybrids which are commonly grown under that name will be found under *Crocosmia* while the plant with rather small pink flowers often offered as *M. rosea* will be found under *Tritonia.* Only one species *M. laxiflora* is left which is known at all in this country and even that is very rarely grown now. It requires cool greenhouse treatment.

† **M. laxiflora.** Stem up to 1½ ft., branched with a loose spike of creamy-pink *fl.* tubular at base, distinguished by the unequal spreading segments, the upper one of which is slightly hooded, pale pink inside, lower ones pinkish-orange, with a horn-like spur arising from centre of the inside of each and pointing upwards and inwards. Autumn. *L.* linear in 2 ranks, narrow. S. Africa.

# MORAEA *Iridaceae*

PROBABLY NONE of the S. African plants are more beautiful or jewel-like than the brilliant and iridescent peacock moraeas. Yet, how rarely does one see them, although one species at least, *M. glaucopis*, is regularly offered by nurserymen although frequently under the erroneous name of *Iris pavonia. Moraea* has three large wide-spreading outer petals, rounded at the edge and three small, almost rudimentary, inner ones. The three outer ones are divided to the base and thus the genus is separated from *Iris* in which they are united into a tube at the base. In the case of the peacock moraeas there is a prominent blotch of glistening darker blue, indigo or purple at the base of each outer petal. This is usually irregular in outline at the edge and sometimes has a margin of lighter colour. The corm is small and covered with a coarse net-like tunic. Some plants with a rather thin rhizomatous rootstock were formerly also placed in the genus but now are more frequently separated under *Dietes*. Being without bulbs or corms they are not treated here. The leaves are linear and rush-like, sometimes as in *M. villosa* with a ciliated edge. Only one species *M. spathulata* with tall stems and bright yellow flowers in spring is reasonably hardy and it is not one of the peacock group. But nevertheless it is a very valuable plant for the really warm border under a wall, since it is tolerant of winter wet and does not begin to grow before the spring. It comes from a different part to the peacock moraeas described.

In this country the peacock moraeas all need cool or even cold green-house treatment with plenty of moisture and ventilation during the warmer spells of the winter. They are winter growers and their enemy, as with many of the gladiolus and watsonia species, is winter fog and damp which sets up mildew and rot in the leaves. They should not be watered in very cold weather. A sandy compost with very good drainage is desirable and those who have been most successful have generally grown them in raised beds in the greenhouse, rather than in pots. They should be lifted and divided about every third year. The flowers appear from March to May and although each flower only lasts a short time, the spike carries a number of buds which follow on and so keep up the season.

For further information on the peacock moraeas readers should consult T. T. Barnard's excellent article in the R.H.S. Journal for 1950 and that of E. Cahn in the issue for August 1943.

Moraeas hybridise freely and many of those supplied by bulb merchants or seen in this country and also in gardens in S. Africa will probably be hybrids. Moraeas can easily be raised from seed but usually take four years before flowering.

**M. gigandra.** *Fl.* large, closely allied to *M. pavonia* and *M. villosa*. Creamy-white or soft lilac-blue with base of orange blotched with green and surrounded by an inner dark blue narrow rim and an outer peacock-blue one on slender stem, distinguished by the large and completely glabrous segments and by the large anthers. Rare in its native habitat. One of the finest *fl.* of the group. Var. *purpurea* has dark purple *fl.* and almost black base, surrounded by a peacock rim.

**M. glaucopis.** *Fl.* white or very pale blue with a deep peacock-blue spot, rimmed like a peacock's eye at base of each outer petal. 1 ft. May-June. Often offered as *Iris pavonia*. Corm small, globose. Smaller than *I. pavonia*.

**M. papilionacea.** A dwarf sp., only a few in. in height. *Fl.* bright orange-red, yellow or salmon-pink with yellow blotch. Very fugacious. Common in S. Africa. March-May.

**M. pavonia.** *Fl.* large, orange-red or yellow up to 1½ in. across with royal blue eye. Inner segments entire. There are many hybrids between this and

*M. villosa.* ' Magnifica,' an unusually fine form with large deep chrome-orange *fl.* and blue base to the three outer petals. (Pl. **23**)

**M. spathulata.** *Fl.* bright yellow on 2 ft. stems, 1½ in. across, outer petals curving downwards, long with wavy edge and clawed at base, quite distinct from the peacock moraeas and distinctly hardier and worth planting in a warm south border. April-May. In general appearance it is closer to an iris than the other moraeas. Corm with distinct dark tunic and *l.* very long after flowering, and spreading by stolons into large clumps occasionally. Better known under its more appropriate syn. *M. spathacea.* S. Africa, Eastern Province of Cape, Natal, Transvaal.

**M. villosa.** Closely allied to *M. pavonia* but with foliage more hairy. *Fl.* very variable in colour, mauvish-purple with iridescent blue blotch at base of outer petals or pale mauve, cream, yellow or orange. Inner segments tricuspidate with a long central cusp, a distinguishing character from *M. pavonia* in which they are entire. May. A number of colour varieties have been separated. Stem slender up to 1½ ft. with a succession of *fl.* One of the most brilliant of this group and the parent of a very varied range of hybrids, a bed of which in flower has been decribed when the sun opens them as like " a flight of big butterflies just about to alight." (Pl. **23**)

# MUSCARI *Liliaceae*

THE GRAPE hyacinths form one of the best and most frec-flowering groups of spring bulbs. In fact in many gardens some species increase so rapidly that they tend to be regarded as weeds and a menace to more delicate plants. This applies particularly to *M. racemosum*, which is a rare native of this country but also has a wide distribution in Europe and Asia Minor. In all there are probably between 50 and 60 species but many of them are so similar that a botanical monographer, of which the genus is very sadly in need, might well reduce their number. Only a small proportion of these are in regular cultivation in this country and this account will be restricted to them, although it is likely that many of the others could also be grown without difficulty.

The genus is distinguished by the flask-like shape of its small bells which are borne in dense racemes. The bells are narrowed both at the base and at the mouth so that Farrer, not inaptly, referred to their " characteristic Rugby-football shape." Their predominant colouring is in either light or dark blue but there are also some with pale yellow flowers. The bulbs are globose and fleshy and with rather thin tunics and most species spawn off little bulbs with great freedom. The clumps should be divided every third or fourth year. The leaves are mostly grass-like, linear and channelled and begin to grow in the autumn, but generally survive the winter without damage. In a few species the leaves are broader and strap-shaped. The less vigorous species such as *M. botryoides* and *M. tubergenianum* are very suitable for the rock garden while the others, particularly the lovely ' Heavenly Blue ', the colour of a rather deep and almost stormy sky, deeper than its name suggests, should be grown in quantities in front of shrubs or among them or even naturalised in grass. One of the most impressive bulb sights I have seen was at the Keukenhof Park, the display garden in Holland of the Dutch bulb growers, where it was used as a small blue river several yards wide among the scarlet tulips and yellow daffodils. A more subtle combination is probably the growing of it among the stems of the dwarf almond *Prunus tenella* and the two will flower together. All species should be planted in full sun and are tolerant of lime in the soil.

**M. armeniacum.** One of the best sp. with dense racemes on short stout stalks, 8–10 in., of very bright azure-blue with a narrow white edge at the mouth, varying in depth of colour; scented. April-early May. Northern Asia Minor. A very easy plant in nearly all gardens and spreading freely both by division and seed.

* ' CANTAB ' A paler blue form and more dwarf.

' HEAVENLY BLUE ' A form of this and very close to the type. It is recorded that all the stock of millions of bulbs now grown has been derived from an original 6 bulbs received by Messrs. Barr from H. J. Elwes under the incorrect name of *M. conicum.*

' BLUE MOUNTAIN ' A rarely seen form with darker *fl.*

' EARLY GIANT ' Very close to ' Heavenly Blue ', but tending to flower slightly earlier. A fine form but rare in cultivation.

**M. szovitsianum.** From N. Persia and the hills around Tiflis is very close to this sp. but is a smaller plant with bells less restricted around the mouth and of a paler colour. The *fl.* also are more closely bunched together.

**M. aucheri.** A slender sp. with *fl.* of very deep indigo-blue, edged with white and much constricted around the mouth. Close also to *M. armeniacum,* but not so fine. Turkey and Asia Minor.

* **M. botryoides.** A dwarf sp. of considerable beauty with almost globular *fl.* of pale China-blue. Not so vigorous as *M. armeniacum* and so more suitable for the Rock Garden among other choice plants. The white form is very attractive and is sometimes known as " Pearls of Spain." April-May. S. Europe.

**M. comosum.** A common plant of cultivated ground and wayside banks throughout S. Europe and Asia Minor and rather distinct from other sp. Stem up to 1½ ft. with a combination of olive-green fertile *fl.* and dark purplish-blue sterile ones above. The sterile *fl.* grow upright, the others horizontal or nodding. *L.* broader than in preceeding sp., strap-shaped; bulb rather larger and with pinkish tunic. May-June.

Var. **monstrosum.** This is the variety generally seen in gardens and really living up to its name since all the *fl.* are sterile and converted into dark mauvish-blue tufts of quite long filaments. It is often known as var-*plumosum* or as the " Feather " or " Tassel Hyacinth."

**M. latifolium.** A dusky but slightly coarse beauty from the Troad, Turkey and N. Asia Minor. *Fl.* dark indigo-blue with a dark purplish bloom, pendulous but aggregated into a close head, uppermost sterile *fl.* pale bluish-lilac. Stem stout up to 15 in. *L.* broad, usually solitary but sometimes 2 up to 12 in. long by 1½ in. broad, narrowed at tip. April-May. This is usually the largest of the sp. described though it may be rivalled in size by *M. moschatum.* The plate in the Botanical Magazine, however, shows an unusually large and robust specimen and with *fl.* even darker than is usual. (Pl. **24**, 11)

**M. macrocarpum.** Probably the finest of the yellow-flowered sp. and close to *M. moschatum* under which it has often been placed as var. *flavum.* It is, however, left as a separate sp. in a recent volume of the Botanical Magazine. Stem stout up to 9 in. with 20 or more nodding *fl.* of a good bright yellow with a deeper brown rim at the mouth and almost fleshy in texture. Sterile *fl.* at the top bluish-purple. April-early May. Bulb large with irregular scales. *L.* strap-shaped, wider than in most other sp. Aegean Islands. It is hardy in a sunny position in the South of England but still rare in cultivation. The bulbs should, however, be given a summer resting period if possible.

**M. moschatum.** The most sweetly scented member of the genus, having something of the musk scent after which it is named. This is its best character since the *fl.* are rather dull purplish-olive, maturing to a yellowish-olive lower down the stem which is stout and about 10 in. high. April. Bulb large like the preceding. *L.* broad for the genus. Asia Minor. Quite hardy in a sunny position. The name *moschatum* has unfortunately in the literature been a source of confusion and is now discarded by some botanists being replaced by *M. muscarimi*, but this has not generally been adopted by horticulturists. (Pl. **24**, 4)
    Var. **flavum.** A syn. of *M. macrocarpum.*
    Var. **major.** A slightly larger and more vigorous form.

**M. neglectum.** *Fl.* deep indigo-blue, closely bunched on rather short stems up to 9 in. Scented. April. S. Europe. Closely related to *M. racemosum* but larger in all its parts. (Pl. **24**, 15)

**M. paradoxum.** A more robust sp. from N. Persia and the S. Caucasian region of U.S.S.R. *Fl.* deep purplish-mauve outside, closely aggregated. Inside yellowish-green which shows at the mouth, which is little constricted, and also at the base outside. May. Bulb large; *l.* strap-shaped, long up to 1½ ft. and up to ½ in. broad. (Pl. **24**, 3)

**M. polyanthum.** *Fl.* deep blue on a slender stem up to 8 in. March-April. Greece.

**M. racemosum.** *Fl.* dark blue, rather small, white at the mouth, fragrant, on stem up to 8 in. Widespread in Europe including Britain. Spreading very freely in garden but probably the least desirable sp. of those described. March-April.

**M. szovitsianum.** See under *M. armeniacum.*

\* **M. tubergenianum.** A spectacular plant often known as the " Oxford and Cambridge grape hyacinth," because of the contrast of its deep blue *fl.* at the apex of the spike above the paler blue lower ones. Stem up to 8 in. March-April. Mountains of N.W. Persia. One of the best sp. for the rock garden and not spreading as freely as *M. armeniacum* or *M. racemosum.* (Pl. **24**, 2)

# NARCISSUS (Daffodil) *Amaryllidaceae*

To MANY spring implies daffodils and it is hardly realised that apart from the many fine garden varieties *Narcissus* is a vast genus including species flowering from autumn till late spring and found wild over most of the countries bordering the Mediterranean. Their main concentration is, however, in Spain and Portugal.

Daffodils are probably the most widely grown of all bulbs and certainly they are among the easiest and most rewarding. The cult of the exhibition daffodil is widely followed and every year the Daffodil Show is one of the most popular of the R.H.S. Shows.

In a separate part of this book I deal both with the subjects of daffodils for naturalising, for which both the large and the small ones are un-rivalled, and also with the growing of daffodils in bowls for the house.

Since the place in the garden of the large-flowered varieties and of the smaller-flowered species is very different it seems best to divide this account into two separate sections and to deal first with the species and a few hybrids which are of a size comparable with the species and then with the garden varieties. Among the former are some first-rate garden plants.

## (*a*) Narcissus species with a few hybrids of comparable size

When Wordsworth wrote of his daffodils dancing in the breeze he was probably referring to the wild lent lilies *N. pseudo-narcissus* which grow so freely in the lake district. There are few more lovely sights. Again at Wisley the alpine meadow covered with thousands of the little yellow and cream-coloured hoop petticoats of *N. bulbocodium* (Pl. **18***a*, **25**, 6, 8) is a spectacle as beautiful and as treasured as any the garden can present, although in the mountains of Spain I have seen them at the beginning of June covering the higher meadows like buttercups stretching for miles. Even earlier in the spring the rich golden-yellow reflexed petals of *N. cyclamineus* on the damp banks of the old woodland is a sight to cause envy in most gardeners. It all appears completely natural and over the years the seedlings have spread so freely that now there are thousands. Each year these sights give me every bit as much pleasure as do the serried ranks of the exhibition varieties in the Shows.

For the rock garden these smaller species and their hybrids are particularly suitable, especially in a raised situation where they may be brought up nearer to eye level. While *N. cyclamineus* seems to thrive best in a damp and even peaty situation the majority of the others do well in a place that is well drained and may even become dry in the summer as long as they have sufficient or even ample moisture in their growing periods. All the most beautiful meadows with dwarf daffodils growing freely that I have seen either in this country or in the Pyrenees, where one finds fields of *N. poeticus* or in the Spanish mountains seem to be in places which are rather on the damp side in spring. This, however, is not essential, except perhaps for *N. cyclamineus*. (Pl. **25**, 9)

As subjects for growing in pots or pans for the alpine house or even in bowls of fibre they are most rewarding and in this way the very early flowering subspecies of hoop petticoat daffodils from N. Africa which are tender to frost can be successfully grown for January decoration. In many ways for a dinner table they make better decoration than the bigger ones since it is possible to see over them.

*Narcissus* is such a large genus that it has seemed best to deal with these miniature species in groups such as *cyclamineus* and dwarf trumpets like *pseudo-narcissus* (Pl. **25**, 4) where the whole group of species and hybrids may be easily grouped around one particular and often variable species.

As a genus *Narcissus* has several times been reclassified and it is one of the most difficult from a taxonomic point of view, it seems best here to adopt the nomenclature used in the last edition (1961) of the R.H.S. Classified List of Daffodils which in the case of these miniatures has been largely based on the work of Dr. Fernandes of Portugal, than whom perhaps no one has studied them more thoroughly both cytologically and in their native habitats. E. A. Bowles' *Handbook of Narcissus* should also be consulted since it is by far the most scholarly book on the genus.

These dwarf species are easily raised from seeds and often this is the best way of building up a stock. The seed should be sown thinly as soon as it is ripe, i.e. about the end of June or in July in deep boxes, pans or even in the open ground and the seedlings may be left in situ for the first two years until small bulbs have been formed. They should then be pricked out in beds about three inches apart or even placed in their permanent situations. The majority should flower in the third or fourth year.

# *Narcissus*

The bulbs of these species vary much in size but the smaller ones should be planted 2–3 in. deep and the larger 3–4 in. Since all narcissus bulbs in the ground start to make roots in the late summer it is very desirable to plant them in good time; August is not too early and is better than September while September is better than October. A light dressing of bone meal on planting and again in the spring will help them, and dried blood or hoof and horn may also be used but on no account fresh farmyard or stable manure.

## (1) BULBOCODIUM GROUP

These are the hoop petticoats and they are nearly all subsp., varieties or forms of *N. bulbocodium*, a very large and variable sp., the exception being the early white-flowered forms known as *monophyllus* and *foliosus* which have now been separated under the name *N. cantabricus*.

**N. bulbocodium.** Distinct from all other sp. in the large funnel-shaped corona, the narrow, almost rudimentary perianth segments and the curved stamens. It is indeed like a horizontally placed little hoop petticoat blown up in the wind. The petticoats vary from the globular with a narrow hoop to the very wide open with a flaring almost trumpet hoop. *L.* narrow, almost filiform; bulbs small to medium in size. The majority of the subsp. and varieties will increase freely by division of the bulbs and then the clump should be lifted every third or fourth year, however, in grass like the alpine meadow at Wisley they seem to grow and increase most satisfactorily without ever being lifted or divided. The majority also grow freely from seed and will increase from self-sown seedlings once a patch is established. They seem to do best in a site that is not too dry. It is unfortunate that the nomenclature has become so cumbersome and I only deal with a selection of the forms here. The three most commonly grown and most successful garden varieties belong to the subsp. *vulgaris*. These are:

* Subsp. **vulgaris** var. **citrinus**. *Fl.* pale lemon-yellow, broadly funnel-shaped, corona about 1 in. across hoop at mouth and widely expanded. Perianth segments narrow, ray shaped and with green stripe at base on outside. Up to 6 in. tall or more and taller than the next variety. One of the best garden forms.

* Subsp. **vulgaris** var. **conspicuus**. *Fl.* deep yellow but variable both in size, shape and colour. Height 4–6 in. but generally more dwarf than the preceding. This is the variety most commonly seen. Generally flowering later than the preceding in early April. It is the combination of hybrids and forms of these two varieties that gives the alpine meadow at Wisley so long a spell of beauty. (Pl **25**, 6)

Subsp. **vulgaris** var. **nivalis**. A low growing and small variety rarely exceeding 3 in. in height. *Fl.* pale yellow, corona rather shorter and constricted towards mouth. Early flowering but not so vigorous as preceding.

Subsp. **obesus**. As its name implies one of the largest and fattest of this group. *Fl.* rich deep yellow, corona widely open at mouth, rather globular and up to 1½ in. across. A robust grower but rarely seen. *L.* narrow, semi-prostrate, and often twisting. (Pl. **25**, 8)

# Narcissus

†* Subsp. **romieuxii.** One of the gems of this section. *Fl.* Large, widely flaring, pale lemon-yellow. Dec.-Jan. Atlas mountains and consequently tender and only fit for alpine house cultivation. Like *cantabricus* subsp. *monophyllus* it seems to flower better when completely dried off in the summer after the *l.* have died down. Some excellent hybrids have been raised between this and *monophyllus*, notably ' Tarlatan '.

Var. **mesatlanticus.** A good deep yellow and with a slightly larger *fl.*; rather flat. Jan.-Feb.

Var. **tenuifolius.** Fl. small, narrowly funnel-shaped, rich yellow, *l.* narrow, long and semi-prostrate or prostrate.

Subsp. **tananicus.** *Fl.* small, white, erect and opening to face upwards.

**N. cantabricus** subsp. **monophyllus.** *Fl.* Snowy-white, corona almost translucent and slightly pleated, mouth wide open and stamens exserted. (Pl. **25,** 13). The N. African var. *foliosus* flowers early in December or January, but is not such a clear white and is too tender for successful cultivation in the open except in specially sheltered and warm situations. It is, however, a splendid plant for the alpine house. The bulbs seem to require a good summer dry period for successful flowering. Forms from S. France and Spain have often been distinguished as var. *foliosus* or var. *clusii* and are hardier and later flowering, but it is difficult to draw any hard dividing line between the two. By no means invariably are they restricted to only 1 *l.* per bulb, frequently having 2 or 3. An unusually fine form has been shown recently with the mouth of the corona flatly recurved and forming a wide white ruff 1 in. or more across round the mouth of the hoop from which the curved stamens project for ¼ in. or more, the whole *fl.* being the size of a half-crown. This has recently been named *N. cantabricus* var. *petunioides.* (Pl. XVIII)

## (2) CYCLAMINEUS GROUP

* **N. cyclamineus.** One of the most beautiful of all Narcissus sp. *Fl.* of a bright rich yellow unsurpassed for colour in the genus. Corona long, tubular; segments recurved completely forming a crown above the corona, or, as E. A. Bowles remarks, " like the ears laid back of a kicking horse." Height 4 8 in. Early flowering, Feb.-March, generally starting to flower 10 days or a fortnight before the bulbocodiums. Spain, Portugal. Definitely a plant for damp places, where it often seeds and spreads freely. In the old wild garden at Wisley it is most beautiful, especially when seen on slopes against a background of deep green moss. It will grow happily in semi-shade. (Pl. **25,** 9)

From crosses between it and trumpet daffodils have been raised a long series of garden hybrids of which the smallest but perhaps the best is *Minicycla, a hybrid with *N. asturiensis.* In its best forms it is a most perfect miniature, deep golden-yellow, trumpet with only very slighty reflexed outer segments. (Pl. **25,** 5). Much larger, up to 12 in. or even more in height and with *fl.* in proportion is *' February Gold,' a *fl.* which often lives up to its name and a most valuable garden plant. Intermediate between these in size and a lovely clear deep yellow is the newer ' Jana ', so named for its early flowering. More recent and even larger hybrids with longer coronas but of the same type, with self-coloured deep yellow *fl.*, are *' Bartley ', ' Caerhayes ' and ' Peeping

Tom '; while as graceful bicolours raised from a cross between *N. cycla-mineus* and ' Mitylene ' the varieties ' Jenny ' and *' Dove Wings ' are very lovely. *' Charity May ' is a good clear yellow. Snipe ' (Pl. XVIII) is one of the best of the smaller hybrids.

## (3) THE JONQUILS

* **N. jonquilla.** Renowned for its scent, probably the sweetest in the genus, this sp. and its forms deserve to be grown far more widely than they are. The rich golden-yellow *fl.* are very short-cupped and are borne up to 6 on a 1 ft.-high stalk. *L.* deep green, rush-like, semi-cylindrical in cross section. Bulb small, very dark brown. Spain, Portugal, Balearic Isles, N. Africa. *N. jonquilla florepleno* is the double form often known as Queen Anne's Double Jonquil and is also very close to the fine double jonquil named ' Pencrebar '. Close also to the jonquil is *N. odorus* and *N. odorus* var. *rugulosus*, the Campernelle jonquil and the largest variety. It is distinguished from the jonquil by its wider *l.*, up to $\frac{1}{8}$ in. across, and by a longer corona. It has been suggested on good authority that it is likely to be a hybrid between *N. jonquilla* and *N. pseudo-narcissus*. It has been known and featured as a garden plant since the 16th century although it has never been found wild.

**N. juncifolius.** A charming miniature sp. from the Pyrenees, Spain, Portugal and Southern France with 2, 3 and occasionally up to 5 clear deep yellow little *fl.* on a 3–5 but sometimes 8 in. stem. The *fl.* are short cupped, not more than $\frac{3}{4}$ in. across, and well scented. *L.* narrow, semi-cylindrical, greener than in *N. rupicola*. A lovely plant for a pan in the alpine house but also growing well enough on the rock garden.

    **N. calcicola.** Closely allied to *N. juncifolius* but larger, up to 6 in. in height. *Fl.* several to a stem, deep yellow, corona cup-shaped, sweet scented. *L.* glaucous. March-April. Portugal, where it is restricted to a small area south of Coimbra and another south of Lisbon.

**N. rupicola.** Rather similar to *N. juncifolius* but with larger solitary *fl.* up to 1 in. across, deep rich yellow in colour and more strongly scented. The corona is saucer-shaped, almost flat and indistinctly 6-lobed. Spain, Portugal. *L.* rush-like, glaucous and erect. April. An excellent sp. for a pan in the alpine house but quite hardy and a more effective garden plant than *N. juncifolius*. In the wild it is nearly always found growing against rocks and so is very well named, and probably this form of planting should be followed on the rock garden. (Pl. **25**, 11)

    Var. **marvieri.** *Fl.* soft yellow, resembling in form and size *N. watieri*. Slightly larger than *N. rupicola* and the three outer perianth segments with a white tip and with semi-prostrate *l.* Atlas Mountains. A rare and little known variety but obviously very desirable for the alpine house.

**N. scaberulus.** A rare gem found wild only in one small area of Portugal. 1 or 2 *fl.* to a scape, like *N. rupicola* but smaller, only $\frac{1}{2}$ in. across, and of a deeper orange-yellow. Corona $\frac{1}{4}$ in. across, slightly crenate at margin, corona tube slightly curved. *L.* rush-like but rather prostrate and twisting and curling on the ground, glaucous. Bulbs very small. A plant for the alpine house or scree frame. Late March-early April.

† **N. watieri.** A larger flowered and pure white counterpart of *N. rupicola* from the Atlas Mountains, one of the gems of the genus and apparently hardier than most of the N. African narcissi. *Fl.* single, 1¼ in. in diameter and snow-white, corona shallow and saucer-shaped, unscented. (Pl. **25**, 10). Stem up to 6 in. *L.* narrow-linear but not rush-like, glaucous and erect. April. An excellent plant for the alpine house, requires to be well dried off after the foliage has died down.

A number of excellent hybrids have been raised between the Jonquils and other sp. of Narcissus and among them the following may be selected, all being good garden plants for the rock garden and of a dainty beauty to justify alpine house cultivation in pans.

* * 'APRIL TEARS' (*N. jonquilla* × *N. triandrus concolor*) raised by Alec Gray at present the foremost grower of these delightful dwarf narcissi. *Fl.* deep yellow and pendulous, cup slightly lighter in colour, up to 5 *fl.* on a 6–8 in. stem. April.
* 'BOBBYSOXER' Like an enlarged version of *N. rupicola* which is undoubtedly one of its parents. *Fl.* single, perianth segments overlapping, up to 1½ in. across, butter-yellow with cup a brighter orange. Stem 6–8 in. Late April.
* * 'HAWERA' One of my favourites, *fl.* 2–4 on 8–10 in. stems, pendulous, resembling 'April Tears' but of a slightly paler yellow and flowering two or three weeks earlier. Raised in New Zealand. A *triandrus-jonquilla* hybrid. (Pl. **25**, 2)
* * 'ORANGE QUEEN' *Fl.* 3–4 on a 6–8 in. stem, up to 1½ in. across, orange-yellow, slightly scented, the deepest in colour of all the jonquils. *L.* rush-like. Quite hardy and also an excellent plant for a pan in the house.
* 'PENCREBAR' A double jonquil already mentioned under *N. jonquilla*.
* 'SUN DISC' Close to 'Bobbysoxer' and of the type of *N. rupicola* only larger, *fl.* rich yellow and up to 1½ in. in diameter, corona saucer-shaped.

## (4) THE POETICUS GROUP

**N. poeticus.** The poet's narcissus. This sp. is widely distributed in S. Europe from Spain to Greece and in the lower meadows of the Alps and Pyrenees and is consequently very variable, particularly in the size and width of the perianth segments. In many of the wild forms these appear starry while in the same meadow forms may be found with perianth segments wide and almost overlapping as in the garden forms usually cultivated. I particularly remember one very beautiful meadow in early June in the Pyrenees where *N. poeticus* grew intermingled with purple orchis. It is the latest flowering of all the spring flowering sp. of *Narcissus*, often not before May in our gardens. The perianth segments are always white; the cup shallow and orange-red, sometimes yellow with a red or green rim. The *fl.* are sweet-scented. As with *tazetta* numerous separate sp. of *N. poeticus* have been recognised and described in the past but under the latest classification of Dr. Fernandes the better differentiated of these are considered as subsp. and varieties of *N. poeticus*. These names have never, however, been in wide or constant use by gardeners and since the plant is so variable little useful purpose would be served by discussing them here. The form *recurvus*, known as the Pheasant's Eye Narcissus is late flowering and has the perianth segments curving backwards. Its corona has a green centre and a red rim above a yellow cup.

# Narcissus

In *N. poeticus* the garden varieties described are much more vigorous garden plants than are the wild collected forms, which tend to dwindle and flower sparsely. Occasionally, however, they may be seen naturalised in a damp meadow and the late Mr. E. A. Bowles had such a site where *N. poeticus* had spread freely and many were little bigger than the best of the wild forms. It was a lovely sight. The best garden varieties are ' Actaea' and ' Sea Green'.

## (5) THE TAZETTA GROUP

**N. tazetta.** These are the sweet-scented bunch-flowered narcissi, a very varied sp. which has by far the widest distribution of any sp. of Narcissus and is really best considered as a group. It extends from N. Spain and Portugal through the Mediterranean regions on both north and south coasts as far as China and Japan, intermediate forms being found in Asia Minor, Persia and Kashmir. As might be expected from such a distribution the forms are very variable and many have been classified as separate sp. in the past. E. A. Bowles records that Haworth recognised no fewer than 54 different sp., but the majority of these names have either been reduced to synonymy or are recognised by the latest classification as subsp. or varieties of *N. tazetta*. Little good purpose would be served by discussing all these names here since many of them have never been widely accepted nor have they been used by gardeners.

Probably for our purpose the simple division into three series proposed by J. G. Baker will serve best since this is dependent on easily observed characters. He divided them into:

(*a*) *Bicolors*, those with white perianth and orange or yellow coronas.

(*b*) *Albae*, those with perianth and corona both white. From this group are descended the sweet scented paper-white Narcissi so widely grown for Christmas.

(*c*) *Luteae*, those with perianth and corona both yellow. From this group come the lovely ' Soleil d'Or ' so widely grown in bowls and for cut *fl.*

All the tazetta group are sweet scented and in the Mediterranean are found chiefly either in damp, marshy meadows or in cultivated ground such as vineyards. Unfortunately for our gardens they start into growth early in the autumn and are too tender to flower satisfactorily unless grown in the shelter of a wall, except in the warmer areas such as Cornwall and the Scilly Isles, where very large numbers are grown for cut *fl.* Those forms from China and Japan are the largest in flower and also have very large bulbs. There used to be a large trade in the import of these under such varying names as " Chinese sacred lily," " the Grand Emperor " etc., for growing in water and among damp pebbles. Double forms are also known.

The perianth segments are regular and saucer-shaped and vary from 1 in. to $1\frac{1}{2}$ in. in diameter. The corona is short cupped and up to 10 *fl.* may be found on a stem. The usual height of the wild forms is under 1 ft. but in gardens many will grow up to 2 ft. and flower from November onwards until March if weather permits.

The large-flowered forms such as ' Cragford ', ' Geranium ', ' Soleil d'Or ' and ' Grand Monarque ' are excellent for growing in bowls. Two small-flowered forms are also worth mentioning here:

**N. canaliculatus.** Regarded as a form of the subsp. *lacticolor* of *N. tazetta*, a perfect miniature tazetta of the bicolor group and very well suited for growth either in pans in the Alpine house or in the rock garden. Perianths white, about 1 in. in diameter; cup egg-yolk yellow and rather small. Height up to 9 in. but generally less and carrying up to 6 *fl.* to a stem. It is very sweetly scented and the bulb increases well in a favourable situation blooming rather later than other members of the group, often not until April. It seems to do best on a light warm soil in a well-drained position. (Pl. **25,** 7)

**N. dubius.** This is now thought to be a natural occurring hybrid between a white *N. tazetta* and *N. juncifolius* and the number and form of its chromosomes supports this theory. *Fl.* snow-white, very small perianth segments up to ¾ in. in diameter, corona cup-shaped and nearly hemi-spherical under ½ in. deep. *L.* glaucous and narrow. S. France. A beautiful but not very vigorous or free-flowering plant in cultivation, probably best in pans in the Alpine house and requiring a good baking during the summer.

## (6) THE TRIANDRUS GROUP

This section includes some of the prettiest and most graceful of the smaller Narcissus sp. and hybrids suitable for cultivation in the rock garden and in pots or pans in the alpine house. They are characterised by loose umbels of one or more pendulous *fl.* on a stem of 6–12 in., occasionally taller and are thus distinct from all the other groups. The perianth is long and hangs downwards while the perianth segments are often reflexed and generally slightly twisted; the corona is cup-shaped, half as long or more than the perianth segments and nearly always pendulous. The section was misnamed triandrus by Linnaeus since like all narcissi it really has 6 stamens although in some varieties the 3 outer stamens are larger than the others and project with the stigma beyond the corona.

In colour the members of this group vary from the pure white of some forms of *N. triandrus albus*, the Angel's Tears, to the deep golden-yellow of *triandrus* var. *concolor* and are native to Portugal and Western Spain with an interesting outrider on the Isles of Glenan off the west coast of France. They do not generally require such damp positions as the *cyclamineus* or *bulbocodium* groups although in Spain I have seen *N. triandrus albus* growing at the edge of running water in a damp meadow. They are generally found, however, on sloping banks and good drainage is important for their cultivation in this country. The bulbs are conical or rounded, generally with a pale outer skin and the *l.* are narrow. The following varieties have been distinguished and all are worth growing, although several are still rare plants.

\* **N. triandrus var. albus.** Angel's Tears. *Fl.* up to 6 on a stem, though more frequently 1–3. White to cream in colour sometimes very pale yellow towards the base of the perianth and corona. Up to 1 ft. high, generally less. April, late May on Spanish mountains. A very variable and lovely plant, very suitable for cultivation in pans in the Alpine house and as such delightful for table decoration. Not a very vigorous grower, but easily raised from seed. Widespread in the mountains of N. Spain. The name Angel's Tears is said to have been derived from a guide called Angelo who was employed by the late Peter Barr who first introduced it into England. After climbing for a long time he was very tired and burst into tears—and there was found this delightful daffodil with its pendulous almost tearful *fl.* (Pl. **25**, 1)

N. **triandrus** var. **aurantiacus.** *Fl.* deep golden-yellow, rather resembling var. *concolor* which is a much commoner and better-known plant but slightly deeper in colour and generally flowering a little earlier, 1–3 to a stem. *Fl.* smaller than in var. *triandrus albus* and the plant more dwarf. Corona cup-shaped and ½ in. long. N. Portugal. March-April.

N. **triandrus** var. **calathinus.** A syn. of *N. triandrus* var. *loiseleurii.*

N. **triandrus** var. **concolor.** Pale golden-yellow. *Fl.* small, cup globular. L. narrow, rush-like. Sweet scented.

\* N. **triandrus** var. **loiseleurii.** *Fl.* white to pale cream, slightly larger than those of var. *albus* and with a longer bell often up to ½ in. in length. Only recorded from the Isles of Glenan, off the west coast of France and some distance from the nearest stations of var. *albus.* This is the plant figured twice by Redouté. L. almost prostrate and curled, unlike those of var. *albus.*

N. **triandrus** var. **pulchellus.** Now a rare plant but apparently more plentiful in the last century. Corona almost white and paler than the perianth segments. Sometimes rather pale forms of var. *concolor* are confused with this.

Hybrids with *N. triandrus* as one parent are some of the most beautiful of all the dwarf daffodils and in the majority of cases have more vigour than the *triandrus* parent. Two of the finest, 'April Tears' and 'Hawera', have already been described under the jonquils. They are truly intermediate between the two sections. The following is a small selection of the best of those not already described:

'RAINDROP' Raised by Alec Gray from *N. dubius* and *N. triandrus loiseleurii.* A very lovely miniature not more than 5 in. high, snow-white with up to 5 *fl.* to a stem. It is reported by its raiser to have a good constitution. It looks like a miniature polyanthus narcissus with pendulous *fl.*

\* 'SILVER CHIMES' A hybrid of *N. triandrus loiseleurii* and *N. tazetta*, rather larger, up to 15 in. and with 6 or more *fl.* on a stem, creamy-white with a pale yellow corona. A vigorous grower, very suitable for the rock garden or alpine house and even for exhibition, but slightly tender in very cold places. L. broad and bright green. A *fl.* of real distinction.

'THALIA' *Fl.* rather larger than 'Silver Chimes' and stem taller, white, drooping.

**johnstonii** This is thought to be a naturally occurring cross between the trumpet *N. pseudo-narcissus* and *N. triandrus.* It is also known as 'Queen of Spain' while a vigorous form has been known as 'King of Spain'. *Fl.* lemon-yellow with reflexed perianth and narrow, pendulous funnel-shaped corona up to ½ in. long. Stem up to 1 ft. in height. Now a rare plant.

*Plate XI. Iris orchioides*, one of the most vigorous of the later Juno irises

*Plate XII. Lilium brownii*, a very beautiful group in a Sussex garden

*Plate XIII. Lilium canadense*, a most graceful lily with drooping
bell-shaped flowers

*Plate XIV. Lilium regale,* one of the easiest species to grow satisfactorily

# Narcissus

'NIVETH' *Fl.* white, like a smaller short-cupped narcissus, 12–18 in., 1 or 2 to a stem. A delicate *fl.* of fine quality.

'TRESAMBLE' *Fl.* white, slightly larger than 'Niveth'.

## (7) DWARF TRUMPET DAFFODILS

These belong to the sub-genus of narcissus called Ajax and from them have been derived our garden hybrids of the trumpet type, but the wild Lent lily *N. pseudo-narcissus* is still one of the best of all garden bulbs for naturalising in grass and in the wild or woodland garden, flowering usually several weeks before the larger garden hybrids. Members of this group can be grown successfully in much less damp situations than are required for *bulbocodiums* or *cyclamineus*. As presently considered the group is clearly divided into three well separated sp. and a number of plants formerly regarded as separate sp. are now included as subsp. of *N. pseudo-narcissus*, which thereby forms a large and very varied group of its own.

**N. alpestris.** See under *N. pseudo-narcissus.*

\* **N. asturiensis.** This is a perfect miniature of a large trumpet daffodil but only 2–4 in. in height. *Fl.* deep golden-yellow, mouth of the trumpet deeply indented, almost frilled, the throat being rather narrow and constricted. (Pl. 25, 12). Unfortunately, the stem tends to be weak and after any rain the *fl.* will often be found lying on the ground. It flowers very early, often in mid-February, or even in January in the alpine house to which it is well suited. It grows abundantly on the higher slopes of the mountains of northern Spain and there I saw it recently in flower as late as the end of May with the snow only just melting above it. It likes very well-drained spots, often almost in scree and there is one form we saw there with twisted leaves and almost prostrate *fl.* In this country the little bulbs need a specially well-drained position and are best seen in a raised bed. They tend to increase slowly and one rarely sees a large patch here, although in the wild it seems to increase and seed freely. It is frequently listed under its syn. *minimus*, a most appropriate name since it is indeed the smallest of all this section of daffodils and nearly of all daffodils. Its attractive hybrid with *N. cyclamineus*, Minicycla, has already been described under that sp.

**N. cernuus.** See under *N. pseudo-narcissus.*

**N. lobularis.** See under *N. pseudo-narcissus.*

**N. minor.** A small and variable bicolor trumpet daffodil. *Fl.* up to 8 in. high but often leaning, segments nearly 1 in. in diam. and pale yellow, trumpet $\frac{1}{2}$–$\frac{3}{4}$ in. long, not constricted at the throat, soft yellow but darker than segments and usually 6-lobed. Forms with little differentiation of colour are however often found. A stronger and larger plant than *N. asturiensis*, flowering a little later, generally towards the end of March but in a favourable season sometimes at the end of February. *L.* glaucous, wider, up to $\frac{1}{4}$ in. wide.

The plant usually sold under the name *nanus* is now regarded as synonymous with *N. minor* var. *conspicuus* although it is a little smaller in all its parts. At times the term *nanus* has also been applied to forms of *N. pseudo-narcissus.*

*N. minor* var. *pumilus* is also smaller than the other forms of *N. minor* and can be readily distinguished by the golden-yellow, not bicolor, trumpet, the mouth of which is deeply indented. Scented. March. Portugal. This is generally regarded as not being such a strong grower as other forms of *N. minor*.

**N. pseudo-narcissus.** A large and varied omnibus group sp. including both the small white trumpets, the bicolored trumpets such as our own native Lent lily (Pl. **25**, 4), the more self-coloured Tenby Daffodil and the larger bicolored and self-coloured forms of the Pyrenees and Spanish Mountains, often known as *pallidiflorus, hispanicus* and *nobilis*. Of these the last named is particularly fine, often with long-nosed deep orange trumpets and occurs over large areas of the Picos de Europa mountains of Northern Spain either in scrub or damp meadows. The bicolored subsp. such as the Lent lily and the golden *obvallaris* (Pl. **25**, 3) are particularly suitable for naturalising in grass or in open woodland and will maintain themselves longer and spread more freely than many of the larger garden varieties. While they do not have the broad outer segments or the regular smoothness of *fl.* of the modern show varieties this does not affect the charm and grace of their early spring flowering and their short height, generally under 1 ft., enables them to stand up better to the storms. The typical Lent lily, the English wild daffodil, is the form most commonly supplied. The outer segments are creamy-yellow and the trumpet a deeper yellow, but the forms are very variable in colour. In the subsp. *obvallaris*, often known as *lobularis*, the Tenby Daffodil, the general effect is one of a deeper and more self-coloured golden-yellow. It appears to be an equally vigorous grower. The *fl.* are generally less drooping than in the Lent lily but of about the same size. Closely allied to these is subsp. *pallidiflorus* sometimes known as *pallidiflorus praecox*, which has larger generally drooping *fl.*, either bicolored or rather pale yellow and occurs widely but sparsely over a wide area of the Pyrenees and N. Spain. In cultivation as in the wild it is not a very vigorous plant and the stem is generally short and the outer segments rather narrow and waved. Subsp. *nobilis* of the mountains of N. Spain is a much finer plant, generally a bicolor, and often reaching a height and size of *fl.* which would be almost comparable with that of a good garden variety while the very deep yellow or pale orange trumpet of some forms is very striking.

The two creamy-white subsp., *alpestris* and *moschatus*, are both beautiful little *fl.* but are rare in nature and distinctly lacking in vigour in the garden. In both cases the *fl.* are drooping. *Alpestris* is the smaller and less vigorous of the two, rarely maintaining itself or spreading satisfactorily in English gardens. The scape is 4–6 in. high and the neck long and curved so that the *fl.* appear almost pendulous, with the outer segments tending to droop round the long narrow trumpet. Pyrenees. April, after the Lent lilies. *Moschatus* is slightly larger, 6–8 in. high and more vigorous, and the *fl.* droop a little less but they are of a less pure white being slightly tinged with a very pale sulphurous yellow. Its wild origin is unkown. This is the plant also known as *N. cernuus*.

' W. P. MILNER ' A dwarf variety of 8–10 in., with similar drooping *fl.* of a pale greenish-sulphur colour, is a much better garden plant than either of the white subsp. and also very suitable for growing in bowls or pans. We always try and have at least one bowl of this for flowering in the house in February. ' Santa Maria ' is another dwarf trumpet with deeper

# Narcissus

yellow *fl.*, rather drooping habit and twisted outer petals and an undeniable charm but it is rarely seen now, although there used to be a large colony in the wild garden at Wisley.

## (8) AUTUMN FLOWERING SPECIES

These are all natives of the countries bordering the Mediterranean both north and south and unfortunately have a poor constitution and little vigour when grown in England, where they seldom flower. A flowering narcissus is, however, unusual in September or October. The trumpets or coronas of this section are hardly developed at all while the outer segments are narrow and spidery. Their best characteristic is generally their sweet scent. They should be given some protection for ripening during the summer. The three best known species are:

**N. elegans.** *Fl.* one–several on a stem each 1½–2 in. in diameter, perianth segments greenish-white and wavy, corona very shallow, saucer-shaped, pale orange. Italy, Sicily and Algeria. *L.* flat and narrow, produced before the *fl.* (Pl. **32**, 4)

**N. serotinus.** *Fl.* unusually solitary, occasionally 2 to a scape, smaller than those of *N. elegans* and usually under 1 in. across but with perianth segments of a much clearer white, corona shallow but deeply lobed, yellow, described by Mr. Bowles as having a touch of orange, leafless at flowering time. *L.* when produced rush-like or filiform, sometimes deeply channelled. Mediterranean regions, widely distributed. (Pl. **32**, 7)

**N. viridiflorus.** A really green daffodil but of a dull olive green; *fl.* 1–4 to a scape, occasionally more, corona shallow, 6 lobed, height 6–8 in. at flowering time but in this and the proceeding sp. the scape lengthens and remains green after flowering. *L.* rush-like, and generally single and not appearing with the *fl.* Oct.-Nov. Restricted in its distribution to Gibraltar, southern Spain and Morocco. This *fl.* has been known for a long time and was figured by John Parkinson in the 16th century. (Pl. **32**, 1)

## (b) Garden varieties

The number of these now registered amounts to several thousands and large numbers of new names are added to the list each year. The majority of these varieties are now the result of a complicated medley of crosses with a parental tree as long as that of any prize animal. Consequently it seems better to arrange them here according to the classification of Daffodils used by The Royal Horticultural Society and drawn up and revised by their Narcissus and Tulip Committee in agreement with the General Bulb Growers Society of Haarlem. This classification is admittedly an artificial one drawn up for Show purposes but it is used throughout the world in arranging Daffodil Shows and in catalogues and serves well. In the lists which follow I have endeavoured to make a small selection out of the great mass of varieties, based both on experience in the garden and on observation over a number of years at the London Shows of the R.H.S. and at the Wisley Trials.

Since new varieties of daffodils are all clones and propagated solely by vegetative division from the one original bulb it inevitably takes a number of years before a good stock is built up and consequently, although the variety may have been exhibited in the London Shows for some years, the price per bulb remains high since the number of bulbs available is still small. The following lists are therefore divided into two categories and the division is *solely* a financial one. In the first category are bulbs now sufficiently well tried and in sufficient supply to be priced currently (1961) under ten shillings a bulb while in the second category headed " promising newer varieties " are some of those which show considerable promise and have won high awards at the R.H.S. Daffodil Shows but are still too expensive for general planting. The price per bulb may still be as high as twenty guineas or even more. All those listed in my first category are strong growers which should do well and increase in the garden and are also very suitable for picking for the house while some of them may still win prizes in Daffodil Shows. They are probably not, however, the most suitable selection for naturalising in grass. The qualities which make a superb show flower are not always those which make the best garden plants, although now the majority of modern daffodils will qualify in both categories, as may be seen from the results of the Wisley Trials. The modern daffodil has advanced or at any rate been changed very considerably from the wild species and the developments have been in the direction of larger flowers; broader and overlapping petals; cleanness, brightness and purity of colour; regularity and balance of form and above all in the development of a thicker, more substantial and smoother perianth segment. The daffodil enthusiast talks of smoothness in his flowers in much the same way as the wine connoisseur talks of it in his wine and it is a quality best conveyed by this analogy. Probably no flower has shown greater returns to the raiser of seedlings and the developments within the last thirty years have been a triumph. Now, however, the standard is so high that only a very small proportion indeed of new seedlings will be considered worth naming and growing on into stocks. It is sometimes possible to buy from raisers stocks of their discarded seedlings and these are generally well worth having for garden and woodland decoration.

# Narcissus

*Cultivation*

Daffodil bulbs begin to root early and therefore are best planted early, if possible in August, if not then, in September. October will suffice but the earlier months are definitely better. Lifting of stocks should be done at the end of June or early in July after the last of the foliage has died down. The exact depth of planting is not important and will vary with the type of soil, being deeper in a light soil. The depth in general should not be less than 3 in. from the top of the bulb to the surface and not more than 6 in. Large bulbs should be planted 5–6 in. apart, smaller bulbs an in. or so closer.

For Show purposes daffodils should be grown in well-cultivated land that has been manured not less than one year previously. Fresh animal manure should never be given to them. A dressing of bone meal in autumn and again in spring will help to build up the bulbs and on light soils a dressing of dried blood in the early spring will help to build up both size of flower and bulb. Sulphate of potash and hoof-and-horn are also suitable fertilisers for daffodils. They should be lifted every third or fourth year and divided. Many growers take this opportunity of submitting them to the hot water treatment against the grubs of narcissus fly at the same time. Daffodils grown for Show purposes may also need some protection against strong winds and hail or snow and there are various methods of providing this through hedges, hurdles or even scrim stretched on poles, but this is not very attractive in the garden.

For garden decoration no such protection need be provided. Daffodils will do well in a wide variety of positions from the completely open exposed hill-top to the semi-shade of a woodland or even a grass meadow. They also do well in a wide variety of soils from the whitest chalk to a heavy clay or peaty soil. They are certainly among the most easily grown and tolerant of all bulbs in this respect. It is important that the soil should not, however, be waterlogged and good drainage is desirable. A period of ripening in summer is also desirable but knowing the success of daffodils in many parts of Cornwall one would hesitate to call it essential. In very heavy soils or in peaty areas where the drainage is poor a layer of sand on which the base of the bulbs rest will be an advantage and the beds may be raised a little above the level of the surrounding soil. The bulbs will undoubtedly benefit if the spaces between can be kept clean of weeds by regular hoeing, and by covering up any hole in the ground which may be left when the dead foliage is pulled away the points of entry into the bulbs of the narcissus flies will be lessened. Many experiments have also been made in the case of commercial crops in the use of pre-emergent herbicides and these are promising also for the amateur.

# *Narcissus*

The classification divides daffodils into eleven divisions and each division is sub-divided according to the colour of the flowers and where relative measurements of perianth and corona are involved it is stated that " the length of a perianth segment is the extreme length measured on the inside from its junction with the corona along the midrib to the extreme tip and the length of the corona is the extreme length measured from its junction with the perianth to the end of its furthest extension when the edge is flattened out."

## (1) TRUMPET NARCISSI OF GARDEN ORIGIN

One flower to a stem, trumpet or corona as long as or longer than the perianth segments.

*(a) Perianth coloured, corona coloured, not paler than the perianth.* These are the typical golden daffodils.

‘ CROMARTY ’  A very fine yellow trumpet for all purposes, growing strongly in the garden.  Medium-large.

‘ GOLDCOURT ’  Very smooth, deep golden-yellow *fl.* suitable for exhibition and cutting, although by now superseded in size by some of the later raised varieties, medium size.

‘ GOLDEN HARVEST ’  A very prolific variety widely grown for market and forcing.  Medium-large, good deep yellow colour, but lacking the substance of petal and smoothness required for exhibition *fl.*  A good variety for planting for garden decoration.

* ‘ KINGSCOURT ’  Very deep pure gold in colour, *fl.* of fine smooth substance and beautiful form, very popular as an exhibition *fl.* and for cutting. Medium-large.  One of the most lovely of all varieties and a good garden plant in addition.  (Pl. **26**, 3)

‘ KING ALFRED ’  An old variety but still one of the most popular for garden decoration, forcing and for market.  A vigorous grower, generally flowering a little later than ‘ Golden Harvest ’.  Large.

‘ MAGNIFICENCE ’  Early flowering.  A good variety for forcing and market. A vigorous grower, medium-large, but not in the same class as ‘ Kingscourt ’ or even ‘ Cromarty.’

‘ MILANION ’  A very fine trumpet variety for exhibition and cutting, slightly paler yellow than ‘ Kingscourt.’  Medium-large.

‘ REMBRANDT ’  Early flowering and suitable for growing in pots and bowls.  A vigorous grower although not of exhibition standard.  Medium-large.

* ‘ ULSTER PRINCE ’  Very fine deep golden-yellow trumpet of exhibition standard.  Large.

‘ UNSURPASSABLE ’  Very large trumpet of good deep yellow colour, vigorous and suitable for market, although not of exhibition standard.  A good garden plant, but in exposed positions the blooms are so large that they may be beaten down.

246

# Narcissus

*Lemon-yellow trumpets*

These are a very recent development and some very beautiful *fl.* have been produced from the crossing of golden-yellow varieties with bicolors. To develop their best colour they need to be picked and open in water unless they are specially protected and their colour seems to change from day to day as the *fl.* matures. Their colour is soft in most cases and not so strong as the phrase lemon-yellow suggests.

' HUNTER'S MOON ' Medium size, perianth pale mimosa-yellow in colour, trumpet pale sulphur-yellow with the colour strongest at the mouth of the trumpet. A fascinating and beautiful *fl.* (Pl. **26**, 4)

' MULATTO ' A striking variety both for pots and in the garden. Colour sulphur-lemon yellow, slightly deeper than in ' Hunter's Moon ' but not a *fl.* of the same perfection of form or subtle colouring. Early flowering.

*Promising newer varieties*

' KING'S RANSOM ' A very magnificent deep golden-yellow trumpet with smooth solid perianth and trumpet and fine form. Bred from ' Kingscourt ' and ' Goldcourt ' on both of which it is likely to be a noticeable improvement when better known.

' MOONSTRUCK ' Very large, sometimes 5½ in. in diameter, pale lime-lemon in colour fading almost to white as the *fl.* matures. A very lovely *fl.*

(b) *Perianth white, corona coloured.* These are the bicolor trumpets and really good flowers have always been scarce in this section.

' BONYTHON ' Early flowering and suitable for growing in pots. Medium size. Perianth creamy-white, trumpet pale primrose-yellow. A good variety for garden decoration.

' CONTENT ' Large. Corona pale canary-yellow, paling to cream at its base. Vigorous.

' PREAMBLE ' An unusually fine *fl.* Very large. Perianth pure white, corona canary yellow paling to lemon-yellow in strong contrast to the perianth. One of the best varieties in this section yet raised. (Pl. **26**, 7)

\* ' TROUSSEAU ' Large and vigorous. Perianth milk-white, trumpet pale yellow, fading to an unusual cream. A lovely *fl.* of good exhibition quality.

*Promising newer varieties*

' LAPFORD ' Early flowering and of good exhibition quality. Trumpet soft yellow.

(c) *Perianth white, corona white, not paler than the perianth.* In this section of the white trumpets great progress has been made, particularly by raisers in Ireland and some very beautiful varieties have been raised. Some of the earlier white trumpets produced large *fl.* but the perianth and corona were thin and papery and as the *fl.* aged these tended to wrinkle and become " crepey." This fault has been surmounted in the later varieties, but the best of these still come into the very expensive class.

\* ' ARDCLINIS ' Large and clear white. One of the best of the white trumpets for pots and garden decoration.

'BEERSHEBA' A general favourite and excellent both for growing in pots or bowls for the house or for garden decoration. The trumpet is rather long and slender. Its only fault is a tendency to grow with rather short stems in a dry season.

'BROUGHSHANE' Very large but still with fine form and texture, often 5½ in. in diameter, trumpet widely flanged and somewhat frilled at mouth. A giant white trumpet which always attracts attention in Shows. Vigorous.

* 'CANTATRICE' Widely acknowledged as one of the *fl.* of most perfect form yet raised and probably still wins as many prizes in Daffodil Shows as any other variety. In colour a clean, pure white. Perianth segments rather pointed and the trumpet rather long; both have a waxy, velvety appearance that gives the *fl.* much of its distinction. An excellent variety for growing in pots for the cool greenhouse but as a garden plant it is also sufficiently vigorous to win an award in the Wisley Trials. It should be included in every collection. *Fl.* is not so large as that of some of the varieties mentioned later but it is only surpassed among some of the new varieties which are still very expensive. (Pl. **26**, 5 and Pl. XVI)

'KANCHENJUNGA' *Fl.* very large, widely flanged and serrated at mouth. The texture, however, is a bit thin and tends to wrinkle as the *fl.* ages, but its great size, often 5½ in. in diameter, marked it as one of the parents through which many of the best of the newer *fl.* in this section have come.

'MOUNT HOOD' Probably one of the most vigorous and the best white trumpet daffodils for general garden decoration, though the *fl.* is not quite of exhibition smoothness and perfect form. *Fl.* large, trumpet ivory-white, very slightly flushed with pale primrose-yellow when it first opens.

*Promising newer varieties*

* 'EMPRESS OF IRELAND' Probably the most lovely white trumpet yet raised. *Fl.* large, well described as ice-white, very large and of perfect form with pointed but widely overlapping perianth segments and trumpet of medium length and approximately of the same length as the perianth segments and frilled at the margin. The texture, to which the *fl.* owes much of its distinction, is very smooth and velvety with an almost waxy thickness and substance. Unfortunately it is still a scarce and expensive plant.

'HINDUSTAN' A very fine white trumpet for exhibition. Large, pure white trumpet, flanged and serrated at the mouth, perianth segments widely overlapping.

'RASHEE' *Fl.* of the same class and type as 'Empress of Ireland' but not quite so large and with pointed perianth segments. Texture of petals very smooth and thick. Well described as " Ice-white with a touch of cold sea-green at the base of the trumpet." Very lovely.

'VIGIL' *Fl.* large, pure white, often 5 in. in diameter, well proportioned and of good texture with wide overlapping perianth segments. A good variety for exhibition. Described by one enthusiast as " One of the flowers in this world perfect enough for the next."

# Narcissus

*(d) Trumpet of any colour combination not falling into categories a, b or c*

\* ' SPELLBINDER ' A unique and fascinating *fl.* very large, vigorous and most promising. A reversed bicolor trumpet of a pale lemon or lime-yellow colour; the strongest colour of the corona is at mouth of the trumpet, while inside of corona pales almost to white. Perianth segments wide and overlapping, sulphur-yellow, paler towards their base. Deeper in colour than ' Moonstruck ' but somewhat similar in form and differing in the reversed colouring. A fine exhibition variety. (Pl. **26**, 1)

## (2) LARGE-CUPPED NARCISSI OF GARDEN ORIGIN

One flower to a stem; cup or corona more than one-third but less than equal to the length of the perianth segments.

*(a) Perianth coloured, corona coloured, not paler than the perianth.* This section includes the most widely grown daffodils and probably those in which there have been the greatest advance in recent years. Included in this section are both those with yellow cups and those with red cups but I have divided them although it is possible that one class may grade into the other.

*Varieties with yellow cups and without red or orange in the cup*
' AMBERLEY ' Perianth broad and overlapping; *fl.* a uniform clear golden-yellow. A vigorous grower, still fairly new but showing considerable promise. (Pl. **26**, 8)
' BROADWATER ' Perianth canary-yellow, corona deep aureolin-yellow, vigorous and a good garden variety, but also a *fl.* of exhibition quality.
\* ' CARLTON ' Clear golden-yellow. *Fl.* large, the cup longer than most in this section and almost qualifying as a trumpet. A very vigorous and very adaptable variety, excellent for garden decoration and for planting in bowls and for forcing. Early flowering. With ' Fortune ' this might well be reckoned as one of the best garden varieties introduced since ' King Alfred ' and it should be very highly recommended.
\* ' CROCUS ' A very fine clear golden-yellow *fl.*, a little deeper in colour and a better Show variety than ' Carlton ' but probably not quite so vigorous in growth. However, it is one of the best varieties obtainable at a moderate price.
' GALWAY ' Deep golden-yellow *fl.*, tall, large and vigorous. Perianth deep aureolin-yellow, corona deep lemon-yellow, long for this section and almost a trumpet.
' HAVELOCK ' Paler yellow than the two preceding, perianth primrose-yellow, and a smaller more delicate *fl.* Good for garden decoration and also for growing in bulbs and forcing.
' ST. EGWIN ' Tall. *Fl.* large, egg-yolk yellow with wide spreading perianth and rather small cup in proportion. A distinctive variety and a fine *fl.* for cutting. Perianth tends not to open quite flat.

*Promising new varieties*
' ST. KEVERNE ' Medium size, perianth deep aureolin-yellow with smooth
249

widely overlapping segments, corona deep lemon-yellow with frilled and expanded mouth. A very beautiful exhibition variety.

*Varieties with orange or orange-red in the corona*

\* ' ARANJUEZ ' A distinctive *fl.* for cutting and garden decoration. Large. Perianth clear yellow; cup shallow, widely expanded, deep yellow with wide rim of deep orange-red. Vigorous and a good garden plant. One of the finest varieties to be obtained at a moderate price.

' ARMADA ' *Fl.* large, very striking, perianth rich canary-yellow, smooth, corona deep orange-red (H.C.C. orpiment orange) mouth frilled and widely expanded. A fine exhibition variety, likely to become a widely grown garden plant.

' BAHRAM ' A very striking *fl.* Perianth deep yellow; cup large, deep orange-red, frilled at mouth. A fine variety for cutting and for pots.

\* ' CARBINEER ' Very vivid colouring. Perianth deep yellow, smooth ; corona deep orange-red, large. Vigorous. An excellent variety both for garden decoration and for cutting, which has often headed the R.H.S. ballot in the class of varieties for garden decoration listed in a retail catalogue at a price sufficiently low to allow of their being obtained in reasonable quantities. ' Rustom Pasha ' has often shared this distinction.

\* ' CEYLON ' One of the finest varieties yet raised in this section. *Fl.* large, very conspicuous in colour and of outstanding exhibition quality. Perianth deep canary-yellow; segments smooth, wide and overlapping; corona cadmium orange-red, large and deeply indented round the mouth. Full colour of the cup is not developed until *fl.* is mature. Sunproof. Vigorous. (Pl. **26**, 2)

' DUNKELD ' A good yellow and orange-red *fl.* with symmetrical smooth perianth. Vigorous, free-flowering and good for cutting.

' FIREMASTER ' Another striking *fl.* of similar colouring to ' Ceylon '. Medium size.

' FORTUNE ' A very striking *fl.* Perianth deep yellow, cup large and fiery orange-red. An excellent variety for market and probably now the most widely grown for that purpose. Vigorous and striking as a garden plant, but the *fl.* tend to be knocked over after a storm. Early. When introduced this variety created a considerable sensation and bulbs fetched very high prices. Now among the cheaper varieties.

' NARVIK ' Perianth canary-yellow, corona goblet-shaped, deep orange. Fine variety for cutting.

' PORTHILLY ' Striking *fl.* of medium size with clear deep yellow perianth and open frilled cup of vivid orange-red. Very good variety for garden decoration and for cutting.

' RED GOBLET ' Perianth deep yellow; corona almost globular, deep orange-red. A striking variety of unusual form in its corona, excellent for cutting and growing in pans. (Pl. **27**, 8)

' ROUGE ' An unusual variety of distinctive colouring, the perianth having an apricot-red flush overlaying a yellow base, corona almost brick-red. *Fl.* rather small but worth growing for its peculiar colouring.

\* ' RUSTOM PASHA ' One of the best of the deep yellow and red-cupped varieties obtainable at a moderate price. Perianth smooth with wide overlapping pointed petals, corona large, fiery orange-red. One of the most nearly sunproof varieties in this section. Vigorous and a good garden plant.

* 'SUN CHARIOT' One of the most brilliant and striking Show daffodils yet seen. *Fl.* large, perianth deep golden-yellow, segments pointed; corona goblet-shaped, deep orange-red. Sunproof and vigorous.

*Promising newer varieties*

'ATATURK' Striking colour and good form. Perianth mimosa-yellow, 3½ in. across; corona ¾ in. long, deeply ribbed, orpiment orange. A vigorous grower. (Pl. **27**, 3)

'FIRECRACKER' A new variety of striking colouring, perianth deep golden-yellow, segments slightly pointed, corona deep orange-red.

(*b*) *Perianth white, corona coloured.* For descriptive purposes I have divided this section into those with red and orange-red cups and those with yellow, pale orange or pink cups.

*Red cupped*

* 'FERMOY' *Fl.* large and of fine texture. Perianth pure white, segments pointed; corona wide, fiery orange-red at the mouth, paling to deep golden-yellow at base. Vigorous, a good garden plant and excellent for cutting or growing in pans. One of the best varieties at a moderate price. (Pl. **27**, 6)

'HADES' An older variety but still worth growing for striking contrast of pure white perianth and fiery orange-red cup.

'KILWORTH' A striking *fl.*, again at a moderate price. Corona deep orange-red. Vigorous.

*Promising newer variety*

'ARBAR' *Fl.* large, perianth pure white, of good substance and show quality. Corona shallow, saucer-shaped, deep orange-red.

*Varieties without red or orange-red in the corona*

'BRUNSWICK' Early flowering. Perianth creamy white; corona long, white at base, shading to primrose-yellow at the mouth. An unusual *fl.* of delicate colouring. Vigorous. Almost a trumpet.

'GREETING' *Fl.* medium-large in size. Perianth segments pure white, wide, overlapping, smooth; corona pale canary-yellow, goblet-shaped, small. An older variety but still unusual and worth including in the collection.

'MRS. R. O. BACKHOUSE' An old variety now but one of the first to show pink colouring in the corona and still nearly the only one to come below our general price limit. Perianth ivory-white; corona like a short trumpet, pale apricot-pink, deepening towards the mouth.

'PENVOSE' Perianth white, of good substance; corona like a short trumpet, pale yellow at first then turning to a coppery buff-yellow. A distinctive *fl.*

* 'POLINDRA' One of the best varieties for cutting and garden decoration. Tall and vigorous. Perianth pure white, smooth; corona deep mimosa-yellow. (Pl. **27**, 1)

*Promising newer varieties*

'BLARNEY'S DAUGHTER' Somewhat resembling 'Blarney' (p. 253), but

251

with a larger-shaped corona of deeper apricot-orange, edged with mimosa-yellow and much deeper than in 'Blarney'. Perianth pure white with broad overlapping segments. A very lovely and promising Show variety. (Pl. 27, 7)

'DEBUTANTE' A very fine flower with broad rounded perianth and a large cup of bright coral pink, frilled at the mouth. One of the deepest pink varieties yet introduced but still an expensive bulb.

'GREEN ISLAND' A very unusual and distinctive *fl.* whose price at present is only just above the general figure. *Fl.* medium large, perianth smooth with pure white, broad and overlapping segments; corona shallow, greenish-white at base with white band in the centre and rim of sulphur-yellow at mouth. (Pl. 27, 4)

'SALMON TROUT' Probably the best and most acclaimed 'pink' variety yet raised. *Fl.* large and of very good substance, perianth white, segments broad, overlapping; corona almost a short trumpet, salmon-pink, developing its best pink colour after it has been open a day or two. Claimed by its raiser to be a robust grower but still a rare and expensive plant.

'TUDOR MINSTREL' *Fl.* very large, perianth white with broad overlapping segments of unusual quality and substance, corona deep aureolin-yellow, frilled at mouth. A very beautiful exhibition variety.

*(c) Perianth white, corona white not paler than the perianth*

'LUDLOW' A lovely *fl.* of medium size, almost pure white but with a pale greenish-yellow base to the corona, which is almost trumpet-shaped and deeply indented at mouth. A fine *fl.* for cutting and growing in pans.

'NIPHETOS' Perianth white, corona trumpet-shaped, pale primrose-yellow on opening, fading to cream. An older variety but one still worth growing for cutting and in pans.

'TRUTH' A very fine white daffodil with perianth segments smooth and overlapping, corona white, trumpet-shaped and with pale yellow inside at base.

*(d) Any other colour combination in this division*

'BINKIE' A very unusual *fl.* which is best described as a reversed bicolor, raised in Tasmania. *Fl.* of medium size, perianth segments primrose-yellow, paling almost to white at base; corona primrose-yellow with a sulphur-yellow edge but paling almost to white as the *fl.* matures. Vigorous. (Pl. 27, 2)

### (3) SMALL-CUPPED NARCISSI OF GARDEN ORIGIN

One flower to a stem; cup or corona not more than one-third the length of the perianth segments.

*(a) Perianth coloured, corona coloured, not paler than perianth*

'CHUNGKING' A fine variety and probably still the best in its section.

Perianth deep yellow with smooth overlapping segments; corona shallow, vivid orange-red. Vigorous. A fine Show *fl.* and excellent for cutting.

### (b) Perianth white, corona coloured

* '**BLARNEY**' An unusual *fl.* Perianth white with broad, smooth overlapping segments; corona shallow, saucer-shaped, pale salmon-orange in colour with a primrose-yellow rim. A charming *fl.* for cutting.
'**MAHMOUD**' A distinctive medium-sized *fl.* with very thick, smooth, almost waxy perianth and small cup of very deep reddish-orange. A fine show *fl.* (Pl. **27**, 5)
'**MATAPAN**' A fine Show *fl.* of medium size with broad smooth perianth segments of pure white and a small shallow corona of deep orange-red. Early flowering.

### (c) Corona white, not paler than the perianth

* '**CHINESE WHITE**' One of the most outstanding Show varieties yet raised. *Fl.* large, pure white with broad smooth overlapping segments; corona small, saucer-shaped, fluted at rim, white with a faint green eye.
* '**FRIGID**' Ice-white, a fine scented *fl.* of medium size, which is distinctive and valuable for its late flowering, often well into the second half of May. Corona small, pure white with a small emerald-green eye. An unusual *fl.* of considerable charm which should prove a good garden variety.

## (4) DOUBLE NARCISSI OF GARDEN ORIGIN

These lack the charm of the single daffodils but are useful for making an effect in bowls, while the old double ' Van Sion ' is still a good variety for mass woodland planting in woodland or in grass, making a lovely golden show at a distance. Apart from this old favourite they are not to be recommended for outdoor decorative planting since the heavy heads are inclined to be knocked down in storms or rough weather.

'**CAMELLIA**' Soft primrose-yellow, fully double. An old variety said to be a sport from ' Emperor.'
'**MARY COPELAND**' Outer petal creamy-white, centre cream but interspersed with a few orange-red petalodes.
'**MRS. WILLIAM COPELAND**' Outer petals pure white, inner petalodes pale canary-yellow and waved at the edges.

*Promising newer variety*

'**DOUBLE EVENT**' A fine Show *fl.* rounded and full with regular overlapping petalodes, outer perianth segments white, inner petalodes mostly white but interspersed with some of lemon-yellow.

## (5) TRIANDRUS NARCISSI OF GARDEN ORIGIN

The majority of these varieties are close to the sp. and are dwarf-growing plants suitable for the rock garden and have been described under the section dealing with *N. triandrus* and its varieties.

*(a) Cup or corona not less than two-thirds the length of the perianth segments*

' Niveth ' An old variety but still worth growing. *Fl.* small–medium in size, pure white.

' Tresamble ' A delightful variety with 4–6 *fl.* to a stem, perianth white cup rounded, pale creamy-yellow with a small green eye, waved at mouth. Taller and slightly larger than ' Niveth.'

*(b) Cup or corona less than two-thirds the length of the perianth segments*

* ' Silver Chimes ' A very fine variety with more vigour than is usual in this group. A triandrus-tazetta hybrid. Stems stout up to 15 in. with 6 or more *fl.* with white perianth and corona of primrose-yellow. *L.* wide, deep yellow-green, not glaucous. Very suitable for the larger rock garden and for growing in pans for the house. Said not to be quite hardy in cold situations.

' Thalia ' Slightly taller and larger than ' Silver Chimes '. Perianth and corona white, *fl.* nodding, 2–4 to a stem. Late flowering.

## (6) CYCLAMINEUS NARCISSI OF GARDEN ORIGIN

The smaller varieties have already been described in the section dealing with the sp. and its varieties but the recent hybrids raised by C. F. Coleman between *N. cyclamineus* and larger garden varieties are plants of great charm and distinction.

* ' Charity May ' Height 12–15 in. *Fl.* soft clear yellow, 3½ in. in diameter. Perianth segments broad and overlapping, corona slightly frilled. Increases freely and is also a delightful plant for exhibition and for growing in pots and pans for the house. A very promising variety.

* ' Dove Wings ' A bicolor with slightly waved creamy-white perianth segments and canary-yellow corona. Height up to 18 in. *Fl.* 3 in. in diameter. A very good garden plant, increasing rapidly, and a variety of great charm.

' Jenny ' Perhaps the most charming of this attractive trio of sisters, although reputed not to be so vigorous as the other two. Perianth segments smooth, white, slightly reflexed, corona pale primrose-yellow (Pl. **26**, 6). A very fine exhibition *fl.*

## (7) JONQUILLA NARCISSI OF GARDEN ORIGIN
### WITH CHARACTERISTICS OF ANY OF THE NARCISSUS JONQUILLA GROUP CLEARLY EVIDENT

Several of these jonquils with small flowers have already been described under the section dealing with the sp. The main characteristics of this group are the clear golden-yellow flowers, one or several to a stem and the fine scent. They are particularly suitable for growing in bowls or pans for the house.

## Nerine

(*a*) *Cup or corona not less than two-thirds of the perianth segments*

'GOLDEN SCEPTRE' An old variety but still worth growing. 1 or 2 *fl*. deep buttercup-yellow, corona tubular, 1 in. deep. Scent very sweet.

(*b*) *Cup or corona less than two-thirds the length of the perianth segments*

* 'LANARTH' A beautiful variety, tall, with buttercup-yellow perianth and a deeper orange-yellow corona. *Fl*. 1–3 to a stem of medium size.

* 'TREVITHIAN' One of the best jonquils yet raised. A self-coloured *fl*. of buttercup-yellow, sweetly scented. An excellent garden variety.

Divisions 8 to 11 deal with (8) Tazettas of Garden Origin, (9) Poeticus of Garden Origin, (10) Species and wild forms and hybrids, (11) Miscellaneous narcissi not falling into any of the foregoing divisions. The majority of the best plants in these divisions have been already described under the species and their related hybrids see pp. 232–243.

# NERINE *Amaryllidaceae*

A MOST decorative genus of S. African bulbs, allied to *Amaryllis* and *Brunsvigia* and flowering in the autumn. The flowers are borne in umbels and in most groups are developed before the leaves have grown to any extent. The segments are mostly regular and strap-shaped and the stamens and style stand out stiffly together in the centre at right angles to the perianth segments. The majority of nerines and particularly *N. sarniensis* and its varieties have a wonderful quality of iridescence in the petals, sparkling especially in electric light. This is due to a peculiar shape of the epidermal cells which are shaped like a lens and concentrate the light on to drops of pink sap at the base of the cells. In consequence they are lovely as cut flowers and they are also long lasting.

Nerines in pots will need repotting every fourth or fifth year since the bulbs increase freely by division but some crowding in the pots will be beneficial. Any repotting should be done in August or early September before they show new flower spikes. At this time a sprinkling of bone meal or other fertiliser should be added to the compost and during flowering and growth they may be fed with weak solutions of fertilisers or natural manures to build up the bulbs.

The two most widely grown groups are *N. bowdenii* of which there are several varieties and *N. sarniensis* of which there are numerous varieties and hybrids. There are also several species characterised by narrow filiform leaves and smaller pale pink flowers with undulating margins to the petals. The *bowdenii* group is hardy but in most gardens does best if planted in a sunny border under a warm wall. The bulbs should be left undisturbed and only divided when the groups become very thick and begin to flower poorly. *N. sarniensis* and the majority of the other species and hybrids are best treated as cool greenhouse plants and the most important part of their cultivation is the complete rest in a dry condition after the leaves have died down. They should then only be watered when the flower spikes begin to show about September. During the winter while the leaves are active they will not withstand frost. If, however, the bulbs are to be potted into larger pots without shaking out the soil and giving fresh compost this may be done soon after flowering, taking care not to injure the young leaves. The bulbs should not be planted deeply and the neck of the bulb should be above the soil of the pot. Good drainage is important. Old pots may be top dressed with new compost with advantage when starting into growth, about 1 in. of the old compost being removed. High temperatures are not necessary nor even desirable but as much fresh air and sunlight should be admitted as possible. The seeds are fleshy and should be sown as soon as they are mature. They are best sown on the surface of the soil and often germinate very quickly. In fact germination has sometimes been observed before they have fallen from the parent seed-head.

† **N. angustifolia.** Stem up to 2 ft. with an umbel of up to 12, but generally fewer, delicate, deep pink *fl.* with undulating perianth segments about 1½ in. long. Pedicels, ovary and scape covered with short glandular hairs. *L.* linear, up to 10 in. long but only ¼ in. wide. Cool greenhouse or even unheated frame, almost hardy. Close to *N. filifolia* but larger.

† **N. appendiculata.** Close to preceding sp. but *fl.* pale pink and with irregular perianth segments, the lowest one bending downwards or horizontal while the others are ascending. It also has a small strap-shaped process with apical teeth at the base of each filament. *L.* narrow, linear, up to 2 ft. Stem up to 2 ft. with up to 20*fl.*, the pedicels being hairy. Cool greenhouse. Almost hardy.

**N. bowdenii.** This is probably the most valuable plant in the genus since it is hardy in most areas but flowers better in a warm border. The bulbs should be planted 6 in. deep. Stem up to 2 ft. stout with up to 8 *fl.* on rather long pedicels in a loose umbel. Perianth segments strap-shaped, up to 3 in. long, slightly undulating and recurved near ends, pale pink with a darker line down centre of each segment. The colour range tends to contain a very little blue in the pink and no orange or warm colour. *L.* strap-shaped, only first appearing with the *fl.* but lasting over much of the next summer. Late Sept.-Nov. and standing a small degree of frost when in *fl.* (Pl. XIX)

\* ' FENWICK'S VARIETY ' An unusually fine and vigorous form with stems up to 2½ ft. and slightly larger *fl.* heads than the type. ' Pink Beauty ' deeper pink with a faint dusting of gold and silver, a very fine variety. †' Aurora ' and †' Hera ' (Pl. XX) are hybrids between *N. bowdenii* and *N. sarniensis* (*N. fothergillii*) and have tall stems and large umbels of satin-pink or pale crimson *fl.*; ' Hera ', being the deeper in colour, has been described as cherry-red. Each segment has a median stripe of deeper colour. Although slightly less hardy than *N. bowdenii*, they have been grown successfully outside in a number of gardens, particularly in the

*Plate XV*. Above, Lilium 'Crimson Queen', one of the most striking deep crimson varieties of the cross between *L. auratum platyphyllum* and *L. speciosum* 'Melpomene'
Below, *Lilium wilsonii* var. *flavum*, sometimes known as 'Marlyn Ross', a bright, heavily spotted lemon-yellow lily

*Plate XVI.* Narcissus 'Cantatrice', one of the best of the white daffodils,
both for growing in the garden and for Show

*Plate XVII.* A meadow naturalised with white narcissus

*Plate XVIII.* Above, a well grown pan of *Narcisuss cantabricus* var. *petunioides,* which flowers very early in the year and so is especially suitable for the alpine house. Left, narcissus 'Snipe', a dwarf variety with pale yellow flowers, very suitable for growing in pans

West of England. Unfortunately they appear to be slower of increase than the sp. and have remained rare and expensive. When first opening the *fl.* are more tubular than in the parent sp.

**N. curvifolia.** A syn. of *N. sarniensis.*

† **N. filifolia.** A pretty dwarf plant with filiform *l.* and rather slender stems generally less than 1 ft. high and loose umbels of delicate rose-pink *fl.* with narrow wavy perianth segments about 1 in. long. Oct.-Nov. Bulbs small. Cool greenhouse but probably worth trying outside in a very warm and sheltered position. *L.* almost evergreen. Does not require such a complete summer rest as *N. sarniensis.* Very common in S. Africa.

† **N. flexuosa.** A vigorous plant with stems up to 3 ft. though generally less and umbels of up to 12 pale pink *fl.* with narrow, wavy perianth segments about 1½ in. long striped with deeper red. *L.* strap-shaped up to 1½ ft. long and growing with the *fl.* Sept.-Oct. Cool greenhouse. Var. *alba* with pure white *fl.* Numerous hybrids have also been raised between *N. flexuosa* and *N. sarniensis.* Syn. *N. pulchella.*

**N. fothergillii.** A syn. of *N. sarniensis.*

† **N. humilis.** Close to *N. flexuosa* but with *l.* usually not more than 6 in. long and generally a smaller plant. Stem up to 1 ft. with up to 8 deep pink *fl.* in a loose umbel. Perianth segments narrow, much recurved, undulating. Sept.-Oct. Cool greenhouse.

† **N. lucida.** Dwarf with stout stems up to 6 in. and large globular umbels of up to 20 pale pink *fl.* each 1½ in. across. Perianth segments narrow, strap-shaped with a median ray of deeper pink. Pedicels long, hairy. In habit said to resemble a dwarf *Brunsvigia* and rather distinct from other sp. Dry western regions of Cape Province and northwards into Transvaal. Cool greenhouse but very rare in cultivation.

† **N. masonorum.** A dwarf plant with small bulbs, narrow filiform *l.* and small umbels of crisped, undulating pale pink *fl.* on narrow stem up to 6 in. high. Hardy in sheltered positions in South and West of England; practically evergreen. Close to *N. appendiculata* but a smaller plant.

† **N. pudica.** Rather larger than the preceding and with linear, slightly glaucous broader *l.* Stem slender up to 1 ft. with a loose umbel of rather funnel-shaped and sometimes drooping white *fl.* each perianth segment having a median red stripe. Cool greenhouse; rare in cultivation.

†* **N. sarniensis.** The Guernsey Lily. The most beautiful sp. Large umbels of iridescent *fl.* on stout stems up to 2 ft. Unfortunately not hardy outside in this country, but apparently so in the Channel Islands, where it is much cultivated. Its popular name of Guernsey Lily is said to have been derived from bulbs shipwrecked on the coast of that island and growing in the sand of the shore. The ship was said to have come from Japan and it became falsely believed that the bulbs were Japanese. They are in fact native only to S. Africa and can be found on Table Mountain where they flower in March. Numerous varieties have been raised with large umbels of *fl.* with wide petals

varying greatly in colour from pure white, through pale pink and orange-scarlet, to pale purplish-magenta. Bulbs are large, shaped rather like those of a narcissus and with several papery tunics. *L.* broad, strap-shaped, appearing almost immediately after the *fl.* The most widely cultivated form is that known as *fothergillii* or *curvifolia*, which has salmon-scarlet *fl.* in Sept.-Oct. Recently polyploids with even larger *fl.* heads have been raised and should be the precursors of a new race of nerines. A good list of cultivars will be found in the R.H.S. Dictionary of Gardening Supplement but since very few of these are offered by name in catalogues they are not quoted here.

† **N. undulata.** *Fl.* rose-pink in quite large umbels on stems up to 1½ ft. Perianth segments narrow, wide spreading from base, very wavy and crisped at edges. *L.* rather narrow, almost evergreen. Oct.-Nov. Cool greenhouse. Its hybrids with *N. sarniensis* flower later than the varieties of that sp. In S. Africa it is said to flower in mid-winter.

# NOMOCHARIS *Liliaceae*

SOME CONSIDER these the queen of all liliaceous plants, since the flowers have a grace and delicacy combined with an orchid-like and exotic appearance that is almost unique. The genus is very close both to *Lilium* and *Fritillaria* and now that under a recent botanical rearrangement the members of the more dowdy and almost drab *lophophorum-oxypetalum* section have been placed in *Lilium*, where they will be found described in the second part, *Nomocharis* is represented by a small and fairly uniform group, all of great beauty. The bulbs are without tunics like those of *Lilium* and are composed of relatively few scales; the flowers are pendulous and generally open face downwards on long pedicels although sometimes held horizontally. The segments are divided to the base and the flowers open wide like a flat saucer, the predominating colours being pale pinks and whites, the flowers often being fringed at the edges of the inner segments and heavily spotted with deeper pinks or purple. The Eunomocharis section, to which most of the species now included in the genus belong, is characterised by the swollen bases to the filaments of the stamens and by the almost crested nectaries at the base of the segments. The leaves are narrow and generally borne in whorls up the stem with a few scattered leaves above.

Nomocharis are native to the higher mountain regions of W. China, S.E. Tibet and the Eastern and Central Himalayas. They have unfortunately proved difficult in cultivation in the majority of gardens particularly in the south and the only continued success with them has been in gardens in Scotland, where they can be grown in full exposure provided there is ample moisture during the growing period preferably from a high water table, combined of course with excellent drainage above the level of the water table. In the South of England they need to be grown in partial shade and are seldom so fine or very long lived.

Their beauty is such, though, that they are worth considerable effort. The seeds usually germinate freely but the seedlings need to be treated with great care in moving. Probably the most successful practice is to sow them very thinly in a box or large pan and then plant the whole lot out together without breaking up the soil, after the second season. Others prick out the seedlings very early after they have germinated and then plant out the bulbs when they are almost mature.

In the gardens where they have been grown successfully they have hybridised freely among themselves and probably the greater part of the plantings are represented by a race of hybrids which may indeed have more vigour than the original species, typical members of which are now rare. All the species flower in June-July.

**N. aperta.** Stem up to 3 ft., generally less with up to 6 nodding *fl.*, up to 4 in. across, pale pink but spotted and blotched with deeper crimson or purplish-crimson. The outer segments are ovate and broad with a dark blotch at the base, the inner segments with a dark basal raised gland. Yunnan and S.E. Tibet. A white form without spotting is also recorded but is not known in cultivation. This sp. is closely related to *N. saluenensis*.

**N. basilissa.** A fabulous sp. with " salmon-scarlet " *fl.* according to Farrer the collector. Unfortunately it has never flowered in cultivation, but he did record its colour in one of his most charming paintings which is reproduced in the book of his plant introductions. N. Burma and Yunnan. It is apparently allied to *N. meleagrina* but quite distinct from all other members of the genus in its colour. Probably not now in cultivation.

**N. farreri.** Closely allied to the commoner *N. pardanthina* and sometimes regarded as a variety of it, this is nevertheless one of the most beautiful plants in the genus. It differs from *pardanthina* in the narrower *l.* and in the absence of fringing on the edges of the inner segments. It is said also to have a stronger habit. Stem up to 3 ft. with narrow *l.* in whorls except just below the *fl.* which are white marked with purplish-red, saucer-shaped and pendulous, up to 4 in. across. N.E. Upper Burma.

**N. mairei.** A beautiful sp. of the Eunomocharis section, distinguished chiefly by the very prominent fringing of the edges of the inner segments. *Fl.* drooping, saucer-shaped, white, usually heavily spotted with rose-purple, up to 4 in. across. The outer segments are much broader than the inner ones. Stem usually not more than 2½ ft.

Var. **candida.** *Fl.* white and unspotted, a very beautiful *fl.*

Var. **leucantha.** *Fl.* slightly larger than in the type, heavily spotted with rose-purple.

This sp. and its varieties are among the best members of the genus to attempt and a specimen has been grown in Scotland up to 6 ft. with 16 *fl.*, the largest of which was 5¾ in. across. This is, however, very unusual. Yunnan.

**N. meleagrina.** Stem up to 3½ ft. with large drooping *fl.*, white or rose coloured and with numerous deeper spots and with segments blotched at the base, the inner and the outer ones being almost equal in size. The base of the filaments of the stamens is inflated and the basal gland is crested and lobed, brownish-red in colour. This sp. is rare in cultivation and appears to be closely related to *N. pardanthina* but is distinguished by the spotting over the whole of the segments, suggestive of that in *Fritillaria meleagris*, hence the name. W. China, Yunnan and Szechwan and S.E. Tibet between 10,000 and 13,000 ft.

**N. pardanthina.** The first discovered member of the genus and still probably the finest. Stems up to 3 ft. or more with up to 10 *fl.* opening almost flat and pendulous, pale pink, spotted with small spots of darker crimson or purplish-crimson especially towards the base of the inner segments which are unusually broad and also slightly fringed; the three outer segments are unspotted. W. China, Yunnan. Distinguished from *N. mairei* by the less deep fringing of the inner segments and by the main bulk of the spots being towards the base instead of all over.

**N. saluenensis.** Stems up to 3 ft., generally less with up to 6 wide, open, bowl-shaped *fl.* up to 3½ in. across, pale rose-pink or white, the central ones carried erect and facing upwards, the lower horizontally, spotted with purple, the inner three segments have a purplish-red blotch at base. W. China, Yunnan and Szechwan, S.E. Tibet and N. Burma between 9,000 and 14,000 ft. It is closest to *N. aperta* but distinguished by the absence of fringing and by a very short style. Deeper coloured forms with rose-purple *fl.* have also been recorded. (Pl. XXI)

# NOTHOLIRION *Liliaceae*

A SMALL genus closely allied to both *Lilium* and *Fritillaria*, in both of which genera its species have been placed from time to time. It is now, however, generally accepted as a separate genus and it seems best to treat it so. It is confined to the Himalayas, S.E. Tibet and Western China and four species are known, all of which have been in cultivation. None of them, despite considerable beauty, has however established itself regularly as a good garden plant in this country. They tend to begin to grow and put out new leaves in the late autumn or early winter and such leaves are easily damaged with corresponding weakness to the plant and the build up of the bulbs. The bulbs are distinguished from those of *Lilium* by the fewer scales of which they are composed and particularly by the hard scaly outer tunics and by the habit of producing innumerable rice grain bulblets on the inside of the scales and before the main bulb reaches flowering size. This character undoubtedly postpones their flowering in

# Notholirion

many English gardens often to infinity, though they can, of course, be propagated from this source. After flowering the main bulb dies. In their basal leaf they are also distinct, these being long and almost grass-like. The flowers are bell-shaped or broadly funnel-shaped and are distinguished from those of *Lilium* by the definitely trifid stigma. The four species are well portrayed in Part 7 of the Supplement to Elwes' Monograph of the genus *Lilium*. Generally best grown under the same conditions as *Nomocharis*.

**N. bulbuliferum.** This is the sp. better known both in literature and garden under the name *N. hyacinthinum* though unfortunately this name has had to be discarded owing to a prior name. Stem stout, up to 5 ft. but generally less, with up to 30 broadly funnel-shaped *fl.*, pale pinkish-lilac or mauvish-lilac in colour and with green tips to the segments. The *fl.* are borne horizontally on short pedicels, thus distinguishing them from the bell-shaped pendulous *fl.* of *N. campanulatum.* Only very slightly scented. July-August. Bulb ovoid and producing many small bulblets, basal *l.* long, up to 1½ ft. Alpine meadows of W. China, S.E. Tibet, N. Burma and recorded westwards as far as Nepal, up to 14,000 ft. It should be planted in a sheltered position with as good drainage as possible. The best recorded specimens have always been from gardens in areas specially favoured with regard to winter climate and rainfall.

**N. campanulatum.** This is undoubtedly the finest of the sp., having pendulous deep crimson or purplish-red bell-shaped *fl.* on stout stems and in outline resembling a dark red *Galtonia candicans*. Unfortunately though it is a very rare plant in English gardens and has really only succeeded in a very few gardens in favoured parts. Stems up to 4 ft. with up to 20 *fl.*, each segment being tipped with bright green and the *fl.* being up to 2 in. long, scentless. June. Bulb ovoid with outer membranaceous tunic. Basal *l.* long, up to 2 ft. and 1 in. broad. W. China, Yunnan, N. Burma. Monocarpic but persisting through the numerous bulbils. In the wild it is recorded as growing in damper alpine meadows between 12,000 and 14,000 ft. than the other sp. In the past there has been much confusion between this and *N. bulbuliferum* and there may even be intermediate forms.

**N. macrophyllum.** The smallest and daintiest of the sp. with lilac-mauve or violet-mauve nodding open funnel-shaped *fl.* on slender stems, rarely exceeding 1½ ft. in height with up to 6 *fl.* each 1½–2 in. long and as much across when wide open. Bulb small, ovoid. Basal *l.* up to 15 in. long and ½ in. wide, narrowly linear. May-June. Central Himalayas, Nepal and Sikkim in sub-alpine and alpine regions between 8,000 and 13,000 ft. Rather tender in cultivation but apparently tolerant of lime.

**N. thomsonianum.** A stout plant from the North Western Himalaya and Afghanistan. Stem stout up to 4 ft. with up to 30 horizontal wide open funnel-shaped *fl.* of pale pinkish-lilac, the segments being divided right to the base and being tinged with a deeper purplish-crimson towards the base inside, but tipped with pale green at the apex. Fragrant. April-May. Bulb larger than in the other sp., up to 2½ in. high, ovoid; sometimes producing more than one stem. Basal *l.* up to 2 ft. long and 1 in. wide. Although early flowering this sp. seems to have a better constitution in English gardens than the others and records of its flowering are much more frequent. Owing to its earlier season of flowering, and in order to protect the winter *l.*, it is often recommended that it should be grown in a cool greenhouse or even in an alpine house. Very good drainage is always essential.

# ORNITHOGALUM *Liliaceae*

A LARGE genus in which 100 or more species have been named, mainly from S. Europe, Asia Minor and S. Africa. The flowers are predominantly star-shaped or cup-like, white or white with a green median stripe down the segment or yellow or orange in the case of some of the S. African species and are generally borne facing upright in a flat corymb or in a rather densely aggregated raceme. The best known of the European species is *O. umbellatum*, a native of this country and widespread in Europe, known as the Star of Bethlehem. Practically all the European species are quite hardy and should be planted in full sun. Of the S. African the best known is *O. thyrsoides*, the Chincherinchee, which is sent all over the world in boxes at Christmas, the flowers having been packed in bud and the stems waxed. It is not hardy in this country but may be grown for summer flowering like a gladiolus then lifted and stored for the winter. For this, however, it is hardly sufficiently spectacular to become widely popular.

None of the ornithogalums are very striking in flower but their white stars look well in a semi-wild open patch or in the front of a border and the European species flower early in the year, generally between March and May. They grow well in light sandy soil. The bulbs are globose or ovoid and fleshy and the leaves basal, linear or strap-shaped, often with a silvery line down the middle like a crocus. Most of the bulbs increase freely and form large clumps which should be divided from time to time. They also grow readily from seed. The distinctions between many of the species are rather fine and not such as to appeal to the average gardener and so only a few are dealt with here.

† **O. arabicum.** One of the finest of the genus. Stem stout, up to 1½ ft. with up to 12 *fl.* pearly-white but with a prominent dark ovary in the centre, quite large, 2 in. or more across. May-June. Bulb rather large, ovoid, about size of a walnut. *L.* broadly-linear. Mediterranean regions. Hardy in warmer areas though not very free flowering in this country except from freshly imported bulbs, the plant sometimes sold as *O. corymbosum* is probably only a good and freer-flowering form of this sp.

**O. aureum.** See under *O. thyrsoides* var. *aureum*.

**O. balansae.** A pretty dwarf sp. from Asia Minor with small umbels of rather long-petalled star-like *fl.*, white with a green stripe. Stem very short. Bulb ovoid. *L.* linear, keeled. Early flowering. March-April.

**O. comosum.** Large heads with up to 30 greenish-white *fl.* on short stems, generally under 6 in. Bulb ovoid. *L.* linear. S. Europe and E. Mediterranean.

**O. corymbosum.** See under *O. arabicum.*

**O. fimbriatum.** Distinguished by its narrow, hairy *l.* Stem short up to 5 in. with an umbel of medium-sized, white star-like *fl.* about 1 in. across and with a green median band to centre of each segment on both sides. Early flowering. February-March. Asia Minor including Southern U.S.S.R. and Crimea.

† **O. lacteum.** A beautiful sp. from the Cape Province of S. Africa. Stem stout and tall, up to 3 ft. with a close raceme up to 1 ft. in length of white, quite large *fl.* nearly 2 in. across. Distinguished from *O. arabicum* by the taller habit, the absence of the dark ovary and the more racemose inflorescence. Suitable for the Cool Greenhouse. June-July.

**O. latifolium.** Distinguished among European and Mediterranean sp. by the very broad *l.* up to 2 in. across, bright yellowish-green especially when young and appearing usually well before the *fl.* Stem up to 2 ft. with a long raceme of numerous white star-like *fl.* on long pedicels. June. Asia Minor. Hardy.

**O. montanum.** Allied to our common Star of Bethlehem but generally with a bigger and more upright raceme. Variable however in height from a low growing plant with narrow *l.* as found in Italy to much larger plants up to 1½ ft. and up to 20 *fl.* from Syria and Asia Minor with broad *l.* up to ¾ in. across. *Fl.* white inside with outer sides of segments green with only white margin. Widespread in S. Europe and Asia Minor. April-June. Hardy.

**O. narbonense.** A common sp. round the Mediterranean with long, keeled *l.* and tall stems up to 1½ ft. with terminal racemes of numerous white, rather small, star-like *fl.* with green central stripes and green outside. Hardy. April-May.

\* **O. nutans.** One of the most beautiful plants in the genus and very distinctive with quite large rather drooping *fl.* giving more impression of soft jade-green than white. Delightful for flower arrangements. Stem up to 1½ ft., generally less. April–May. S. Europe but naturalised in a few places in Britain. Hardy and increasing freely and growing equally well in semi-shade.

**O. pyramidale.** Closely related to *O. narbonense*, but rather more vigorous and with larger *fl.* Stem up to 2 ft. Later flowering. May-June.

**O. pyrenaicum.** Rather small and inconspicuous but numerous *fl.* on long stem up to 2 ft., star-like, pale greenish-yellow inside, green outside. May-June. S. Europe but naturalised in Britain. Hardy. The young shoots are eaten by the French as Asparagus.

**O. subcucullatum.** An attractive sp. from Central Spain with tall stems up to 1½ ft. with dense heads of pure white *fl.* borne without the *l.* in its native habitat but not always so in this country. May-June. Doubtfully hardy.

† **O. thyrsoides.** The Chincherinchee from S. Africa. Widely grown there for cutting. *Fl.* white with prominent yellow stamens, cup-shaped in dense

racemes. Very long lasting. Not hardy but may be grown outside to flower in summer and then lifted and stored in sand for the winter or grown in a cool greenhouse.

Var. **aureum.** Rather more dwarf and with deep yellowish-orange *fl.*

**O. umbellatum.** Our native Star of Bethlehem. Very widespread and increasing rapidly like *Muscari racemosum* or a weed but attractive with large umbels of snow-white *fl.* opening flat on short stalks. Only the outside has green stripes and hardly shows when the *fl.* are open. April-May. Europe and Asia Minor. *Fl.* only open late in morning and close again early.

# PAMIANTHE *Amaryllidaceae*

A MONOTYPIC genus of bulbous plants closely allied to *Hymenocallis* and *Pancratium*, but distinguished by its peculiar winged seeds and also by the false stem made up of the elongated tops of the bulb scales as in *Worsleya* and by the sheathing leaf bases. The bulb spreads with stolons. It is named after the late Major Albert Pam of Wormley Bury in Hertfordshire who first introduced the only sp., *P. peruviana*, from Peru. The flowers are large, white, with a very long perianth tube and strongly scented. It is a very beautiful and distinctive plant. At one time another tropical plant, *P. quitoensis*, was placed in this genus but it has been removed to another genus, *Leptochiton*, on the basis of a substantial difference in the seeds. As far as I know the latter is not in cultivation.

**P. peruviana.** False stem enclosing scape up to 2 ft. with a small umbel of up to 4 *fl.* Perianth tube very long, up to 4 in., green, outer segments with broad lobes with an apiculate tip, up to 4 in. long, white with a central yellowish-green stripe, central staminal cup or corona bell-shaped with pointed tips to segments, 3 in. long and 2 in. across at mouth, white with green median lines. *Fl.* strongly scented. Feb.-March. Bulb large, ovoid, with olive-brown tunic. *L.* linear, keeled, bases sheathing false stem. N. Peru, warm temperate zone. Suitable for a warm greenhouse with a humid atmosphere. Evergreen. Unfortunately rare in cultivation but can be propagated from seed.

# PANCRATIUM *Amaryllidaceae*

A SMALL genus of summer and autumn flowering bulbs allied to *Hymenocallis*, but native to the Mediterranean regions, particularly near to or even on the sandy sea shores, but extending also to the Canary Islands, Tropical Africa and India. The S. American plants often included in this genus such as *P. calathinum* should, however, now be found under *Hymeno-*

# Paradisea

*callis.* The bulbs are unusually large, globose, the leaves strap-shaped, often glaucous and arranged in two ranks, the flowers white, in a large or small umbel, the outer petals rather narrow and recurved, the inner joined together into a staminal cup, the tube usually long; flower borne in an umbel on a stout stem. Two species, *P. illyricum* and *P. maritimum*, which are both widespread in S. Europe, are reasonably hardy in very warm situations under a wall. They tend, however, not to be very free flowering unless the bulbs are well ripened. They are strongly and sweetly scented. Only the two European species mentioned are in general cultivation in this country and even these are rarely seen. Probably, however, *P. canariense* would also be worth growing in a cool greenhouse.

**P. calathinum.** A syn. of *Hymenocallis calathina.*

† **P. canariense.** Stem up to 2 ft., flattened. *Fl.* in a spreading umbel with up to 12 *fl.*, each about 3 in. across; tube shorter than in other sp., staminal cup shorter and toothed at edge between the stamens, outer segments narrow, recurved. White. Only slightly scented. Sept. Bulb of medium size. *L.* strap-shaped, glaucous. Canary Islands. Cool greenhouse, though there are records of its surviving winter outside in S. England.

**P. illyricum.** Stem up to 1½ ft. with a compact umbel of large star-shaped white *fl.* up to 12 to an umbel and each 3 in. across, tube long and green, outer segments pointed, staminal cup short-toothed at edge, very fragrant. May-June. Bulb very large, pear-shaped or almost globose. *L.* slightly glaucous. S. Italy and Central Mediterranean regions. Hardy in warm and sheltered positions if bulb is planted deep, but requires good ripening to flower. Generally more successful in a cold frame.

**P. maritimum.** Stem 1 ft. with a loose umbel of very sweetly scented white *fl.* with long perianth tubes, outer segments long, narrow with a green stripe on outside, staminal cup long, tubular, toothed at edge. Bulb more globose than in *P. illyricum*. *L.* slightly glaucous, persistent throughout year. Later flowering than preceding sp. July-Sept. Probably not quite so hardy. Mediterranean regions particularly on or near the seashore, often in very sandy positions. Common. Known by the Greeks as the " Sea Lily."

# PARADISEA *Liliaceae*

A MONOTYPIC genus closely allied to *Anthericum* and containing the lovely white St. Bruno's Lily of alpine meadows, *P. liliastrum*. Although rarely seen in English gardens it is quite hardy and grows without difficulty and is well worth establishing in large groups in the rock garden or front of the border.

**P. liliago.** A syn. of *Anthericum liliago*, St. Bernard's Lily.

**P. liliastrum.** St. Bruno's Lily. Stem 1½ to 2 ft., wiry with a loose spike of 6 or more translucent pure white funnel-shaped *fl.* 2 in. long and as much across the wide open mouth, with a green spot at tip of each petal. Scented. June-July. Root-stock a short tuber with fleshy roots. *L.* linear, narrow, keeled. Alps, Pyrenees and mountains of S. Europe 6,000–7,000 ft. Farrer describes it well as an " understudy for the Madonna Lily."

# PHAEDRANASSA *Amaryllidaceae*

A SMALL genus of S. American bulbous plants with pendulous flowers from quite high zones of the Andes from Colombia to Peru, allied to *Stenomesson*. The flowers are long and tubular, generally brightly coloured with red and green zones and extruding stamens and style. The segments are joined through most of their length and the lobes hardly spread out at all at the tips. They are borne in loose umbels on long arched pedicels. The bulbs are globose with thin brown tunics and the leaves which are mostly produced after the flowers are broadly oblong or elliptic. Unfortunately none of the species are hardy in this country and are most suited to cool or even intermediate greenhouse treatment where they are reputed not to be difficult. Unfortunately also they are very rare in cultivation. Probably the finest is:

† **P. carmioli.** Stem up to 2 ft., stout, with a loose umbel of up to 12 *fl.*, drooping, tubular, 2 in. long and ½ in. wide at the mouth, green at base, bright crimson for the larger part and then with a bright green zone around the mouth. In bud the *fl.* are yellow at the base. This curious *fl.* has something of the look of *Bilbergia nutans*, although larger and more brilliant. Late spring. Bulb globose. *L.* with a long petiole, oblong-elliptic, produced after the *fl.* Probably Peru and Costa Rica in gardens. Rare.

# POLIANTHES *Amaryllidaceae*

THIS IS a monotypic genus from Mexico containing the tuberose of florists, one of the most sweetly scented of all plants. The flowers are white in a terminal raceme and the bulbs may be forced into flower at nearly any season, being started with a temperature of 60°F. or more. However, in a cool greenhouse they can be grown quite adequately. The double variety is the one most commonly grown by florists under the name ' The Pearl ' and its flowers are larger than in the single form.

† **P. tuberosa.** Stem up to 2½ ft., with a terminal raceme of funnel-shaped white rather waxy *fl.*, the perianth lobes of which open flat into a star-like

*fl.* in the single forms.  Very fragrant.  Bulb ovoid, knobby like a tuber.
*L.* linear, deeply channelled, slightly glaucous.  Mexico.  In general these
are grown from newly imported bulbs and old ones tend to take a year to
recover after flowering.  Possibly if they were ripened completely they would
flower well each year.

# PUSCHKINIA  *Liliaceae*

A VERY small genus of two or three species of early spring flowering bulbs
but only one, *P. scilloides*, the striped squill is at present known in cultivation.  Closely allied to *Scilla* and *Chionodoxa* and should be treated in the
same way in the garden, being separated botanically by the segments
being joined together at the base into a bell-like tube before opening flat
and with a central tubular nectary of six lobes around the stamens and
style.  This is sometimes referred to as a corona.

> **P. scilloides.**  Stem short, 3–6 in. with about 6 or even more medium-sized
> *fl.* on rather long slender pedicels, very pale blue or whitish with a darker
> greenish-blue median stripe down centre of segments, thus having some
> resemblance to *Scilla tubergeniana*.  March.  Caucasus, Asia Minor and
> Lebanon.  Generally found in damp places.  The form from the Lebanon is
> probably the best and there is also a fine white form.  Syns. *P. libanotica,*
> *P. sicula, Adamsia scilloides, Scilla sicula.*  (Pl. **24**, 19)

# ROMULEA  *Iridaceae*

A LARGE genus with small corms and flowers resembling those of *Crocus*,
but distinguished from this genus by a stem which appears out of the
ground at flowering time and bears one or occasionally two flowers
on short pedicels.  They are readily divided geographically into two
groups, (*a*) those from S. Europe, N. Africa and Asia Minor and (*b*)
those from E. and S. Africa.  The former are for the most part hardy,
but less free flowering than most crocus and require the same conditions.
Many are collected as crocuses, but the flowers are generally smaller and
have the disadvantage of only opening in bright or warm sunlight and
closing early.  They flower in spring and early summer and are delicate
little flowers only emerging a few inches above the soil but often brightly
coloured.  None of the S. African species are in regular cultivation in this
country and probably would prove less hardy, being best suited for pans
in the cool greenhouse or a frame, but they tend to be slightly larger in
flower.  The corms are for the most part small and reticulated, often
no larger than a pea and the leaves linear and channelled with a central

## Romulea

silvery stripe though less prominent than in *Crocus*, thus making them easily recognisable in the wild. Formerly many of the species were known as *Trichonema*.

### (*a*) Species from S. Europe, N. Africa and Asia Minor

**R. bulbocodium.** The best known sp. among gardeners. *Fl.* small, cup-shaped, bright violet with conspicuous yellow base, but white forms with varying markings are also recorded. Stem and pedicel up to 6 in. but generally less. Feb.-April. Common in S. Europe particularly in sandy places. Hardy. Suitable also for pans in Alpine house.

**R. clusiana.** One of the finest European sp. *Fl.* rather larger than preceding, bright violet-mauve with white zone in centre and prominent yellow base, trumpet-shaped on very short stem. Spring. Spain, especially near the sea.

**R. columnae.** *Fl.* small, whitish or pale mauve with deeper mauve streaks, yellow at base. March-April. Our only British native sp. but rare and inconspicuous as a garden plant.

**R. crocea.** *Fl.* bright golden-yellow with streaks of deeper tawny colour outside. A handsome plant closely allied to *R. bulbocodium*. Spring. Asia Minor.

**R. requienii.** *Fl.* small, rather globular, deep violet-purple outside, paler inside with deeper veins. Stem up to 5 in. often bent with 1–3 *fl.*, rather variable in size up to 1½ in. long by 1½ in. across when fully opened. March-April. Corsica and Sardinia. Hardy.

### (*b*) S. African species

These are little known in cultivation in this country but should be regarded as being less hardy and except in very warm situations or where the stock is sufficiently plentiful to experiment with, should be treated as plants for the cool greenhouse, although in their native country many are mountain plants. The following is only a very small selection of the recorded species. They are said to require plenty of water during the growing period but none during the resting time.

† **R. bulbocodiodes.** *Fl.* golden-yellow, small, star-shaped, only 1 in. across when fully open. Stem up to 4 in. with several *fl.* to a stem. White forms are also known. Common in all Cape districts where it flowers from June to Sept.

† **R. citrina.** *Fl.* small, star-like, bright yellow, only 1 in. across, stem up to 5 in. Namaqualand.

† **R. hirsuta.** *Fl.* bright crimson with deeper base, 1½ in. across. Stem only a few in. Common in all Cape districts flowering from July to Oct. A handsome sp.

† **R. macowanii.** *Fl.* golden-yellow, reddish-orange near tips, large for the genus, about 1 in. across, stem short. Spring. Corms globose of medium size. *L.* narrow, sickle-shaped, recurved. Mountains of Eastern Cape Province and probably hardier than other S. African sp. but very rare in cultivation.

† **R. pudica.** *Fl.* deep pink with white base and striped with deeper crimson, larger than in other sp., up to 2 in. across when fully open. Stem 4 in. with 2–3 *fl.* August, but this is recorded from an isolated imported corm; corm small, dark, reticulate. *L.* narrow, twisted. Cape districts.

† **R. rosea.** A striking *fl.* deep pink with large golden cup-shaped base and deep blue rim to base and streaks on base of segments, 1½ in. across when fully open, stem slender to 5 in. with 1 *fl.*; June; corm small, round. *L.* filiform, long. Cape districts. Cool greenhouse.

† **R. speciosa.** Close to *R. rosea. Fl.* deep carmine-pink with deeper striping but without prominent deep golden cup-shaped base, 1½ in. across. Outer segments striped pale green and deep crimson on outside. *L.* long, rush-like. Cape districts. Cool greenhouse.

# SANDERSONIA *Liliaceae*

A MONOTYPIC tuberous genus from Natal, related to *Gloriosa* and requiring rather similar cultivation in cool or intermediate greenhouse, but nearly hardy in a protected place. Root tuberous, small.

† **S. aurantiaca.** Stems slender up to 2 ft. straggling and needing some support. *L.* narrow, long, often with tendrils at tip. *Fl.* urn-shaped, rather globose, pendulous, several to a stem, constricted at base and also slightly at mouth, pale orange, about 1 in. long and ½ in. across mouth. July-August. In S. Africa it flowers in Nov.-Dec. and dies down soon afterwards, remaining dormant for quite a long period. It is known there as " Christmas Bells."

# SAUROMATUM *Araceae*

A SMALL genus of tropical aroids, one species of which, *S. guttatum*, has been widely imported for sale in this country as a popular curiosity since the large round tuber will flower once without soil, just grown in a saucer in a room. Proper cultivation, however, requires a greenhouse.

† **S. guttatum.** Monarch of the East. Spathe very large up to 2 ft. in length, purplish or green with large purple spots, tubular for first half, then opening with upper part recurved, spadix pale purple, long and curving in upper half. *Fl.* produced before *l.* which are deeply divided. Himalaya. More peculiar than really beautiful. Var. *venosum*, inside of spathe pale yellowish-orange towards base with deep crimson spots. Spathe up to 2 ft. long, fleshy.

# SCHIZOSTYLIS *Iridaceae*

A SMALL genus of S. African plants known as Caffre or Kaffir Lilies and most valuable for their late autumn flowering. Although not strictly bulbous but rather with a small slightly bulbous rhizome and numerous fibrous roots the schizostylis are generally sold by bulb merchants and included in bulb catalogues as are some of the anemones and so have been included here. The flowers are star-like, up to 2 in. across and borne in a terminal raceme, red or pink, the leaves narrow and ensiform. Schizostylis are best grown in a warm sunny border under a wall but they do not require to be dried out during the summer or indeed at any resting period. In S. Africa they grow along the banks of rivers and in damp places. Only one sp., *S. coccinea* with several forms, is in cultivation. They may also be used as cold greenhouse plants and grown successfully in pots.

* **S. coccinea.** Stem up to 2 ft. with up to 10 *fl.*, star-like with a long basal tube, opening flat, up to 2 in. across, scarlet. Sept.-Nov. S. Africa, N.E. Cape district, Natal, Transvaal. (Pl. **32**, 3)
  * Var. **major.** Distinctly larger *fl.* and more vigorous.
* ' MRS. HEGARTY ' *Fl.* rose-pink. (Pl. **32**, 2)
* ' VISCOUNTESS BYNG ' *Fl.* pale shell-pink.

# SCILLA *Liliaceae*

A LARGE genus of bulbous plants containing a number of attractive small spring flowering bulbs such as the well-known *S. sibirica*. They are closely related to *Chionodoxa*, being distinguished by the complete division of the perianth segments. The distribution of the genus is very wide, extending throughout Europe and also much of Asia and both N. and S. Africa, but excluding the really tropical parts of both Africa and Asia. The S. African species, with the possible exception of *S. adlami*, are too tender to be grown outside in this country. Their chief merit lies in their decorative striped foliage and they are best grown in the cool greenhouse. Here they are treated in a separate section. Formerly the bluebells were also included under *Scilla* but these are now generally split off and although the subject of many nomenclatural changes and recommendations recently, they are here treated under *Endymion*, being separated especially by the hypogeal cotyledon in the germination of the seedlings in *Endymion* and an epigeal cotyledon in *Scilla*. Much further

# *Scilla*

discussion of interest on these morphological characters in the whole tribe of allied genera will be found in a lengthy paper of Prof. P. Chouard in the *Annals de Sciences Naturelles de Paris* (vol. 13, 1931) and if followed would lead to a wide revision of the species assigned to these genera. The spring flowering species are for the most part quite hardy and are easily cultivated. They should be planted in a sunny position with the bulbs about 3 in. deep. The summer and autumn flowering species are generally less showy than the spring ones and are more rarely seen. These also are treated in a separate section. Some of these such as *S. lilio-hyacinthus* are woodland plants. All Scillas can be grown from seed or from offsets of the bulbs. These are not, however, usually very freely produced. The bulbs are usually fleshy and globose, although varying from this considerably in such plants as *S. lilio-hyacinthus*, where they are made up of a number of untunicated scales, just like a lily, and whose leaves also resemble those of a lily.

## (*a*) Spring flowering species

**S. amoena.** The Byzantine Squill. A small bulb from Central Europe, suitable for the rock garden but not nearly as striking in size of *fl.* or in brightness of colour as *S. sibirica*. Several stems to a bulb up to 6 in. with small, deep indigo-mauve, star-like *fl.* about ¾ in. across. Late April-early May.

**S. bifolia.** One of the finest sp. but very variable, usually a bright turquoise-blue, but pink and white forms are also found. (Pl. **24**, 12, 13). Widespread on the mountains of S. Europe, but excluding the Alps, generally flowering as the snow melts. Not generally such a vigorous grower as *S. sibirica* but a finer plant in most cases and flowering usually a few weeks earlier. Stem often reddish, up to 8 in. with up to 8 *fl.* usually fewer. *Fl.* star-like, about 1 in. across, on long pedicels facing horizontally or upwards. *L.* 2 but frequently more, green, keeled, shorter than the stems at flowering time, slightly fleshy. A well-drained position is necessary. A number of separate varieties have been distinguished and an account will be found in R.H.S. Journal 51, 339 (1926). The hybrid with *Chionodoxa* will be found under × *Chionoscilla*.
> Var. **alba.** White.
* Var. **praecox.** Earlier than the type and rather more robust, a very good bright blue and spreading freely in some gardens, combining beautifully with the early dwarf narcissi such as *N. asturiensis* and *N.* ' Minicycla '.
> Var. **rosea.** *Fl.* pale purplish-pink.
* Var. **taurica.** *Fl.* bright violet-blue with purplish anthers on very long pedicels, on stout reddish stem, up to 12 to a stem. A very fine variety but usually not so free to increase as var. *praecox*, which for that reason would be preferred for most gardens. The *fl.* of *taurica* are very slightly deeper blue and it is distinguished also by the colour of the anthers from var. *praecox* and by the long deep pink base to the *l.* which sheathe the stem, but unfortunately it is very rare in cultivation.

# Scilla

**S. bithynica.** Very close to *S. amoena*, but taller and with more purplish-blue colour in the *fl.* Mountains of N.W. Asia Minor and Bulgaria. Stem up to 12 in. with up to 15 *fl.* each ½ in. across in a rather compact inflorescence. April. Quite hardy.

**S. campanulata.** See under *Endymion hispanicus*.

**S. cernua.** See under *S. sibirica*. Probably most plants under this name are *S. sibirica*, but some may be *S. bifolia*.

**S. hispanica,** the Spanish Bluebell. See under *Endymion hispanicus*.

**S. italica.** *Fl.* small, fragrant, in a conical spike of up to 30 *fl.*, pale blue with darker blue stamens. May. Italy, S. France. Hardy but not a very striking plant. Distinct from other Scillas by the hypogeal germination of its cotyledons and so placed by Prof. Chouard in *Endymion*.

* **S. messeniaca.** *Fl.* pale blue-mauve, starry, on 6 in. stems. Late March-April. Often spreading freely and useful for naturalising. Greece. The plant featured in the Botanical Magazine (t.8035) is much stouter and with larger *l.* than that usually grown. Distinguished from *S. italica* by its shorter bracts, under ¼ in.

**S. nutans.** The English Bluebell. See under *Endymion non-scriptus*.

**S. sibirica.** The best known member of the genus and distinguished for the very brilliant, almost violent, prussian-blue colour of the *fl.* (Pl. **24**, 14). It is best planted by itself or in company with orange or white *fl.* rather than other paler blues. Stem up to 8 in. with 3 or 4 *fl.* on short drooping pedicels, several stems to a bulb, each *fl.* about 1 in. across. The Siberian Squill which apparently also extends to S. Russia and the Caucasus, is also an excellent plant for naturalising in grass. *S. cernua* from Turkey is very close, if not synonymous, and has *fl.* of the same brilliant blue but is generally a less vigorous plant. There is also a white form. (Pl. **24**, 10)
    *Var. **atrocoerulea,** often known as ' Spring Beauty ' is usually earlier to flower and more robust than the type. (Pl. **24**, 7)
    Var. **taurica,** from Asia Minor, paler blue with deeper tips to petals. (Pl. **24**, 9)

* **S. tubergeniana.** One of the earliest of spring flowering bulbs and quite distinct. *Fl.* very pale blue, sometimes almost bluish-white, but with deeper blue-mauve backs to the perianth segments and with a narrow central band down the centre of each segment. Stems short at flowering time, generally less than 4 in. several to a bulb and with up to 4 *fl.* to a stem. Each *fl.* 1 in. across with broad starry segment. (Pl. **24**, 17). *L.* bright green, broad. Bulb globose with grey papery tunic. Hardy but owing to its early flowering, generally Feb.-early March very suitable to pans in an Alpine house. Free-flowering. Mountains of N.W. Persia around Tabriz whence it was sent to Messrs. Van Tubergen by their collector G. Egger mixed with *Puschkinia scilloides*, which it rather resembles in colouring.

**S. verna.** A British native plant and extending through most regions of N. Europe. *Fl.* pale blue-mauve but with brighter blue ovary and anthers, star-

*Plate XIX. Nerine bowdenii*, one of the best flowering bulbs for the early autumn

*Plate XX*. Nerine 'Hera'

*Plate XXI. Nomocharis saluenensis*

*Plate XXII. Tulipa orphanidea*

like, small on short stems, generally found near the sea and hardly striking enough to be worth garden cultivation.

## (b) Summer and autumn flowering species

**S. autumnalis.** A British native plant. *Fl.* numerous but small, star-like, purplish-blue or pinkish-lilac, variable in colour, on short stems up to 8 in., generally produced before *l.* July-September. Bulb globose, up to ¾ in. across. Found in dry short grass near the sea. Distribution extends to most of N.W. Europe and W. Mediterranean. Not a very striking plant for the garden.

**S. hyacinthoides.** A woodland plant of the Mediterranean regions, chiefly distinguished for its broad, shining *l.* up to 1½ ft. long when mature. Flower-spike up to 1½ ft. with numerous *fl.* of pale lilac-blue in a dense raceme, but individual *fl.* are small and star-like and the spike comes rather as an anti-climax after the promise of the fine foliage. June-Aug. Hardy. Bulb large.

**S. lilio-hyacinthus.** Resembling the preceding sp. but with *fl.* slightly larger though still rather disappointing. June-July. W. Mediterranean regions. For its foliage quite an attractive plant for an open woodland. Bulb large and with conspicuous yellow scales like a lily bulb.

**S. monophylla.** A small plant from Spain and Portugal allied to *S. verna* but flowering slightly later in May and June. Spike up to 8 in. with small but bright blue star-like *fl.* *L.* generally 1 only. Hardy.

**S. odorata.** Also from Spain and Portugal. Stem slender, up to 9 in. with numerous, deep sky-blue, sweetly scented bell-shaped *fl.* on long pedicels. May to early June. An attractive plant but not very common in cultivation.

**S. peruviana.** A handsome plant with a large broadly conical head of deep lilac-blue *fl.* like the upper half of a small football, but much misnamed since it is a native of the Central Mediterranean regions and quite unconnected with either Peru or Cuba although it has sometimes been called the " Cuban Lily." The story is that it was named by Clusius who made a special journey to see it at Bristol and was told it had come in the *Peru*, a ship. Stem stout, up to 9 in. Head up to 6 in. across with up to 100 densely-packed star-like *fl.*, variable in colour. May-June. Should be grown in a sunny and warm position. Bulb large, ovoid, up to 2 in. across; *l.* broad, lorate and glaucous. A white form is also known.

**S. pratensis.** Spike up to 1 ft., slender, with a dense raceme of small bluish-lilac bell-shaped *fl.* Scented. May-June. Not a very conspicuous sp. but attractive in a wild meadow in full sun. Yugoslavia. Var. *amethystina*, brighter blue.

## (c) Cool greenhouse species

The following species from S. Africa are not quite hardy and are chiefly grown for their handsome, rather fleshy, striped and coloured foliage.

The flowers are generally small and inconspicuous. They seem to do adequately in an unheated Alpine house and may be left in their pots until the bulbs are thickly clustered on the surface. *S. natalensis* is much larger and distinct from this group.

† **S. adlamii.** *L.* 8–9 in. long, broadly linear, fleshy; *fl.* small purple. April. E. Natal. Hardy in very sheltered areas.

† **S. cooperi.** *L.* up to 1 ft., broadly linear, green but streaked with purple and spotted towards base. *Fl.* bright purple, small, in a short raceme on 8 in. stems, star-like. Spring. S. Africa, Natal.

† **S. natalensis.** Rather divergent from the rest of this group in the possession of very large bulbs and forming tall spikes up to 3 ft. of small lilac-blue or deep blue *fl.* Early autumn. Cool greenhouse but has proved hardy in a few sheltered gardens in a hot sunny position. S. Africa where it is known as Blue Squill and where it is regarded as the best of its genus.

† **S. tricolor.** *L.* broad up to 1 ft., dark green with blotches of lighter green and dark reddish-purple. *Fl.* green. Spring. Natal.

† **S. violacea.** Dwarf. *L.* entirely violet-purple below and above blotched with green. *Fl.* green. Spring. Cape Province. Increases freely from bulblets. One of the finest foliage plants in the genus.

† **S. zebrina.** *L.* glaucous, marked with bars vertically and basal blotches of purple. *Fl.* green. Summer. One of the best for its unusual foliage. Tender. S. Africa, hillsides north of Durban.

# SPARAXIS *Iridaceae*

A SMALL genus of S. African plants with corms; flowers of very varying but nearly always bright colours. In S. Africa they are sometimes known as 'Harlequin flowers.' The perianth has only a short tube and the flowers open wide and flat, the segments being equal. They are closely related to *Ixia* and also to *Freesia* and require rather similar treatment. In all except the very warmest parts of the country they are best grown in pots or raised beds in a cool greenhouse. They usually start growing in our winter and flower in April or May. There are two main species which may be found, *S. grandiflora* and *S. tricolor*, but more often sparaxis are grown as mixed hybrids either between these species and their varying forms or with *Streptanthera cuprea*, giving them a striking bicolour effect from a deeper coloured base. The corms are small with light tunics and the leaves narrow and fan-like as in freesias.

† **S. grandiflora.** Stem up to 1½ ft., wiry with several *fl.* 1½–2 in. across, purplish

or white and with a dark blotch in centre. Cape Districts. Common and flowering Aug.-Oct.

† **S. tricolor.** Stem up to 15 in. with several *fl.* open together, orange with yellow throat but variable, ranging from red through pink to bright purple. The central markings are usually prominent and dark in colour. A white form is also known. April-May. Aug.-Oct. in S. Africa.


# SPREKELIA  *Amaryllidaceae*

A MONOTYPIC genus closely related to *Hippeastrum* but differing in the always solitary, irregular flower with lower petal two-lipped. Its only species is one of our most striking and decorative Amaryllids and hardy in really warm situations although more often grown as a pot plant in the cool greenhouse. It is best potted or divided in August. It should be rested dry during the winter and given water again in the spring and bulbs outside should if possible be given some protection against rain and frost.

S. **formosissima.** Stem up to 1 ft., often less, with generally 1 but occasionally 2, really large deep scarlet-crimson *fl.* up to 5 in. across and as much deep, upper petal broadest, lateral petals strap-shaped, lower petals narrowing at base and curving round into a tube, lanceolate, green at base; filaments bright red. May and early summer but rather variable in season of flowering. Bulbs roundish with a long neck and dark scaly tunic. *L.* narrow, linear, produced after *fl.* Mexico and Guatemala. Sometimes known as the Jacobean Lily. Syn. *Amaryllis formosissima.*


# †STENOMESSON  *Amaryllidaceae*

A SMALL genus of S. American bulbous plants from the Andes of Peru and Chile with usually pendulous, long and narrow, tubular flowers in umbels, the perianth usually red or orange in colour and often tipped with green. None of the species is recorded as reliably hardy although they come from 8,000–13,000 ft. and they are best suited for pots in the cool or intermediate greenhouse where they flower in early summer and require the same treatment as a *Hippeastrum*. Further trials for hardiness might, however, yield more information and be worth while. None are sufficiently showy to have become popular and so they are rarely seen in cultivation. The bulbs are shaped like those of a *Hippeastrum* but generally are smaller, while the leaves are strap-shaped and usually appear

## Sternbergia

with the flower. After the leaves have died down a late summer resting period should be given before restarting the bulbs in late autumn. Re-potting is not necessary every year. A few rather unusual species have flowers which are almost stemless, but none of these are in cultivation.

**S. aurantiacum.** Stem up to 1 ft. *Fl.* reddish-orange in small umbels of 2–3 *fl.* only, horizontal or even erect, 1½ in. long. Andes of Ecuador up to 6,000–13,000 ft. where it flowers in Oct. before the *l.* appear.

**S. coccineum.** *Fl.* bright orange-red or crimson, with very slender tube, constricted near base, drooping, 1½ in. long, in small umbels on 1 ft. stem. Late Autumn. *L.* narrow, linear. Andes of Peru up to 10,000 ft. Syn. *Coburgia coccinea.*

**S. humile.** Dwarf with solitary large *fl.* on 4 in. stems, tube sulphur-yellow and segments orange-red with yellow central stripe, tube long but narrow so that *fl.* are up to 4 in. long. Andes of Peru up to 12,000 ft.

**S. incarnatum.** Stem stout, up to 2 ft., with small umbel of quite large *fl.* bright red usually but variable in colour, 4–5 in. long with long tube, pendulous or horizontal. Late autumn or early winter. Andes of Peru and Ecuador up to 10,000 ft. Bulb very large. *L.* strap-shaped, wide. An attractive pink-flowered form with green markings at the tips of the segments is shown in the Botanical Magazine (t.3867) and a similar plant is recorded from Lake Titicaca in the Peruvian Andes.

Var. **trichromum.** *Fl.* scarlet outside, pink inside, tube narrow near base. A handsome variety. Syn. *Coburgia trichroma.*

# STERNBERGIA *Amaryllidaceae*

THIS SMALL genus contains bulbs with some of the most brilliant golden-yellow crocus-like flowers of the Eastern Mediterranean and Middle East but they are easily distinguished from *Crocus* by the possession of six stamens instead of three. It has been suggested that *S. lutea* is the flower of the "Lilies of the Field," since in autumn it flowers widely in Palestine as in other countries around the Mediterranean, particularly Turkey and Greece. The genus has only four species which have been in cultivation, three of which are autumn flowering and one spring flowering. Only one, *S. lutea*, is in general cultivation. Apart from the division into spring and autumn flowering they can also be divided into two separate groups, those that flower with the leaves, such as *S. lutea* and *S. fischeriana*, and those which flower well before the leaves and have a long cylindrical tube to the flowers such as *S. clusiana*. This is the finest of all the species, a great golden globular egg of richest satiny-yellow, more often known as *S. macrantha*, but originally described in 1808 by Ker-Gawler under

276

*Amaryllis clusiana*, hence the adoption of this name, which is the earlier by 80 years.

All are hardy but they only flower satisfactorily in a really warm sunny place, such as a border under a house or greenhouse wall. Like *Amaryllis belladonna*, they seem to flower best after a really hot summer; undoubtedly they need a good baking. The bulbs should not be planted too near the surface: 4–6 in. deep is best and then they should be left alone until they become congested and form large clumps when they may be divided. *S. lutea* is much the easiest species and is permanent in most gardens, but the others are intolerant of too much wet and many prefer to grow them in a frame or in pots where their summer rest and control of watering can be ensured. The flowers are solitary, erect, globular or egg-shaped, with six petals. They are never more than 6 in. above the ground, often less. The bulbs are covered with a black tunic and the leaves strap-shaped.

One other species *S. pulchella* is recorded from Syria, the Lebanon and Palestine but is still little known. It has small flowers like *S. colchiciflora* but has leaves with the flower.

* **S. clusiana**. The finest sp. *Fl.* bright golden-yellow, globular and opening widely with broad, overlapping petals; *fl.* up to 4 in. across and as long, with a long cylindrical tube up to 2 in.; peduncle often enclosed in dark membranous upper extension of tunic of bulb, thus giving to the *fl.* the appearance of a stem. Sept.-Oct. and even into November. Bulb large, globose with a prominent long neck and dark membranous tunic extending upwards. *L.* strap-shaped, slightly glaucous, produced in spring after the *fl.*, up to 1 ft. long and 1 in. across. Asia Minor, Turkey, Syria, Palestine and Western Persia. It differs from *S. lutea* by the larger *fl.* and much longer perianth tube and by flowering before the *l.* appear. Unfortunately rare in cultivation, especially outside, but it should be quite hardy. As a pot plant in a cool greenhouse it is quite satisfactory provided it gets a good summer rest and is not allowed to get too moist in winter. Syn. *S. macrantha*, under which name it is better known, also probably *S. stipitata* from Lebanon and Syria which is now usually regarded as only a smaller form.

**S. colchiciflora**. The smallest sp. *Fl.* almost sessile on the ground, crocus-like, tube about 1 in. petals pale yellow, rather narrow, about 1 in. long. Sweet-scented. Sept.-Oct. *L.* appearing in spring after flowering, narrow, up to 4 in. long, keeled. Balkans, Hungary and Roumania, U.S.S.R., Crimea, Turkey, N. Palestine. Very rare in cultivation and with the reputation of being a difficult plant to keep long. The variety sometimes described as var. *aetnensis* is very barely distinct.

**S. fischeriana**. Spring flowering, otherwise close in appearance to *S. lutea*. *Fl.* bright yellow, funnel-shaped, petal oblong, 1½–2 in. long, tube short. Stem 4–6 in., generally several *fl.* to a bulb. March-April. Bulb, large, ovoid. *L.* numerous, appearing in spring with *fl.*, linear up to 6 in. Caucasus, Persia. Not very free-flowering in cultivation.

\* **S. lutea.** One of our finest autumn flowering bulbs. *Fl.* crocus-like, rich golden-yellow with a satin sheen, about 2 in. long and as much across when open, egg-shaped, standing generally above the foliage which is dwarf at this time. Late Aug.-Oct. (Pl. **32**, 10). Bulb shaped rather like a narcissus, tunic dark. *L.* strap-shaped, deep green up to 6 in. after flowering. Eastern Mediterranean from Sicily through Greece to Turkey, Palestine and Persia. In Greece it is a plant of the mountains among rocks and in short grass. It is variable both in size of *fl.* and in width of leaf and it is always claimed that the narrower leaved forms from Greece flower best in this country. These have been distinguished as var. *augustifolia* and var. *graeca*, of which the former is said to have very slightly larger *fl.* but there is really little to choose between them. A good summer ripening and good drainage are essential and it does very well on chalk.

# STREPTANTHERA *Iridaceae*

A SMALL genus of S. African plants with corms close to *Ixia* and also to *Sparaxis* with which it has been hybridised. It is distinct in the twisted form of the anthers. The treatment is the same as for *Ixia* and *Sparaxis* or *Freesia* and five to seven corms should be planted in pots in a cool greenhouse in late autumn. There are two species.

† **S. cuprea.** Stem short, about 9 in. but each having several *fl.* though each has a separate spathe. The tube is short and the perianth lobes wide spreading and overlapping 1–1½ in. across. *Fl.* coppery-yellow with a purple base and a paler yellow spot on each side on a darker, almost black, band. An orange variety is recorded and the one known as ' Coccinea ' is also to be recommended.

**S. elegans.** *Fl.* white with a yellow centre outside which is a band of black and yellow, 1–1½ in. across and several *fl.* to a stem. Corms small. *L.* ensiform and arranged in a fan as in a freesia.

# TECOPHILAEA *Amaryllidaceae*

A SMALL genus of only two species but containing one of the great and fickle beauties of the bulb world, *T. cyanocrocus* with its rich gentian-blue flowers. The peculiar generic name is derived from the unusual Christian name of a daughter of the Italian botanist Prof. Colla, presumably a friend of Bertero the botanist who first described and named the genus. In addition to the *Amaryllidaceae* it has been variously attributed to the family *Haemodoraceae* and also to a special family of its own *Tecophilaceae*. Both species are native of S. America and *T. cyanocrocus* has become rare in its native country of Chile, having been killed out partly by grazing cattle and partly, one fears, by collectors.

\* **T. cyanocrocus.** Chilean Crocus, a dwarf spring flowering plant with short stems 3 or 4 in. long with a single *fl.* of deepest gentian-blue like a *G. verna* and with a white throat. The 6 petals are spreading and divided to the base of the *fl.* which is about 1½–2 in. across when fully open. Corm with fibrous reticulate tunic; *l.* narrow, linear, partly sheathing stem. March-April. Chilean Andes at about 10,000 ft. Var. *leichtlinii, fl.* with the white of the throat spreading out through a large part of the petals. Var. *violacea*, deep purple.

The Chilean Crocus has always had the reputation of being difficult of cultivation in the open although there are records of its having settled down and spread freely in gardens as widely separate in climate as Norfolk and Co. Wicklow in S. Ireland, the former in a very sandy soil at the foot of a wall, the latter also under a wall where it is top dressed with sheep manure, as near as it is possible to get in this country to its native llama manure. It starts into growth early in the year, but appears to be hardy in all except very exposed areas but obviously needs very good drainage. In its native habitat it is thoroughly ripened by the summer sun during a long dry period after flowering and then rested under snow during the winter but it is doubtful whether this is required here. There it flowers in October and November. As an Alpine house plant it can more easily be grown and maintained and a pan of it is always much prized in March or early April.

† **T. violiflora.** *Fl.* smaller than the preceding and violet-mauve in colour. From lower coastal regions of Chile, also in Peru and S. Brazil. Probably not now in cultivation and unlikely to be hardy. Not nearly as conspicuous a *fl.* as the preceding.

# TIGRIDIA *Iridaceae*

THESE GORGEOUS beauties from Mexico and S. America are well named Tiger flowers since the great spotted flowers of *T. pavonia* are among some of the most striking which we can grow in the garden. The three outer petals seem to float on the stems like a great butterfly with three wings. Only one species, *T. pavonia* (Pl. **28**), is widely grown and it is probably the finest. There are, however, a number of other species with rather smaller flowers also from Mexico and S. America.

The corms are ovoid and covered with a coarse tunic. Normally they should be planted in April or early May about 3–4 in. deep and the usual practice is to lift them in the autumn after their flowering and store them dry in sand or peat moss for the winter like a gladiolus corm. In protected places in the South and West of England it has, however, proved possible to leave them over winter in the ground. While they are growing tigridias require plenty of moisture and may be mulched with richer soil. The leaves are ensiform and plicate like those of a gladiolus, only narrower and the stems grow up to 1½ or 2 ft. with the buds enclosed in a terminal spathe. The segments are divided into two very distinct ranks, the outer and larger petals forming a small concave cup at the base and then spreading outwards with a large flat ovate blade, the inner much smaller and with a distinct waist. The stamens and stigma with filaments joined in a long tube are held erect. Each flower only lasts a single day but a stem will bear six or more flowers from a spathe and they are so handsome that it is well worth while planting a group.

The Tiger flower formed one of the early plates in the Botanical Magazine and the author was so excited by it that he wrote : "It has no scent, but in splendid beauty it appears to us, at least when assisted by rarity and singularity, to surpass every competitor; we lament that this too affords our fair countrywomen another lesson, how extremely fugacious is the loveliness of form, born to display its glory but for a few hours, it literally melts away."

† **T. lutea.** *Fl.* much smaller than those of *T. pavonia*, 1½ in. across, pale lemon-yellow, the broad claws of the segments forming a cup, marked with deeper yellow markings. Stem slender. *L.* narrowly linear, plicate. Mountains of Chile and Peru. Probably tender and very rare in cultivation.

†\***T. pavonia.** *Fl.* large, up to 4 in. across, very variable in colour, the type being orange-scarlet with the blade of the outer segments broad and glowing scarlet-red, spotted with deeper crimson towards base. Other forms are orange, deep yellow, white, pinkish-crimson, and violet-mauve. The white form, although very beautiful, is not usually considered as vigorous as the others. There are also unspotted orange and white forms. Different varieties have been distinguished by name in the past but the plant is very variable and as corms are now usually sold as a mixture there is little advantage in describing these. Stem up to 2 ft., generally less, with up to 6 *fl.* in the spathe. July-Sept. depending on the time of planting and the season. Mts. at about 6,000 ft. of Central and S. Mexico and parts of Peru.

† **T. pringlei.** A fine *fl.* resembling *T. pavonia*, bright orange-scarlet with broad blade to the outer segments differing from *T. pavonia* in the possession of a larger blade to the inner segments as well as the outer, though this is much smaller. Mts. of N. Mexico at 6,000 ft., and having a range north of that of *T. pavonia*. Very rare in cultivation.

† **T. violacea.** *Fl.* small, 1½–2 in. across, pale violet-mauve with deeper purplish-red markings at base of blade of outer segments and around cup formed by bases of both inner and outer segments. Stem slender, sometimes forking near top, up to 1½ ft. with 4–5 *fl.* to a spathe. July. Mts. of Mexico, Yucatan. Very rare in cultivation. Probably requiring similar treatment to *T. pavonia*.

# TRILLIUM *Liliaceae*

A GENUS of 30 or more species, mainly N. American; only a few are in cultivation, the best known and probably also the finest horticulturally being the Wake Robin, the lovely white *T. grandiflorum*. A few species are also found in Japan and the Himalayas but these are not in general cultivation in this country and would probably be of lesser horticultural value than the American ones.

The genus is distinguished by having all its parts very clearly in threes, leaves, sepals and petals. The three outer segments or sepals are always green and pointed and the three larger and more conspicuous inner segments or petals are white or pale yellow, purple or reddish and either held erect or spreading horizontally. The root consists of a knobbly tuber or rhizome and the leaves are borne in a whorl below the flowers. All trilliums should be planted early in autumn, about 4 in. deep in a dampish position, and they do best in a peaty or acid soil either in open woodland, in which they look peculiarly at home, or even in the open. They rarely succeed, however, in hot dry situations. They increase slowly but are quite hardy and usually long-lived, especially in the case of *T. grandiflorum*.

The species are often difficult to separate botanically and in many cases rather ill-differentiated and probably many natural hybrids occur. They can, however, be divided into larger sections by the upright or spreading petals and by the absence or presence of a pedicel between the leaves and the flowers. This is several inches long in *T. grandiflorum* and entirely absent in *T. sessile*.

**T. cernuum.** The nodding Wood Lily. *Fl.* small up to 1 in. across on short pedicels, drooping petals white or pinkish, rather narrow. Stems strong, usually two or three together, up to 1½ ft.; leaves broad, almost sessile. April-May. Eastern N. America including Newfoundland and eastern Canada.

# *Trillium*

**T. discolor.** A syn. of *T. sessile* var. *wrayi*.

**T. erectum.** *Fl.* erect like those of *T. grandiflorum* on stout pedicels but rather smaller. Petals slightly fleshy, 1 in. long by ½ in. wide, pointed, colour very variable, white, pale yellow, pink, dark or even mahogany-red. An interesting plate of these colour variations will be found in *The Wild Flowers of Western Pennsylvania and the Upper Ohio Basin.* Stem slender, up to 1 ft.; *l.* broadly ovate, sessile. The white form is sometimes distinguished as var. *album* and a pale yellowish-green form as var. *viridiflorum* or *ochroleucum.* May. Eastern N. America. From its scent when damp it is sometimes known as the " Wet-dog or Ill-scented Trillium."

**T. erythrocarpum** Michaux. A syn. of *T. undulatum.*

\* **T. grandiflorum.** The Wake Robin. The largest sp. and much the finest for gardens. Once established in a damp semi-shady position it is usually long-lived and looks particularly well among groups of ferns or such woodland plants as *Smilacina.* *Fl.* large, up to 3 in. across, on stout pedicels up to 3 in.; petals broad and overlapping, spreading flat from a campanulate base, pure white, fading to pinkish-purple. Stems stout, up to 2 ft. *L.* with short stalks, broadly ovate. April-May. Some forms are tinged with rosy-purple towards base of petals and var. *roseum* has been distinguished for a particularly pinkish form. Eastern and Central N. America, a woodland plant spread over a wide area.

**T. luteum.** A form of *T. sessile.*

**T. nivale.** Dwarf and distinguished by the distinct petioles to the *l. Fl.* on short pedicels, petals white, ¾ in. long by ½ in. broad. Stem up to 5 in. only, slender. *L.* ovate-oblong. March-April. S.E. United States. An attractive plant for the not too dry rock garden but rare in cultivation. Should probably be planted in a rather drier position than the other sp.

**T. ovatum.** *Fl.* erect, quite large on 1 in. pedicels, petals white then changing to pinkish-purple. Stem short, up to 10 in. *L.* ovate or almost round, sessile. Early flowering, March-April. Western N. America, the " Coast Trillium."

**T. recurvatum.** Close to *T. sessile* but with downward-curving sepals. Petals narrow, tips often curving inwards, deep maroon. *L.* much mottled. Central northern U.S.A. The " Prairie Trillium."

**T. rivale.** Very close to *T. nivale* but distinguished by numerous small purple spots at base of petals. Oregon.

**T. sessile.** Petals of dark crimson-purple or maroon, narrow and erect, up to 1¼ in. long, the *fl.* without pedicel. Stem up to 1 ft. *L.* sessile also, oval, marbled attractively; otherwise not a very conspicuous plant. April. N. America. Widespread in open woods and sometimes known as the "Toad Trillium."

Var. **californicum.** Petals white or purplish-pink.

Var. **luteum.** Petals greenish-yellow or lemon-yellow.

Var. **wrayi.** Petals dark purple but often mixed with green and variable. Syn. *T. discolor.*

**T. undulatum.** *Fl.* of medium size on short erect pedicels, petals white but conspicuously striped or blotched with purple or crimson at base forming a rough " V " shape. Stem rather slender up to 1 ft.; large ovate *l.* with acute tips, slightly mottled. Margins of both petals and *l.* wavy. April-June. Eastern N. America, including Canada, in cool damp woods. Known as the " Painted Trillium " or the " Painted Wood Lily." Syn. *T. erythrocarpum* Michaux. Rather a rare plant in English gardens and much less robust than and not so easy to grow as *T. grandiflorum.*

# TRITONIA *Iridaceae*

A GENUS of very beautiful and brightly coloured S. African plants with corms, allied to *Ixia, Sparaxis, Streptanthera* and *Freesia* and requiring similar cool greenhouse treatment and some support in the form of twigs. Although there are quite a large number of species recorded only one is generally grown in English gardens, namely *T. crocata* but *T. rosea* is also sometimes seen. Some of these are now more often assigned to other genera such as *Crocosmia.* This includes also the garden montbretias which have sometimes in the past been included in *Tritonia.* The flowers are cup-shaped, all facing upwards on a thin wiry stem which bends over like a freesia. Other species which might be worth a trial are *T. hyalina* with deep salmon or coral-coloured flowers and *T. squalida* with pink flowers stained deeper at the throat.

† **T. crocata.** Blazing star. Stem up to 1 ft. growing out of a fan of *l.* like a freesia. The *fl.* are 1½ in. across and several open together, cup-shaped with very brilliant coppery-orange rounded petals, marked with yellow at the base. Corm small. *L.* rather narrow. ' Prince of Orange ' is the variety usually grown, but ' Princess Beatrix ' and ' Orange Delight ' are also to be recommended while there is an unusual and rather pretty white form known as ' White Beauty'. May-June. Oct.-Nov. in S. Africa. Plenty of water and fresh air is required during the growing season but they will not stand any appreciable frost. All forms last well when cut.

**T. rosea.** Stem slender, wiry often arching over, up to 1½ ft. *Fl.* rather cup-shaped, smaller than in preceding sp., pale pink, 1 in. long and as much across with yellow markings edged with crimson on three lower segments. Corm globose with matted tunic. *L.* narrow, linear. Hardier than *T. crocata* and sometimes grown outside in a warm border. S. Africa, Cape Province, Natal.

# TULIPA *Liliaceae*
## (*a*) Tulip species

THE WILD tulips are native to the Mediterranean regions, Asia Minor and the Caucasus and extend as far east as China, with the centre of a group of particularly fine species around Bokhara and in Turkestan. They have the same magnificent quality as the old carpets from that region.

The tulip was not known in mediaeval European gardens or pictures but it is generally considered that it was introduced from Turkey in the time of Clusius, in the middle of the 16th century, through the auspices of ambassador Busbeq. The great age of tulip discovery was, however, the last decade of the last century through the travels of the botanist Regel in Turkestan and Central Asia. He described many of our most magnificent species including *greigii*, *kaufmanniana* and *eichleri*. Their introductions to gardens, however, we owe to the enterprise of the Dutch nursery firm of van Tubergen and the Hoog family. They employed collectors who travelled widely in Central Asia and sent back large quantities of bulbs. Among the most enterprising of these was a German named Graeber who lived at Tashkent and travelled and collected for van Tubergen for nearly 35 years. It must have been a wonderfully fertile ground and the following quotation from Regel is taken from the description in the Botanical Magazine of *T. lanata*. He wrote : " every ravine in the red sandstone slopes reveals new forms which break the monotony of the leathery leaved pistachia and almond scrub. From the first days of spring there sprout here anemones, crocuses, irises, tulips, fritillarias and long shafted eremuruses." It is only sad that these wonderful hunting grounds in Asiatic Soviet Russia have been for so long closed to western European collectors.

They are nearly all plants of areas with a hard and long cold winter, a short spring and a hot dry summer in which the bulbs are well baked. In this country it is difficult to ensure the baking and consequently the majority of the species are better lifted in late June each summer and carefully cleaned and then dried off; although there are a few, mostly the European ones, which have been successfully naturalised. They are tolerant of a wide range of soils provided the drainage is good and seem to do as well in lime regions as in those without it. Unlike narcissi they do not benefit by being planted early. On the contrary late October or early November is generally regarded as the best time. In this way the leaves do not become too much developed before the colder weather.

In the wild the bulbs are generally found deep, often up to 1 ft. down, but here planting 5–8 in. deep is quite sufficient.

All tulips should be planted in open sunny situations and many of the species are specially suited for growing in the rock garden or in pans in the Alpine house. A few species such as *T. fosteriana* and *T. greigii* and their hybrids with very large scarlet flowers are magnificent as bedding plants and I have seen few more brilliant floral displays than the massed beds of these at the Keukenhof, the Dutch Associated Bulb Growers' display park in Holland. The inner side of the petals in these as in many tulips has a shiny, satin-like texture which in some way saves the large scarlet blooms from appearing vulgar or garish.

Tulips are usually classified into two main groups, those with hairs on the base of the filaments and those without. The late Sir Daniel Hall, the leading authority on the genus, stated that the two groups would not hybridise together. These characters, however, are not clearly represented in their horticultural characteristics and so it has seemed to me better to describe them here in a simple alphabetical list, grouping together those species which are so similar that in a further revision of the genus, which is undoubtedly needed, they might well be merged. The genus is one of complicated taxonomy with a number of highly variable species and also a number of naturally occurring polyploids. The flowers also do not show well in the dried state and many of the specimens are without bulbs; in consequence as more specimens are collected showing the range of each species, some of the former interspecific distinctions tend to loose their meaning.

**T. acuminata.** The Horned Tulip. A most distinct plant with both yellow and red forms with long, very narrow, pointed almost spidery, twisted petals up to 3 in. long. It is probable that these tulips, which appear almost freakish, have been developed from garden seedlings and have no true separate existence as a wild sp., although often so classed. They are usually classified with the Neo-Tulipae, a large group of doubtful origin to many of which have been given specific names without any corresponding wild distribution. They are not very vigorous but otherwise not difficult to cultivate under the same conditions as the main garden hybrid tulips.

**T. aitchisonii.** Closely allied to the better known *T. clusiana*, a polyploid of which it may well be the diploid ancestor. A smaller plant with short stem up to 3 or 4 in. 1 or 2 *fl.*, outer petals white outside flushed with crimson, inner petals whitish, all petals white inside, *l.* crinkly. Forms with entirely yellow petals (Pl. **29**, 11) and forms with yellow petals in which the three outer petals are flushed with red have also been found. Bulb small, nearly round with a tuft of wool at the apex, a characteristic of the Clusiana section. Chitral and Kashmir above 8,000 ft. In this country best suited to Alpine house culture. Subsp. *cashmeriana*, petals yellow and without any red colour. A taller-growing plant. Kashmir.

# Tulipa

**T. aucheriana.** See under *T. humilis*.

**T. australis.** See under *T. silvestris*.

**T. bakeri.** See under *T. saxatalis*.

\* **T. batalinii.** *Fl.* single, clear creamy-yellow on 6–10 in. stems. One of the most lovely and suitable of the smaller tulips for cultivation both in the rock garden and in the Alpine house. Perianth segments rather pointed and the same colour both inside and out but with deeper yellow basal blotch, $1\frac{1}{2}$ in. long, anthers yellow. Bulb small, rather globose, tunic thin with a tuft of brown hairs inside at apex. *L.* linear, lanceolate on stem. Turkestan. (Pl. **29**, 9). Closely allied to the scarlet *T. linifolia* from which it only appears to differ in colour and of which it may be an albino form. Hybrids have been raised between this and *T. linifolia* and *T. maximowiczii* (a scarlet sp. very close to *T. linifolia*) and show a range of intermediate shades of pink and buff-yellow and apricot. (Pl. **29**, 10)

**T. biflora.** *Fl.* small, white with yellow basal blotch on inside. Outside whitish stained with green and sometimes a little crimson, up to 5 *fl.* to a slender stem, 5 in.–1 ft. high. (Pl. **29**, 16). Anthers yellow but with a purple tip. *L.* linear, slightly hairy. Bulbs small, ovoid with yellow-brown silky hairs at apex. S. Russia, Caucasus. An inconspicuous plant allied to *T. turkestanica*. Early flowering. March.

**T. boetica.** A fine scarlet flowered sp. found sometimes plentifully in the cornfields of S. Greece. Like a small Darwin tulip in appearance. Perianth segments crimson-scarlet with inside a dark olive-green blotch at base. Anthers black. Bulbs medium-sized, dark brown with a few silky hairs at apex, tunic thin. *L.* broad, glaucous. In the wild they tend to grow very deep, at least 10 in. in rather heavy clay soil. One of the Gesneriana group.

**T. celsiana.** See under *T. silvestris*.

**T. chrysantha.** A variety of *T. stellata*.

\* **T. clusiana.** The Lady Tulip. One of the most lovely and graceful of all tulips. *Fl.* medium size, on tall slender stems, white ground with prominent pinkish-crimson streak on outside of petals. (Pl. **29**, 1). Sir Daniel Hall has shown that it is a pentaploid but that a tetraploid form of it has been described under the name *T. chitralensis*. Perianth segments narrow, pointed, *fl.* rather star-like when open, inside segments have a prominent purplish-crimson basal blotch. Anthers purple. *L.* narrow, linear, often edged with red. Persia through Afghanistan to Kashmir, naturalised also in several Mediterranean countries but probably not originally wild there. The Lady Tulip has been known since the time of Clusius as a desirable garden plant. Rarely seeding but spreading by underground stolons, it needs a warm, well-drained position but is one of the few tulip sp. which have spread freely in some English gardens. In others, however, it has proved singularly impermanent.

**T. cretica.** See under *T. saxatilis*.

**T. dasystemon** (of gardens). A syn. of *T. tarda*. The true *T. dasystemon* of Regel is a different plant which is not in cultivation.

# *Tulipa*

* **T. eichleri.**  One of the finest of the scarlet large-flowered sp. from Bokhara, Transcaucasia, Turkestan and N.W. Persia, and also a reasonably good garden plant increasing well in warm situations. *Fl.* large, up to 4 or 5 in. across when fully open.  Perianth segments broad but pointed at tip, outside pinkish-buff reddening more as the flower matures, inside brilliant shining scarlet, the three outer ones with a prominent blackish blotch at base margined with yellow. (Pl. 30, 1).  The *fl.* shows a prominent waist when in bud, later opening wide with perianth segments reflexing near the tips. Anthers violet-black.  *L.* broad, glaucous, sometimes with a faint crimson edge.  Stem stout, up to 15 in.  Bulb large and ovoid with a red-brown tunic.  Middle to end of April.

* **T. fosteriana.**  Perhaps the largest flowered and most spectacular of all the species tulips.  A bed of these is a sight not quickly forgotten. *Fl.* very large, up to 10 in. in diameter when fully open.  Perianth segments broad, bluntly pointed at apex.  Outside bright vermilion-scarlet, inside glowing crimson-scarlet and glossy with a silky sheen, basal blotch dark purplish-black, irregular in shape and with a yellow margin. Anthers purplish-black.  *L.* broad, glaucous, floppy.  Bulb probably the largest of any tulip sp., globose, reddish-brown, tunic thin, papery.  Height 1–1½ ft.  Early mid-April.  Central Asia around Samarkand and Bokhara.  Several selected forms of this fine sp. have been put into commerce.  Perhaps the finest one with the largest *fl.* is ' Red Emperor ', also sometimes listed as ' Madame Lefeber '.  It is liable, however, to be knocked down by the wind in an exposed situation where it would be better to grow the rather sturdier and more dwarf ' Princeps ', which also blooms slightly later.  This truly magnificent sp. is a robust grower but in most areas is better lifted and dried off each year.

**T. gesneriana.**  There is still much mystery surrounding the origin of the garden tulips which are assumed to have sprung from plants of this group, possibly by a mutation which brought the white ground into the flower petal as well as the yellow ground.  As defined by Sir Daniel Hall in a rather more limited sense than is often used, *T. gesneriana* must be the term used for the orange or crimson-scarlet tulip with large, cup-shaped *fl.* with pointed perianth segments and dark basal blotch with yellow margin, and bulbs large with thin tunics but without any obvious tuft of hairs at the apex, and *l.* broad and glaucous.  Such tulips have been found in many locations in Asia Minor but it is not certain whether they are truly indigenous or not.  Cultivation is similar to that for garden hybrid tulips.

* **T. greigii.**  Another magnificent scarlet tulip of the same series as *T. fosteriana* and also from Central Asia but easily distinguished from all other sp. of this group by the prominent dark mauvish-purple mottled and streaky markings on the broad glaucous *l.*  Stem stout, up to 2 ft. *Fl.* very large, opening to a wide cup with the tips of the segments reflexed.  Perianth segments broad, bluntly pointed and often with a very small tuft of hairs at the tip.  Both outside and inside brilliant vermilion-scarlet, crimson-scarlet or deep golden-orange with red markings outside and inside, inside with a rounded dark olive-green or blackish blotch at base broadly margined with light yellow.  Anthers black but with yellow pollen.  *L.* glaucous, broad, always with conspicuous dark purplish streaks or markings.  Bulb large, tunic brown, papery.  Turkestan.  A much more variable sp. with regard to colour than *T. fosteriana.*

287

It is also a stouter and often taller sp. The *fl.* is as large, globular in outline and has more the appearance of a Darwin tulip, though in brilliance of colour and general magnificence it undeniably excels them all. Recently a number of very fine hybrids have been raised between *T. fosteriana, T. greigii* and various Darwin hybrids and these will be described under the garden forms. Those descending from *T. greigii* can nearly always be recognised by the dark markings on the *l.* A vigorous tulip and a good garden plant, thriving in good soil but still it is better lifted annually in most situations.

**T. hageri.** See under *T. orphanidea.*

**T. hoogiana.** A very magnificent large-flowering sp. from the mountains of Central Asia, unfortunately very rarely seen. Distinguished from the *fosteriana-greigii* group by the thick covering of felted wool on the bulbs underneath the papery tunics, thus bringing it into the *oculis-solis* group as differentiated by Sir Daniel Hall. *Fl.* stem tall, up to 15 in., *fl.* very large, perianth segments brilliant scarlet inside and outside but with a median lighter stripe, up to 4 in. long with a narrow dark olive-green blotch with pale yellow margin at the base, outer segments broader than inner ones, anthers black. *L.* glaucous, upper becoming narrower. Bulb large and ovoid. Late flowering. Probably closely related to *T. lanata.* This fine sp. fittingly commemorates the Hoog family of the van Tubergen business, the introducers of so many magnificent tulips. It is reputed to require as warm a corner as possible if grown outside.

\* **T. humilis.** A small dwarf sp. of very variable but often very brilliant, almost shocking colour, always in the pink-magenta shades, from the mountains of N.W. Persia and N.E. Turkey. Very early flowering, often in February, and opening to a low flat star with a yellow centre, in bud looking like a large deep pink egg emerging from the *l.* Perianth segments broad, 1½–2 in. long, blunt at apex generally with a dark olive-green basal blotch margined broadly with yellow, but like the petal colour this is very variable. Some forms have been found with the petal colour almost white while in others it is a purplish-violet. Anthers purplish olive-green. Bulb with yellow to light brown tunic and only a few hairs at top, *l.* slightly glaucous, narrow and sometimes lying flat near ground, but not developing much till after *fl.* (Pl. **29**, 19)

\* **T. pulchella** from Asia Minor with *fl.* slightly later and pinkish-crimson on the inside and \* **T. violacea** (syn. *T. pulchella violacea*) (Pl. **29**, 17) also from North Persia and Kurdistan with a definite violet-purple colour in the *fl.* were in the past distinguished as separate sp. on the grounds of differences in colouring and separateness of geographical distribution, but from subsequent collections it seems very doubtful if these specific or geographical distinctions can be usefully maintained although they still appear in most catalogues. *T. violacea* is very early flowering.

**T. humilis** and its allies are excellent for the Alpine house and will do adequately in the rock garden, but seldom seem to become established there although there is no other comparable display of colour at this early season. Undoubtedly they need very good drainage and a warm position, and are easily damaged by early storms.

\* **T. aucheriana,** also from Persia, with *fl.* slightly smaller and more slender, and of a less brilliant colouring, opening to a lovely pink star with a yellow

*Plate XXIII. Tulipa sprengeri*, the latest tulip species to flower

*Plate XXIV. Zantedeschia aethiopica,* a beautiful group of white arum
growing at the edge of a pond

base, but flowering later, generally in April. Seems to be rather easier as a garden plant and has been recorded as establishing itself and spreading in the open. It is also distinguished by a broad greenish-yellow stripe on the outside of the three outer perianth segments and always has a deep golden-yellow base. (Pl. **29**, 21). Bulb small, ovoid. *L.* prostrate, narrow. It is a mountain plant from 5,000 to 10,000 ft. and flowers in its native habitat from May-July where it is said to vary " in all shades from a deep rose-purple to white with just a flush of pink." In the Botanical Magazine *T. aucheriana* is treated as a syn. of *T. humilis.*

**T. ingens.** This sp. from Central Asia and the mountains of Samarkand is very close to *T. eichleri* but larger in *fl.* and one of the most handsome of all sp. *Fl.* very large but with rather narrow pointed perianth segments, deep scarlet-crimson both inside and outside; the dark, almost blackish, basal blotch on the inside of the perianth segments has no yellow margin and is thus distinguished from *T. eichleri* and *T. hoogiana.* This is still unfortunately a little-known member of the outstanding group which includes *eichleri, fosteriana* and *greigii* but is well worth attempting. Mid-April in a cold frame. Height 2 ft. *L.* glaucous.

\* **T. kaufmanniana.** The Water-lily Tulip. From this sp., both through selection of forms and hybridisation with other sp., there has been produced in recent years a great range of most lovely and valuable early flowering tulips. A selection of these is discussed under the list of garden varieties. *Fl.* medium-large, perianth segments rather narrow, reflexing widely in the sun, white or yellow with some crimson markings on the outside but very variable in colour, anthers yellow. Height 6–15 in. Bulb with brown papery tunic, medium-large. *L.* slightly glaucous, broad. Undoubtedly this is one of the most vigorous and easily grown of tulip sp. and it is fortunate that it is also one of the most beautiful; in most areas it is, however, safer to lift the bulbs in the summer. (Pl. **30**, 2*a*)

**T. kolpakowskiana.** This lengthy name covers a variable but always slender, graceful and beautiful tulip from eastern Turkestan and the steppes around the Aral Sea. In height it grows up to 1 ft. with a slender stem. The perianth segments are lanceolate, pointed and rather narrow, up to 1¾ in. long by ¾ in. wide, generally yellow outside with a heavy central streak of dull pinkish-red on the outside of the three outer petals. Inside the *fl.* are bright yellow and the segments are without a basal blotch. Bulbs rather globose with thick purple-brown tunic. *L.* narrow, glaucous, with wavy margins, generally lying flat. Mid-March to April. Quite a good garden plant though not as spectacular as many of the other sp., the *fl.* always seeming proportionately a little small for the length of the stem. (Pl. **29**, 13)

**T. lanata.** A magnificent but unfortunately little-known sp. from N.W. Persia and the mountains of Central Asia. *Fl.* very large, cup-shaped with perianth segments up to 4½ in. long by 2½ in. broad, brilliant scarlet both inside and out, slightly lighter outside, basal blotch large, deep olive-green with a yellow margin. Bulb large with brown papery tunic with a thick coat of straight hairs inside, stoloniferous. *L.* basal, broad and glaucous, upper narrower. Height up to 2 ft. Stem with very short pubescence. April.

# Tulipa

A triploid not setting seed. A member of the Oculis-solis groups only suited to a very warm and sheltered situation outside.

* **T. linifolia.** One of the most charming and brilliant of the smaller tulips, this is a scarlet-flowered equivalent of the primrose-yellow *T. batalini*. *Fl.* medium in size, perianth segments unequal, outer up to 2 in. long and pointed at apex, inner shorter, outside dull red but inside brilliant scarlet and silky, reflexing widely as the *fl.* opens and displaying the large, dark purple basal blotches. Anthers blackish-violet. (Pl. **29**, 12). Bulb small with leathery light brown tunic and conspicuous tuft of yellowish-brown wool projecting at apex. *L.* narrow, linear, slightly glaucous and wavy and with a faint red margin. Late April-May. Turkestan around Bokhara. This is an excellent sp. for the rock garden providing a very brilliant splash of colour after the majority of the sp. are over. It is not, however, a very vigorous grower and tends to die out unless frequently renewed. A much more graceful and delicate plant than the large-flowered members of the *fosteriana* group.

* **T. maximowiczii.** Also from Bokhara, is very close to *T. linifolia*, which is the prior name, and has similar brilliant scarlet *fl.* on a graceful stem but it tends to flower slightly earlier in mid-April. Both sp. are lovely in pans in the house although perfectly hardy.

**T. marjolettii.** This is a member of the Neo-tulipae and doubtfully distinct as a sp. It is, however, generally listed as such in catalogues. *Fl.* of medium size, pale yellow, almost white, tinged with purplish-red on the outside. 1½ ft. Mid-May. Quite hardy.

**T. maximowiczii.** See under *T. linifolia*.

**T. montana.** A fine, bright cherry-red or crimson-scarlet sp. from N. Persia. *Fl.* medium in size, perianth segments broad and overlapping, spathulate, 2¼ in. long by 1 in. wide, scarlet inside and outside, but slightly darker in colour than *T. fosteriana* ; basal blotch very small, an olive-black ; anthers yellow but with scarlet filaments becoming black towards the base. Height 9–12 in. Bulb medium size with a purplish skin and a tuft of wool projecting from the top, thus bringing this tulip into the same section as *T. clusiana* and *T. linifolia*. *L.* glaucous, with a narrow red margin, basal leaves waved at edge, upper stem *l.* narrow. *T. montana* resembles a slightly larger *T. linifolia* with broader petals but it flowers rather later and does not appear to be such an easy plant to grow satisfactorily. The name *T. montana* has also been used for a scarlet-flowered member of the Oculis-solis group, easily distinguished from this group by the thick coat of woolly hairs beneath the outer tunic in the bulb and these plants have now been re-classified by Sir Daniel Hall under the name *T. systola*. They are rarely seen in gardens although widespread in the Middle East. A good citron-yellow form is also found in Persia, particularly on the Elburz Mountains where it grows between 8,000 and 10,000 ft. on steep slopes surfaced with scree. The scarlet form is commoner on Mt. Dermavend at about 6,000 ft. Syn. *T. wilsoniana*.

* **T. orphanidea.** Under this name I propose to discuss a group of very closely related tulips from Greece, Turkey and the nearer Middle East. They are among the best garden plants among the sp. in the genus and have been

290

successfully naturalised in quite a number of places. While not having any-thing like the spectacular display of the large, scarlet-flowered sp., their drooping *fl.* have a considerable charm and variation in colour which makes them well worth a place both in the rock garden, in front of shrubs and also in the Alpine house.

**T. orphanidea** is very variable in colour. *Fl.* medium in size on stems up to 15 in., generally less, stem often slightly drooping, star-like when open, perianth segments up to 2 in. long by $\frac{1}{2}$ in. broad, inner and outer segments clearly differentiated, outer ones buff-orange on outside flushed with green and a little pinkish-purple, generally towards the base, inner segments broader and with a more well-defined central streak along the outside, inner surface tawny-orange to buff-orange generally but not invariably with a slight dark basal blotch of irregular outline without yellow margin. Anthers dark olive-green or greenish-yellow. (Pl. **29**, 2 and XXII). Bulb with dark reddish-brown tunic and a few hairs at top and base. *L.* long and narrow, mostly basal but with a few stem *l.*, green with a narrow darkish purple or deep crimson edge. End March-April.

**T. hageri** is very closely allied to *T. orphanidea* and is also found on the same mountains in Greece, particularly Mt. Parnes. They are both mountain and not lowland plants. *Fl.* rather similar in colouring and size but outer segments more clearly marked on the outside with green along the centre and deep crimson bordering it. Sometimes found with 2 or more *fl.* on a stem branching near the base. *Fl.* not quite so star-shaped when open, coppery-brown inside with variable basal blotch, often with a distinct yellow border. (Pl. **29**, 6). The form with several *fl.* to a bulb has sometimes been distinguished as *T. hageri splendens*.

\* **T. whittallii** is a very fine tetraploid form of the same group from Smyrna. The *fl.* are slightly larger than in the two previously described and more globose. The outside of the three outer segments is tawny-buff marked with green while the inner segments are orange with a yellow centre. Inside the *fl.* are bright orange or tawny-orange with a dark olive-green base margined with yellow, filaments dark olive-green and anthers very dark. April ; generally flowering before the other two described, it is a finer, more vigorous and distinctive garden plant than either.

**T. ostrowskiana.** Another scarlet-flowered sp. from E. Turkestan though slightly smaller and more slender than those of the *fosteriana* group and in fact belonging to the same group as *T. kolpakowskiana. Fl.* of medium size, bright scarlet both inside and out with yellowish olive-green to dark green basal blotch on the inside rather irregularly bordered with yellow. Outer segments a little reflexed, with slight purple sheen on the outside. Bulb with thick reddish-brown tunic. *L.* mostly green, slightly glaucous. (Pl. **29**, 7)

**T. persica hort.** See under *T. celsiana*, described under *T. silvestris* group. The Persian tulip, *T. persica* of Clusius, however, is *T. clusiana*, the Lady Tulip.

**T. praecox.** A tall member of the Oculis-solis group. Stem up to 18 in. or more, stout ; *fl.* medium-large, dull scarlet both inside and out, perianth segments uneven in size, outer the larger, up to $2\frac{1}{2}$ in. long by $1\frac{1}{4}$ in. broad, pointed at apex, marked with dull green or yellow with a basal blotch showing through yellow at base ; inner segments bluntly rounded at tip with a median yellow streak on the inside, otherwise vermilion-scarlet, basal blotch large, deep olive bordered irregularly with yellow. Bulb large with thin tunic and covering of woolly felt inside tunic, stoloniferous. *L.* large, glaucous. End of March to April. Reported to be a triploid, setting no seed but spreading freely by its stolons. It has established itself in various mediterranean regions including the Riviera and N. Italy but its original location is probably further east and it has been recorded from Iraq.

\* **T. praestans.** A member of the *fosteriana* group but easily distinguished by the smaller *fl.* of vermilion-scarlet, which are without the satin gloss of others of this group and are generally borne several, up to 4 on a stem. Stem stout, up to 12 in. *Fl.* cup-shaped, perianth segments bluntly pointed at apex, up to 2½ in. long and 1¼ in. broad, light vermilion-scarlet or capsicum-scarlet and without basal blotch. Bulb with thick leathery tunic, medium-large in size. *L.* green, slightly glaucous, closely set at base, keeled, slightly pubescent, broad. A good garden sp. growing vigorously and making a bright mass of colour on the rock garden. Early April.

**T. primulina.** A well-named creamy-yellow sp. from the mountains of Algeria in N. Africa, closely allied to the *silvestris* group. Stem up to 1 ft. but generally less, bearing 1 or 2 *fl.* of medium size, often slightly drooping. Perianth segments rather narrow and pointed, pale creamy-yellow on both surfaces, deeper yellow inside towards the throat, outer segments with some greenish markings and slight pink flush on the outside, texture rather thin and papery. Anthers pale yellow. (Pl. **29,** 8). Bulb of medium size and with reddish-brown tunic. *L.* long and narrow. Quite an easy sp. to grow : apparently quite hardy and has naturalised itself in some gardens. *Fl.* only open fully in the afternoon.

**T. pulchella.** See under *T. humilis.*

**T. saxatilis.** A very distinctive plant from Crete with cup-shaped *fl.* of an unusual pinkish lilac-magenta opening in sunshine to reveal a deep egg-yellow centre and throat and also easily distinguished by its shining bright green leaves. Stem up to 1 ft., generally less, with 1 or occasionally 2 *fl.*, perianth segments uneven, outer segments paler on the outside, about 2 in. in length by ¾ in. broad, colour variable in intensity, but always in the same pinkish-lilac to magenta range, outside flushed green at base, the three inner segments have a narrow median green stripe on outside. Basal blotch deep egg-yellow, large, extending up to one-third of the perianth segments. March-April. Bulb of medium size with yellowish-brown tunic, very stoloniferous. *L.* bright shining green, broad, produced early in winter but apparently quite undamaged by frost. *T. saxatilis* is a triploid and sets no fertile seed but spreads very freely by underground stolons. It is quite hardy but does not tend to be very free flowering except in a few gardens where it occupies a very warm position. It is best to restrict the area over which the stolons can wander by confining the patch with slates buried in the ground to the depth of at least 1 ft. and to ensure that the bulbs get as good a summer ripening as possible. Dykes reported that he lifted his bulbs each year and baked them in the kitchen cupboard and that they then flowered well afterwards. The unusual colouring of the *fl.*, produced rather early in the season, makes it a striking plant in the garden.

**T. bakeriana** is a diploid very similar to *T. saxatilis* with the same peculiar colouring of *fl.*, though often a deeper shade, and with slightly smaller *fl.*, sometimes 2 to a stem, setting fertile seed. *L.* green, narrower than in *saxatilis*. It is a mountain plant confined to Crete while *T saxatilis* is a lowland sp. I have seen *T. bakeriana* growing in large patches on the plain of Omalo in the White Mountains of Crete and in early May at 3,000 ft. it was just passing out of flower, but it had been an early season.

**T. cretica.** A much smaller plant than either of those previously mentioned. The stem is short and the *l.* often appear almost sessile. Perianth segments white, but outer segments flushed with purplish-red on the outside, inner surface white, flushed with a smaller yellow basal blotch. Bulb small with some pinkish-brown on tunic, stoloniferous. *L.* dark green, generally with a definite purplish-red margin and usually lying flat on the ground. *T. cretica* is a very rare plant in the mountains of Crete, its native habitat, and lacks the vigour of the two previously described. In this country it is probably best treated as an Alpine house plant.

**T. silvestris.** The most abundant and widespread European tulip, though spreading as far eastwards as northern Persia and south into N. Africa. Very variable and spreads freely by stolons. In some forms quite strongly scented. It forms a large aggregate group, some forms of which have been distinguished in the past by specific names. It is a tetraploid and for the most part a *fl.* of the lowlands, thus differing from the very closely related and similar *T. australis* which is a diploid and a plant of the hills and mountains. The stem is rather weak and the bud generally drooping, though the *fl.* tends to open upright, up to 15 in. but generally less, sometimes with 2 *fl.* to a stem. Nearly always scented. Perianth segments yellowish-green outside, with some reddish markings generally towards the tip, very variable in colour and size, up to $2\frac{1}{2}$ in. long by $\frac{3}{4}$ in. broad, inside soft bright yellow, anthers yellow. (Pl. 29, 4). Bulb small, with dark reddish-brown tunic, stoloniferous. *L.* rather straggling, long and narrow, keeled, slightly glaucous. Although naturalised in some parts of England and even considered by some as a native *T. silvestris* in gardens is very shy flowering although growing and spreading by stolons freely. Probably it should be confined by slates in the ground, as with *T. saxatilis*, and it should certainly be given as warm a spot as possible where it can be dried off well in the summer. In S. Europe it flowers much more freely and bunches of *fl.* are often sold in the streets. The form from Persia known as *'Tabriz' is very fine, a good yellow and the largest *fl.* I have seen in this sp.

**T. australis** has a more slender habit and is generally a mountain plant extending throughout Europe and into Central Asia. Very variable. *Fl.* narrow with pointed petals and generally more strongly marked with red outside than *T. silvestris*, but again very variable, inner surface clear yellow with no basal blotch. (Pl. 29, 5). Bulb small, reddish-brown, often rather flattened or elongated, generally very deep in the wild and often growing through spinous dwarf bushes. *L.* narrow, keeled, generally lying flat on ground.

\* **T. celsiana.** A tall, yellow-flowered form of the same aggregate from N. Africa. (Pl. **29**, 15). The outer perianth segments are flushed red, but the general effect, especially when open is of a yellow star about 2 in. across. It is probably a better garden plant than either *T. silvestris* or *T. australis* and quite hardy. I have seen it naturalised in a Midland garden and flowering freely. Mid-April to early May, later than the two previous sp.

\* **T. sprengeri.** The latest flowering of all tulips, generally towards the end of May. Stem up to 18 in. but giant forms up to 2½ ft. are sometimes seen. *Fl.* single, globular, mahogany-red both inside and out but slightly lighter outside, perianth segments up to 2½ in. long and ¾ in. broad, without basal blotch, pointed. Bulb small-medium size with dark brown papery tunic often growing very deep. *L.* green, long and narrow, shining. *T. sprengeri* is a good garden plant, quite hardy and has been naturalised successfully in a number of gardens. It seems to grow equally well in semi-shade. Asia Minor, Turkey. (Pl. XXIII)

**T. stapfii.** A scarlet-flowered sp. from Asia Minor with a rather short, stout stem, broad, glaucous basal *l.* and narrower pointed stem *l.* Recently reintroduced but seldom seen in cultivation, basal blotch purplish with yellow margin. Perianth segments up to 3 in., pointed, slightly lighter in colour on outside than inside. Its garden merits still await further trial. A member of the Oculis-solis group.

**T. stellata.** A member of the Clusiana group from Kashmir and Afghanistan. A delicate and graceful sp. with white *fl.* flushed pink on the outside, resembling *T. clusiana* but with a slightly smaller *fl.* and less clearly defined in colour. Stem slender, up to 10 in. *Fl.* star-shaped when open; perianth segments 1½ in. × ½ in., pointed at tips, white, outside tinged with red as central stripe, variable in amount of marking, inside white with small pale yellow blotch around throat, anthers yellow. Mid-April. Bulb small with thick tunic woolly inside tunic and with an apical tuft of wool protruding. *L.* narrow and wavy, often pinkish-crimson on the margins. (Pl. **29**, 3)

Var. **chrysantha,** often known as *T. chrysantha* of gardens, is a variety with bright yellow basal colouring instead of white, generally heavily flushed with pinkish-crimson on the outside of the three outer segments. A very lovely garden plant, rather more showy than *T. stellata.* In some places it has been satisfactorily established on the rock garden. Mid-April. (Pl. **29**, 14)

**T. tarda.** An attractive dwarf sp. with a bunch of small yellow and white *fl.*, perhaps still better known in gardens under its syn. *T. dasystemon.* Stem short, up to 6 in. with 4–6 *fl.*, each opening star-like. Perianth segments up to 1½ in. × ¾ in., outside white, heavily tinged with yellowish-green and sometimes a little red, inside white at tip while lower half is yellow. Anthers deeper yellow. Bulb medium in size with thin, yellowish-brown tunic. *L.* long and narrow, often almost prostrate on the ground, not glaucous. E. Turkestan. Rather late flowering: late April to early May. *T. tarda* is

# Tulipa

one of the easier sp. to grow satisfactorily and is a pleasant rock garden plant. (Pl. **29**, 20)

**T. tubergeniana.** Another large, deep scarlet and very handsome sp. from Central Asia around Bokhara, probably very closely allied to *T. ingens* and slightly less closely to *T. fosteriana* in which group it belongs, but distinguished from both by the undulating margin to the petals. Stem stout, up to 2 ft. *Fl.* single; perianth segments up to 4 in. × 1½ in., pointed at tip, inner surface glossy, bright scarlet; basal blotch very dark olive-green narrowly margined with yellow, showing yellow outside of basal blotch. Bulb large with thin reddish-brown tunic. *L.* broad, glaucous and somewhat pubescent. To estimate the relative garden value and range of these obviously closely related sp. requires both further importations from their native habitat and more widely spread experiments in cultivation. So far, however, none of these has surpassed the best forms of *T. fosteriana* and *T. greigii* in magnificence and garden value, although *T. ingens* and *T. tubergeniana* undoubtedly equal these sp.

**T. turkestanica.** A small flowered sp. with up to 7 *fl.* to a stem, closely allied to *T. biflora* but with larger *fl.* and generally more vigour for garden purposes. Stem slender, up to 1 ft. *Fl.* star-like when open, perianth segments up to 1½ in. × ¼ in. wide, whitish flushed with cream and green markings, inside white with a yellow blotch. Anthers dark purplish-brown. Bulb small with purplish-brown tunic. *L.* long and narrow, slightly glaucous. Early flowering, Feb. to early March. Turkestan. *T. turkestanica* is a tetraploid while *T. biflora* is a diploid.

**T. urumiensis.** *Fl.* star-like, butter-yellow inside, outside flushed pale purple or dull red. Height 9 in. 1–2 *fl.* to a stem. *L.* strap-shaped, green, slightly glaucous. N.W. Persia. (Pl. **29**, 18)

**T. violacea.** See under *T. humilis.*

**T. whittalli.** See under *T. orphanidea.*

**T. wilsoniana.** See under *T. montana.*

## (b) Tulip varieties

Although the Darwin, the Darwin Hybrids and the Lily-flowered varieties comprise the main bulk of the tulips planted for late April and May decoration, there are also a number of other divisions in the classification Scheme prepared jointly by delegates from the Narcissus and Tulip Committee of the R.H.S. and the Royal General Dutch Bulb Growers Society. This is not a botanical classification in the strict sense but rather one designed for general use at Shows and in the garden and to facilitate easy catalogue descriptions. It is now divided into 23 divisions of which the first three are early flowering, the next are mid-season and the remainder either May or late flowering or varieties based on the varieties and hybrids of a particular species. The list of tulip varietal names registered under

# *Tulipa*

these divisions is already a long one and is published by the Royal General Dutch Bulb Growers Society and is available from them or from the R.H.S.

## (1) DUC VAN TOL TULIPS

Very early flowering, generally of bright colours, single, not often 6 in. in height. These were much used formerly but are now little grown to-day and no longer generally listed in catalogues having been superseded by the next division.

## (2) SINGLE EARLY TULIPS

These are much used for growing in bowls or for forcing but are also valuable for planting outside when they will flower usually about mid-April, but varying with the season and also with their variety. Among the best are:

'BRILLIANT STAR' One of the earliest to *fl.* Dwarf. Bright red with a large *fl.* Much used for forcing.

* 'COULEUR CARDINAL' An outstanding variety, glowing velvety crimson-red with a dusky grey bloom on outside. Always conspicuous and much to be recommended, well named.

'FRED MOORE' Brownish-orange. Early flowering.

* 'GENERAL DE WET' Bright orange suffused with gold. Tall stems and much to be recommended. Sometimes listed as ' De Wet '.

'KEIZERSKROON' Bright scarlet, broadly edged with yellow. Conspicuous but not a good mixer with other plants. A large *fl.*

'MON TRESOR' Bright yellow, early flowering.

'ORANGE HAWK' Bright orange, tinged with carmine.

'PRINCE CARNIVAL' Bright scarlet edged with yellow, a sport from ' Prince of Austria.' Not quite so harsh in colour contrast as ' Keizerskroon.'

'PRINCE OF AUSTRIA' An old favourite, bright red suffused with orange. Tall, sweet scented.

'WHITE HAWK' Early-flowering. White with a yellow flush at base. A large globular *fl.*

## (3) DOUBLE EARLY TULIPS

These are specially suitable for growing in bowls and flower like small paeonies early in the year. For the most part the stems are stout and sufficiently strong to carry the large flowers which often measure up to 4 in. across. Many of them are very suitable for forcing. Among those most usually grown and which can be safely recommended are:

'BONANZA' Carmine-red with a broad yellow edge.

'CALIPH OF BAGDAD' Deep golden-yellow, flushed with orange as *fl.* ages. A good variety for forcing.

'DANTE' Deep blood-red.

'GOYA' Salmon-scarlet with yellow base.

'MARÉCHAL NIEL' Yellow, flushed orange.

'MURILLO' White, flushed pink.

'MURILLO MAXIMA' Similar to ' Murillo ' but with a larger *fl.* and slightly earlier.

296

# Tulipa

'ORANGE NASSAU' Orange-red.
'PEACH BLOSSOM' Deep rose-pink.
'SCARLET CARDINAL' Bright scarlet. One of the earliest.

## (4) MENDEL TULIPS

These are rather dwarf tulips with single flowers resulting from crosses between Darwin varieties and Duc van Tol. They seldom are taller than 20 in. They flower outside a little later than the Early varieties of divisions 2 and 3 above, but distinctly earlier than the Darwins and are usually described as mid-season, usually mid-April. They are for the most part also good for forcing. They are not, however, so widely grown as the Triumph tulips which have partly superseded them. Among the best, however, are:

'ATHLEET' Pure white, good for forcing.
'HER GRACE' White, with broad rosy-lilac edge.
'ORANGE WONDER' Bronzy-orange with scarlet shading. Also known as the 'Tulip of Albany'.
'SULPHUR TRIUMPH' Primrose-yellow.

## (5) TRIUMPH TULIPS

Derived from crosses between single early flowering tulips and late May flowering varieties. Usually flowering before the Darwins and not so tall. Stems usually stouter and flowers with more substance than the Mendel varieties, but seldom more than 20 in. in height. They are used where it is necessary to clear out the tulips in bedding schemes early to make room for summer arrangements. Mid-season.

'AUREOLA' Bright red with deep yellow margin.
'BANDOENG' Mahogany-red, flushed with orange, paler at edge.
'CRATER' Bright red, vermilion near edge.
'ELMUS' Cherry-red with a white edge.
'KORNEFOROS' Bright carmine-red. Very brilliant colour.
'MAKASSAR' Deep canary-yellow. A very fine variety.
'OLAF' Scarlet.
'SULPHUR GLORY' Pale sulphur-yellow, large globular *fl.*
'TOPSCORE' Geranium-lake with a yellow base and black stamens.

## (6) DARWIN TULIPS

The most popular class of tall May flowering tulips, generally up to 2 ft. Flowers rather globular and petals mostly rounded at edge.

*White, cream and pale yellow varieties*

* 'ANJOU' Pale canary-yellow inside and at edge of petals, pale buttercup yellow outside. A strong grower.
* 'GLACIER' Pale cream outside, pure white inside, a very fine tulip.
  'JOAN OF ARC' Pale ivory, becoming white.
  'NIPHETOS' Soft lemon yellow, an old favourite.

* ' SWEET HARMONY ' A most distinct variety, pale lemon-yellow with a white edge to each petal.
' WHITE GIANT ' Pure white, a large *fl.*
' WHITE STANDARD ' Pure white with yellow stamens, of medium height.
' ZWANENBURG ' A good white with black anthers.

### Deep yellow and golden or orange-yellow varieties

' GOLDEN AGE ' Deep yellow, the edges of petals becoming pale orange.
' GOLDEN HIND ' Deep golden-yellow, of medium size but with unusual substance to petal. (Pl. **31**, 7)
' MAMASA ' Deep buttercup-yellow with long petals.
' SUNKIST ' Deep golden-yellow.
' YELLOW GIANT ' Deep yellow with conspicuous black anthers. *Fl.* of medium size.

### Pale to deep pink

' CLARA BUTT ' An old favourite and a smaller *fl.* than many of the newer varieties, bright rosy-pink. Combining well with forget-me-nots.
' DRESDEN CHINA ' Soft rose-pink with paler pink rim to petal, a delicate colour.
' MR. VAN ZIJL ' Soft pink becoming paler towards edge of petals.
' PRUNUS ' Deep rose-pink. (Pl. **31**, 1)
* ' QUEEN OF BARTIGONS ' Rich salmon-pink, an unusually lovely colour and of good form. Strongly recommended. (Pl. **31**, 8)
' WILLIAM PITT ' Strawberry-red, slightly tinged with purple. Much used for forcing.

### Scarlet and crimson

' BARTIGON ' Geranium to lake red. An old variety much used for forcing.
' BREITNER ' Petals slightly pointed, inside blood-red with blue blotch at base, with a white edge, outside blood-red darkening at centre of petal to dark bluish-red. A very striking variety.
' CHARLES NEEDHAM ' An older variety and not so large as some, bright scarlet-red.
' ECLIPSE ' Deep scarlet-crimson with deep violet base inside, another older variety of medium height.
' NOBEL ' Dark geranium-lake. A very striking colour.
' PAUL RICHTER ' Geranium-lake, good for forcing.
' SCARLETT O'HARA ' Bright geranium-lake, appearing scarlet.

### Mauve, lilac, purple and maroon

' ACE OF SPADES ' Purplish-black, maroon.
' ARCHBISHOP ' Deeper purple than ' Bishop,' from which it is a sport.
' BISHOP ' Deep lavender-purple, a large *fl.* on a tall stem; an old favourite. (Pl. **31**, 5)

'BLEU AIMABLE' Lavender-mauve, shaded purple but with brighter blue base inside.

'DEMETER' Plum-purple with a glossy sheen. Early flowering for a Darwin.

'DORRIE OVERALL' Dark petunia-violet, edged with mauve.

'GIANT' Deep reddish-violet. Large *fl.*

'LA TULIPE NOIRE' An old favourite, deep maroon, almost black but not so large a *fl.* as 'Queen of Night' or 'Ace of Spades'.

'QUEEN OF NIGHT' Deep velvety maroon, appears almost black. Large *fl.*

## (7) DARWIN HYBRIDS

This class includes probably the finest as well as the largest tulips raised in recent years and is the one in which the greatest advance has been made, due largely to the work of Mr. D. W. Lefeber and Messrs. van Tubergen. *T. fosteriana* has been used for one parent. They have great vigour often growing up to 2 ft. and flower rather earlier than the Darwin tulips but are excellent for bedding. From *T. fosteriana* has been inherited a brilliant glowing scarlet-red colour with a satin sheen in most cases, combined with great size of flower while from the Darwin side has come a tall and strong stem and a rather globular shape of flower. Several of the named varieties are very similar in the garden in their effect but it is one of undeniable and oriental magnificence. They can be grown successfully also in a cool greenhouse but this is not generally necessary.

* 'APELDOORN' Bright scarlet with a pale mauvish sheen on outside, base black, bordered with yellow ; one of the best.

'CANOPUS' Glowing scarlet-red with black base.

* 'DOVER' Oriental scarlet or poppy-red with purple-black base, bordered by yellow ring, a very large *fl.*

'FRANKLIN D. ROOSEVELT' Deep orange-scarlet with black base, bordered yellow ; a large *fl.*

'GENERAL EISENHOWER' Orange-red with yellow base.

'GUDOSHNIK' Creamy-yellow, splashed and flecked with rose-red, base inside grey. A distinct *fl.*

* 'HOLLAND'S GLORY' Orange-scarlet with pointed petals, very brilliant colour and very large *fl.*, 7 in. across when open. Early flowering. One of the most distinct and conspicuous varieties yet raised.

'LEFEBER'S FAVOURITE' Bright glowing orange-scarlet with yellow base inside ; not so tall as 'Apeldoorn' or some of the others, nearer to *T. fosteriana*, but very conspicuous.

* 'LONDON' One of the largest, early flowering, vermilion-scarlet with black base edged with yellow.

'OXFORD' Deep scarlet-red with yellow base inside, a very large bloom.

* 'RED MATADOR' Intense fiery scarlet with yellow or black base, close to *T. fosteriana.*

'SPRING SONG' Cochineal-red flushed with salmon outside and black base with white edge.

'WINDSOR' Signal-red overlaid outside with mauvish bloom, brownish-green blotch at base bordered by yellow.

# *Tulipa*

## (8) BREEDER TULIPS

May flowering single varieties with oval flowers and ranging in colour from yellowish-orange through brown dull red and purple to violet with a paler base of white or yellow, sometimes stained with blue, green or black. While not so suitable for bedding their more unusual colours make them interesting for decoration. In stature and size they correspond to the Darwins, but the flowers are more oval and globular. Among those best known are:

'BACCHUS' Dark purple with a violet-blue bloom on the outer petals.

'DILLENBURG' Orange and terracotta.

* 'LOUIS XIV' Bluish-violet with a tawny golden-bronze margin. A very distinctive and handsome *fl.*

'PAPAGO' Poppy-red with a yellow base.

'PRESIDENT HOOVER' Orange-scarlet, paler inside. One of the brightest colours in this division. An old variety.

## (9) LILY-FLOWERED TULIPS

These are distinguished by the long pointed petals reflexing as they open and taller and narrower flowers than in the Darwins. As a group they have been much developed in recent years and can be most strongly recommended for bedding or for mixing with other plants in groups, growing to an equal size and with equal vigour in the case of the larger varieties such as 'Mariette' and 'Queen of Sheba'. They tend to flower slightly earlier than the Darwins but about the same time as the Darwin hybrids. As yet there are no double lily-flowered varieties and many prefer them to the Darwin for their extra grace and delicacy of form.

'CAPT. FRYATT' Reddish-purple with a purple flush. A distinctive graceful variety of medium size.

'CHINA PINK' Rose-pink with a deeper flush on outside. One of the best varieties. Medium size and height.

'DORA M. BOND' Deep red, a new and promising variety.

'DYANITO' Bright red with a yellow base. Probably the brightest colour yet developed in this section.

'GOLDEN DUCHESS' Deep golden-yellow. A larger *fl.* than the old 'Mrs. Moon'.

'MARCELLINA' Deep pink with a rose-pink sheen.

* 'MARIETTE' Deep China-rose. Very large *fl.* on a stout stem and very long lasting, sometimes as much as 3–4 weeks. One of the best varieties for massing in beds with forget-me-nots. (Pl. **31**, 2)

* 'QUEEN OF SHEBA' Very large and one of the most striking tulips raised in recent years. Glowing rusty-red with an orange edge. Very conspicuous in *fl.* and much to be recommended. Stem tall and stout.

* 'RED SHINE' Deep red with a blue base, a glowing colour. Of recent introduction but very promising.

'SEBASTIAN' Deep buttercup-yellow. Probably the deepest yellow available. (Pl. **31**, 3)

# *Tulipa*

'STANISLAUS' Orange-vermilion with a yellow base and edge. Medium size but always conspicuous.

' WHITE TRIUMPHATOR ' Pure white, an elegant *fl.* of medium size.

## (10) COTTAGE TULIPS

These are late flowering single varieties with flowers often long or egg-shaped and the group includes rather a mixture which do not fit into the previous divisions. In size and height they correspond to the Darwin varieties and include some old favourites for bedding where it is not necessary to clear the bed too early. The viridiflora tulips with green as a base to the flowers such as ' Artist,' ' Groenland ' and the various forms of viridiflora are particularly popular with flower arrangers. Among the best are:

' ARTIST ' One of the viridiflora tulips, inside green and rose, outside green striped with purple and salmon-rose.

' BELLE JAUNE ' Dark golden-yellow. An old favourite.

' CHAPPAQUA ' Dark violet-rose.

' GEISHA ' Greyish or light lilac-mauve outside, soft reddish-lilac inside. An unusual colour.

' GOLDEN HARVEST ' Deep lemon-yellow. A very old favourite.

' GROENLAND ' Green edged with rose. One of the viridiflora tulips.

* ' G. W. LEAK ' Geranium-lake with a yellow centre. A very bright colour. (Pl. **31**, 4)

' MARJORIE BOWEN ' Salmon-pink flushed with buff-pink.

* ' MARSHAL HAIG ' Bright scarlet. A very reliable and strong colour for bedding.

' OSSI OSWALDA ' Creamy-white with pink flush and flecks stronger on margin of petals.

' PALAESTRINA ' A lovely terracotta-pink.

* ' ROSY WINGS ' Clear pink with a white base. Long pointed petals. One of the most lovely tulips for bedding and cutting.

' VIRIDIFLORA PRAECOX ' Pale yellow and green. Early, with a large *fl.* with wavy petals.

' ZOMERSCHOON ' Rosy-carmine splashed liberally on a creamy base. A very old variety and rather small in *fl.*, but an unusual and distinctive combination of colours. Not very vigorous.

## (11) REMBRANDT TULIPS

These are broken Darwin tulips.

## (12) BIZARRE TULIPS

These are broken Breeder or broken Cottage tulips. Striped or marked with brown, bronze, maroon or purple usually on a yellow ground.

## (13) BIJBLOEMEN TULIPS

These are broken Breeder or Cottage tulips, striped or marked rose, pink, violet or purple on a white ground.

# *Tulipa*

All these three groups consist of tulips which are infected with virus and so are best grown apart from the other tulips. They do not possess the same vigour as other varieties but in some cases the flowers are very beautiful and make lovely flower decorations. During the old days of the Tulipomania in Holland bulbs of this type were sold for enormous sums. To-day the Darwins and self-coloured varieties are more grown and appreciated, but generally a few of these are still to be seen among the others at the Chelsea Show. An excellent article on them by Mr. G. R. Barr will be found in the R.H.S. Daffodil and Tulip Year Book for 1951–2. Among the best are:

'ABSALON' A fine yellow, flamed and feathered with mahogany. (Bizarre).
'AMERICAN FLAG' Deep red with white stripes, a large *fl.* (Rembrandt).
'CORDELL HULL' Blood-red with white blotches and streaks, a distinctive *fl.* Much better than its description sounds. (Rembrandt).
'MME DE POMPADOUR' White overlaid with reddish-purple flaming (Rembrandt).

## (14) PARROT TULIPS

Those with fringed or laciniate petals, generally with very large *fl.* but unfortunately tending to be a little weak in the stem for the heavy *fl.*, but very effective when cut for flower decorations. May flowering. Many are sports from well-known Darwin varieties. Among the most distinctive are:

'ADVENTURE' A very large *fl.* which needs support. Light scarlet.
'ALLARD PIERSON' Crimson-maroon.
'BLACK PARROT' Very dark maroon, almost black with bronze bloom outside.
'BLUE PARROT' Lavender-mauve with bronze bloom outside. A very large *fl.* with deep frillings.
'FANTASY' Salmon-pink with green at base and edge of petals. An old favourite.
'GADELAN' Deep violet-mauve.
'ORANGE PARROT' Bronzy-orange. A very striking *fl.*
'RED PARROT' Deep raspberry-red with a stout stem.
* 'THÉRÈSE' Bright rose-red. A striking *fl.* (Pl. **31**, 6)

## (15) DOUBLE LATE TULIPS

Their name adequately describes this group and they include the so-called " paeony-flowered " tulips. In many cases when fully open the *fl.* are very large and sumptuous and the stems are quite strong, but of course they are susceptible to damage in stormy weather owing to the weight of the *fl.* and to my eye lack the grace of the single Darwins or Lily-flowered tulips. Among the most popular are:

'BLUE FLAG' Light violet-blue. Sometimes known as 'Bleu Celeste'.
'BRILLIANT FIRE' Bright orange-red.
'EROS' Rose-pink, fading to a slightly bluish-pink.
'GERBRAND KIEFT' Deep reddish-purple with a white edge.
'HERMIONE' Light violet-rose with a white base.
'MOUNT TACOMA' White. An old favourite.
'SYMPHONIA' Cherry-red.

# Tulipa

The remaining divisions 16 to 23 are devoted to varieties and hybrids of particular species: (16) *T. batalinii.* (17) *T. eichleri.* (18) *T. fosteriana.* (19) *T. greigii.* (20) *T. kaufmanniana.* (21) *T. marjolettii.* (22) *T. tubergeniana.* (23) other species. Of these, the varieties and hybrids of *T. fosteriana, T. greigii* and *T. kaufmanniana* are by far the most important, and it is in these groups that great advances have been made in recent years. The hybrids of *T. fosteriana* and *T. greigii* are of great size and usually have great brilliance of colour, while those of *T. kaufmanniana*, the Water Lily tulip, are early flowering, very varied in colour and have graceful long pointed petals. There are no hybrids either from *T. batalinii* or *T. eichleri* in general distribution, although they would seem to offer good scope for further work, nor are there at present any hybrids in general distribution from sections 21 to 23.

## (18) *T. fosteriana*

The Darwin hybrids derived from crosses between Darwin tulips and *T. fosteriana* have already been discussed in Division 7, but a number of other varieties remain which are very good garden plants and of great value in the border.

' ALBAS ' White inside, flushed pale pink outside, base yellow. Early flowering.

' FEU SUPERBE ' Cardinal-red with a black base edged with yellow. A magnificent plant with very large *fl.* of the strongest brightest colour.

* ' MME LEFEBER ' Fiery-red. Probably the best selected form of *T. fosteriana.* Also known as ' Red Emperor.' *Fl.* very large, of flaming scarlet with a glossy sheen, base yellow.

* ' PURISSIMA ' Milky white. A beautiful *fl.*

## (19) *T. greigii*: VARIETIES AND HYBRIDS

These are of great brilliance with almost dazzling scarlet or deep golden-yellow flowers and can nearly always be distinguished by the blotched and streaked leaves. They rival the hybrids of *T. fosteriana* in garden display and the very large flowers are borne on good stout stems and the flowers are long lasting. A number of very promising new hybrids have also recently been raised in this group but since they are not yet on the general market they are not included here. The work of Mr. D. W. Lefeber in raising new hybrids in this group and in the *fosterianas* has contributed very greatly to our garden decoration.

' BOKHARA ' Orange-red with black base rimmed with yellow. *L.* with a red edge. A very striking *fl.*

' FATUMA ' Orange-scarlet with a greenish-black base. *L.* only slightly mottled.

' KARATAU ' Orange-scarlet with black base.

' MARGARET HERBST ' Scarlet with yellow base.

303

# *Tulipa*

'ORIENTAL SPLENDOUR' Outside carmine-red edged with lemon-yellow, inside lemon-yellow with black base.

'TASHKENT' Orange-scarlet with black base and a pronounced bloom on outside of *fl*. A very striking variety.

## (20) *T. kaufmanniana*: HYBRIDS AND VARIETIES

These are certainly among the most attractive and brilliant tulips introduced in recent years. While not so large as the former group they are distinguished by the pointed petals, often short stems and very early flowering, often even towards the end of March. Many have strongly mottled or striped leaves, which have arisen from crosses with *T. greigii*. Mixtures of these tulips are sold under a variety of names such as Peacock tulips, Colour Parade or Rainbow Mixture. The named varieties are now very numerous and are nearly all striking in early spring in the rock garden or part of the border. The majority do not exceed 1 ft. in height and are often less when they first open. A long series have been named after musicians.

'ALFRED CORTOT' Deep scarlet with black base. *L.* mottled.

* 'BRILLIANT' Scarlet with golden-yellow base.

'CÉSAR FRANCK' Carmine-red edged with yellow outside, deep yellow inside. Early flowering. (Pl. **30**, 2*b*)

'EDWIN FISCHER' Outside carmine-red edged with lemon-yellow, inside lemon-yellow flushed with deep red.

'FRITZ KREISLER' Deep pink with a deeper yellow base and carmine-red blotches, outside flushed mauve with a yellow edge. One of the taller varieties. (Pl. **30**, 2*e*)

'GLUCK' Sulphur-yellow with deeper yellow base, outside banded carmine-red. (Pl. **30**, 2*d*)

'GOUDSTUK' Carmine-red and gold. A large *fl*.

'JOSEPH KAFKA' Deep golden-yellow with red blotches at base. Mottled *l*.

* 'LADY ROSE' Pale rose flushed with scarlet. Tall and a large *fl*. To me the most beautiful in this section but unfortunately not always a very vigorous grower. (Pl. **30**, 2*c*)

'ROBERT SCHUMANN' Outside pale carmine-red, edged yellow. Inside deep golden-yellow with red blotches and bronze base.

* 'SCARLET ELEGANCE' Scarlet with yellow base.

'SPARKLING EYE' Outside carmine-rose edged with cream, inside creamy-white with bronzy-green base and scarlet blotches.

* 'STRESA' Outside deep golden-yellow with orange-red vertical band on outer petals, inside deep yellow with red markings at the base. One of the tallest in this group and a very striking *fl*.

'THE FIRST' Ivory-white with yellow base and some red flushing on outside. Very early flowering and close to original sp.

'VIVALDI' Deep yellow edged with carmine, sulphur-yellow inside.

# VALLOTA *Amaryllidaceae*

A MONOTYPIC genus containing one of the most beautiful of autumn flowering Amaryllids from S. Africa. It differs from *Amaryllis* and *Brunsvigia* in its more regular perianth. Unfortunately the only species is not quite hardy but is an excellent plant for the cool greenhouse. The bulbs are best planted about July and can then be left undisturbed for several years provided that while in growth they are given some feeding and ample water. Very fine specimen plants of *Vallota* have even been grown on window sills. They should be given rather a sandy compost.

> **V. speciosa.** The Scarborough Lily. The name Scarborough Lily was given to it because some bulbs were washed up there from a wrecked ship. Stem up to 2 ft. with large inflorescence of up to 10 very bright, glowing scarlet-red funnel-shaped *fl.* of which usually several open together, up to 3 in. across, regular. There is also a rare but very beautiful form with pink *fl.* Bulb large, up to 3 in. across, ovoid. *L.* broadly linear, up to 1½ ft. long produced with the *fl.* Aug.-Sept. S. Africa, Cape Province where they bloom in Nov.-Dec. and are known as " George Lilies." Syn. *V. purpurea.*
>
> Var. **elata.** *Fl.* smaller, bright cherry-red. Sometimes regarded as a distinct sp.

# †VELTHEIMIA *Liliaceae*

A SMALL genus of S. African bulbous plants with long drooping tubular flowers on a rather fleshy stem, generally in the slightly blue or muddier shades of pink. It is probably this that has prevented them becoming popular although they remain in flower for a long time. The flowers are borne in rather dense racemes and remind one of an aloe, or, except for the colour, of a kniphofia. They are not difficult of cultivation in a cool greenhouse and there will flower during the winter months. None, however, are hardy enough to plant outside. The bulbs should be dried off after the leaves have died down and restarted in September.

The best-known species is *V. capensis.* In S. Africa it flowers from July-September and there it is recommended that it should be planted in the shade.

The bulbs are large, rather globose and the leaves radical and slightly fleshy.

> **V. capensis.** Sometimes listed as *V. viridifolia* and with the largest *fl.* in the genus. Stem up to 1½ ft., fleshy, dark purplish-crimson with small yellow spots, raceme of *fl.* up to 5 in. long. *Fl.* pendulous, tubular, deep pink or dull

red, sometimes described as " crushed strawberry " lighter towards mouth and showing white mottling there, rather variable in colour, up to 1½ in. long. March-April. Bulb large with prominent old bases of *l.* and often projecting above soil. *L.* oblong with slight wavy edge, bright green above, slightly glaucous beneath, basal. S. Africa. Cape Province in Coast regions by seashore. Cool greenhouse, generally fairly easily grown. Syn. *V. viridifolia, Aletris capensis.*

**V. deasii.** Close to *V. glauca,* but smaller and distinguished by the prominent crisped waviness of the edges of the grey *l.* Stem glaucous, up to 1 ft., with pendulous tubular pale pink *fl.* 1 in. long and yellowish-green at tips, tinged yellow on inside, stamens inserted below middle of corolla tube. This is a distinguishing character. Raceme of *fl.* about 3 in. long. Corolla tube slightly constricted near middle. December. Bulb broad with persistent brown rings in upper part from base of old *l. L.* strap-shaped, very glaucous, crisped at edge, undulating. S. Africa, Cape Province. Cool greenhouse.

**V. glauca.** A larger plant than the preceding. Stem up to 1½ ft., mottled with red, raceme of *fl.* up to 6 in. long. *Fl.* pendulous, tubular, white or whitish with purplish-crimson spotting, bracts pink. Nov.-March. Bulb large, oblong-ovate. *L.* strap-shaped, broad with undulating edge, glaucous but not so much as in preceding sp., sheathing stem at base. S. Africa, Cape Province. One of the earliest sp. in cultivation. Cool greenhouse.

Var. **rubescens,** with a dense raceme of dull crimson *fl.* tipped with dark mauve has also been recorded.

# WATSONIA *Iridaceae*

WATSONIA IS a large genus of S. African plants with corms, closely allied to *Gladiolus* and containing members of considerable beauty. Unfortunately, however, none of these are reliably hardy in most parts of Britain, though in the milder parts some have been grown successfully in a warm situation such as a border under a wall. The majority are suitable for growing in a cool greenhouse or a frame where they can be given some frost protection in winter and the corms ripened at their correct season. They can be divided into four separate groups:

(*a*) Tall winter growing species from the S.W. Cape Districts such as *W. ardernei* and *W. aletroides.* These tend to suffer from both damp and cold during our winters although they do not flower until the May or June following. They are best, however, permanently planted and left rather than taken up each year like a gladiolus as is sometimes recommended. Even so they cannot in this country be described as free flowering although in S. Africa they are among the best garden plants. All species seem to require plenty of moisture while they are in growth and in S. Africa they are not found in areas of very low rainfall such as the Karroo. Apart from the tall winter growers the following groups can also be distinguished.

(*b*) *Short winter growers from S.W. Cape.* These are best grown in a cool greenhouse and should be planted in September/October to flower the following April/May. These include some beautiful species such as *W. humilis* and the scarlet *W. spectabilis* and it is unfortunate that they are so rarely seen in this country since as greenhouse plants they are rewarding.

(*c*) *Summer growers from Transvaal and neighbouring areas.* These can be treated like gladioli and lifted and dried off in the winter. They should be planted again in late March or early April. Unfortunately records of their trial in this country are very meagre and corms would need to be imported from S. Africa. They should, however, be well worth the experiment. The main species are *W. alpina*, *W. transvaalensis*, *W. wilmsii* and *W. densiflora*.

(*d*) *Evergreen species from the eastern districts of S. Africa.* These should be planted in as warm a situation as possible and left permanently in the ground. Their hardiness is borderline in most districts and any protection that is possible will be a help. Probably outside they will survive a number of mild winters but then may be lost in a severe one. If planted in a cold frame they need plenty of height between the soil and the glass, although the lights can be taken off during the summer when most of them should flower. They should never be dried off completely. The flowers are often conspicuous and very lovely and they are well worth more trial than they appear to have had so far in sheltered gardens. Among the best are *W. beatricis*, *W. galpinii* and *W. pillansii* but the species, hybrids and colour forms are very numerous.

All watsonias are easily raised from seed and flower in about three years. The first season it is better not to disturb the very small cormlets. Corms divide readily and tend in some species to make large clumps which should then be divided. The account of this genus in Mrs. Sima Eliovson's excellent book *South African Flowers for the Garden* should be studied by those considering a trial of this genus.

*Watsonia* is distinguished from *Gladiolus* by a small difference in the stigmas, those of *Watsonia* dividing twice and making six branches while those of *Gladiolus* only divide once into three branches. The flowers have usually a long curved tube cylindrical in the lower part and the six segments are regular or nearly regular spreading out into rounded lobes. The spikes vary in height from 1 ft. to about 4 or 5 ft. and are usually

# Watsonia

strong in colour varying through shades of scarlet, orange, pink and terra-cotta with a few white or mauve species or forms. The flowers tend to be arranged in two regular ranks on each side of the stem, both facing outwards but this is not invariable. The larger species rival the gladiolus in conspicuousness and in brightness of colour. The corms are usually globular and have coarse reticulate coverings while the leaves are sword-like and resemble those of the gladiolus though often they have a narrow dark red or yellow edge.

In the following account only a few species are included since neither space nor my unfortunately rather limited experience of this genus permits a full account. A number have, however, been portrayed in the Botanical Magazine, particularly in the older issues and also in the volumes of the Flowering Plants of S. Africa. The letter after the species indicates the group to which it belongs as given above. There are many other species which may well be their equal as garden plants if tried and there are also numerous hybrids.

† **W. aletroides.** (*a*) *Fl.* variable in colour from pale salmon to deeper red in a long spike, 1½–2 in. long, drooping, tubular with very short lobes and widely spaced on the stem. Stem usually not more than 2 ft., branched. May-June in this country, Sept. in S. Africa (Caledon Division). This sp. is very distinct in the tubular shape of the *fl.* thus resembling rather a lachenalia than a watsonia. Corm globose with a reticulate tunic. *L.* narrow and inflorescence rising from the 2 upper *l.*

**W. alpina.** (*c*) A slender sp. with deep pink *fl.* each segment being striped with deeper colour. *Fl.* rather bell-shaped and with only a short tube, and nodding, each about 1¼ in. long. Stem branched, up to 2½ ft. and usually requiring a stick. Summer. Feb.-March in S. Africa. E. Transvaal in mountainous districts. Corm large with tough wiry tunic; *l.* broad.

† **W. ardernei.** (*a*) Tall, up to 3 ft. Stem branched, large, up to 3 in. long, pure white with long curved tube, broadly trumpet-shaped in upper part with spreading lobes. Summer, Oct.-Nov. in S. Africa. Tulbagh district of Cape Province. Apparently only found wild as a single clump but now one of the best known in gardens.

†*W. beatricis.** (*d*) Tall, up to 3 ft. with a rather dense spike of large apricot or orange-red *fl.* up to 2 in. long and 2 in. across, tube long and lobes of segments wide spreading. Stem generally unbranched. Cape Districts. Summer flowering and requiring plenty of water when growing. Jan.-March in S. Africa. Evergreen. Probably the best known in gardens of this group. Almost hardy. A very beautiful and conspicuous plant.

† **W. bulbillifera.** (*a*) Very tall, up to 5 ft., with a spike of widely-spaced pale yellow *fl.* which are orange inside and flushed with deeper colour around margins outside. Early summer, Oct. in S. Africa. Cape Province in Paarl mountains. Unusual in its production of small cormlets in axils of bracts and stem *l.*

# Watsonia

† **W. coccinea.** (*b*) Dwarf, with stem up to 1 ft. *Fl.* blood-red with long curved tube, large up to 2½ in. long, spike with only a few *fl.* and these widely spaced, but nevertheless a conspicuous plant. Lobes broad, rather pointed. Cape Province. June-July, Sept. in S. Africa.

† **W. comptonii.** (*d*) Evergreen, a rather slender plant up to 2½ ft. with apricot-flame *fl.*, loosely spaced. Summer. Nov.-Jan. in S. Africa. Cape districts.

**W. densiflora.** (*c*) Stem up to 2 ft. with a long double-sided spike of thickly packed deep pink *fl.* Tube horizontal with dark brown prominent membranous bracts. White and purple forms have also been recorded. June-Aug. Jan.-Feb. in S. Africa. Natal, Orange Free State.

† **W. fourcadei.** (*d*) Tall, stem up to 4½ ft., branched. *Fl.* large with long tube and 3 outer lobes, deep salmon-red while inner lobes are much lighter in colour. Cape Province. Nov.-Dec. in S. Africa. A very beautiful sp.

† **W. galpinii.** (*d*) Evergreen, rather slender sp. with stems 2–2½ ft. *Fl.* bright orange-scarlet, grouped at top of spike. Late summer, August, Feb.-March in S. Africa. Cape Province.

† **W. humilis.** (*b*) Dwarf, up to 1½ ft. Stem slender with widely-spaced *fl.*, deep pink with a bluish tinge, lobes wider. Autumn and winter growing. May-June, Sept.-Oct. in S. Africa. Cape Province.

† **W. marginata.** (*a*) Tall winter-growing sp. up to 5 ft. *Fl.* stem slender, branched with dense spikes of rather small rose-pink or lilac-pink *fl.* about ¾ in. long, tube short, curved with lobes opening wide, salver-shaped. July. Oct.-Nov. in S. Africa. Cape Province. *L.* distinct, wide glaucous with broad yellow margins.

† **W. meriana.** (*a*) Variable from 9 in.–3 ft. *Fl.* salmon-pink to mauvish-pink, large, up to 2 in. long with spreading lobes. May-June, Oct. in S. Africa. Cape Province but extending into Natal.

† **W. pillansii.** (*d*) Tall, up to 4 ft. *Fl.* orange-red with overlapping green bracts; tube long but lobes only slightly developed. Evergreen. Late summer. Eastern districts of Cape Province.

† **W. pyramidata.** (*a*) Probably better known as *W. rosea*. Stem tall, up to 5 ft., branched. *Fl.* large, rose-red or mauvish-pink or mauve, 2 in. across, tube strongly curved, segments wide spreading, with rather pointed lobes. June. Sept.-Nov. in S. Africa. S.W. Cape districts. Abundant on mountain slopes, especially in a year following a fire.

**W. rosea.** A syn. of *W. pyramidata*.

† **W. spectabilis.** (*b*) Stem only up to 2 ft. with large but loosely spaced glowing scarlet *fl.* 2¼ in. long with prominent lobes, the lowest of which points downwards and is recurved, making the *fl.* irregular in appearance. Late spring. Cape Province.

† **W. stanfordiae.** (*d*) Stems tall, up to 4 ft. *Fl.* deep rose-purple on branched inflorescences, lobes wide spreading. Summer; November in S. Africa. Cape

Districts in the mountains. A scarlet form or closely related sp. is also known. Evergreen.

† **W. tabularis.** (*a*) Tall, up to 5 ft. Inflorescence branched, with large *fl.* deep coral red outside but paler salmon-coloured inside, lobes broad and wide-spreading, tube long, horizontal. Summer; Nov.–Feb. in S. Africa. Cape district on mountains in cloud belt where it is described as abundant.

**W. transvaalensis.** (*c*) Closely allied to *W. alpina*, rather dwarf. *Fl.* deep pink, slightly smaller than those of *W. alpina*. A white form is also known. E. Transvaal in mountains. Summer growing and autumn flowering.

† **W. versfeldii.** (*a*) Tall, up to 5 ft. Inflorescence branched with large pale rose-pink *fl.* stained crimson at throat, up to 3½ in. across, petal lobes narrow, strap-shaped. May-June; Oct. in S. Africa. Cape Province. A white form has also been recorded.

† **W. wilmaniae.** (*d*) Tall, up to 4 ft. Inflorescence branched with many rose-purple or lilac-purple *fl.* of medium size, tube curved through a right angle. Summer. Cape Province, Knysna District, by streams. Evergreen.

# WORSLEYA *Amaryllidaceae*

A MONOTYPIC genus containing one species of very beautiful amaryllis type with the unusual distinction of having bluish-mauve flowers, *W. rayneri*, better known under its synonyms of *W. procera* or *Hippeastrum procerum*. It is a native of Brazil and in this country can only be treated as a warm greenhouse plant and is regarded as difficult to flower regularly. The bulbs have a prolonged aerial neck which gives the flowers the appearance of having a stem. The late Major A. Pam of Wormley Bury was, however, very successful with this plant and recorded its flowering on several occasions in the R.H.S. Journal. It is sufficiently distinctive, however, to be an event when it flowers. *Worsleya* is distinguished from *Hippeastrum* by the unusual structure of the seeds (if you get them!), which do not have the wing seen usually in seeds of *Hippeastrum*, by the false aerial stem which is often up to 3 ft., and by the prominently falcate leaves. The false stem consists of tightly folded leaves covered by membranous skins which peel off. A somewhat similar false stem is found in *Pamianthe*. *Worsleya* should be grown in an orchid mixture with Osmunda fibre, loam and charcoal and should never be allowed to become dry. In Brazil it has a very restricted distribution, growing in pockets of black leaf-mould on the northern slopes of the Organ Mountains in full sun.

**W. rayneri.** False stem up to 3 ft. with up to 6 large, funnel-shaped *fl.* with long pointed petals 5–6 in. long and with wavy edge. Heliotrope-blue in

colour with paler base shading to white but with mauve spots. Bulb large
with prolonged neck merging into the false stem. *L*. falcate, up to 3 ft. long
and 2 in. wide. July-August. Brazil. Warm greenhouse. Syns. *W. procera,
Amaryllis procera, Hippeastrum procerum*.

# ZANTEDESCHIA *Araceae*

A SMALL genus of S. African aroids, all most decorative in flower. The
best known is the white Arum Lily formerly included either in *Arum,
Calla* or *Richardia* and widely used as a cut flower especially at Easter.
None are really hardy in this country though the white Arum grows well
in the South and West in damp situations or even in the mud at the
edge of a pond where it may be submerged in winter. The flowers are
monoecious, the female below but adjacent to the male on the spadix, thus
differing from *Arum* in which there are two kinds of flower separated by a
sterile portion. All are excellent plants for the cool or intermediate
greenhouse and do best in rich soils, well fed and with plenty of moisture
in the growing period. The white Arum can be kept growing almost con-
tinuously but the others from the Summer Rainfall areas of S. Africa
require a definite resting period.

The genus was better known as *Richardia* but unfortunately this name
had to be discarded, having previously been used for quite another genus
in another family. The white Arum was also erroneously placed in *Calla*
but is considerably different morphologically from the bog *Calla palustris*.

† **Z. aethiopica.** White Arum, Lily of the Nile. Spathe very large up to 10 in.
long and recurved in upper part, snowy-white; spadix also white, extending
above spathe. Stem up to 3 ft., generally less; *l*. hastate, rich green without
any mottling. Spring to summer flowering, but depending on the amount of
heat given. After flowering the pots are usually stood outside for ripening
but it does not need to be completely dried off. Frequent division is necessary
and cultivation in large pots. It may be grown outside in warm areas at the
edge of ponds or in well manured sheltered borders. A hardier form is also
known and marketed under name 'Crowborough', which can be grown
successfully in the open border in the Home Counties while there is also a
dwarf form known as 'Little Gem' which rarely exceeds 1½ ft. (Pl. XXIV)

† **Z. albomaculata.** Dwarf, spathe milky-white with greenish base, less widely
expanded and narrower than in preceding sp. and with a purple blotch at base
inside. *L*. hastate, mottled with translucent spots. Natal and Transvaal.
A pale yellow form is also known but neither are in general cultivation nor
are they as decorative as other sp.

†\***Z. angustiloba.** This is the sp. with large deep golden-yellow spathes and
unmottled *l*., cordate at the base. More often known as *Z. pentlandii*, it is

311

probably unsurpassed in the genus. The spathe has a dark blackish patch at the base inside and is up to 6 in. long, recurved at end. Spadix short, only 2 in. long, golden-yellow. Stem up to 2½ ft. June-July. Intermediate or warm greenhouse. E. Transvaal where it flowers Nov.-Dec. *Fl.* very long-lasting, either on the plant or cut.

†\***Z. elliottiana.** Spathe deep yellow but not quite so rich a colour as in the previous sp. Distinguished from it by the transparent silvery blotches on the *l.*, which are broad and cordate at base and by the absence of a dark patch at the base inside the spathe. Spadix also golden-yellow, about 3 in. long. Stem up to 2½ ft.; spathe up to 5 in. long. Intermediate greenhouse. Summer flowering. Transvaal.

**Z. melanoleuca.** Spathe pale yellow with a dark spot at base which is exposed by spathe being cleft at the base. *L.* arrow-shaped with oblong translucent silvery-white blotches. Var. *tropicalis*, rather larger and deeper in colour, but variable. A fine form flushed with deeper apricot colour has been named 'Helen O'Connor'. N. Transvaal and Rhodesia on the mountains in areas of high summer rainfall and it flowers there in Dec.-Jan. (their summer).

**Z. rehmannii.** Dwarf. Stem up to 1½ ft. but generally less. Spathe variable from pale pink to a deep purplish-pink, tightly rolled especially near base, 4 in. long. *L.* unmottled or slightly mottled, slender, hastate. Hills of E. Transvaal and Natal where it flowers from November to January.

# ZEPHYRANTHES *Amaryllidaceae*

AN ATTRACTIVE genus of bulbous plants from N. and S. America and the Caribbean area, hence their names 'Flowers of the Western Wind.' They are nearly related to *Habranthus* and *Hippeastrum* but the flowers are always solitary on short erect stems and emerging from a sheathing spathe and open erect or only slightly inclined to the horizontal. Perianth funnel-shaped with six equal segments, united at base only, overlapping and recurving slightly in their upper part. The majority flower in late summer but only *Z. candida* can reasonably be described as hardy although other species such as *Z. grandiflora* have been recorded growing success-fully out of doors in this country. They are, however, excellent in the cool greenhouse and should be allowed to become pot bound when they are likely to flower better. When the leaves die down they should be rested like a *Nerine*, although probably they do not require quite so much baking. Many of the species flower before the leaves appear.

**Z. andersonii.** See under *Habranthus andersonii*.

† **Z. atamasco.** The Atamasco Lily. Spring and early summer flowering with *l. Fl.* white with pale pink stripes, flushed green at base, opening pale pink

but quickly fading; petals rather narrow and pointed, 2 in. long. Stem up to 10 in. U.S.A. from Missouri to Florida in damp woodlands. Reported hardy in some gardens in a well-drained sunny position, but more usually grown in a cool greenhouse.

† **Z. aurea.** A pretty sp. with deep golden-yellow *fl.* 1½ in. long and up to 2 in. across on stems 6–12 in. from Peru. *Fl.* erect and funnel-shaped. *L.* narrow, linear, glaucous beneath, bulb globose. Probably not now in cultivation and likely to require cool greenhouse culture, but would be worth re-introduction.

* **Z. candida.** The best known sp. Pure white *fl.* about 1½–2 in. long, on stem up to 8 in., erect and somewhat crocus-like. Perianth segments green at base. Bulb ovoid with a dark tunic and multiplying rapidly from offsets and so forming large clumps. *L.* rush-like, narrow, linear, longer than stem. Sept.-Oct. S. America, Argentina, particularly in marshes round La Plata. Hardy in warm sheltered situations and often very free flowering as in the narrow borders alongside some of the greenhouses at Kew where it is used as an edging. (Pl. **32**, 8)

**Z. carinata.** A syn. of *Z. grandiflora.*

† **Z. citrina.** *Fl.* bright golden-yellow on short stems 4–6 in. with pedicel 1 in. ; perianth segments 1½ in. long, ½ in. across; *fl.* tubular at base. Bulb large, 1½ in. in diameter with rush-like *l.* A very distinctive plant, unfortunately very rarely seen in cultivation. Autumn. Probably suitable for the intermediate or cool greenhouse. Origin uncertain but reported to have been found near Demerara in British Guiana.

†*Z. grandiflora. Probably the finest sp. in the genus with large, rosy-pink *fl.* 3 in. long, on stems up to 1 ft.; *fl.* borne at angle of about 45° from the horizontal, spathe also flushed with pink. *L.* broader than in *Z. candida,* but still linear, keeled. Late summer and autumn. Mexico, Guatemala, W. Indies but widely planted and sometimes naturalised in tropical and semi-tropical countries. Cool greenhouse, though it has been reported as flowering outside in very warm situations in England. (Pl. **32**, 6)

† **Z. rosea.** A pretty sp. with smaller *fl.* and of a paler rose-pink than the preceding. *Fl.* veined with deeper pink and with a long green tube. Late summer and autumn. W. Indies and Cuba in the mountains. Cool greenhouse but almost hardy.

**Z. texana.** See under *Habranthus texana.*

† **Z. tubispatha.** A handsome *fl.,* white, sometimes flushed pink near tips of petals outside, strongly flushed green at base, 2 in. long to base of tube, funnel-shaped, outer segments opening flat in upper part, longer and wider than inner segments, tube short. Bulb sub-globose, about 1 in. across. *L.* linear, very slightly channelled. Stem 6–8 in., pedicel up to 2 in. and longer than the spathe. West Indies, Cuba, Jamaica in the Blue Mountains. Intermediate or warm greenhouse. July-August.

**Z. verecunda.** Known as " The Modest Zephyranthes." Rather similar to *Z. atamasco* but with smaller *fl.,* white, fading to pinkish, flushed green at base and narrow rush-like *l.* Mountains of Mexico.

# BIBLIOGRAPHY

## (1) GENERAL

*The Royal Horticultural Society.* Dictionary of Gardening. Edited by F. J. Chittenden. 4 vols. and Supplement. 2nd edition edited by Patrick M. Synge. 1956. Clarendon Press.

*The Botanical Magazine* 1787–, (now published by *The Royal Horticultural Society*)·

ANDERSON, E. B. Dwarf Bulbs for the Rock Garden. 1959. Nelson.

BAKER, J. G. Handbook Amaryllidaceae. 1888.

BOWLES, E. A. My Garden in Spring. 1914. T. C. and E. C. Jack.

BOWLES, E. A. My Garden in Summer. 1914. T. C. and E. C. Jack.

BOWLES, E. A. My Garden in Autumn and Winter. 1915. T. C. and E. C. Jack.

ELIOVSON, SIMA. South African Flowers for the Garden. 1956. Howard Timmins, Cape Town.

*Flowering Plants of S. Africa.* 1921–.

GREY, C. H. Hardy Bulbs. 3 vols. 1937–8. Williams and Norgate.

HORT, SIR ARTHUR F. The Unconventional Garden. 1928. Edward Arnold.

HORT, SIR ARTHUR F. Garden Variety. 1935. Edward Arnold.

MUNZ, P. A. in collaboration with KECK, D. D. A Californian Flora. 1959. Univ. Calif. Press.

ROWNTREE, LESTER. Hardy Californians.

STERN, SIR FREDERICK C. A Chalk Garden. 1960. Nelson.

WEATHERS, T. The Bulb Book. 1911. Murray.

*The New Flora and Silva.* 12 vols. 1929–40.

*Ministry of Agriculture, Bulletin No. 117.* Diseases of Bulbs.


## (2) SPECIALISED WORKS

*Calochortus*

OWNBEY, M. Monograph of the Genus *Calochortus*. *Ann. Missouri Bot. Garden, Vol. 27, p. 371.* 1940.

*Colchicum*

BOWLES, E. A. A handbook of Crocus and Colchicum for Gardeners. Revised Ed. 1952.

*Crocus*

BOWLES, E. A. A handbook of Crocus and Colchicum for Gardeners. Revised Ed. 1952.

MAW, G. A monograph of the Genus *Crocus*. 1886. The Bodley Head.

*Cyclamen*

BOWLES, E. A. Cyclamens in the Garden. *Jour. Roy. Hort. Soc. Vol. 74, p. 325.* 1949.

DOORENBOS, J. Taxonomy and Nomenclature of Cyclamen. *Bulletin No. 87* Wageningen, Holland. 1950.

# Bibliography

HILDEBRAND. Die Gattung Cyclamen. 1898.
PALMER, THE HON. LEWIS. Cyclamens. *Jour. Roy. Hort. Soc. Vol. 85.* May 1960.
SAUNDERS, DORIS E. Cyclamen. *Quart. Bull. Alpine Garden Soc. Vol. 27, p. 18.* 1959.

*Cyrtanthus*
DYER, R. A. A review of the Genus *Cyrtanthus. Herbertia, Vol. 6, p. 65.* 1939.

*Erythronium*
ANDERSON, E. B. The Genus *Erythronium,* in *The Lily Year Book, p. 32.* 1958.
APPLEGATE, PROF. E. Key to the Western American Species of *Erythronium. Madrono, Vol. 3,* pp. *58–113.* 1935. Key only reprinted with notes by E. H. M. Cox in *New Flora and Silva, Vol. IX, pp. 265–73.* 1937.

*Fritillaria*
BECK, CHRISTABEL. Fritillaries. 1953. Faber and Faber.

*Galanthus* (Snowdrops)
BOWLES, E. A. *Jour. Roy. Hort. Soc., Vol. 43, p. 28.* 1918–19.
STERN, SIR FREDERICK C. Snowdrops and Snowflakes. 1956. R.H.S.

*Hippeastrum*
TRAUB, HAMILTON P. The Amaryllis Manual. 1958. Macmillan, New York.

*Iris*
DYKES, W. R. The Genus Iris. 1913. Cambridge University Press.
*The Iris Society* now *British Iris Society.* The Iris Year Book, 1930–(formerly *Bulletin 1–7,* 1924–9).

*Leucojum* (Snowflakes)
STERN, SIR FREDERICK C. Snowdrops and Snowflakes. 1956. R.H.S.

*Lilium*
ELWES, H. J. Monograph of the Genus Lilium. 1880.
GROVE, A., and COTTON, A. D. Supplement to Elwes' Monograph of the Genus Lilium. *Parts I–VII.* 1933–40. Dulau.
MAXWELL, ALICE C. Lilies in their Homes. 1953. Collins.
TURRILL, W. B. Supplement to Elwes' Monograph of the Genus Lilium, *Part VIII.* 1960. R.H.S.
WOODCOCK, H. DRYSDALE, and STEARN, WILLIAM T. Lilies of the World. 1950. Country Life.
The Lily Year Book. 1932–. R.H.S.
The Lily Year Book of the *N. American Lily Soc.* 1947–. North American Lily Society.

*Moraea*
BARNARD, T. T. Peacock Moraeas. *Jour. Roy. Hort. Soc. Vol. 75, p. 323.* 1950.

*Narcissus*
BOWLES, E. A. A handbook of Narcissus. 1934. Martin Hopkinson.
FERNANDES, A. *Sur la phylogénie des éspèces du genre Narcissus L. Boletim da Sociedada Broteriana Ser. 2a XXV, 113–90.* 1951.
GRAY, ALEC. Miniature Daffodils. 2nd Ed. 1961. Collingridge.
JEFFERSON-BROWN, M. J. The Daffodil. 1951. Faber.

# Glossary

The Daffodil and Tulip Year Book. 1913–. [1931–.] R.H.S.
Classified List and International Register of Daffodil Names. 1961. R.H.S.

*Tulipa*
DYKES, W. R.  Notes on Tulip Species. 1930. Herbert Jenkins.
HALL, SIR A. DANIEL.  The Genus *Tulipa*. 1940. R.H.S.
The Daffodil and Tulip Year Book. 1913–. R.H.S.
Classified List of Tulip Names. 1958. *Roy. Gen. Dutch Bulb Growers Ass.*

# GLOSSARY

*Acid:* Applied to a soil in which there is a preponderance of peat, leaf mould or humus and in which the pH value is below 7.  The opposite to alkaline.  In horticulture it does not necessarily imply sourness.

*Acuminate:* With the tip drawn out into a long narrow point.  Generally applied to leaf shape.

*Alkaline:* Applied to a soil derived from chalk or other calcareous deposits in which the pH value is over 7.  The opposite to acid.  Most bulbs do well in such a soil.

*Anther:* The pollen-bearing end of the stamen, generally two-lobed.

*Apiculate:* Ending abruptly in a short point, applied to the tips of leaves or petals.

*Aril:* An extra covering of the seed coat, often hard and knobbly as in the seed of an Oncocyclus iris.

*Axil:* The angle formed by the base of the leaf as it joins the stem.

*Axillary:* Growing out of the junction of leaf and stem as a lateral branch or as the flower of a Juno iris.

*Basal plate:* The lower surface of a bulb from which the roots are developed.

*Basal rot:* Rot of the basal plate of a bulb, particularly common in lilies and nearly always fatal.

*Bifid:* Two-cleft, divided from about half way into two.  Applied to shape of leaf or petal.

*Bulb:* An underground, round or fleshy storage organ derived from the modified base of a stem.  It consists of a basal plate bearing modified scale-like leaves, with a bud in the centre from which a shoot or flower will be developed.  (See p. 36.)

*Calcareous:* Limy, containing chalk or other lime, applied to an alkaline soil.

*Campanulate:* Bell-shaped, applied to the shape of a flower.

*Carpel:* A division or part of a pistil, the female organ of a flower.  This develops into an ovary or part of an ovary.

*Caudate:* Having a tip shaped like a tail, applied to the shape of a leaf.

*Chequered:* Having a pattern of alternating dark and light squares or patches, as in the flower of a fritillary.

*Chromosome:* The basic structure on which the genes are carried in a cell.

*Cirrhose:* Having a tendril applied to the tip of a leaf.

*Clone:* Plants which are derived by vegetative propagation, i.e. division of a bulb, from one individual and so identical in all respects.

*Convolute:* Wrapped round each other, applied to the way in which the leaves appear above ground (the vernation) in such plants as snowdrops.

*Cordate:* Heart-shaped, applied to the base of a leaf which has two equal rounded lobes with a distinct notch between.

*Cordiform:* Heart-shaped.

*Corm:* A solid swollen base of a stem used to store food material below ground as in crocus or gladiolus where it takes the place of a bulb.  (See p. 37)

# Glossary

*Corolla:* The inner part of a perianth, the petals which may be free or joined together.

*Corona:* A cup placed between the petals and the stamens as in a daffodil.

*Cup:* Used as the equivalent of corona in flowers such as the daffodil.

*Cuspidate:* Narrowing abruptly into a long point ; used to describe the tips of some leaves, often used for ending in a sharp rigid point.

*Dendate:* Toothed, used to describe the margin of a leaf or corolla.

*Dioecious:* With male and female flowers on separate plants.

*Diploid:* The double number of chromosomes, normal in a cell other than a gamete which has only a single set after a reduction division.

*Distichous:* Arranged in two vertical ranks, applied either to leaves or flowers as in many Watsonias.

*Elliptic:* About twice or more as long as wide and with the broadest part in the centre, used to describe the shape of a leaf.

*Endemic:* Confined to a particular region.

*Entire:* Undivided and without teeth or lobes, used to describe the shape of a leaf.

*Fall:* The outer and lower perianth segments of an iris, generally drooping.

*Family:* A group of plants with common characters, more comprehensive than a genus and containing often a number of genera.

*Filament:* The basal part of stalk of a stamen, often thread-like.

*Filiform:* Thread-shaped, very narrow, used to describe a leaf.

*Gene:* Thought to be the basic units of heredity, spread along the chromosomes in the nucleus of a plant cell.

*Genus:* A group of species with common characters, a smaller group than a family and bearing the same generic name.

*Glaucous:* Grey with a waxy bloom, used to describe the colour of a leaf.

*Grex:* A group of individuals derived from a similar cross, propagated by seed and not all identical.

*Haft:* The basal part of the fall or standard of an iris.

*Hastate:* Spear-like, used to describe the base of a leaf which has two equal, rather triangular lobes pointed outwards like the base of a spear.

*Inflorescence:* The arrangement of the flowers on the stem, more loosely used for flowers and top of stem together.

*Lanceolate:* Much longer than broad and broadest below the middle, but tapering at both ends; used to describe the base of a leaf.

*Linear:* Narrow with sides nearly parallel; used to describe the shape of a leaf— roughly grasslike.

*Monoecious:* Having male organs in one flower and female in another flower but both on the same plant.

*Nectary:* A gland which gives out a sugary solution which serves to attract insects to the flower. Usually at the base of the flower.

*Oblanceolate:* Applied to the shape of a leaf which is long and narrow in the proportion of at least 3 : 1 of breadth to length and having the broadest part above the middle.

*Oblong:* Applied to the shape of a leaf or petal which is twice as long as it is broad and about the same width throughout and with blunt ends.

*Obovate:* Egg-shaped but with the broadest end above the middle, applied to the shape of a leaf.

*Ovary:* The basal part of the pistil which encloses the ovules, often used for an immature fruit. An inferior ovary has the other floral parts inserted above it, as in the *Amaryllidaceae*; a superior ovary has the other floral parts inserted below it, as in *Liliaceae*. (See p. 39)

*Ovate:* Egg-shaped with the broadest part near the base, applied to the shape of a leaf.

# Glossary

*Palmate:* Lobed or divided like a hand by its fingers, applied to the shape of a leaf in which all the leaflets begin at the top of the petiole.

*Pedicel:* The stalk of a single flower, in an inflorescence the last stalk before the flower.

*Perianth:* The outer non-sexual parts of a flower, including the petals or sepals or both.

*Petal:* One section of the corolla of a flower, usually coloured and the most conspicuous part of a flower.

*Petiole:* The stalk of a leaf.

pH: The symbol for the measurement of acidity or alkalinity especially in a soil. The scale ranges from 0 to 14: figures below 7 are acid, 7 is neutral and figures above this alkaline.

*Pinnate:* With leaflets arranged on each side of the petiole, applied to the shape of a compound leaf.

*Pistil:* The female organs of a flower, consisting of ovary, style and stigma.

*Polyploid:* Applied to the number of chromosomes in a cell nucleus and implying a multiplication of the normal diploid number.

*Reduplicate:* Folded back, applied to the edges of a leaf.

*Reniform:* Kidney-shaped.

*Rhizome:* A creeping underground stem, generally swollen and sending up successive leaves or flowering stems.

*Sagittate:* Arrow-shaped, applied to the shape of the base of a leaf.

*Scale:* Any thin membranous body on a plant, but applied more specially to the parts of which a lily or fritillary bulb is made up.

*Scape:* Stalk of a flower or flowers arising directly from the ground, generally leafless.

*Sepal:* One of the sections of the calyx of a flower, often green, the outer sections of the perianth in which sepals and petals can be differentiated.

*Serrate:* Edged with teeth pointing forward, applied to the margin of a leaf.

*Sessile:* Without a stalk, applied to a flower which sits on the ground.

*Spadix:* A fleshy spike carrying flowers either in small pits or on the surface, applied to the central club-like organ of an aroid flower.

*Spathe:* A bract enclosing one or more flowers, applied to the membranous covering at the base of a daffodil flower or the slightly fleshy outer part of an aroid flower surrounding the spadix.

*Spathulate:* Oblong with the lower end narrowed, with the shape of a spatula, applied to the shape of a leaf or petal.

*Species:* A group of individuals having similar distinctive characters, smaller than a genus, larger than a variety.

*Stamen:* The male organ of a flower bearing the pollen, it consists of anthers and filament.

*Staminal Cup:* A cup-shaped structure in the flower bearing the stamens as in *Hymeno-callis.*

*Staminode:* A rudimentary stamen without any pollen.

*Standard:* The three inner segments of an iris flower which are erect.

*Stigma:* The tip of the pistil, the female organ of the flower, the part which rceeives the pollen, often covered with a sticky fluid.

*Stolon:* Used with reference to bulbous plants for an underground horizontal stem bearing further small bulbs and stems.

*Style:* The " stalk " of the female organ of a flower joining the carpel to the stigma.

*Subspecies:* A division of a species, differing from other subspecies in more characters than a variety, often used for a well marked geographical race.

*Tepal:* A segment of the perianth of a flower in which the sepals and petals are not readily distinguishable.

*Tessellated:* Covered with a pattern of alternating dark and light spots or squares, as in the flowers of some colchicums, usually less clearly defined than " chequered."

# Glossary

*Tetraploid:* Applied to the chromosomes of a plant in which the normal diploid number for the species or genus is doubled and the single gamete number is multiplied by four. Often a tetraploid is larger in its parts than a diploid.

*Trifid:* Partly divided into three parts, applied to the divisions of the stigma or style as in some species of crocus.

*Trifoliolate:* With three leaflets arising from the end of the petiole.

*Triploid:* Applied to the chromosomes of a plant which has three times the basic single number of the gamete cell. Triploids generally arise through an aberration from the normal reduction division and are rarely fertile.

*Tunic:* The outer covering of a bulb or corm, generally membranous, but sometimes hard.

*Umbel:* An inflorescence with stalked flowers arising from one point, as in the flower heads of an onion.

*Variety:* A group of plants within a species usually separated from other plants in the species by only one or two characters, such as colour. In the case of plants which have arisen in cultivation through selection or hybridisation it is used for a group of plants sufficiently distinct to be given a separate name, often a clone.

*Vernation:* The arrangement of the leaves in relation to each other when they emerge from the ground, an important character in snowdrops, or the arrangement of leaves round a bud.

*Whorl:* An arrangement of parts of a plant all in one plane as in the leaves of some lilies where they are inserted round the stem in tiers.